W9-DGR-673

Staking Her Claim

The Life of

Belinda Mulrooney,

Klondike and

Alaska Entrepreneur

Staking Her Claim

Melanie J. Mayer & Robert N. DeArmond

Swallow Press

Ohio University Press

Athens

Swallow Press/Ohio University Press, Athens, Ohio 45701
© 2000 by Melanie J. Mayer
Printed in the United States of America
All rights reserved. Published 2000

Swallow Press/Ohio University Press books are printed on acid-free paper ⊗ ™

09 08 07 06 05 04 03 02 01 00   5 4 3 2 1

Library of Congress Cataloging-in-Publication Data

Mayer, Melanie J., 1945–
    Staking her claim : the life of Belinda Mulrooney, Klondike and
Alaska entrepreneur / Melanie J. Mayer and Robert N. DeArmond.
      p. cm.
    Includes bibliographical references and index.
    ISBN 0-8040-1021-8 (acid-free paper). — ISBN 0-8040-1022-6
(pbk. : acid-free paper)
    1. Mulrooney, Belinda, 1872–1967. 2. Klondike River Valley
(Yukon)—Gold discoveries. 3. Alaska—Gold discoveries.
4. Women pioneers—Yukon Territory—Klondike River Valley
Biography. 5. Women pioneers—Alaska Biography.
6. Businesswomen—Yukon Territory—Klondike River Valley
Biography. 7. Businesswomen—Alaska Biography. 8. Frontier and
pioneer life—Yukon Territory—Klondike River Valley. 9. Frontier
and pioneer life—Alaska.
I. DeArmond, Robert N. II. Title.
F1095.K5M295 1999
971.9'1—dc21
  [B]   99-36187

"That which does not kill me makes me stronger."

—*Friedrich Wilhelm Nietzsche, 1888*

Contents

Illustrations

Chapter 9: Winds of Change

Chapter 10: A Fair View in Dawson

Chapter 11: The Skagway Caper

Chapter 12: Racing with Winter

Chapter 13: Charles Eugene Carbonneau

Chapter 14: Belinda at Her Peak

Chapter 20: Mining Gold Run

Chapter 21: Starting Over in Fairbanks

Chapter 22: The Dome City Bank

Chapter 23: Retrenching in Yakima, Washington

Chapter 25: Belinda Matures

Preface

If Horatio Alger had imagined a female protagonist in the same mold as one of the young male heroes in his rags-to-riches stories, she would have resembled Belinda Mulrooney. Belinda was smart, spunky, ambitious, self-assured, hard-working, competitive, and courageous. In the late nineteenth and early twentieth centuries, her legendary pioneering in the wilds of the Yukon basin led her to found towns and many businesses. She built two fortunes, supported her family, was an ally to other working women, and triumphed in what was generally considered a man's world. Realistically, unlike fictional heroines from the nineteenth century, Belinda also had "faults" or darker aspects. She was aggressive, hard-headed, ambivalent in her relationships, prejudiced, and sometimes emotionally defensive or physically violent. Though basically honest, at times she lied and broke laws. Not all episodes of her life were admirable. Perhaps heroines can be human now?

Belinda's saga unfolded during a dynamic era for women in the United States and Canada. Traditionally women had been excluded from public life, but in the late 1800s those prohibitions were being challenged on legal, political, social, and economic fronts. Belinda was among the increasing number of single women looking to make their own ways in the world. But they found that most occupations were gender-segregated, and that the pay for women's work did not reflect productivity.[1] To understand Belinda's unusual entrepreneurial solutions to the bind of women's work, we explore her personal traits along with the circumstances that hindered most women in those times from achieving financial independence.

How then did Belinda manage to succeed against the odds? It was through a felicitous combination of the personal and situational. First, she benefited from the earliest steps then being taken toward more egalitarian laws and attitudes. And then she discovered that even within general restrictions, there were circumstances where rules were less likely to be enforced or where boundaries were not so firmly established. Belinda was adept at finding permissive niches that allowed her to flourish.

For Belinda the most important of these unique environments was the newly opening northwest of North America. The Yukon River basin included both Canadian (English) and United States territories. At the end of the nineteenth century when Belinda was in her twenties, this hitherto isolated region was about to experience dramatic events that would drastically change its material and social landscapes. Belinda became a significant player in that drama.

Like any good Horatio Alger hero, Belinda had many obstacles to overcome. Among these were poverty; early loss of her mother and father; alienation from her family; limited education; financial disasters; no great beauty nor inclination to develop "feminine wiles"; and prejudices against her Irish background, her gender, and her mental aptitudes that were inconsistent with gender stereotypes. Belinda's responses to these challenges became the bases for her notable strengths. Though physically small and intensely private, she became a powerful person, as any number of people who knew her would attest. This is the story of a woman who developed inner strength and used it to effect a positive impact on her outer world.

Acknowledgments

We thank the following people who have generously helped us over the last nineteen years to reconstruct and understand the life of Belinda Mulrooney Carbonneau.

Granting interviews and relating their personal knowledge of Belinda have been Janet Noble Bouillon; Carol Gilge Cribbs; Virginia Cummings Devine; Gladys Gue Wilfong; Marjorie Gue Lambert; Quail Hawkins; Ann Hughes; Charles, Emogene and Christine Johnston; Sarah and Dale Kroll; and Betty Mulrooney. Rose Dougher Vitzthum has been especially interested in the project and generous in her sharing of family information.

Enlightening us with their special knowledge and relevant materials have been Dennis Andersen, Norman D. Anderson, Constance Backhouse, Frank Barron, William Berry, Norm Bolotin, Sara Holmes Boutelle, Sybil Brabner, Michael Cirelli, Jack Frazelle, Michael Gates, Claudia Goldin, David S. Good, John M. Gould, Lewis Green, Jane Haigh, Ray Hall, Myra Hart, Martha Hoppin, Angel Kwolek-Folland, Jean Lester, Norman Lezin, James McCurdy, Lael Morgan, Phyllis Movius, Clause-M. Naske, Bruce Parnam, Anthony Pratkanis, Alyce Prudden, Jim Robb, Pat Roppel, Virginia Rusinak, Tom Sandry, Eileen Tanner, Louis Waddell, and Christianne Young. Candy Waugaman has been especially generous with her time, materials, and alertness to new sources of information.

We could not have carried out this research without the skilled assistance of the staff members of libraries and archives throughout the United States, Canada, and England. In particular, we thank . . .

University of California, Santa Cruz, especially the reference librarians and Alice Morrow, Julia Graham and Erik Stricker at Interlibrary Loan; and Don Harris at Photography Services;

University of California, Berkeley, Bancroft Library, particularly for access to and permission to quote materials from the Hawkins Collection;

University of Washington, Seattle, and especially Richard Engeman and Kris Kinsey in Special Collections;

Yukon Archives, Whitehorse, and especially Angela Wheelock and Heather Jones;

Alaska State Library, Juneau, and especially India Spartz, Kay Shelton, and Gladi Kulp;

University of Alaska, Fairbanks;

California State University, Fresno, and especially Jean Coffey of the Sanoian Special Collections Library;

Puget Sound Regional Archivists Deborah Kennedy and Phil Stairs;

as well as Megan Murphy, Maya Chaffe, Jill Ten Cate, Terri Mitchell, Steve Alexander, Susan Goldstein, and Serge Barbe;

and an unidentified librarian at the Court Library, Yellowknife, Northwest Territories.

For general encouragement, guidance, and assistance we thank Don Coyne; Dale DeArmond; John Dizikes; Julie Dryden; Baukje Altena and Stan Klein; Jean Lester; Marcia Millman; Tina Moss; Florence Nelson; and Billie Jo, Tony, and Erik Cole.

We are indebted to Nancy Basmajian of Ohio University Press, whose expert editing, good taste, and sense of style grace these pages.

Finally, MJM would like to thank the Academic Senate Committee on Research at the University of California, Santa Cruz, for research support for the final stages of the book.

Concerning Sources

IN 1927–28 HELEN LYONS HAWKINS conducted a series of interviews with Belinda Mulrooney Carbonneau. Ms. Hawkins prepared at least three manuscript versions of these interviews, which she deposited along with notes and supporting materials in the Bancroft Library of the University of California, Berkeley. The Hawkins Collection contains factual errors typical of reminiscences and handwritten interviews, as well as instances of faulty memory and some obvious obfuscation on Belinda's part. It is nonetheless the most complete single source of information about Belinda's life from her own perspective up to the year 1900. Whenever possible we have cross-checked facts with other sources, and documentation of such appears in our notes. All quotations not otherwise attributed are from material in the Hawkins Collection.

The "New and Wonderful" manuscript (cited as NW) by Carbonneau and Hawkins is, in many ways, the most complete version of Hawkins's 1928 interviews. Its pages are numbered by chapter and the page within the chapter (e.g., 10:3). Starting with chapter 14, there are also sequential page numbers, although the numbering is not continuous. We append these sequential numbers, when available, in parentheses, as in 20:1(133).

In quotations from all sources, we have edited punctuation and spelling where it does not alter the meaning. Editorial emendations and glosses appear in square brackets.

Parenthetical citations in the text use shortened titles or author's last name only when not ambiguous. Full bibliographic information for all sources cited appears in the References section.

Abbreviations

FOR A FEW frequently cited sources, we use the following abbreviations:

ASL	Alaska State Library
AYIC	Alaska-Yakima Investment Co.
AFKS	Anglo-French Klondyke Syndicate
CSUF	California State University, Fresno
DAPR, PS	Division of Archives and Public Records, Puget Sound Regional Branch
GR(K)M	Gold Run (Klondike) Mining Co., Ltd.
Hawkins	Hawkins Collection, Bancroft Library of the University of California, Berkeley
NW	Carbonneau and Hawkins, "New and Wonderful" manuscript
NWT	Northwest Territories
RCMP	Royal Canadian Mounted Police
UAF	University of Alaska, Fairbanks
UCB	University of California, Berkeley
UW	University of Washington Libraries

In specifying locations of claims, we use the following:

A/D	Above discovery
A/U/D	Above upper discovery

A/L/D	Above lower discovery
B/D	Below discovery
B/U/D	Below upper discovery
B/L/D	Below lower discovery
RL	Right limit (specified looking downstream)
LL	Left limit (specified looking downstream)

Staking Her Claim

1

Ireland

Fostering Self-Reliance

THE DAY BEGINS moist and fertile, with air and water mingling in a soft Irish rain. It soaks gradually into the soils of the small farms about the village of Carns, District of Castleconnor, County Sligo.[1] Stone fences that separate farmyards from the surrounding fields gleam silver in the dampness. The mist collects on the tightly thatched roofs of whitewashed stone cottages. It glides down the long, bundled fibers, dropping steadily to the ground, wearing a graveled depression around each house. Four miles to the southeast, the pressuring clouds squeeze against the steeper slopes of the Ox Mountains. Droplets coalesce into rivulets, then streams, then rivers, one of which, the Carns, flows beside the village of the same name on its way to Killala Bay. The soft rain nourishes the spring wildflowers and the vivid green grass, as well as the crops—potatoes, beets, carrots, oats—of the farmers who make up most of the two hundred souls calling Carns their home.

The date is 16 May 1872,[2] and a new resident has just arrived. The newborn girl is christened Bridget, but her name is soon changed to Belinda.[3] Belinda Agnes Mulrooney is the first child of Maria (later called Mary) Connor[4] and John Mulrooney of County Mayo.[5] Belinda's birthplace is on the twenty-one-acre farm of Maria's parents, James and Alice Howley Connor.[6] The Connor

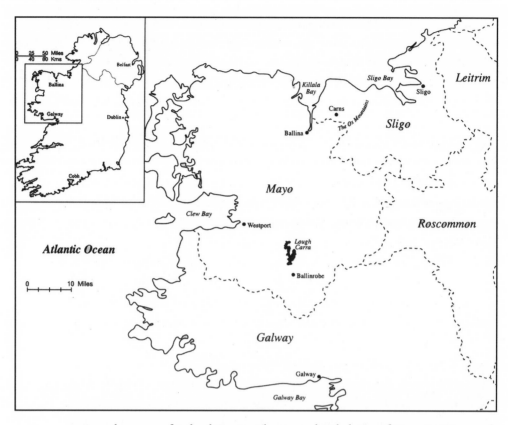

1.1. A modern map of Ireland (*inset*) with a more detailed map of Counties Mayo and Sligo. Carns is located northeast of Ballina, just inside the Sligo County line.

and Mulrooney families are both Catholic Irish, with roots winding round proud Gaelic ancestors.

The Connor family name hints of noble connections, even if Belinda's grandparents' tenant farm is far from grand. Their parish is Castleconnor, and seven centuries before Belinda's birth, Rory / Roderic O'Connor ruled the province of Connacht, which included the present counties Sligo and Mayo, as well as Leitrim, Galway, and Roscommon. Under King O'Connor, Connacht frustrated British attempts to dominate the region. Henry II prudently decided to concentrate his governing efforts on the provinces closer to England and so agreed to acknowledge O'Connor's title, second only to Henry himself.

Connacht was certainly "beyond the Pale." Western Ireland resisted the English on land and by sea. In the centuries that followed, the "Irish enemies" maintained a belligerent independence even while occasionally paying lip service to the British. Girls born in the province of Connacht could identify with the fighting spirit of Ireland's legendary "Pirate Queen" Granuaile, or Grace O'Malley, of County Mayo, who captained trading ships in the sixteenth century and defended her castle against the troops of England's Elizabeth I. Granuaile supplemented her income by leading a fleet of swift galleys to rob the hated British merchant ships on the west coast of Ireland, thereby increasing her popularity with the native Irish.[7]

John Mulrooney's family was from Granuaile's County Mayo. We know very little about John's life before he married Maria Connor. Their marriage certificate gives his townland as Carra.[8] There was a barony of Carra in County Mayo, bordering on Lough Carra,[9] about thirty miles southwest of Carns. This may have been John's family's home. We do not know how or why he came to County Sligo. We can only speculate that he may have ended up in Carns searching for food and work, one of the thousands displaced by Ireland's potato famine.

Both of Belinda's parents were born during the harsh beginnings of the famine in 1845 through 1851. Potatoes had been introduced in Ireland 250 years earlier—one of the benefits of explorations of the new world of South America. By the beginning of the nineteenth century, Ireland enjoyed relative prosperity, due in large part to the highly nourishing, easily grown tuber. In many areas of Ireland it was the primary food crop, supplanting oats, wheat, barley, and beans on much of the arable land. The abundant potatoes supported a large population of well-fed peasants, but the monoculture left them very vulnerable to crop failure.

The first blight of the potatoes hit Ireland in 1845, reducing yield by 33 percent. With the spread of the black rot that only later was understood to be a fungus, even more of the potato crop was lost in subsequent years. When John Mulrooney was born, in 1846,[10] the blight was devastating—75 percent of the harvest was lost. A 37 percent loss followed two years later.

These crop failures caused widespread malnutrition, as well as ecological and social disruption. What came to be called the Great Famine could as well be described as the Great Upheaval. Relief efforts from England and the United States were inadequate; many people died. By 1851, when Maria Connor was one year old, it is estimated that the potato blight, with its accompanying famine and diseases, had doubled the death rate in Ireland for all ages. Approximately one million lives had been lost during the preceding five years. The province of Connacht was one of the hardest hit, with deaths in County Mayo estimated at over one quarter of the population.[11] Somehow John Mulrooney and Maria Connor survived.[12]

Throughout these desperate years western Irish peasants struggled to find something, anything, to eat. Much of the countryside was stripped of edible natural resources—rodents, birds, fish, game, shellfish, plants. Neighbors who were formerly comrades were now competition. Anyone who managed to plant a crop that survived had to guard it closely from starving thieves. Families who had farmed a plot of land for generations left their homeland to crowd into areas that seemed to have more food or more charity. But often the suffering and disorder only grew as the new locale's resources were overwhelmed. Eventually, many Irish peasants decided their only hope lay in the United States and Canada, to which they sailed in great, miserable waves.

If the food shortages were not enough to wreak havoc, societal changes in Ireland were also having a profound effect upon John and Maria's generation. At about the same time as the Great Famine, the inheritance patterns in Ireland were changing. The prevailing practice of dividing estates equally among all the children insured a place for everyone but reduced each individual's holding with successive generations. Gradually there was a shift to impartible inheritance, with the estate usually going to the eldest son.[13]

The potato blight that caused the Great Famine and Upheaval reappeared in cycles for nearly fifty years. The uncertainty of the crops together with impartible inheritance convinced increasing numbers of young Irish to try to make a life elsewhere. Between 1846 and 1854 nearly 2.5 million Irish left their country.[14] Most went to the United States. There they, along with both earlier and later nineteenth-century migrants from the tiny troubled island, would become the second-largest group of immigrants from any country in the world.[15]

John and Maria Mulrooney were part of the Irish diaspora. According to Roman Catholic Church records, they married on 21 January 1871, in the Parish of Castleconnor.[16] John left for the United States the following year,[17] shortly after Belinda, his first child, was born. Maria joined him in a couple of years[18] to settle in Archbald, Pennsylvania, a coal mining town near Scranton. Belinda was left in Ireland to be raised by her Connor grandparents, who were still occupied with rearing Maria's younger brothers, some only slightly older than Belinda.

Another new resident of Carns, born on the same day as Belinda, became her "twin" (NW 2:1). It was a donkey. He began his life dedicated to the service of the Church, for he was offered as the prize in a fund-raising raffle. Someone bought a ticket for baby Belinda. She won, but the drawing was disputed. The raffle was run again. Again Belinda won. So it was that Belinda and the little ass became constant companions.

The fact that Belinda also describes the donkey as her best childhood friend hints that despite her loving grandparents, Belinda was a little girl who needed comforting and reassurance. Because Belinda's father left soon after she was born, she had no childhood memory of him. Her first two years, the time when a stable, responsive caretaker is so important to healthy psychological development,[19] Belinda spent with her mother. These two years gave Belinda a sound beginning, from which she could grow to become more independent. However, even a secure two-year-old feels a keen sense of loss if her mother, upon whom her whole world depends, suddenly disappears. That blow for Belinda was eased somewhat by her close relationship with her Grandmother Connor, and by the cultural support in Ireland for fostering by a family member. At least Belinda was not taunted for being raised by someone other than her mother. But Belinda undoubtedly missed her mother, and her young mind was troubled to make some intuitive sense of Maria's disappearance.

Belinda's solutions to her emotional trauma set patterns for a lifetime. She found solace and trust in the company of an animal. Her dependable donkey friend helped ease her loneliness and fear of further abandonment. And rather than slipping into depression or withdrawing or becoming very clinging, as some abandoned children do, Belinda managed her fear of loss of love through hearty toughness. Only with animals was there a softening of this shield. The toughness would insulate her from the vagaries of others' judgments and emotions. It would help her to become a daring leader, an aggressive competitor, someone who was comfortable being in front and not unduly hampered by others' opinions about what she should be doing. At the same time, her warrior mode was less compatible with sympathetic empathy for others, and it did not prompt a free-spirited nor open-hearted approach to life.

Belinda's recollections of her childhood in Ireland illustrate these developments. Her stories are humorous and usually emphasize rough-and-tumble but affectionate relationships with her uncles, along with experiences that helped to build her independence and leadership. She explained, "Anyone born with a donkey for a twin doesn't grow up to be a 'yes man' (NW 2:1). About her uncles she said,

> My whole life was influenced by them. I played ball with them. . . . I had a
> fight when there was a fight. They treated me just like a boy. One trick they
> used to tease me was to throw an arm around my neck when I wasn't looking
> and rub my nose hard.
> Seriously, what I learned from my uncles was useful later in Alaska. Never

to expect any favors. To know that a woman around men who couldn't do her share was a nuisance and was left behind. So that is why I tried to be in front always, to lead.

The uncles, the donkey, and I grew up together. That donkey's back was bent from being ridden when he was too young. . . . He took all of the fear out of me. I'd been kicked so often by him and knocked down so much, I stopped being afraid. (NW 1:3, 2:1)

Like most farm children, Belinda had her chores to do, responsibilities that contributed to the family's livelihood. She saw and participated in the daily routines of a small farm—caring for animals, planting and harvesting crops, milking cows, making butter, gathering eggs, slaughtering animals for food, planting and tending a garden, washing in water hauled in buckets from a stream, and gathering fuel for a stove. These experiences would serve her well in later life, for they made her familiar with animals and comfortable with simple living off the land. Conditions that urban dwellers might view with trepidation, Belinda saw as familiar and not only survivable but full of possibilities.

Although Belinda had responsibilities on her grandparents' farm, she also had a lot of freedom and enough imagination to get herself into mischief.

When I grew up a little bit, I started catching birds. . . . I'd get a little basket and prop it up with a (stick) and tie a string to the stick. . . . I'd put lots of food inside for bait. [When the bird hopped in] I'd pull the string and down would come stick and basket.

I used to . . . turn them loose in Grandmother's milk room. It's what we would call a spring house here. Those birds started flopping about. Nearly all of them got into the cream. [When] someone told Grandma . . . the birds and myself were thrown out.

Belinda did attend school when she got older. The one-room schoolhouse was of whitewashed stone with a cement floor. Students sat on benches with no backrest. Belinda and her uncles either walked or rode Belinda's donkey friend the four or five miles to school (NW 1:4).

[My first teacher] was lame and grouchy. He was the most disagreeable thing that ever happened. . . . He had a rod of cane splits . . . that he kept to wallop the kids over the back whenever he felt bilious. He'd hit without cause or anything.

One of his ideas was that we had to take to school every day two sods of turf. [These were] fuel, you know, [for the school stove]. We had to bring the darn dirty things under our arm to school. After you had trotted [or walked] a lunch and two sods of turf . . . four miles you had done a hard day's work. I was seven then.

The second or third day, I was crossing the river with my donkey. . . . Well I lost one of my sods of turf. It floated gracefully down the river. The teacher would always sit at the window to see that everyone had his share of fuel. Before I came close to him, I broke my one sod of turf in two and stuck the two good ends out under my arm. But when I threw them on the pile, he saw the two raw ends.

. . . He called me and told me to bring it in. I took one piece in. He explained to the whole bunch what I had done, what I had tried to put over on him. . . . [Then he] gave me a good wallop. That darn rod thing, when it spread, it felt as though it were a bushel of them. I looked up, and I saw my uncle with fire in his eye. I was stunned, but I wouldn't cry. I saw he expected something. I picked up the sod and let it fly. It struck that teacher above the glasses and knocked 'em off! I was frozen for a minute, but there was nothing left but to fly. The teacher started up and dropped his stick. His game leg wouldn't work. He could only shuffle along without his stick. By that time I was on the donkey and beating it for home.

Belinda's fiery temper was not necessarily cooled by the family conferences that followed this incident. It was several months before Belinda was convinced to go back to school. Nevertheless, when she did return, she tried to stay out of trouble. And her uncles helped her, she claimed: "I got something out of that school. [But] not very much because every time I looked at that teacher I was ready to fight. My uncles took an interest in my studies. [They] tried to keep me ahead of the game so I wouldn't get licked any more."

When Belinda was about nine, three of her uncles—John, Bryan, and Patty Connor—followed her mother and father to Archbald, Pennsylvania, to work in the coal mines. At about this time, Belinda started working for others in Carns. She was beginning to strive for better things, and she saved her wages to buy the first oil lamp in the village.[20] The lamp was a gift for her grandmother, whom she loved dearly. It is also the first indication we see of her budding enterprise and of her appreciation for the beauty of light in her environment.

In early 1885, when Belinda was almost thirteen, her uncle John sent her the fare for passage to the United States.[21] By then her parents had other children in America—Patrick, born in about 1879,[22] and Helen/Nellie, born in 1884.[23] (Two other children born before Helen died in infancy.[24]) According to Belinda, her mother sent for her to help with the younger children.

For Belinda's parents and uncles, the experience of emigration was an act of desperation as well as of hope. For them, going to America offered the promise of new opportunities, of creating a more prosperous life. For Belinda, there was not much to recommend it. She was secure in her childhood world, and except for her uncles, all those folks in Pennsylvania were strangers. When she recounts her departure for America, there is no remembrance of eager anticipation of a better life or of being reunited with her parents. We hear instead of the difficulty of the uprooting. "Leaving my uncles was bad. Leaving my grandmother was worse. But leaving the donkey—I threw my arms around his neck. And (I) cried for hours and hours after I left him" (NW 2:1).

Belinda made the long, trans-Atlantic crossing on her own. And despite the pain of leaving the security of her childhood home, she was drawn almost immediately into the new experiences offered by the ship.

> Of course, I was all curious, everything was new. And I loved the sea. . . . I loved the wind blowing and the spray. . . . I'd spend every minute I was awake out of my cabin and on deck. . . . I spent [much of my time] in the bow on a pile of rope, looking into the water. . . . A flying fish came up once and knocked me silly. There was something in my blood, something [about] the storm [that] appealed to me.

BELINDA'S CHILDHOOD in Ireland laid the groundwork for her later life. Her naturally robust constitution was nourished by good care and a healthy environment. She found that meaningful work as a member of a self-sufficient, rural family was satisfying to her, and so she focused her considerable energy on hard work that interested her. She learned how to protect and take care of herself physically and emotionally; consequently she grew to have confidence in herself —her imagination, intellect, and actions. By competing with her older uncles within the family, she found expression for her aggressiveness. At the same time she enjoyed the support of her uncles' affection and discovered the value of family solidarity in the wider world. She also learned she could hold her own and even excel compared to her contemporaries. These traits and inclinations would serve her well in the life she was to build for herself in America.

2

Pennsylvania

Unhappiness, Deceptions, and New Opportunities

BELINDA WAS AGOG as her ship entered New York harbor. She had never seen such a huge city. And there on a tiny island in the harbor construction was underway on the largest statue in the world. The colossus on its pedestal was over 305 feet tall and proclaimed the ideal of liberty for all. Belinda was impressed with the new Statue of Liberty as much for its size and beauty as for its symbolism. Since she was interested in construction techniques, she was fascinated that someone had figured out how to build so huge a structure.[1] Similarly, the tall buildings of the city were a wonder: "I was stunned. It seemed like such a lot of stone. [And] I couldn't understand one high building and then a squatty one, after the uniformity of Europe."

Belinda did not have time to explore New York on this first visit. She was met by a relative who put her on a train to Philadelphia. From there she traveled north to Archbald,[2] a small town in the steep valley of the Lackawanna River, about nine miles upstream from Scranton. This was the gloomy heart of the rich Pennsylvania anthracite coal mining area. It was also the center of a large Irish settlement where everyone, even the few German immigrants, spoke English with an Irish brogue.[3]

Belinda's reaction to her new home was strong and unequivocal. "The dirtiest hole in the world it seemed to me. I didn't like . . . my family or the dirt and coal dust." Her parents and her siblings were really strangers, and Belinda was not motivated to get to know them. "I was afraid I would have to stay there," she explained.

Like most of the families in Archbald, Belinda's depended on mining the coal buried beneath the surrounding hills. Her father was a contractor who had a few men working for him. John Mulrooney got up at 4 A.M. to crawl underground and drill, then set dynamite in the area to be mined that day. After he set off the charge, his men dug and hauled out the loosened material while John installed cribbing to stabilize the ceiling and walls. If they uncovered a seam of coal, they would make some money. The profits were seldom large, but they were enough for the growing Mulrooney family to live on.[4] Ever since the financial panic of 1873, the U.S. economy had been volatile, with intermittent crashes and periods of labor unrest. But the coal dug in Pennsylvania fueled the burgeoning, if changeable, industry and transportation of the entire nation. So there was some security in supplying coal. Having seen so many perish during the hard times in Ireland, Belinda's parents did not take even a small income for granted.

In Ireland Belinda had been the youngest child in the Connor family, with all the attention and special care that status conferred. In Archbald she was the oldest of the Mulrooney children. Now she was expected to take responsibility not only for herself, but also for the younger children and the household. Furthermore, the cramped, disrupted, coal-dust-coated environment around the mines was a far cry from the pastoral loveliness she had loved to roam.

> I couldn't get used to just one house and one lot for all those people [her family]. After the wide spaces and the beauty of Ireland, and my own way so much, to be with such a flock! There was always a lot of neighbor's kids around too. I hated the sight of them. . . . I had only one set idea from the first, to find enough money to get out of there.

Belinda's feelings of alienation were reinforced by experiences at her new school. While the teacher was interested in her bright new pupil, the other children plagued Belinda. In the following recollection there are clear signs of Belinda's ambition and competitiveness, as well as her aggressive defensiveness.

> I had a beautiful bunch of brogue that seemed to be the wonder of the rest of the bunch of dirty little faces. . . . Every kid picked on me, repeated after me, and razzed me. I think I had thirty fights a day. . . . I never said anything in

school. But God help any kid after school. I'd had so much boxing and sport around my uncles and their friends that I sent those kids to [their] mother to be patched after every fight.

The climax of the season came when they were giving a little play. I wanted to be in it but didn't want to say so. Teacher knew it and asked me if I didn't want to recite something. She gave me a little piece.

I studied and studied because I wanted to be so much better than the rest. I recited it. It was a serious thing for me, but I suppose my brogue was funny. They howled their heads off. I was boiling mad. I didn't wait to get them outside. I took them in the hall. The first one I met I pasted. And I would not after that go back to that school for man or woman.

When Belinda did not attend school, her parents expected her to help more at home, where her responsibilities increased with the arrival of two more sisters—Margaret Ann in April of 1886[5] and Agnes in August of 1887.[6] Belinda, on the other hand, was determined to get back to Ireland as fast as she could and was always on the alert for ways to finance her escape. There were few if any regular jobs in Archbald for girls outside the home, but she used her ingenuity to make the best of every opportunity.

One source of funds was berry picking, an ideal occupation for Belinda because it allowed her to be on her own and outdoors, away from the coal dust. In the summer there was a market for ripe huckleberries, for which she earned eight cents a quart. So Belinda was off to the hills with her buckets, competing with the other children to get the most berries. She became the acknowledged berry champion, earning about eighty cents per day, by going further into the hills than the other children dared. They were afraid they would run into rattlesnakes.[7]

Me, afraid of them? I just thought the rattlesnake would have to take care of himself. . . . I killed rattler after rattler. I'd take an old crooked stick, try to cut a piece of limb with it. [I'd] get his head, snap it off. You had to wait until he was coiled, ready to strike. But there were always more berries where the rattlesnakes were. I traveled alone always. The rest were afraid of the snake district, so I got two pails to their one.

Belinda also crossed social boundaries that seemed senseless to her. When a boy who drove a mule team hauling coal into town got sick, Belinda pleaded with the owner of the coal wagon to hire her. He was very much opposed to the idea at first, for not only was it against custom, but females specifically were prohibited by Pennsylvania law from holding any job having to do with the coal mines, except for office work.[8] Yet when Belinda showed up with coal dust on her face and dressed in a boy's cap and coat, the coal man let her try. Later he admitted she handled the mules better than anyone else. Nevertheless, when the regular driver recovered his health, Belinda lost her job. Still, the coal man hired her to help whenever there was a rush of business, and for his own as well as for Belinda's protection, he never told anyone what she was doing. Eventually, after a couple of years of occasional driving, Belinda had earned twenty-five dollars. In the late 1880s, a typical male, adult farm laborer would have needed to work about seventeen ten- or eleven-hour days to earn as much.[9]

Belinda saved much of the money she earned and hid it in a coffee can she buried in the backyard: "I saved, hoarded and buried it. If I'd banked it, I couldn't take it out and count it every day. It was my own secret. I knew the family wouldn't stand for it. It was out of the question for me to go out on my own."

Belinda's separate cache was prohibited not only by family rules but also by common law, the legal system governing areas not covered by legislation, based in the eastern United States on the centuries-old traditions of English common law. While many aspects of common law in the United States were being slowly modified in the nineteenth century, especially with respect to the family, the status of the earnings of a minor living at home was not one of them. By common law, the money Belinda earned was not her own but belonged to her father. Belinda knew this by custom if not explicitly. Circumventing the rules by hiding her profits was her only hope to save enough on her own to finance her return trip to Ireland.[10]

Belinda somehow managed to account for her absences while earning outside money. When at home, she looked after her younger siblings and helped with the housework. But her heart was not in either task.

> . . . I tried to keep the children in good humor, never gave them any chance for argument. If things looked stormy inside, I'd go out to the garden and hoe and root. There was a second little house, a small one for rough work, laundry, and in summer we'd cook out there. I'd go out there and pretend to study. My thoughts were all my own. They never got a look in on them.

Religion was no comfort to Belinda either. "My mother was so darned religious, trying to drive us all to church. I was all off it. You can't drive an Irishman anywhere. He's like a pig. Drive him one way, and he'll run another."

Belinda's description of her life in Archbald is striking in its sense of unrelenting isolation. Most teenagers are caught up in the intrigues of relationships with best friends, the beginnings of sexual attractions, and peer bonding. But Belinda seems to have experienced none of these. She was developing a sense of her own identity primarily in terms of conflicts. She felt alienated from her siblings and from the other teenagers in town. The uncles who had been her pals in Ireland had found work in a gender-segregated industry—mining—so there was no opportunity for Belinda to join them. Belinda resented the stereotypical feminine roles she was assigned by her family and community. The natural environment around her was so altered by the mining operations, it offered her no solace. And she could not confide her innermost thoughts to anyone, least of all her family. To survive she added more layers to her psychological armor. These gave her the strength of self-reliance that would facilitate her economic ascendance. But the cost was lack of intimacy and loss of emotional flexibility.

By the time Belinda was about seventeen years old, she was ready to make her break from Archbald. She told her family that she wanted to visit an aunt who lived in Philadelphia. Her mother was angry and mystified by her oldest daughter. "You are the queerest human being I ever saw in my life," she exclaimed. "I don't understand you" (NW 2:2). Nevertheless, her parents supplied the ticket to Philadelphia, not realizing Belinda intended never to return.

Belinda went to the home of her mother's sister,[11] Bridget Agnes Connor Gowran, and her husband James. Aunt Bridget earned money by taking in boarders, as did about 16 percent of all married households in Philadelphia at that time.[12] But Aunt Bridget could not tell Belinda how other women got jobs in the city, because neither she nor her married friends had experience working outside the home. More and more in the nineteenth century, as the Industrial Revolution shifted production of goods out of the home and into factories, married women gave up proprietorships and performed labor at home that was not officially acknowledged, such as running a boardinghouse. The 1890 census counted only 4.6 percent of married women in the labor force.[13]

What Belinda eventually gleaned was that when unmarried women like herself found work, more than 80 percent were employed in gender-segregated jobs as domestic servants, manufacturing operators, or farm laborers. For example, factories making boots and shoes, clothing, and woolen and cotton goods employed predominantly females, while those making agricultural implements, building materials, metal products, and modes of transportation hired predominantly males. According to one estimate, by 1900 the manufacturing sector in the United States was gender segregated to an extraordinary degree not equaled since. Furthermore, Belinda found that she could expect to earn about half what a male working equivalent time made;[14] therefore, whatever employment she found was not likely to be very rewarding.

But Belinda was not picky. Apparently she discovered odd jobs on her own for a while. Then she asked one of her young acquaintances how to find better employment. The tactic she used to get the information, while it is manipulative and calculating, shows she understood what motivated others.

> I remember a nice big fat girl came to play with me. I asked her how people made money in a big place like that, and she said she thought you went to an employment office. I told her if she would take me and show me the way, I'd repay her. I had quite a little money sewed all over me, and I treated that great big old fat slob to candy, ice cream, and soda water because she could tell me things I wanted to know.

Thus bribed, Belinda's acquaintance led her to a nearby employment office. When asked what types of work experience she had had, Belinda described taking care of her brother and sisters. Consequently she was tentatively identified as a nursemaid. When a woman came to the agency looking for someone to help care for her infant son, Belinda was called in for an interview.

The potential employer was Belle Brown Cummings, wife of George King Cummings, a prosperous industrialist. Belinda told Mrs. Cummings she wanted to work and would do what she was told. "I guess I was young and healthy, " Belinda explained, "and that appealed to her. I never asked what she would pay me."

Belinda was hired for three dollars per week[15] and taken to the Cummings home in Chestnut Hill, one of the northern, well-to-do neighborhoods of Philadelphia.[16] Although in many ways different from her humble previous homes, this place of quiet parks, green lawns, and graceful old trees was one where Belinda felt more in her element.

> It was wonderful, beautiful country. I went all over it. Jack . . . was a young, year-old baby. I must have pushed [him] miles and miles and miles, gaping at everything. Every building [site] we came to, I stood and watched the working men. I couldn't see enough of how they built things. Jack used to get hungry, and I would go to a milk shop and buy him some milk. His mother used to worry at first, but he thrived. . . . I had a pal in Jack. He took the place of the uncles and the donkey probably, and we would go anywhere we wanted to. It was the happiest life.

As Belle Cummings got to know Belinda better, she liked her very much. With Mrs. Cummings's warm support, Belinda became more independent and knowledgeable about the wider world. Belle encouraged Belinda to read during her time off, so Belinda made the most of the Cummingses' extensive library. And Belle helped Belinda with practical matters as well, such as what to do with a paycheck.

> It was the first check I ever saw. I asked her, "What's this?" She told me it was my money, and I asked her if she'd save it for me. She said yes, but told me how to put money in a bank. I told her I had a little [other money] and that I needed clothes. She helped me get some and went with me to put my money in the bank.

During the two years Belinda worked for the Cummings family, she got to see a style of life she had not had access to before, and she began to develop the idea of creating something similar for herself. Perhaps more importantly, Belinda was able to reveal more of her inner world without fear of censure. With Belle Cummings it was not necessary for Belinda to hide her needs, her savings, her dreams of returning to Ireland, or, as they gradually took shape, her growing ambitions about life in America. Belle became a trusted advisor and ally. And she introduced Belinda to an ever wider world of her influential friends and illustrious family.

Belle's parents, who lived in New York City, were Mary Owen and John George Brown.[17] Belle's father was a famous artist, best known for his paintings of the city's street urchins. The Cummings family visited the Browns often, and the Brown family also took an interest in Belinda. She, in turn, admired their generous, optimistic spirit, and joined happily in the family fun and jokes.

> I remember how [J. G. Brown] laughed one day. [The Browns] were driving in the park when they came across [Jack and me]. I always hated the bustle things of wire and tape girls were supposed to wear at that time. I'd start out with one and then slip it off the first chance I got. Well when the family drove up that day they found us with me sitting on a bench looking a lot thinner in spots, and Jack sitting in his carriage folding and unfolding that bustle like an accordion. (NW 2:3)

While she was visiting the Browns one day, J. G. Brown painted a picture of Belinda with Jack. It is perhaps them we see looking out the window of the family home[18] at "The Sidewalk Dance" (1894). The composed young woman

2.1. J. G. Brown's painting, "The Sidewalk Dance," dated 1894. We believe the pair inside the house at the window to be Belinda Mulrooney with her young charge Jack Cummings, J. G. Brown's grandson. *(Manoogian Foundation)*

rests her chin in her hand. Her dark hair is wound on top of her head. The child looks to be under three years old.

Until about 1891 Belinda's life with the Cummings family was "just heaven" (NW 2:3). Then began a series of nationwide financial crashes that gravely affected G. King Cummings's business interests. People were thrown out of work as factories began to run on shortened hours or closed entirely, and many businesses failed. Suddenly the Cummings family was no longer very wealthy.[19] Belinda was so concerned that she offered to give them the money she had been saving. They refused, of course. Then she naively suggested to J. G. Brown that she peddle some of his paintings. He laughed heartily and explained that his works were not marketed in that way. But he did sell some of his paintings and gave the proceeds to his daughter.

Feeling that the Cummings family could no longer afford to pay her, Belinda informed them, "As Jack is old enough to look after himself now, I'll go to Chicago. There's a fair there [and] I want to go into business" (NW 2:3–4). Belinda had formulated the plan to go to Chicago after talking with two German women, a cook and a housemaid, who worked in the residence next door. They were going to open a restaurant, and Belinda decided to go with them.[20] Belinda collected her savings, amounting to about six hundred dollars,[21] and headed for Chicago and the World's Columbian Exposition of 1893.[22]

A Turning Point

Belinda's move to Chicago marks an important transition in her life. Her early years in Pennsylvania had been filled with conflicts, isolation, and constant reminders of all the ways she just didn't fit in with her new surroundings. Her time with the Cummings family had helped her to see new possibilities, new ways of thinking about what she could do with her life. When Belinda set her sights on Chicago she was ready to create a place for herself that would be defined by her work. Work became not just a way to get money for the return fare to Ireland, but the means for taking charge of her life and making it what she wanted it to be. Now Belinda began to work for herself.

Besides altering the goal, Belinda also changed the type of her work. The fact that she worked as a teenager was not out of the ordinary. While 19 percent of women were in the labor force in 1890, among single women fifteen years and older participation was 40 percent, and among foreign-born single women it was 71 percent.[23] Belinda was also typical of unmarried working female immigrants in that she had usually performed domestic work. But this would change when she moved to Chicago.

Belinda's personality supported her shift to more independent employment. By the time she was twenty years old, Belinda was self-assured (at least outwardly), imaginative, intelligent, nonconformist, action-oriented, hard-working, independent, often uncomfortable working with others, and a calculated risk-taker. She liked to be in control of her life and her relationships. These characteristics are typical of successful entrepreneurs,[24] which Belinda was about to become. Entrepreneurship would insulate her somewhat from the strong gender segregation and wage discrimination prevailing in wage-earning jobs of the time. As her own boss she could hope to make good money, despite her gender and her relative lack of education.

Although gender discrimination was deeply ingrained in American culture, legal and social conditions in 1890 were not entirely unsympathetic to Belinda's transformation into an independent businesswoman. Women had succeeded in

loosening some of the legal restrictions on their independent business and professional activities.[25]

Some historians view the colonial period of America as a "golden age" for the
economic status of women.[26] They cite as evidence surveys showing an impressive variety of occupations for women in the late 1700s. For example, in Philadelphia colonial women could be found working as silversmiths, tin-workers,
barbers, bakers, fish picklers, brewers, tanners, rope makers, lumberjacks, gun-
smiths, butchers, milliners, harness makers, potash manufacturers, upholsterers,
printers, morticians, chandlers, coach makers, embroiderers, dry cleaners and
dyers, woodworkers, stay makers, tailors, flour processors, seamstresses, net
makers, braziers, and founders.[27] Such occupations were rare in Belinda's day.

Ironically, America's political revolution, founded on the principles of equality of opportunity, coincided with a shift to more restrictive roles for women in
business. One factor contributing to this trend may have been that with national independence, the laws governing businesses and families became more
codified, professionalized, and conservative, for the models turned to were not
those derived from experience in the New World, but those of England. Sir
William Blackstone's *Commentaries on the Laws of England,* first published in
1765, became the guide for legal education in the United States.

One tenet of English common law especially burdensome to independent-
minded women was "coverture," the principle that the married man and woman
were a single entity, and that only the husband was legally recognized. According to Blackstone, "the very being or legal existence of the woman is suspended
. . . [and] incorporated and consolidated into that of the husband."[28] All property was his; all money earned, whether by himself, his wife, or their children,
was his; all contracts were to be made and executed by him alone; the place of
residence was where he lived; the estate was his to be willed as he saw fit.[29]
Under coverture, a married woman would find it impossible to run a business,
for she could not own and dispose of property, enter into contracts, sue, or be
sued in her own right.

Also contributing to the decline in women's business fortunes during the first
half of the nineteenth century was the Industrial Revolution.[30] Industrializa-
tion transferred production out of the home, where it had been in the purview
of women as well as men, into factories where the goods could be made more
economically but where married women often were barred from employment.
Restrictions on a married woman's employment, rationalized as being for her
own and her family's good, were reinforced by the revival and elaboration of
cultural myths about "separate spheres of influence" for men and women. That

is, while women were denied power in the legal, political, and economic world, they were compensated by a more central role in the home; that revised domestic role, however, permitted them agency only through the lives of others. As Marlene Stein Wortman summarizes the prevailing attitudes, "Women were depicted as physically delicate, sexually passive, and selfless. They were the opposite of the colonial image. Woman's role was to supply the immediate physical needs of husbands and children, to socialize the new republic's citizens, and insure the continuity of culture and morality" (*Women in American Law,* 1:4).

An unmarried woman who was of age did not have the legal disabilities of a married woman. But still she faced the cultural myths about what was appropriate for her to do. From the advantage of a broader perspective, French statesman Alexis de Tocqueville on his tour of America in the 1830s noted that "inexorable public opinion carefully keeps woman within the little sphere of domestic interest and duties and will not let her go beyond them" (592), which fact he attributed to America's religious and industrial traditions. Furthermore, neither married nor single women could vote,[31] hold office, or serve on a jury. That is, a businesswoman had no legitimate way to directly influence the business climate in which she operated. Also the fact that a single woman might eventually marry and thereby forfeit control of her business because of coverture often meant that her options were limited in fact if not by law. To make a long-term contract with a woman meant that, should she marry, the agreement transferred to her husband, no matter who he might be.

In the middle and later decades of the nineteenth century, a number of factors brought pressure to modify coverture.[32] Financial panics and depressions motivated legislation to allow married women to protect at least some of the family assets from creditors. The desire to encourage women to help settle the frontiers—and, once there, to protect them from financial disaster should their husbands die or disappear—motivated changes in homestead laws specifically and property rights in general. Better education for women, their proven ability to organize and run effective public service groups, and greater political expertise developed through the movements for temperance and women's civil rights also contributed to the legal reform.

The changes were titled Married Women's Property Acts, and by 1888 they had been enacted in some form throughout the United States,[33] though their provisions varied from state to state. Not all barriers were removed; women were still denied the right to sell, sue, or contract without their husband's or other male relative's approval. And the revisions often had little effect in practice because longstanding traditions and attitudes seldom change quickly. Progressive laws often were reversed within a few years and those that stood were interpreted by male judges,[34] an enforcement system, and a citizenry still reasoning within the framework of coverture. Consequently, though the Married Women's Property Acts were a step toward equality, they were not revolutionary, for usually they still assumed an inherent incapacity of women to act rationally.[35]

The uneven, zig-zagging progress of women's rights during the second half of the nineteenth century often led to incongruities. For instance, in 1872, the year Belinda was born, a number of states had passed Married Women's Property Acts. And that year the National Woman's Suffrage Association celebrated the nomination of Victoria Claflin Woodhull as the first woman candidate for president of the United States. At the same time, Susan B. Anthony, on constitutional grounds, claimed the right as a citizen to cast a ballot. She was promptly arrested, jailed, tried, and convicted of having voted illegally. Women would have to wait another forty-eight years to cast uncontested ballots in a federal election. And also in 1872, in a decision denying highly qualified Myra Colby Bradwell the right to practice law in Illinois, a justice of the Supreme Court could confidently opine:

> . . . The civil law, as well as nature herself, has always recognized a wide difference in the respective spheres and destinies of man and woman. Man is, or should be, woman's protector and defender. The natural and proper timidity and delicacy which belongs to the female sex evidently unfits it for many of the occupations of civil life. The constitution of the family organization, which is founded in the divine ordinance, as well as in the nature of things, indicates the domestic sphere as that which properly belongs to the domain and functions of womanhood.[36]

Belinda was destined to challenge the narrowed cultural vision that restricted women entrepreneurs in the late nineteenth century. She was neither timid nor delicate, and her interests were centered in the occupations of civil life. Her motivations were not political. She simply had the strength, and perhaps insensitivity, to act forthrightly, as well as the knack of identifying environments where she was not likely to be squashed for her deviance. Fortunately there also would be enough support in those environments to allow her to succeed at least some of the time. She became part of the process that would gradually lead to legal, social, and conceptual revisions of women's roles, a process that continues in the present.

3

A Young Entrepreneur Exploits
Chicago and the World's Fair of 1893

THE WORLD'S COLUMBIAN EXPOSITION was planned to commemorate the four-hundredth anniversary of Christopher Columbus's arrival in America and to celebrate the accomplishments of modern civilization and the ideals of ordered, urban life. H. H. Bancroft's official description of the exposition captures the ambitious, even ostentatious, tone of the endeavor—"A Display made by the Congress of Nations, of Human Achievement in Material Form, so as the more Effectually to Illustrate the Progress of Mankind in all the Departments of Civilized Life."[1]

Once Chicago had been chosen as the exposition site, its American planners set out to live up to these lofty aspirations. They would design the World's Columbian Exposition to be a showcase not only for the United States as a whole, but particularly for the businesses and citizens of Chicago. Chicago was then the second-largest city in the United States and hoped to promote further development through the exposure and capital outlay from the exposition.

The site for the main grounds of the fair, selected by the leading American landscape architect Frederick Law Olmsted, was an undeveloped lakefront park to the south of Chicago's center. On the north and south sides of swampy Jackson Park were 56th and 67th Streets, respectively. To the east was Lake Michigan.

Rand, McNally & Co.'s
MAP
OF THE
City of Chicago

EXPLANATION:

City Limits................
Parks and Boulevards......
Railroads................
Stations................

RAILROADS.

	Depot No.
Atchison, Topeka & Santa Fe	6
Baltimore & Ohio	7
Chicago & Alton	5
Chicago & Erie	6
Chicago, Burlington & Quincy	3
Chicago Central	7
Chicago & Eastern Illinois	6
Chicago, Evanston & Lake Superior	3
Chicago & Grand Trunk	4
Chicago, Milwaukee & St. Paul	3
Chicago & Northern Pacific	7
Chicago & North-Western	2
Chicago, Rock Island & Pacific	4
Chicago Great Western	7
Chicago & So. Western	6
Chicago & Western Indiana	6
Illinois Central	1
Kankakee Line (C., C., C. & St. L.)	4
Lake Shore & Michigan Southern	4
Louisville, New Albany & Chicago	4
Michigan Central	1
New York, Chicago & St. Louis	1
Pittsburg, Cincinnati, Chicago & St. Louis	3
Pittsburg, Fort Wayne & Chicago	3
Wabash	4
Wisconsin Central	7

Rand, McNally & Co.'s Map of the City of Chicago

Copyright, 1891, by Rand, McNally & Co.

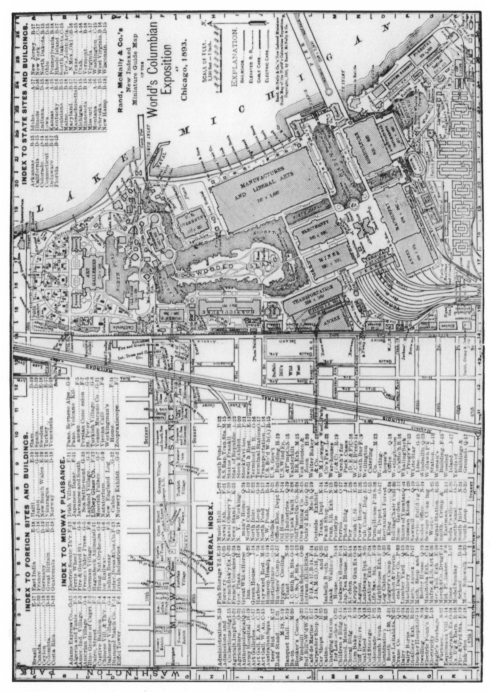

3.1. Map of Chicago in 1891 (*opposite*) with detail of the World's Columbian Exposition grounds (1893) (*above*). In the Chicago map, Jackson Park and the Midway Plaisance are included in the shaded area to the west (*left*) of the "H" in "LAKE MICHIGAN." In the figure above, Cottage Grove Avenue runs north/south along the western margin of the map. The Ferris Wheel location is slightly to the west of the midpoint of the Midway Plaisance. (*CSUF*)

3.2. The magnificent Manufactures and Liberal Arts Building, a centerpiece at the World's Columbian Exposition grounds, located on the north side of the Grand Basin. *(Arnold photog. Photographs, vol. 3, p. III-26, Manufactures Building, c. 1894, platinum print. ©1997, The Art Institute of Chicago. All Rights Reserved. E20822)*

On the west, the main body of the fairgrounds, which housed the formal buildings of the exposition, was bounded by Stony Island Avenue.

Construction for the exposition began with dredging in June of 1891 to create the Lagoon at the center of the main grounds, along with ponds, canals, and more formal basins. Sludge from the dredge was used to build up the higher ground surrounding the waterways, forming the sites for plazas and structures. Within a little less than two years, the large, ornate, neoclassical buildings, some of them supported by engineering masterpieces of modern ironwork, were ready to greet visitors. The names of the principal exhibit halls reflected the most dynamic spheres of late-nineteenth-century American culture—Women, Transportation, Mines, Government, Machinery, Fisheries, Manufactures and Liberal Arts, Electricity, Agriculture, Horticulture, and Fine Arts. Their facades were a dazzling white mock stone made from plaster, fiber, and concrete.[2]

3.3. An interior view of the iron work in the main hall of the Manufactures and Liberal Arts Building, the largest ever constructed to that date. Its 206-foot-high, 368-foot-wide framework allowed an unobstructed interior large enough to contain replica buildings, spires, minarets, and clock towers along with the exhibits. *(Arnold photog.* Photographs, *vol. 1, p. II-20, Manufactures Building, construction interior, 3 August 1892, c. 1894, platinum print. ©1997, The Art Institute of Chicago. All Rights Reserved. E17884)*

Their brightness, so unusual for the smoke-filled, begrimed industrialized world, earned the fairgrounds the nickname of "the White City."

Like Chicago, situated on the margins of a still rough-shod, largely untamed American West, the formal exposition grounds were surrounded by less idealized but no less wondrous exhibits of the world at that time. Between 59th and 60th Streets on the inland side of the main grounds, a mile-long, two-hundred-yard-wide swath stretched westward, connecting the formal exposition grounds with Washington Park. This was the "Midway Plaisance," the carefully planned pleasure strip, the place for "amusing, distracting, ludicrous and noisy attractions."[3] Visitors strolled its wide boulevard to view the exotic belly dancers, glass eaters, and scorpion swallowers of the Algerian Village, or the luxuriously plumed birds, taller than a man, laying eggs large enough to feed a dozen people, at the Ostrich Farm. The admission fees to the exotic exhibits of the Midway Plaisance would prove to be essential to the Exposition's financial success.

At the center of the Midway Plaisance was perhaps the most popular exhibit of the fair—the astounding 268-foot creation of G. W. G. Ferris. Ferris's wheel was many times larger than any previously built roundabout, consisting of two giant wheel frames turning on a horizontal steel axle. Between the two wheels, at their outer edges, were suspended thirty-six cars on pivots, each of which could accommodate up to sixty passengers. As the wheels turned, each car was brought to the top of the rotation, where the view was breath-taking and considered by many to be the highlight of the fair. A single ride lasted about twenty minutes and consisted of two complete revolutions, during one of which the wheel would repeatedly start and stop to gradually exchange passengers on the bottom platform.[4] Ferris's wheel became for the Chicago World Fair what the Eiffel Tower was for the Paris Exposition of 1889—a signature piece, an engineering marvel in steel, a wonder-filled sight in itself, as well as the best place from which to view the rest of the fair.

Outside the fairgrounds to the north of the Midway Plaisance visitors could explore the first few buildings of the newly chartered University of Chicago. The rest of the streets surrounding the fair were lined with independent, unofficial exhibits and businesses, ranging from the elaborate and thrilling Buffalo Bill's Wild West Show to ramshackle booths peddling merchandise, food, and amusement rides.

The Exposition was opened officially 1 May 1893 by President Grover Cleveland. It continued through October 31, with typical daily attendances of 100,000 or more,[5] despite the economic crashes that plagued the financial world throughout the summer. On the specially designated Chicago Day, October 9, as well as the days just before and after, the happy throngs were nearly overwhelming. The Illinois Railroad trains to the fairgrounds on these days alone tallied 541,312 passengers.[6] It is estimated that fourteen million visitors from around the world and as much as one-tenth of the population of the United States attended the fair.[7]

Into this dynamic, expansive atmosphere came Belinda Agnes Mulrooney. She apparently arrived in late 1891 or early 1892, when work on the exposition halls was under way.[8] Belinda first found a place to live with two German women above their bakery on Cottage Grove Avenue[9] and perhaps worked for them briefly. As independent bakers, Belinda's employers were helping to expand the number of woman-owned businesses in America as well as the number of

3.4. G. W. G. Ferris's first colossal wheel was built on the Midway Plaisance of the Chicago Columbian Exposition, 1893. *(CSUF)*

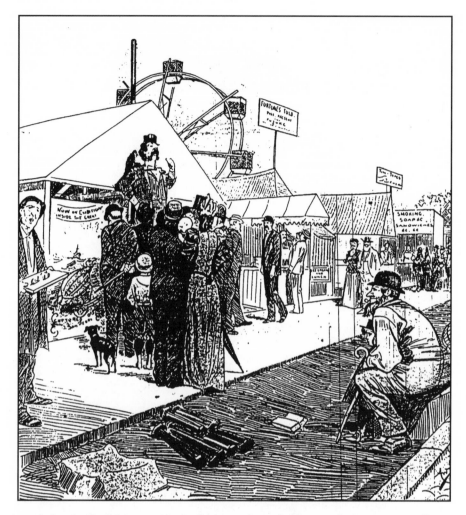

3.5. A sketch of exhibits outside the fairgrounds, probably near the intersection of Cottage Grove Avenue with the 60th Street corner of the Midway Plaisance. (The Inter Ocean, *11 June 1893, cover of Supplement. Anderson Collection*)

woman bakers. According to the United States Census of 1890, while women made up 17.2 percent of the general labor force, they were only 3.8 percent of bakers. This percentage would increase to 5.5 percent by 1900.[10]

Cottage Grove Avenue was a good business location during the fair. The western gate of the Midway Plaisance opened onto the avenue, with Washington Park on the other side of the street. Cottage Grove also carried the north-south cable car line connecting to downtown Chicago, and so it was a major route to the fairgrounds.

Once settled, Belinda set out to observe the marvels of the developments on the fairgrounds. The light-filled, vibrant environment of the Columbian Exposition was exactly suited to her taste. "I do not believe any one ever saw any more than I did when I was young," she recalled. "I would walk down a street, and I believe I could have given you not only a description of the buildings, but the lettering and wording of every sign we passed."

Belinda's nearly photographic memory was always activated by construction methods and details. The exposition's grounds were an ideal schoolroom for observing not only state-of-the-art design, but also basic construction techniques. After careful observation, followed by surveying the developing layout of the fairgrounds and guessing at the needs of soon-to-arrive crowds, Belinda was ready to do some building of her own.

She bought a lot just outside the Midway Plaisance on Cottage Grove Avenue where land was still available at a reasonable price. This was Belinda's first real estate purchase, and she was so naive that she was unsure exactly how the transaction was carried out. She wondered why the real estate agents did not seem bothered that she was underage. When she had paid for the lot, she asked, "What do I get?" and had to have deeds explained to her.[11]

Belinda need not have worried about being younger than twenty-one years, for she was now doing business in one of the few states where she was actually at an advantage in that regard compared to young males. In Illinois women reached majority at age eighteen, while men had to wait until twenty-one. And because she was single and an adult, there was no barrier to her owning and controlling property, as there might have been had she been married.[12] Although Belinda thought what she was doing was illegal, she did not let that stop her. No doubt she reasoned that the age of majority was somewhat arbitrary, and since she was as responsible as any adult, there was no reason for her to obey the letter of what she thought was the law.

Belinda next had a building constructed for speculation on the front part of her land. The lot cost $600, the materials were $1,500, and she paid the laborers by the day out of money earned from rental of the rest of the property. So Belinda's first entrepreneurial undertaking was in an area very much out of the "feminine sphere." While some women did own their own businesses at this time, they were usually in the service sector or related to domestic activities, such as the bakery of her German friends. It was highly unusual to find a woman, let alone a young woman, acting as a real estate developer and contractor. In 1890 in most areas of the building trades, women represented less than one-tenth of one percent of the work force; those proportions increased slightly in the next decade thanks to the activities of women like Belinda.[13]

Belinda was helped by the fact that the building boom surrounding the fair presented unique opportunities. First, the authorities who might otherwise have enforced restrictions were occupied by the hectic construction pace of official buildings. And then more chances for making a quick profit on development appeared as the opening drew nearer. With her natural interest in construction, Belinda acted decisively to take advantage of these conditions. If she had any qualms about invading a masculine domain or about her chances of accomplishing what she set out to do, she did not mention them.

According to Belinda, for a time G. W. G. Ferris rented the back of her lot for a hundred dollars per month to store a small model of his Ferris wheel and his gear; this small wheel, she said, was used as a ride for children.[14] There were, indeed, two small roundabouts on Cottage Grove Avenue near the entrance to the Midway Plaisance. One was begun in November 1892 on the southwest corner of Cottage Grove and 60th Street and was in operation by 1 April 1893.[15] The second opened about June 1893 on the east side of Cottage Grove near Sixtieth Street,[16] and it is this one we think is illustrated in figure 3.5. While both of these small wheels were in locations congruent with Belinda's description of her lot, neither was built by G. W. G. Ferris, and we have been unable to discover whether Ferris's crew had an additional small model wheel such as Belinda described.[17]

After a short time Belinda sold her first building and used the profit to buy a restaurant nearby. She hired an older woman to sell "wienies and a special lunch for 25 cents" (NW 3:1). This became the base for her second self-owned business and may be the location listed as 3025 Cottage Grove Avenue in the 1893 Chicago City Directory. From the directory we also learn that Belinda's associate was named Nannie Langjahr.[18] The restaurant was only part of the business, however, for apparently Belinda also peddled food from it out on the streets.

Belinda spent most of her time working in the vicinity of the fairgrounds, where she could observe the glitter, as would any tourist. The Midway attractions were especially showy. One could see "Gentleman Jim" Corbett, the heavyweight champion, demonstrate the artistry of boxing, or for comic relief, a boxing match between a man and a kangaroo. (The kangaroo won.)[19] Refreshments were available at a Japanese teahouse, at cafes, and at lemonade and beer gardens. There were African, Irish, South Seas Island, German, Austrian, Chinese, Dahomey, and American Indian villages. There was a Bedouin encampment and a replica of a block of a Cairo street with three-story facades and a bazaar, where donkey drivers, veiled women, fakirs, musicians, camels, a wedding procession, or a magician attracted curious spectators. At an Egyptian theater Fahreda Mahzar, "Little Egypt," drew much comment for her performance of a belly dance. Belinda saw them all. But from her longer-term vantage point, she also witnessed the fair's seamier side.

> The shows [along the Midway, such as] Streets of Cairo and such things made me sick. But the police made me sicker. They gave [the shows] concessions, [and] took their money, [knowing] what they were going to do. Then they'd arrest the people and take the balance of their money.
>
> This [one] midnight I found the police were hustling a whole show, children and women and all, into a patrol wagon. So I just told the police, "If you take them, you take me. And I'll tell the judge all about it."
>
> One of the officers had as much of a brogue as mine. "Where are you from?" he asked, and I told him. His name was Mr. [McGuinness].[20] Darned if he hadn't been brought up across the street from where my grandmother lived in Ireland![21]
>
> He let those people go. They brought me tea in long bricks, bottles of wine and attar of roses all summer long, they were so grateful. (NW 3:2)

Officer McGuinness also befriended Belinda. According to Belinda in one later interview, he actually helped her with the arrangements to buy her first piece of property.[22] He was concerned that Belinda had no contact with her family. She still had no use for the crowd back in Archbald, to which another sibling, Jim, had been added in 1892.[23] When Officer McGuinness learned that Belinda had not told her parents where she was, he wrote to them to let them know he was keeping an eye on her, and that she was doing well in Chicago (NW 3:3).

Of course, Chicago was a big city, and the area around the fairgrounds was a lot rougher than the quiet neighborhoods of Chestnut Hill or Archbald. Furthermore, in the years Belinda lived in Chicago, the boom of the World's Fair presented extra opportunities to those who wanted to make their way illegally. Purse stealers, pickpockets, and con artists were common at the fair, and occasionally even parts of exhibits were stolen.[24] And of course, illegal activities were not confined to the exposition grounds. While Belinda was living with the German bakers on Cottage Grove Avenue, she had at least one encounter with thieves, and she showed unusual daring when she dealt with them.

The German girls' rooms had bay windows over their restaurant. Looking out of them one night at midnight, we could see a gang of thieves coming down the street with a wagon. In Chicago at that time, they'd clean up everything on both sides of the street. And never a policeman in sight . . . either.

The old girls were wringing their hands over their money, which was downstairs [in a cigar box] in the cigar show case. A pistol [was] with it.

So I go down in my night shirt and braids and bare feet. I got the money and the revolver out of the box by the light from the street coming in through the upper part of the windows. I tiptoed to the front door where the shade was pulled down almost to the bottom. That was why I had to stoop down to take a peek.

On the other side of the door was a fellow, all dressed up like a cowboy to try to look frightening. He was trying to open the door, stooping down too. I saw him. He saw me. I was so scared that pistol rattled over the glass. We both ran. As I stepped back a rat ran over my foot. I gave a scream. It frightened me more than everything else. . . . Those sisters told the cops. . . . My God, what excitement! (NW 3:2–3)

It was an exciting story—Gun-Toting Girl Foils Burglars—and according to Belinda it got front page coverage in at least one of the Chicago newspapers.[25]

Fire was another danger in the big city. Most heating and cooking was done by wood-fired stoves, and gas lamps and candles were typical sources of light. A stray spark could easily catch and spread through the closely spaced wooden buildings typical in residential neighborhoods. Furthermore, in Chicago any fire triggered anxious memories of the conflagration, set off legendarily by the O'Learys' cow, that had leveled major portions of the central city in 1871 and killed more than three hundred people. Newspaper headlines in the summer of 1893 included a number of reports of life-threatening fires. On 10 July the cold storage building at the southwest corner of the fair grounds went up in flames, killing sixteen firemen. On 1 August a quickly spreading blaze across the street from Belinda's restaurant gutted five buildings and forced two women to a dramatic escape along a narrow plank suspended between the windows of adjoining buildings.[26] And within eight months after it closed, most of the buildings of the Columbian Exposition would be burned to the ground.[27]

Belinda had a close encounter with fire. Her quick action saved her from the disastrous consequences of a potential building fire, but her apparent lack of concern for the distress her impetuous act caused her neighbor is notable in this account.

I threw a burning oil cooking stove out of the upstairs room where I lived. Just took it and threw it—crash!—through the glass of a window, right onto the Dago's fruit stand below. I can see him now, with his hands in the air, bananas and apples flying everywhere. I'd just wanted to separate the fire from the building as quickly as possible. (NW 3:1)

A highlight for Belinda at the World Fair was Chicago Day on October 9.

. . . There were such mobs, all traffic was suspended, people [were] stranded, and nobody even had bread to eat. It couldn't be delivered. So I hired a transfer wagon outside the crowded zone, bought a wagon load of bread, and sold it for 50 cents a loaf.

And who should be in that mob but Mrs. Cummings! The jam had messed her up, so I rescued her. And when I got her on the wagon, [I] acted like a baby bear I hugged her so hard. "How's Jack?" was my first question.

Her feet were all trampled on so I took her into my restaurant and fixed her up. She had a sense of humor always and kept laughing. "Are you telling me the truth? Do you own this building!?" When I took her home [the Cummingses were living in Chicago by then],[28] she kept saying, "Get George [Mr. Cummings) and tell him. My! Oh my!" (NW 3:3)

The Columbian Exposition closed shortly after Chicago Day. In the meantime, promoters in San Francisco had organized an exhibition for the winter of 1893–94. Belinda decided to follow the action to San Francisco. Her enterprises in Chicago had netted her eight thousand dollars—a very considerable sum for those days, when a skilled male laborer could expect to earn about a thousand dollars a year.[29] But Belinda's gains were more than monetary. Chicago had laid much of the occupational groundwork upon which she would build her adult life.

DURING THE YEAR or so she was in Chicago, Belinda had mastered the fundamentals of entrepreneurship—contracts, finance, management, and marketing —as well as the specifics of practicing three kinds of business—restaurant, real estate development, and construction. She had learned how to buy on time and how to develop and sell property for profit. She increased her understanding of construction materials and techniques. She saw the importance of arriving early and anticipating the needs of people who were to follow. She worked hard, but found she could accomplish even more by delegating to others the jobs she didn't have the skills for or didn't particularly like. She learned how to manage these employees effectively. She experienced not only the direct rewards of her efforts, but also the glow from having her accomplishments recognized and praised by someone she admired, such as Belle Brown Cummings. She learned that boldness was often enough to intimidate others and carry the day. She saw that treating people fairly was important and would be appreciated, and that the law and its representatives were not necessarily always fair. These latter observations increased her readiness in the future to take noncompliant and unconventional actions. More generally, Belinda learned that by finding the right niche, she could start and run a business to earn a lot of money, even when the overall economic climate was very poor.

The motivation for her work had also shifted from the time she lived in Pennsylvania. Still determined to be financially independent, she no longer was working to go to Ireland. Now she wanted to stay in America, support herself, and live up to her own high goals of being a success in the world.

Perhaps Belinda's self-confidence also was reinforced by the optimistic spirit and achievements of the women activists at the World's Fair. Though Belinda may have felt an outsider in Archbald, Pennsylvania, in Chicago she saw there were other women like herself who were ambitious, who were not satisfied with the status quo, and who knew how to get things done in the public arena. They had succeeded in getting space designated for a Woman's Building at the Exposition. They commissioned a female architect, Sophia Hayden, to design the building. They planned the exhibits contributed by women from all over the world. And they financed the whole undertaking. Furthermore, during the week of 17–23 May they conducted an International Woman's Congress, discussing women's changing roles in the world and feminist ideals, such as reproductive rights, voting, prohibition, and improvement of working conditions. From these activities Belinda could observe that women can be movers and shakers in the world, and that their talents and achievements would be acknowledged, even though sometimes ambivalently. Perhaps she was encouraged by this to continue to seek her own glory, though her pathway would not be through political or social movements.

All of these were potent lessons. For twenty-one-year-old Belinda Mulrooney, her Chicago enlightenment marked a true coming of age.

4

Launching into the Pacific Northwest

ORGANIZERS OF THE Midwinter International Exposition in San Francisco, held in 1894, hoped to duplicate the great success of the World's Columbian Exposition in Chicago the year before. Despite setbacks in the general economy, huge crowds had been attracted to Chicago, and many of the fairgoers seemed enthusiastic for more travel. The Midwinter Fair, though much more modest than the Chicago exposition, would provide an excuse for well-to-do travelers to go further west, to see the sights, and to enjoy the milder winter weather along the Pacific coast. And the fair could give a welcome boost to the financial doldrums of San Francisco.

San Francisco at this time was the largest city in the American West. Transportation had been the key to the city's growth in the nineteenth century. Sailing ships found safe harbor in its large but well-protected bay, and linked the otherwise isolated outpost with the rest of the continent and the world. The sleepy little town of a few hundred souls got its first big boost from the discovery of gold in 1848 in the foothills of the Sierra Nevada Mountains. The gold fields were a little more than a hundred miles to the east, but they were connected to the bay area by navigable rivers and wagon roads. Within two years San Francisco's population soared to 35,000 as gold, gold seekers, supplies, merchants, bankers, speculators, and con artists filtered through the city. When the gold craze began to wane after a few years, the economic base of central California shifted to more steady mining and to development of its rich agricultural lands. These supported San Francisco's continuing growth as a transportation and financial center. And then the Comstock silver boom in Nevada, on the eastern side of the Sierras, helped to boost the population to nearly 150,000 by 1870. Also by that time, the first transcontinental railroad, terminating in San Francisco, assured continuance of the bay area's position as a center of commerce.

But in 1893 San Francisco's 300,000 residents confronted unemployment, financial panic, and general economic depression along with the rest of the nation. An influx of dollars from tourists attending the Midwinter Fair would be heartily welcomed. Under the direction of M. H. DeYoung and with financial support from city, county, and state governments as well as from citizens of widely varying means,[1] ground was broken in Golden Gate Park on 24 August 1893. After a little more than four months of industrious construction, the fair opened on 27 January 1894.

When twenty-one-year-old Belinda Mulrooney arrived in San Francisco that winter, she was far from her simple Irish village origins—geographically, physically, and psychologically. Physically, her appearance was changing both with maturity and with increased self-assurance and sophistication. She stood five feet three inches tall, and her luxuriant, dark, chestnut-colored hair was wound into a business-like bun at the nape of her neck. She was dressed in plain but well-cut clothes. She walked with an erect, purposeful gait,[2] and her plump girlish figure had filled out to the more buxom contours of womanhood. Though even as a child Belinda's daring exploits suggested inherent confidence, now her self-assurance was based upon the knowledge gained from her rich experiences in Chicago. The money and cashier's check in her purse also insured that she had resources to bankroll her next undertakings.

It was the possibility of setting up a business connected with the Midwinter Fair that had drawn Belinda's attention to San Francisco, but she soon became disillusioned with the exposition. "I found the Midwinter Fair was made up from the flip-over from Chicago. . . . I saw a lot of the old punk stuff."

So Belinda looked around San Francisco for other investments for her Chicago profits. In the meantime, with a mixture of practicality and sentimentality, she deposited her money in the Hibernian Bank. She picked it simply because the name appealed to her, as it no doubt had to other Irish immigrants, a large number of whom had settled in the bay area. Irish workers arrived early in the "Americanization" of the West. They made up a large portion of the laborers constructing the transcontinental railroad. They mined gold and silver in California and Nevada. Some of the most successful, the millionaires of the Comstock lode of Virginia City, Nevada, were prominent figures in San Francisco finance and politics. Perhaps Belinda was encouraged by their example.

For amusement Belinda took long walks and enjoyed the views from atop the hills of the city. She also indulged her love of horses and her yen for a bit of a gamble by going to the races. "I won four hundred dollars at the old race track down by Sutro Heights.[3] I wasn't as excited about the money as I was the race. I think I got the one grand thrill of my life to see that old gray horse stretch himself, going with everything in him" (NW 4:1).

Finally, after about a month of surveying the business scene, Belinda found what she was looking for in the heart of San Francisco's commercial district.

> I located a place on Sixth and Market, on the corner. The building was badly kept up. I got interested, made arrangements with the owner, and rented it very cheaply [because the building was in such poor repair]. So I got a lease for a long term and put the building in shape. I spent a great deal more money on the downstairs, which I sublet for a restaurant . . . .[4] The upstairs was rented to a woman to keep roomers.
>
> That owner got very large insurance on his place after I had fixed it up. And just as my tenants were moving [in], it burned.

Belinda herself was uninsured. Having borne all the cost of the extensive renovations, she lost $7,500 in the fire. When she learned what had happened, she immediately went looking for her landlord. She suspected he had set the fire for the insurance money, and she wanted to hold him to an accounting. "I spent two solid weeks looking for him, but I never saw him after the fire." Here was a business lesson learned the hard way. But the loss of nearly all of her finances did not stop her for long.

At the time of the disaster, Belinda was living at the Fairmount Hotel at the corner of Market, Fell, and Post Streets, about two blocks from City Hall and five blocks from her burned-out investment.[5] Her loss became known to the sympathetic owner of the Fairmount,[6] who befriended Belinda and gave her a temporary job at the hotel (Franklin, 23). Domestic service in a hotel was not Belinda's cup of tea, but the owner's kindness helped ease the shock of Belinda's losses. Eventually she was ready to seek her fortune in new directions. She remembered the joy of sailing on her trans-Atlantic immigration ten years earlier. From the cliffs on the western edge of San Francisco, her imagination was captured once again by the salt-tinged breezes, the view of the vast ocean, and the ships funneling toward the Golden Gate.

At this important juncture, the supporting hand of her friend Belle Brown Cummings reached across the continent to help Belinda get started again. Belle had introduced Belinda to her friend Mrs. Cramp, whose family owned Cramp and Sons, a large shipbuilding yard in Philadelphia.[7] Mrs. Cramp liked Belinda and gave her a letter of recommendation. With this letter, Belinda approached the firm of Goodall and Perkins, at the foot of Market Street, general agents for the Pacific Coast Steamship Company, for whom Cramp had built ships.[8] Belinda talked with George C. Perkins himself, a prominent businessman and former state senator and governor of California. He was sympathetic to her plight and recommended that she talk with Thomas R. Turner, the port steward, about getting a job.

> I went to Mr. Turner's office, determined to stay on his hands until he was rid of me. He was kind of snappy and busy.
>
> "What can you do?" he asked me.
>
> "I don't know," I answered him. "Tell me what I have to do and I will do the best I can."
>
> "What do you want to do?"
>
> "I want to work on one of the ships. I want to work on one going to Alaska." I had seen it on the posters on the dock, and it seemed far away and new to me.
>
> "That's out of the question," he told me. "We don't carry stewardesses there."
>
> . . . Mr. Turner, on account of Mr. Perkins, felt he'd have to find something for me. There was a stewardess sick on the southern run down to San Diego,[9] and I could try that. I made that trip and worked like heck. I did everything, anything, even if it wasn't mine, so he'd have no kick. . . .
>
> . . . When I came back I told him I didn't care for duties on that run. Too many whining women on it. Mr. Turner said he'd try me on the *City of Topeka* on the Alaska run.

Like many hard-working, goal-directed, enterprising high achievers, Belinda was not particularly tolerant of those who traded on privilege. Mr. Turner's assessment that Belinda might do well on the Alaska run was accurate in at least two respects. First, it suited her interest in seeing more of the undeveloped north country. Second, it put her in contact primarily with passengers who were used to living on the frontier, where self-sufficiency was valued, and who thus were likely to have attitudes resembling her own. Belinda headed for Alaska in the spring of 1895.[10]

The *City of Topeka*'s Alaskan run was between Seattle and the ports along Alaska's southeastern panhandle.[11] Southeast Alaska is a long, narrow strip formed by a range of mountains to the west of northern British Columbia. The eastern tiers of the range are high enough to be connected by land to the North American continent, while the band of mountains along the western edge is partly submerged by the Pacific Ocean. The islands in this chain protect the waters between them and the mainland from the brunt of the Pacific Ocean's wind and waves. Irregular shorelines lead into picturesque, rugged fjords and deep bays, and the calm waters serve as a north-south marine highway called the Inside Passage. Abundant rainfall along the coast nourishes thick forests of hemlock, spruce and cedar in the southern regions of the panhandle. To the north, glaciers blanket most of the rugged mountains, scouring and sweeping them into the sea and depositing icebergs that bedevil unwary ships winding through the Inside Passage.

The *City of Topeka*'s main function was to carry mail, freight, and supplies to the residents of Southeast Alaska and to provide them with transportation, for waterways were the only "roads" for the towns and villages on the rugged coast. When Belinda joined the crew of the *City of Topeka*, tourists, eager to explore the newly opening Alaskan territory, were also a growing part of the ship's business.

David Wallace was captain of the *City of Topeka*. Belinda described him as "a Scotsman, a great big red-faced man with two gold teeth, who was very religious and held prayers twice a day at sea."[12] Captain Wallace was not sure what to do with Belinda. The Alaska run had not carried a stewardess before, so he was uncertain what duties to assign her. And he also worried about having a young woman on board. Belinda put him at his ease by talking with him in her competent, no-nonsense manner. Then she set out to make herself indispensable.

> A wreck of a little Spanish fellow kept the officer's rooms in order, brushed their clothes and looked after them generally. "I'm going to use you, Davey," I said to myself, "to do the things I don't want to do."
>
> . . . There were quite a number of women on board, and I introduced Davey to them when there were trays to be hauled. I made a contract with him. "I'll go and get their orders, and you take them the trays. I will not accept tips. I'll clean the silver for you. If they don't pay you, I will." Davey and I got an understanding right away. . . . It put the Alaska and Juneau people in good humor to have the service.

. . . Before we landed on the return trip, I asked the Captain if he thought I had rendered enough service.

"Yes, girl, sure you did all right."

"Would you mind reporting so?" I asked him. "I kind of talked Mr. Perkins into the job."

With Captain Wallace's support, Belinda was hired for a regular position. She was delighted. She liked the officers and crew. She loved Alaska and the sea. And she enjoyed meeting the occasional challenges presented to her: on one trip she was called upon to assist in the delivery of a baby. Though she was eager to please, Belinda evidently knew how to set boundaries on her duties.

There's nothing like being a stewardess to develop your wits when you're just a bit too independent for the job and you have to give the passengers as good as they send when they're sassy. I remember an old Englishman who expected me to black his boots. I told him I wouldn't, and I told him if he put 'em outside his door again I'd be thinkin' he was wantin' ice-water and turn a pitcherful into 'em.

He went to the captain. The captain . . . didn't believe in puttin' on airs; and when the captain sent for me and I went to the captain's room, I found the old gentleman there. Before we came out I had him laughin', and I'd never blacked his boots, either.[13]

A photograph of Belinda taken at about this time shows her considerably heavier than she had been in Philadelphia. In fact, she described herself as, "short and stocky with rosy cheeks, and my chestnut colored hair was always falling down to my heels at the wrong time—a darned nuisance" (NW 1:1). By the time of the photograph she had begun wearing glasses, probably for near-sightedness.

Although Belinda was the official stewardess of the *City of Topeka,* she also was alert to possibilities for sideline businesses. She soon recognized that both on board and on shore, people wanted certain goods that weren't readily available. Belinda the entrepreneur found a way to provide the items at a reasonable price—and with a nice profit for herself.

I pegged away a year and a half at that job. I got very busy with my remaining four hundred dollars. I bought a lot of Alpine sticks and turned them over to Davey and also started him in business with steamer chairs. It was astonishing how much money he cut with me.

Then different families traveled with us who lived in Alaska and did not like the stores, which were just general merchandise. I told them I'd purchase for

4.1. Belinda Mulrooney at about age twenty-four when she was a stewardess on the *City of Topeka* steamship's Alaska run. *(DeArmond Collection)*

them in Seattle anything they wished to have brought up. In six months I had the heaviest bill of lading on the *City of Topeka*. Once I brought back on the same trip canary birds and a cow. The manager's wife of the Treadwell mine [near Juneau] wanted some canaries, and someone else wanted a cow.

Mr. Curtis, the [usually dignified, sober] purser, used to laugh over the bill of lading. "Which have you got in the cage, the cow or the canary?"

. . . There was always someone waiting [with lists] for the steamer going down. . . . McDougall and Southwick [a clothing and dry goods store in Seattle] used to look forward to the docking of the *City of Topeka* in Seattle. They allowed me a good stiff commission, but I would not let them charge the Alaskans more than Seattle prices. They sold [to] me wholesale. I bought eider quilts, fancy linen, [gowns and underwear]. I was nicknamed by the crew, "Purchasing Agent for Alaska."

As a retail merchant, someone who purchased goods for resale rather than simply sold goods belonging to others, Belinda was helping to open new territory for businesswomen. Only about 4 percent of retailers at this time were females, and very few of those were operating in Alaska.[14]

According to some reports, Belinda did not feel bound to uphold the law in all respects when doing business, for she also is said to have supplemented her income by peddling whiskey. Under a provision of Alaska's Organic Law of 1884, the importation, manufacture, and sale of intoxicating liquors, except for medicinal purposes, was forbidden. Although religious advocates in the territory vigorously supported the prohibition, much of the Caucasian population of the territory was against it. As one commentator later explained, "The people of Alaska took the position that Congress passed the prohibition law for the Indians and not for the whites, and consequently felt justified in opposing it."[15]

As a result, smuggled whiskey was widely available and easily bought in saloons and liquor stores. So if Belinda did break the law to bring in whiskey, in the eyes of some she was doing the people of Alaska a great service by supplying a good grade of liquor. According to one informant, Belinda had made a long fur coat with a canvas lining. Into the lining twenty-four pockets were sewn, each of which could hold a half-pint bottle.[16]

Native Americans also were among Belinda's customers (Franklin, 23), but she was very careful not to sell them whiskey. For Native Americans the prohibition law was strictly enforced, and violations carried very stiff penalties. When Alaska was first discovered by Europeans in 1741, the territory that became Southeast Alaska was occupied by the Tlingits, who suffered dreadfully from the contact.[17] By the 1890s they were decimated by warfare and disease, and their traditions were disrupted by the encroachment of trappers, settlers, miners, and missionaries. Many Tlingits shifted from a self-sufficient life-style to an economy based upon selling furs or trading them for goods from Seattle. The following account of one transaction with Belinda reveals her prejudice toward Native Americans, an attitude fairly typical for the time.

> The Indians used to make a great deal of money, and they got to be a nuisance. The darned things lined up, wanting to give me money to buy things.
>
> I remember one fat squaw in Sitka who had seen what she wanted for a bridal outfit in pictures in a magazine. [It was to be of white satin, and] she wanted a picture hat. I told her it would be expensive. She did not care. "I give you money now," she said. I took her measurements for everything, including shoes. I knew they'd have to make up something for her specially, she was so fat.
>
> I'll never forget when the boat got into Sitka. The tide was high and the gang plank steep, but that squaw came aboard. She must see what I had brought. McDougall had put some orange blossoms in with the outfit. She just had to put the dress on and wear it off the boat with her moccasins on. And she was pigeon-toed [and] all smiles.
>
> I'll never forget Captain Wallace. His fat stomach was going up and down with his laughing.

Native Americans were not the only ones to bear the brunt of Belinda's derisive humor. Among her other targets were demanding, complaining women. The following account comes from one of Belinda's passengers.

Making a short stop at Juneau, we went on to Sitka by way of the Muir Glacier, now partially destroyed by an earthquake, making it no longer safe for steamers to go in. It was indescribably grand and beautiful.

. . . The *Topeka* anchored a mile from the face of the glacier, for the great bergs as they calved from the glacier sent great ice-laden waves which might have damaged the ship. The passengers were taken to the shore on the right hand side of the glacier in the ship's boats, carefully counted off and on, that no one might be marooned—a chilly proposition with no food, no wood for a fire, and no shelter.

. . . [Lloyd Valentine] Winter, the Juneau photographer, was with the steamer—a custom in those days—to take pictures of those so inclined. He kindly took mine with my camera—dry plates, no Kodaks then—and I took others.

[Among the passengers going ashore was] a Rhode Island school teacher who was always seeking the limelight, and who appeared in a Swiss Alpine costume of violent maroon—she was not young—Alpine hat, feather and all. Greatly satisfied with herself, she was a source of quiet amusement to the rest.

The *Topeka* stewardess, Miss Mulrooney, [explained later], "She had been so fault-finding and snippy that when she asked me about wearing it, I said 'Sure,

4.2. The *City of Topeka* at Muir Glacier. Walking sticks, perhaps sold to these excursionists by stewardess Belinda Mulrooney, are very much in evidence. Like the trip referred to by William Johns, this scene was photographed by Winter and Pond of Juneau in 1895. *(Library of Congress, 700128, 262–53979)*

it is just the thing.'" She told me [this] with a grin as wide as that of the cat that swallowed the canary. (Johns, 14–15)

With Belinda's successful trading also came complications. Although the company officers stationed in Alaska and their families thought the service a "God-send," "it rolled up to such a volume that the merchants in Juneau resented it and complained to the office of the [shipping] company." Neither Belinda nor McDougall and Southwick wanted to lose her profitable business. Therefore, the company suggested that she simply open a store for them in Juneau. And so we find an announcement on 15 July 1896 in the Juneau newspaper, *Alaska Searchlight*:

> The McDougall and Southwick Company, Seattle dress goods and clothing firm, has opened an order branch in the Schmeig Building in Juneau. Miss Belinda Mulrooney, who has been a stewardess on the *City of Topeka*, is in charge of the branch. Goods ordered through the branch will be delivered to the customer without freight or express charges.

Belinda was too restless to stay long with the static business in town. By the end of September she left Juneau on the *City of Topeka*. She planned to take up a position as a stewardess on a trans-Pacific liner,[18] but it is not clear whether she actually did so. By midwinter she was back in Juneau, where rumors were trickling in from the north about gold discoveries in the Yukon River basin. Belinda was eager to explore trading prospects along the Yukon, where miners would have gold to pay for her goods. On her first attempt to reach the interior, however, she found her equipment and companions inadequate for the formidable journey over the passes (NW 5:1).

Belinda returned to Juneau to regroup and get the necessary equipment. A prospector arriving from the Yukon basin showed samples of the gold being taken from a fabulous strike on a tributary of the Klondike River, which flowed into the Yukon River.[19] Here was an opportunity not to be missed—to be in early on an apparently rich gold strike. Belinda had the connections and the financial resources to pull together an "outfit" quickly. She had enough experience to know what getting to the Klondike would take. And she knew people who were already familiar with the territory and with whom she could team up. Belinda was off to the Klondike.

5

Chilkoot

Going In in 1897

T HE DISCOVERY CLAIM that started the Klondike gold rush was located about 410 miles north by northwest of Juneau as the raven flies, on a creek that came to be called Bonanza. The creek flows into the Klondike River, which, within a mile, joins the mighty Yukon River. Though there were a few trading posts along the Yukon River, cabins of trappers and prospectors here and there, and occasional villages of Native Americans, this interior region of Alaska and of Canada's Northwest Territories was, and still is, mostly wilderness, a world unto itself. To its residents, on the "Inside," the rest of the world is the "Outside."

The main routes Inside to the Klondike gold fields were by way of the Yukon River—one upstream, the other downstream. In the summer shallow-draft boats could steam up the river from its mouth on Norton Sound on the western coast of Alaska. First they churned northeast until reaching Fort Yukon, at the mouth of the Porcupine River. There the Yukon River turned sharply to the southeast. Seventeen hundred miles upstream from Norton Sound, the straining steamers arrived at last at their destination. The town site of Dawson, established shortly after the Klondike discovery, was on the relatively flat, swampy floodplain to the northeast of the junction of the Klondike and Yukon Rivers.

The second route to Dawson, coming down the Yukon River with the current, was by far more popular. This one started from the northernmost inlets of

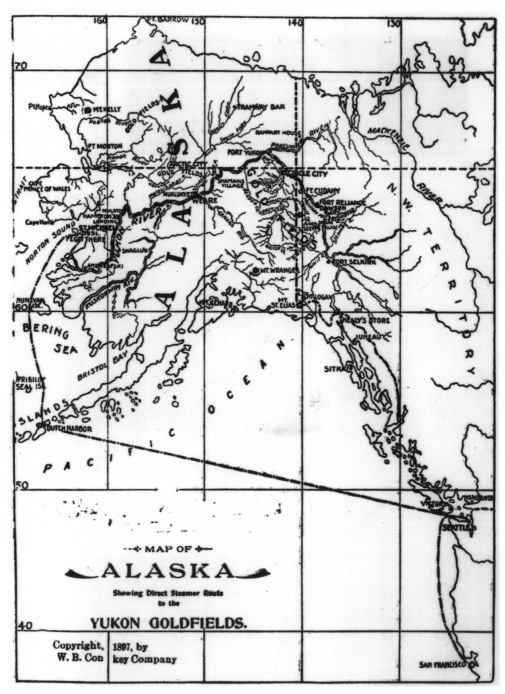

5.1. A map of the northwestern United States and Canada in 1897 showing the location of the Klondike goldfields just east of the Canadian border with Alaska.

(UW, LaRoche photog., 1897, 9075)

Alaska's Inside Passage. The headwaters of the Yukon are in the lakes only thirty-some miles north from the sea and across a range of coastal mountains. Once through the lakes, the flow of the Yukon would carry a boat the 550 miles north to Dawson within a couple of weeks, if it managed to avoid the usual hazards of river travel—rapids, sweepers,[1] and hidden rocks.

During the winter, the Yukon River freezes solid. Then the only way to get to Dawson was by dogsled or snowshoe. The winter trail approximately followed the downstream river route, but took as direct a path as possible between the various outposts along the river.

Prior to 1896 members of the Tlingit tribe had established and controlled for trading several trails from the Inside Passage across the mountains to the interior. These became the routes used by the earliest gold seekers. The Chilkoot trail, starting at Dyea, Alaska, climbing across 3,550-foot Chilkoot Pass, and then descending to Lakes Lindeman and Bennett, was the most popular of these early routes. It was via Chilkoot that Belinda and her party started for the Klondike strike.

But first Belinda had to get her outfit together. She gathered information about what would be needed from Two-Finger McKay, who had just arrived in Juneau from the Interior with news of the gold strike. Then she went to Seattle to get her gear. For the trail she would wear moccasins and high boots, with snowshoes added when needed. Her skirts were tailor-made in Seattle. They were "short" (calf-length) and gored up to a high waistline. "I ditched corsets," she explained, "which was a rash thing to do in those days. But the skirts were whaleboned around the waist and made a good substitute. I suffered a lot from the whalebone stuff. I always had a grudge against it. I had three suits—one of corduroy, one of tweeds, and one of navy . . . serge."

Under her long-sleeved, man's-style heavy shirt and her skirt could be layered light or heavy underwear. She took a fur parka for less active times around camp, but her traveling parka was of denim with a fur lining on the hood to surround the face. Snow glasses were also needed to protect the eyes from sunburn. Belinda's sleeping bag was made of eider quilts on the inside and red fox fur on the outside, with an outermost layer of oiled silk sheets to keep out dampness.

For food she packed mainly lightweight items. The many dried foods available included potatoes and fruits such as apples and peaches. Coffee was the beverage of choice in camp. Heavier items included butter sealed in cans, cornmeal, flour, and bacon. She would depend on fish and the wildlife along the trail for fresh meat.

The rest of Belinda's outfit consisted of goods she expected to sell to the wealthy miners—especially the women—in the gold camps. To limit the weight of her gear she selected mostly silks and packed them in long, waterproof, tin cylinders (NW 1:2). But she also included other luxuries she figured the newly - rich miners would be pining for, such as hot water bottles.[2]

Belinda left Seattle on 25 March 1897, on the steamer *Mexico,* among a large group of passengers curious about the rumored big strike on the Klondike River.[3] She arrived back in Juneau on 29 March, then left on the *Mexico* again the next day for Dyea, where she landed on 1 April 1897.[4] Since Dyea lacked a dock or pier, the ship simply steamed in as far as possible, then off-loaded passengers and cargo into lighters that floated to the beach on the high tide. All the goods were stacked above high-tide line to be packed farther as soon as possible.

In Belinda's party to begin with were Nels Peterson; Nathan Kresge; J. D. and Mrs. Minnick with their three children, aged three, five and seven years; and Joe Barrette.[5] Joe Barrette was a gentle, easygoing, man. He came originally from Quebec and had gone into the Yukon area in 1894 to prospect.[6] Belinda apparently had met him in Juneau.[7] They became good friends and looked out for each other on the trail, although Joe's attempts at gallantry, while flattering, clashed with Belinda's desire to pull her own weight in the party.[8]

5.2. Belinda Mulrooney's party near the beginning of Dyea trail in April of 1897. The two women at the right of the photograph are Belinda on the left and perhaps Mrs. Minnick on the right. *(ASL, Winter and Pond photog., PCA 21–14)*

5.3. Belinda Mulrooney, second in line, sleds goods through Dyea Canyon. Others in the photo have been identified, front to back, as ?? Williams, John Lee, Dan Fraser, Bob Menzie, Gus Biegler, Ed Hutchison, ?? Williams, Clare Gillett, Marlin Mosier, and Bert Bower, according to a note in the Yukon Archives. *(ASL, Winter and Pond photog., 1897, PCA-87–682.)*

In a photograph of the party taken at the lower end of Dyea trail (fig. 5.2), Belinda and another woman appear with twelve men amidst stacked supplies, tents, and a sled pulled by a dog team. No small children are evident, though there may be one peering around the left edge of the tent in the distance near the middle of the photo. There is only light snow on the ground at this point, so pulling the sled must have been difficult, even on this relatively flat terrain.

As Belinda's party progressed toward Chilkoot Pass, the trail became steeper and the spring snow deeper. Both dogs and people were needed to move the sleds carrying supplies along the trail. A photograph taken in Dyea Canyon, about six miles up the trail from the beach, shows Belinda transporting goods with other stampeders (fig. 5.3). Their packs are on sleds pulled by one person while a second person pushes from behind with a pole. Belinda is the pusher for the first sled.

Although there was comradeship on the trail, there was also competition. Everyone wanted to get to the Klondike before the others so they could locate and stake the best claims. Belinda was proud of the fact that her party was in the lead on the Chilkoot trail. But even with members of her own party, her strategy involved getting as much information as possible without compromising her own position. She noted that although they were the first to go In, McKay caught up with them because he was traveling light. "I never got friendly. I held to myself, was nice to anyone with knowledge. I was that way with McKay when he caught us" (Hawkins; NW 61:1).

Packing an outfit to the Yukon headwaters was a major undertaking. Everything had to be carried in backpacks or on sleds. Since each person's outfit weighed between one and two thousand pounds, it could not be taken in one load. It had to be relayed along the trail. Camps were set up at strategic locations, then the round-trips between camps would begin.

> The first trip was from Dyea to Sheep Camp, 20 miles.[9] . . . You packed the outfits first with dogs and sleds. . . . [A second camp was set up] five miles away[10] on the inland side [of the pass] where there was timber for fuel. . . . [To climb the pass] you took a hand ax and cut each step out of the ice, carrying your stuff on your back. . . . In bad places you strung a rope and climbed up like that. . . . The Indians,[11] after we had broken trail for them, got into action by putting stuff over the Summit on their backs. We had to hire them of course.
>
> I picked up six good dogs and trained them to pack with little pockets for freight hanging down on each side of them. The leader followed me (NW 5:2). Poor things! They'd slip and their feet would get full of ice packs. They'd be

On Chilkoot Pass

5.4. By spring of 1898, a year after Belinda and her companions hacked icy steps over Chilkoot Pass, thousands of stampeders followed in their footsteps, ferrying their outfits to the summit. Packers to the left have stepped out of line to catch their breath. Just to the right of the climbers are chutes used to slide to the bottom for the next load of goods. *(UW, Cantwell photog., 46)*

miserable and cry like children. The sharp ice would cut into the tender part of the foot. I'd take it out and had the Indians make them little shoes out of hide. We'd lace them on. I'd do all I could to protect them, but all I could possibly do was to render bacon and pour grease in the cracks. The salt would smart and the dogs would cry. They'd be ready to bite, snap at me, and then lick my hand [to show they] didn't blame me.

Belinda and her companions made about thirty round trips to get their supplies to Lake Bennett (NW 5:2). Not everyone who started up Chilkoot completed the trip.

. . . Relaying was endless. Two or three hundred people were started. After our camp was placed, I got to buying supplies from the disheartened people who looked at the Summit. . . . Such a small percentage made the Summit. A great many returned, some snow-blind, some . . . sick, or homesick. . . . [Or] they'd make one trip up to the top and knew they'd have to relay to get sufficient food for one year. Before they'd make the round trip they'd give up and say, "Impossible." I bought their outfits.

Belinda, on the other hand, had turned back once before. This time she had come better prepared, and she was determined to make it to the Klondike. "There were lots of funny things that happened that anyone looking on and not too tired could see. But we were all in the same predicament—all in. All I wanted was just to get that piece of work done. I never thought of the other end. Between work and sleep the pleasantest part was to be able to lie down and stretch."

In later years, when she had time to be more reflective, Belinda offered some insight on why it was that Chilkoot Pass came to symbolize the gold rush experience for so many stampeders. "The hardest things you have done are the things you are happiest about, and somehow in remembering what you went through, the pride makes you forget everything else."

Belinda crossed Chilkoot Pass on Easter Sunday, 15 April. It is not clear whether this was the first or last of the many relays needed to get her whole outfit across.

Just over Chilkoot Pass is a steep descent to Crater Lake with its treeless, windswept shores. Fourteen miles of hiking are required to reach the first navigable lake, Lindeman. "We hauled our stuff to the head of Lake Lindeman. There was plenty of timber. . . . [But] we figured we'd have a couple of months before the lake would break up. So we decided to pull our stuff across Lake Lindeman and camp at the head of Lake Bennett."

The smooth, frozen surface of Lake Lindeman made yet another type of packing possible.

> We started out with one or two sleds to find out how to go ahead. After we broke the trail we began to get the sun. It had not been entirely dark, but as the sun stayed longer each day and it grew warmer, the ice was slicker.
>
> After one trip we put our tarpaulins on sleds for sails. We didn't need all of the dogs. They had to go to keep out of the way when the wind blew behind those sails.
>
> From Lindeman we found marvelous big timber at the head of Lake Bennett, better timber for the boats. We had the pick of the timber. We set up some logs—had a [whip] saw[12] [to saw planks]. According to the amount of our freight, we contributed towards the cost of the boats. I had materials for boat building, and that stuff they pack boats with, oakum. All I had to do was to exchange that for labor. Pretty soon we had big boats all dolled up and named.

Belinda had had the foresight to bring essential and barterable materials, but she certainly was not idle while the boats were being built. Unlike the other woman in her party who was "always complaining about things that never happened," Belinda took pride in not grousing and making sure she held up her end of work. While she never got overly friendly, she still felt an equal partner in the undertaking.

> The first thing, I got up and made a fire. Then I cooked the dogs' breakfast —fish, corn meal, and pork chopped up. After it was cooked, it was cooled off, and I gave each dog his portion. Then my own breakfast. Then I'd offer my services to the men towards the boats.
>
> Three of the outfit, two men and myself, were assigned to get fresh food— fish and game. We'd wander out into the hills with snow shoes on. The men were always hunting moose and never found any. There was an abundance of fresh fish. All you'd have to do was to chop a hole in the ice and drop in a line. Fish, fish! . . . I was the one to fish.
>
> When they were busy finishing the boats, I used to cook for the whole outfit, eighteen in all.

Although cooking was often a role that female stampeders filled, it was not one that Belinda took on easily. She did not like to cook, even for herself. But for the time being, cooking was what was needed, so she did it. And in return she profited from the knowledge and experience of some of the men in her party.

> When our boats were all set, Joe [Barrette] and [Two-Finger] McKay evened up the freight in them. The men knew what to do. We didn't wait for Bennett to be opened. We put the boats on the sleds and pushed on to the [foot] of Lake Bennett [where the outlet river was flowing]. . . . That lake stuff was easy going. There was quite a number of hours of sun, and if the sleighs stuck, we put a dog on to pull and then had to grab the dog and throw him on the boat [when the wind caught the sails]. (Franklin, 23)

Belinda's party reached Dawson ahead of others, she asserted, because the others waited for the ice to break on the lakes.[13]

Once on the Yukon River itself, the 480 miles to Dawson still had a few surprises. Almost immediately appeared the largest rapids on the river—Miles Canyon followed by Squaw and White Horse rapids. The first was dangerous because of turbulence from the huge volume of water from all of the lakes being forced suddenly through narrow, hundred-foot-wide, nearly vertical walls.

About halfway down, at a slight widening in the canyon, a whirlpool could spin inexperienced boaters crosswise into the boiling current and waves. The second and third rapids were wider but more boulder-strewn and therefore more dangerous. These three rapids were so intimidating that the entire Minnick family walked the five or so miles around them. Apparently Belinda rode through on one of the boats with the rest of the party.

As Belinda progressed closer to her goal, her love for Alaska and the north country grew.

> The beauty of Alaska—you can't possibly overdo it. It seems to me that every day and every night is different. You just feast on it. You become quite religious, seem to get inspiration. Or it might be the electricity of the air. You are filled with it, ready to go.
>
> You couldn't keep your eyes off the heavens. . . . I don't think I was ever as happy and comfortable as after we got to Bennett and [were] able to get boughs for a bed. I would lie in one of those beds—really tired, just breathe the air of Alaska and stare into the heavens, and rest, and think—until my eyes closed. . . . I'd wake up in the morning feeling as fresh, rested and equal to anything. I'd get my towel and go down to the nice cold water and wash up.

Of course, Belinda is playing loose with the term "Alaska." Most of the wilderness she was traveling through was actually in Canada's British Columbia and the westernmost section of the Northwest Territories, which would become the Yukon Territory. But the political boundaries were artificial, for the land was of a whole, a world unsympathetic to boundaries of any sort except those of nature. And Belinda's "mistake" was such a common one that probably the majority of Klondike stampeders from the United States thought that they were headed for Alaska.

Belinda and her companions rode the mighty Yukon north with the advancing spring weather. They got to the mouth of the Klondike River on 15 June at three or four o'clock in the morning.[14] But already the north country was beginning its cycle of twenty-four-hour daylight, so all was laid out clearly as they floated in.

The first little settlement they saw was a collection of low-roofed cabins just before the Klondike River's junction with the Yukon. Known as Klondike City, or sometimes, more derisively, Lousetown, its squatty little cabins looked uninviting to Belinda.

> Joe Barrette turned to me, "I think we go to other side. . . ."

On [that] beach were a few tents. The people who lived in them came down to meet us, full of joy. A woman was on the bank to greet us.

"Come on," she called. "We have a real town."

"It's cleaner anyway," I said to Joe.

The woman was Esther Duffie,[15] and this "real town" was the beginnings of Dawson itself. "After looking around," Belinda recalled, "I saw there was nothing in Dawson I could buy for a quarter. So I threw my last coin into the Yukon and said, "We'll start clean.""

How had Belinda ended up with only twenty-five cents to her name? "I had separated myself from my last twenty-dollar gold piece a while before. As I was always ashamed to admit I had no money, when Joe [Barrette] had wanted to buy something quick, 'Here's a twenty-dollar gold piece,' I told him, 'if that will help you.'" (NW 1:1)

Once Dawson rather than Lousetown had been selected, Belinda picked a spot to set up her tent. "I chose the location I did because it was away from the rest of the town and it was clean. I didn't want to live on Front Street where all the saloons were going up. I wanted to be where I could be by myself" (NW 1:2). When Belinda arrived in Dawson, there was only one log saloon, owned by Joe Ladue. The other saloons were in tents (Ogilvie, 272), though they would soon be in more permanent structures on the main street fronting the river. Belinda's first tent went up on Front Street too, but about two blocks south (toward the Klondike River) from where most of the saloons were being built. According to Belinda, this tent was on the site eventually chosen for the Canadian Bank of Commerce. That would put it on the bank of the Yukon, opposite to where Princess Street eventually intersected Front Street.

DESPITE THE ODDS against her, Belinda had made it to Dawson. She had done it by allying herself with people who had the skills and knowledge to meet the challenges that the journey presented. And she had done it by being a determined, responsible, equally-contributing partner to the group. While she made friends, she also maintained an emotional distance from her companions, a natural reserve that was only partly a reflection of her competitiveness. Her coolness to her human partners is all the more striking when contrasted with the obvious warmth of her feelings for her animal companions and for the countryside she was coming to love.

6

Building Dawson

THE KLONDIKE GOLD was found on 17 August 1896. As soon as the discovery claim was registered at Forty Mile Post, the news spread by word of mouth to prospectors, traders, and trappers in all the nearby areas. The first wave of the rush to the new goldfield was on.

Among the earliest stampeders was Joseph Ladue, a prospector in the Yukon basin since 1882. In 1893, he had teamed up with Arthur Harper, who in 1873 was one of the first to enter the Yukon basin to prospect for gold rather than to trade for furs. Harper prospected extensively, promoting the area whenever he wrote to friends.[1] He supplemented his mining income through trading and, together with Ladue, established a trading post and sawmill at the mouth of Sixtymile River, just forty-seven miles up the Yukon from the mouth of the Klondike River.

When Ladue rushed to the Klondike he claimed a townsite rather than a mine.[2] He quickly built a cabin and warehouse, then moved his sawmill to the new town. Sawn lumber would be needed not only for houses and businesses in Dawson, but also for sluice boxes and flumes at the creeks. Ladue's town claim would prove to be as profitable as many of the richest gold-bearing properties.

Located on the eastern bank of the Yukon River, just north of the mouth of

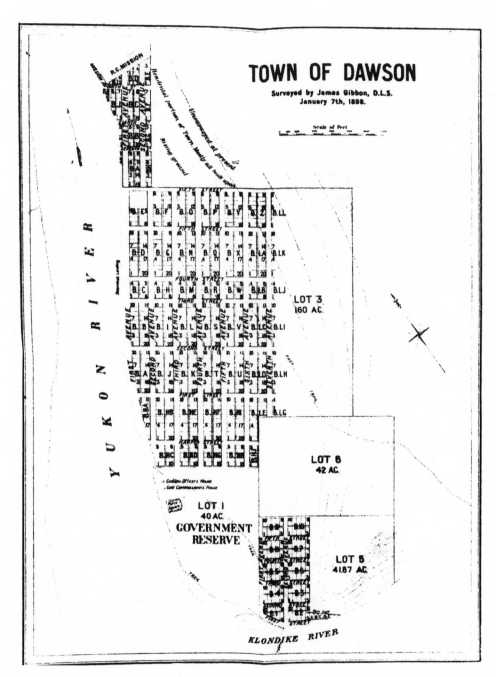

6.1. An early map of Dawson townsite. *(Mayer Collection)*

the Klondike River, about sixteen miles from the discovery claim, Dawson was strategically positioned to act as a supply center for the entire region. The Klondike River and its gold-bearing creeks were unnavigable by large boats. But the Yukon River was the main "highway" of the interior. Equipment and supplies could be delivered directly to Dawson during the months the waterway was clear of ice.

No one seemed concerned that the land in Dawson was poorly drained or that permafrost started only a couple of feet below the surface. The latter was true for all parts of the territory. As for the drainage, perhaps Dawsonites figured that most of the year the townsite simply would be frozen. The Yukon region has, for the most part, a dry climate. Water from the melt of the winter's snow might cause problems for a while, but digging drainage channels would allow the swamp to dry out for the remaining three or four months of summer before freezing solid again.

Ladue claimed about 160 acres, which he laid out in streets and lots. The part of the muskeg closest to the Klondike River became a military reservation housing the barracks, offices, storerooms, jail, and public administration buildings of the Northwest Mounted Police. In the spring of 1897, Arthur Harper claimed most of the remaining flat land adjacent to Ladue's town;[3] and Harper and Ladue along with Thomas Kirkpatrick formed the Dawson Town Site Company. By mid-June, as Belinda and her party were arriving, the Dawson Town Site Company was issued its final certificate of ownership.[4]

At first glance, Belinda found Dawson unimpressive. A dozen buildings were strung along the riverfront; Dawson's six hundred or so inhabitants[5] were living mainly in tents. Most of the townsite was covered with scrub timber, except for a fringe of larger trees along the bank of the Yukon.[6] But these were being cleared to make room for new development along the main street of town. Front Street, as it was called, conceptually was the showpiece of Dawson, the main thoroughfare. It skirted the Yukon for about a mile and was the first sight presented to those arriving from either up- or downriver. On early maps, such as figure 6.1, Front Street is labeled First Avenue, for in imitation of the cities its founders expected it to resemble, Dawson was laid out with avenues running north and south, and streets running east and west. In reality Dawson at the time of Belinda's arrival was quite different from an established city. Front Street then was little more than a pathway through a tangle of roots, stumps, and branches. It was flanked on the east side by an irregular row of tents and some

6.2. Front Street, Dawson, in about July of 1897, was still being reclaimed from the wilderness. This view looking north from about Second (Queen) Street shows a typical one-story log building under construction at right, as well as a framed tent building similar to one Belinda constructed. However, hers was located another block to the south of this location. The buildings in this photo would become the saloons from which Belinda wanted her own businesses to be set apart. The scar from a landslide on the hillside in the distance is the landmark "Moosehide," used by downstream boaters on the Yukon to anticipate landing at Dawson. *(Library of Congress, Fujiwara [?] photog., 807315, Z62–120346)*

buildings under construction. On the river side of the street-to-be was a motley group of beached scows, boats, and rafts, along with more tents.

In the middle of what was to become Front Street stood Ladue's first small cabin, sited before the town survey and used as a residence, storehouse, and trading post before Ladue's larger, two-story cabin was built a few months later.[7] The little cabin was torn down in the spring of 1898 to conform to the plat plan.

6.3. The waterfront and Front Street in about July 1897, taken from a steamer tied up at the Alaska Commercial Company landing between Third (King) and Fourth (York) Streets. The false-fronted building facing the river and partially obscured by the pole in the foreground appears to be the one-story version of the Monte Carlo Saloon. The one next to it sports the sign of the Dominion Saloon. The cabin between the saloons and the river may be the one built originally by town founder Joe Ladue that, after the survey, ended up in the middle of Front Street. It was torn down in the spring of 1898. *(Library of Congress, Fujiwara [?] photog., 807314, USZ62–26039)*

Despite the confusion and primitive conditions, Dawson in June of 1897 was filled with excitement. After years of hard living, prospectors, miners, and mining camp businesspeople were beginning to realize this was really IT—the Eldorado they had been seeking. As the tons of golden treasure, wrested from the surrounding creeks and hillsides, were hauled into the new town for weighing and shipping, Dawson became the focal point for infectious optimism. The atmosphere was intoxicating. Belinda, though a newcomer, recognized the promise of the town. She sensed that Dawson at this time was like San Francisco in 1849, poised to become the business and transportation center for the nearby gold fields. And as in Chicago, Belinda would find this expansive, energetic town to be a tolerant and even supportive environment for her considerable, somewhat unconventional, talents. People were too busy with their own business to be overly concerned about what someone else was doing, even if that someone happened to be a woman.

Belinda had probably missed by just a few days celebration of the arrival of the first steamers of the year, the Alaska Commercial Company's *Bella* and North American Trading and Transportation Company's *Portus B. Weare*.[8]

> When (a steamboat's whistle was heard), the first one let out a yell, "Steamboat!" Then everybody came out of the saloons, [tents], and cabins, whether they had all their clothes on or not. The native dogs took it up with their mouths wide open, "Steamboat, steamboat!" . . . You should hear the dogs. They are part wolf, and they made the same noises. Everyone would trail along the bank in a string, the dogs howling.[9]

A steamboat's arrival was always an event for celebration along the Yukon River, but the ones landing at Dawson in the beginning of the summer of 1897 were even more special. Those prospectors who had staked early claims had been working the frozen ground all winter. When the spring thaw came, they could wash with the running water the earth they had dug and, if they were lucky, in the bottom of their sluice boxes or rockers they found great fortunes. The miners hauled their bags of gold to Dawson and waited eagerly with the town residents for the steamers at the beginning of June. The supplies the boats brought were essential for the summer's work. But also the winter's rewards were to be sent out, mostly to United States banks, to be converted into currency. And many of the successful miners planned to accompany their fortunes to the Outside.

When the first steamers left Dawson bound for Norton Sound and the Outside, they carried more than eighty men and women and literally tons of gold. The arrival of these miners in Seattle and San Francisco in July 1897, with their stories of the great wealth of the Klondike, set off the major waves of the gold rush.

But Belinda was already in Dawson and ahead of the crowd in June. She had no money, but she had her trade goods and plenty of ideas. First, she needed to get settled.

> We divided our food stuffs . . . , each person's pile for himself. And we cooked our food, had dinner and cleaned up. After they'd gotten their stuff out of the boats, I asked the boys if they'd let me purchase [the boats].
> "Mon Dieu! You going to live in a boat? Boys, suppose we give her a boat?" Joe [Barrette] said.

"No," I said. "You wait awhile, and I'll pay you later. We'll make a new deal. You have to see the mines and the country. I'll store your provisions if you will give me your help for about three days."

"What do you want to do?" Joe was curious.

I explained I wanted to fix myself a place to live, protect their food stuffs, and let them be free to look around the country. So we got busy. Pulled the boats apart. Knocked out the lumber [and nails] and built a frame that, as far as it went, was a house for me. We used the old tarpaulin from my tent as a roof. There was no floor. There I kept the goods I'd brought in to sell and their outfits. (NW 1:2)

Now Belinda was ready to set up her business. At first she had some misgivings. "I saw those women in that camp wearing mukluks, short skirts, and men's shirts. I thought I had been a fool in my plans [bringing in the silk clothing]" (NW 1:1). But her fears proved to be unfounded.

The first women I got to know were Esther [Duffie]), Mrs. Harry [Catherine] Spencer, and her sister Mrs. Julius [Lizzie] Geise. They wanted to know what I had in the [long, cylindrical] tin cans.

I opened one to let them look. When the silk things—the dresses, petticoats, night gowns, and underwear—fell out, they couldn't get enough of the feel of them.

"Girls," I told them, "I'm going to start a store, and you folks will have to help me. You know the people here and the gold dust. I don't understand gold dust or the right prices to charge. It's all new to me."

They all volunteered. Practical Esther ran out for a pair of scales. "You can be cashier and head saleswoman," I said.

. . . In no time at all our place came to be the regular headquarters for the [miners who had originally come from Circle City and Forty Mile] as well as for the people from Old Town [Klondike City] and New Town, as Dawson was called. [They would hang] around to see what was in the next tin can. Esther would stand behind the little board counter, and she'd holler, "Next? Who wants a beautiful night dress?" She knew everybody by name, and they'd come up, each in turn, and feel the gown gingerly.

A lot of things the women bought they didn't know how to wear, but they had been so long separated from luxuries, they just wanted to possess them, to feel 'em. They didn't care what they paid either. I just looked on and let Esther run the business.

The squaws started coming. Every time they did, their husbands were separated from their money. . . . I can see those Old Timers now, standing around, be-whiskered and dirty, protesting, "What's that good for?" as Esther would

hold up a silk something. . . . The squaws would just eat the things up. I remember one old duffer grunting when his squaw came back for more. It was a
night gown this time. "That'll be a fine outfit when the mosquitoes get after
you."

I don't believe we ever stopped. Esther wouldn't open [a new] tin until what
was in the others was sold. She was like a child about them herself. "I can't
wait," she'd say. Then I'd open a new can to show her. Things vanished as fast
as Esther showed them. (NW 1:2–3)

Esther Duffie, Lizzie Geise, and Catherine Spencer had been among the Old
Timers living in Circle City before 1896. When news of the strike on the Klondike
reached Circle City, they, like most of the rest of the camp residents, hurried to
the new grounds. Lizzie was the wife of Julius Geise, tinsmith for the camp.
Catherine's husband, Harry Spencer, was a saloon keeper, and Esther Duffie was,
among other occupations, the good-hearted, generous-minded epitome of the
prostitute with a heart of gold.[10]

Esther was a worker. She had mining interests.[11] A girl, no a woman, between forty and forty five—she looked younger. . . . She was friendly with all
the women. They were all her pals. One of the best old hearts God ever put on
the face of the earth! Esther! (NW 1:3)

In her recollections Belinda, perhaps out of loyalty as well as self-protection,
skirted the issue of Esther's practice of one of the oldest forms of entrepreneurship. What Belinda knows is only hinted at by what occurs to her to tell as she
thinks of Esther: "I never saw her with one man, always with a gang. Funny
though, from the first it was my friendship with Esther that made me insist on
the men calling me Miss Mulrooney. My backbone stiffened then and there"
(NW 1:4).

In the 1890s, women's roles were often reduced to simplistic stereotypes based
upon their sexual relationships with men. For example, in Jack London's novel
A Daughter of the Snows, Vance Corliss embodies this pervasive attitude. Here is
his advise to Frona Welse, the heroine of this story of the Klondike gold rush.

"It is only meet that two kinds of women come into this country. Those
who by virtue of wifehood and daughterhood are respectable, and those who
are not respectable. . . . [T]he women who come over the trail must be one or
the other. There is no middle course, and those who attempt it are bound to
fail."[12]

According to Vance's perspective, any "good" woman who associated with a "bad" woman became contaminated. Belinda probably felt she couldn't completely buck this trend in dualistic thinking. She was searching for a position that left no doubt as to her own respectable behavior. At the same time, she was determined not to forsake her friendship with a woman in whom she found much to admire.

Though there were many wealthy people in Dawson, there was very little currency. Most transactions were carried out with gold dust as payment. Since Belinda was unfamiliar with handling gold, she decided to watch Esther to see how it was done. She could hardly have imagined what she would learn.

> Those first days . . . I watched [Esther] with astonishment. She had her little scales, and I don't think she ever changed the weights. After she poured the dust on the empty [pan], she'd pour my share through a funnel into a big sack. How she soaked them, those Old Timers! (NW 1:4)

With Esther's high-handed, enthusiastic dealing, Belinda estimated she netted a profit of nearly 600 percent on the sale of her goods. She used the proceeds to pay her partners for the boats. And within a couple of weeks, she decided to invest some of the rest of her earnings in a restaurant.[13] Though Belinda makes it sound almost accidental, the starting of this business is a good example of how a successful entrepreneur works. First she recognizes a need; then she assesses how the need might be met, whether she has the experience to do it, and if she can reasonably expect a profit. Finally, she needs to be flexible about using the resources at hand—people and materials—to set up and run the business.

> The reason I started so many restaurants in my life . . . was because I was never the kind of woman to be married to a cook stove. . . . The boys who had gone up the river came down . . . [again]. They ate with me at my camp, and the other men began to crowd around wanting to buy a meal. I'd learned how to fix some of the Alaska food by then, thanks to Mrs. Geise. She was [a great talker], about fifty, good humored. All the miners liked her. I liked her husband too, Julius . . . , who was a tinsmith looking around. I guess the banks of the Yukon in the first days of the rush were lined with men looking around.
>
> "Mrs. Geise," I said to her one day, "I don't know much about fixing dried potatoes. I wish you'd show me how to cook them and other Alaskan prepared foods. I'll make you a present of a fine silk dress if you'll take me in hand."
>
> Mrs. Geise said, "All right, I'll show you. But I'll buy the dress." So she helped me cook. The boys wanting to buy meals persuaded me to ask Mrs. Geise, "Won't you go in with me for a restaurant?"

"You're crazy!" Mrs. Geise said. "Where'll we get the grub?"

"I'll get the grub," I told her.

That settled it. She had Mr. Geise fix us up a good stove. We added on to my first little place enough space to make room for a restaurant with some homemade tables. And Mr. Geise fixed us up a real counter. We'd take all the sawdust we could find from where the men had been cutting logs and would sprinkle it on the floor. [When the floor was dirty, we'd put down more sawdust.] The place where I lived was separated from the restaurant by a little canvas wall.

The grub I said I'd get? Well there were two boats from the lower Yukon which gave us supplies twice a year. Also, every time a man with his outfit came up, I traded with him. Where I was on the waterfront, the only desirable beach was back of me. . . . I'd see the men come in and tell them if they'd turn over their food and outfit to us, they'd get credit in cooked food in the restaurant. Or they could sell for cash. They were glad to give up their stuff because they hated individual cooking—all that chopping bacon with an ax and the waste, the packing and re-packing of supplies. (NW 7:1)

Belinda and Lizzie Geise charged a flat two-dollar rate for their meals.[14] Their cooking was "home-style"—whatever was being prepared that day was what their patrons got. During the summer, the long hours of daylight meant customers were likely to arrive at almost any time. So the restaurant was kept open twenty-four hours a day. Business was so brisk that soon a new employee was needed.

In July two girls came up river in a boat. One was Sadie O'Hara, a Canadian, a nice well-brought-up Presbyterian girl. Strict and all that, but she was always laughing. Everything struck her as funny. I got her to helping in the restaurant. The men used to come in just to see her, as she was handsome, and to hear her laugh. She'd laugh at something until she was weak, and then she'd start to cry, with the tears just rolling down her face. I've known one man to buy four meals in two hours just for the fun of sitting in the restaurant and getting Sadie started. (NW 7:2–3)

Belinda also offered an interesting observation on another effect of Sadie's good humor.

She was the most popular girl in Alaska—tall, strong, and handsome. There was this difference about Sadie. The other women, while they were not bad, used to let the men get close to them, whisper in their ear, and grin and such sly things. But Sadie! She was so busy laughing, and she'd turn her face away to hide the tears and then start all over again with her laughing, that the men never got beyond the fun of starting her off. (NW 10:5)

Perhaps feeling a little guilty about Esther Duffie's gold weighing techniques, Belinda made sure that procedures at the restaurant were more conscientious. Julius Geise made up some two-dollar weights so the gold dust could be balanced quickly without error. One customer, Jim McNamee, did not realize what a sore point he was probing when he complained about the gold weighing. Jim had been prospecting in the Yukon basin before the Klondike strike, and was known as a generous, fair-minded man, who was usually good-natured and sensible.[15] But in this incident he definitely got under Belinda's skin.

When I went . . . to my table and was starting on my soup, I heard Mrs. Geise ask Jim McNamee, "How did you like the food?"

"All right, Lizzie," Jim said. "I ain't got no kick coming about the food. But I've thought a lot about your system of weighing gold dust. Look at the dust on that long bar there. I suppose you spill the miner's sacks in the sawdust ever so often, don't you? I can just see you and your partner cleaning up every night."

I have a terrific temper. When I get mad, I can't move. As I heard Jim talk I just froze stiff, like a pointer. I had a big tin salt shaker Julius Geise had made and was holding it over my soup. It dropped with a crash. I couldn't hold it. Then in a second my blood began to circulate, and I grew hot. At that time, I was still growing and was healthy and very strong. I just walked over and took that old sport of a McNamee by the collar and threw him out towards the door, landing him up against the jam. The building was flimsy, and when Jim McNamee landed on that door jam, the whole place just shook. A lot of men were waiting for a place, all lined up, but I didn't see them. I got a good grip on his coat collar. . . . It was high and kind of stiff that collar, and I felt the button give as I sent Jim whirling. "You'll say we are crooks and dishonest?"

He picks himself up. "Good God! Can't you take a joke?"

"If that's your sense of humor, go try it on the natives." I took his poke and gave it to him. "Here's your poke. Now go out and stay out."

"Can't I come back?" he begged. And Mrs. Geise put in, "Ah, Miss Mulrooney, this is just a joke. We are all friends."

"Yes, may be. But it will be told all over Dawson, and I won't stand for it."

Then I noticed that Bill McPhee[16] . . . and some of the other Old Timers . . . were watching the whole thing. Bill McPhee took McNamee by the collar when he started to argue with me. "The drinks are on Jim," he told him. "And the whole town is in on it too." Those men went up and down the street calling in everybody to have a drink. Before they were through, they made Jim spend all that he had. (NW 7:3–4)

Belinda regretted having lost her temper, even though she had won the awe, perhaps even admiration and respect, of a large portion of the town. "I always had a terrific temper. I heard Captain Wallace on the [*City of Topeka*] once tell another officer, 'You can't expect to control anyone else until you have learned to control yourself.' That stuck with me" (NW 7:4).

But though she rued having lost control, Belinda did not soon forgive Jim McNamee, either. She refused him service in her restaurant, even when he returned and begged to be let in a couple of days later (NW 7:5).

While the restaurant became a center for socializing, Belinda still made it her policy to keep to herself. This was not always easy to do, considering that the restaurant was attached to her tent home, but she kept her distance in her demeanor. Mrs. Geise gave Belinda the nickname "schoolteacher" because she was so reserved and formal. And even to her friends, Belinda did not reveal much of her background.

> The reason I didn't get too well acquainted was that when anyone would ask where I came from, I'd say, "It's a long story. I'm awfully busy. Wait until winter and I'll tell you."
>
> . . . I never used to eat in the place when it was full. There would be too much of a crowd during the rush hours. Besides, I'd like to have it quiet and to myself. (NW 7:2–3)

Although Belinda remained somewhat aloof from even her closest human associates, she did become emotionally attached to a dog. Her introduction to her new pal took place at the restaurant. The adolescent Saint Bernard was "all ears, legs and lanky body" when Belinda first saw him (NW 10:3). His owner, a young Englishman, had just arrived, but he had lost his outfit and had nearly lost his life coming In. He stopped at the restaurant hoping for some scraps of food for his ever-hungry, growing pup. Because he was so discouraged, the young man was thinking of leaving, though he worried what to do with his dog. Belinda offered to help find the man a job. Then she struck a deal. She agreed to take care of the dog without pay. When the young man was ready to go, whomever the dog wanted to stay with would be his owner. The young man agreed, for he saw no prospect of being able to feed the huge animal in Dawson. Almost immediately Belinda found the man a job working for one of the miners she knew. But the pup was forever afterward Belinda's. "I didn't know what his name was,

6.4. Belinda's beloved dog Nero. *(UCB, Hawkins Collection, 77/81)*

but someone dubbed him Nero"(NW 10:3–5). And Nero became Belinda's close companion, much as her donkey had been during her early years in Ireland.

Since the restaurant was running well under the care of Lizzie, Esther, and Sadie, Belinda turned her attention to other pursuits. Again she was adept at identifying where there were needs, where there was a market that she had the skills to satisfy. She knew her male companions from the trail would be needing accommodations in Dawson and she figured there would be even more of a demand for cabins when all the new stampeders from Outside arrived. Her experience with construction in Chicago gave her the confidence to start in that business now again in Dawson.

> I went to the men who were figuring . . . out [the] townsite.[17] . . . I told them I'd be willing to pay . . . for some lots fifty dollars and for some a hundred. And [I] would take one block back of Front Street, which was by that time pretty well staked out for business houses.
>
> After the men arrived from the mines, we had a meeting. They told me how they had found conditions in the mining district. I told them they'd all have to have winter quarters, and the first thing we should do was to get plenty of logs so we could build cabins.

" . . . It doesn't matter," I told them, "how many we build. They'll sell. I have money now, and you'll receive your pay. Get a raft out of logs. Make them twelve by sixteen and keep them as complete as you can so we can put them up when they arrive." My idea was to build a cabin first for my men so if they got engaged anywhere in the mines they'd have an option on one cabin they could call home. (NW 8:1)

Once her partners agreed to get logs, Belinda began buying boats and rafts as they arrived at Dawson. She hired a good carpenter, Harry Cribb,[18] who was down on his luck, to act as foreman to a crew of two other men. They began taking the boats apart and readying the lots. When the logs began to arrive, Cribb and his workers were ready to begin construction.

The first cabin built for speculation sold so quickly that Belinda wondered whether she was asking enough. She had figured her costs carefully, then charged double that amount. But her friends advised her the price still wasn't high enough. She felt uncomfortable making so much profit, so she hired a man named Mack to act as agent. He received a hundred-dollar commission on each cabin he sold. Belinda then just drew up the deeds (NW 8:2–3).

Mack quickly sold the next cabin for a thousand dollars. Belinda was still feeling nervous about the high prices, so she decided to put a bit more into furnishing the cabins. All the furnishings came from outfits she would buy from arriving gold seekers.

We'd clean tarpaulins from the packs by tying them to a rope and letting them stay in the Yukon River current. Then we'd take them out, stretch them and dry them. Canvas was useful stuff for lining cabins and making partitions.

"We'll make furniture out of poles, and they shall have windows or at least window casings. [There was little or no glass in Dawson.] If we can find some paint, we'll paint the doors, and if we can find any locks, we'll give them a lock." The noble idea come to me to build a place for their food. And the thing that pleased them the most was a doghouse. (NW 8:2, 4)

The cabin-building enterprise grew. Belinda recruited one woman after finding her crying on the beach because some of the town dogs had eaten all her bacon. She was very young and inexperienced. She had been schooled in a convent. "It seems she had eloped, got married, and came North. No wonder she was wailing!" (NW 9:1). Belinda gave her a job making curtains from calico bought at the Trading Post. And she hired two more men to build furniture from birch poles. When the next cabin was finished, Belinda hung around to listen to Mack's marketing techniques.

"Don't be too sure you can get it," Mack told [the prospective owner.] "It belongs to a lady."

"God," the miner said, "if I could sleep here this night, you could put your own price on it. God! A place to hang clothes and a doghouse. Get me that dame before she changes her mind."

When Mack brought me $3,500 for the cabin, he was moaning. "What a simple-minded ass I was."

I didn't want Mack to think me a hog about the commissions. "I'll pay you double," I told him.

But Mack was thinking only what he could have charged. . . . "If the next cabin don't bring four thousand, kick me all over the place."

"Don't brag," I warned him. "The men will resent it. But find a man jealous of this miner, and we'll offer him something a little better." (NW 9:2–3)

It is obvious that Belinda was enjoying herself, even though her sense of what was fair was stretched by Mack's enthusiasm. There is little doubt that she liked both the game and the profit, and that she was psychologically astute when it came to figuring out how to attract more customers.

The miner who had just bought the thirty-five-hundred-dollar cabin was James "Curly" Monroe. "Curly" had been an early prospector in the Yukon basin and was one of the best of the card game gamblers in the camp (Johns, 147, 134). It is apparently the interior of the cabin Belinda built for Curly that is shown in a photograph published in 1898 by *The Klondike News,* for we are told, "He built and furnished last fall a neat and cozy cabin on Second Street [*sic*][19] in Dawson, where he keeps bachelor's hall, with all the comforts that [a] mortal heart could wish for."[20] In the photo (fig. 6.5) we see a group of people gathered around a table that has on it several large nuggets and a photograph of a woman. The table is round and covered with a cloth. The walls of the cabin are elaborately draped, with swags and tie-backs.

The next order of cabin improvements were artistic ones. Belinda found a German man who had been a theater scene painter. She hired him to paint some scenes on the canvas walls of the next cabin. The painter was skeptical that his work would be appreciated. But the new cabin was quickly purchased by the same miner who had bought Belinda's first cabin, Dick Lowe. Dick was another of the early prospectors in the Yukon basin who was also an accomplished gambler (Johns, 134). He had been lucky enough to stake a small fractional claim, 2A, on Bonanza Creek, which proved to be some of the richest ground per square foot of any in the Klondike. He had already given his first Belinda-built cabin away. His new, improved model included a sitting room with a separate bed-

6.5. The interior of Curly Monroe's cabin, probably built by Belinda and her crew. The woman shown is Mae McKamish Meadows (according to Jean King, *Arizona Charlie*, 197). To her right at the table, examining nuggets, is her husband, Arizona Charley Meadows. The man standing behind Charley and to his right, with his hand resting on Charley's shoulder, appears to be Curly Monroe. *(Klondike News, 1 April 1898, p. 11. Mayer Collection)*

room, a kitchen and storeroom, and a doghouse with door painted to match that of the cabin (NW 9:3).

With each new cabin Belinda introduced more elaborate features.

> The next rich miner had a safe that no one else had, and a porch, so Mack could explain the extra cost. There was even a mattress. . . . Before that we had used canvas and stuffed it with hay. The crew up river brought down some wild hay each trip for our mattress factory. But when we found real mattresses on the steamboats, we bought them.
>
> . . . Julius Geise made candlesticks, which were better than an empty bottle or three nails on a board that the miners had been used to. Dr. Hall Young[21] gave me a Bible for each new house. I sort of treated it as a joke. A Bible for those tough old birds!
>
> We also gave a lot of service. After he bought a cabin, a miner . . . would find the first night he was in possession water in the barrel and a meal prepared. We'd send a cook up from the restaurant and give him moose steak. (NW 9:4)

By this time the building and selling of the cabins was an interesting enough game that Belinda and Mack thought they could set their sights on one of the most flamboyant characters in town, "Swiftwater" Bill Gates. "Swiftwater" Bill had been regarded as a good-natured boaster at Circle City in 1896 (Johns, 138).

> The world read and raved about Swiftwater Gates. He was a foreigner, and I'm sure his name was not Gates. He was dubbed "Swiftwater" because he walked around White Horse Rapids. He was afraid to go through. His stuff was mostly four-flushing, noise. He got a lot of notoriety not coming to him, but he went after it.
>
> . . . To sell the newest cabin I got the old German [painter] to follow Swiftwater around and sketch him and his dog team. We decorated the canvas of the cabin with his own portrait. But we had the canvas only tacked on, so we could turn it around if he didn't buy it.
>
> I got a nice big oak barrel, polished it and set it upside down for a table with a lamp on it. . . . Somewhere we found a bedspread and pillowcases and a pillow. We used hide for backs and seats of chairs and made a dining table and chairs. We had such modern improvements as a nice pail for water with a dipper in it.
>
> . . . A piece of white oilcloth was tacked down on the bedroom floor and painted. "Don't walk on the darn thing," I told everybody. "You'll puncture it." The room was a real dream. I even took a couple of silk night dresses, left out of my cans, for curtains. (NW 9:5)

When Swiftwater got back to town with a shipment of gold, he was lured to the cabin by being told that it had been built especially for him. He was surprised when he saw it, but also a little doubtful. "Say, I could build this cabin in four days." Belinda agreed with him. Then Swiftwater decided to buy it anyway for $6,500. Later he said that he wouldn't give it up for $10,000 (NW 9:5); however, he may have been commenting more on the booming of Dawson's real estate than on his great love for the cabin. In the year between April 1897 and April 1898, land prices in the business section of the new town increased by a hundredfold or more.[22] This particular cabin may be the one entertainer Gussie LaMore said Swiftwater had built for her and Violet Raymond, another entertainer. She bragged it consisted of two rooms and a kitchen, and that he had it built for about $10,000.[23]

AT THE AGE OF TWENTY-FIVE, Belinda helped to create Dawson in the summer and fall of 1897. Belinda's early businesses in the Klondike were examples of the

6.6. An overview of Dawson in August of 1897, taken from the top of the mountain to the north of town and looking south. The Yukon River is to the right. The Klondike River flows from left to right in the far ground. The largest buildings near the center of the photo are the Alaska Commercial Company warehouses in the block bounded by Front and Second Avenues and Third (King) and Fourth (York) Streets. *(Cohen Collection)*

most constructive form of entrepreneurship—creating something of value out of raw materials by devoting time, planning, and effort, and by assuming the responsibility and risks. With each venture, Belinda saw a need or anticipated a market. And she believed in her vision enough to follow it through, to try it wholeheartedly. She recognized the talents of people she met who were looking for work and hired them to carry out her schemes. Her efforts were well rewarded, and she built her capital substantially by reinvesting nearly all of her profits in further development.

Belinda's style of operating had also become more assured, more expansive. Now she could operate several businesses at one time. She sold trade goods and supplies she had transported to Dawson over the Chilkoot trail. She started and managed a restaurant, often bartering for the supplies she needed to keep it going. She planned and contracted to build and furnish a number of cabins on Second Avenue.

While some of Belinda's occupations, such as restauranting, were relatively common for women in the 1890s, the others were more unusual. Only about 4 percent of retail merchants in the United States were women, and women in construction were even rarer, probably accounting for no more than 0.1 percent of all building trade categories.[24]

The new Dawson mining camp was a place where Belinda Mulrooney could be herself—strong, smart, creative, greedy—and not be censured for it. Helping to build Dawson was satisfying for Belinda. For her next project, she would establish a town of her own.

7

Grand Forks, the Heart of Gold Country

WHILE BELINDA WAS RUNNING her restaurant in Dawson, she was also gathering information and dreaming up new plans. "I learned a lot about the country and conditions through that restaurant. You couldn't get information about the strikes or properties by going into the miner's cabins and asking for it. However, when the men came in to eat . . . , Esther and I used to sit and listen to Mrs. Geise and the miners talking things over" (NW 7:5). These overheard conversations were the sparks for many of Belinda's ideas. Perhaps the most important came from her learning of discoveries of gold on the hillsides above Bonanza Creek in July 1897.[1] Immediately she joined a stampede from Dawson to stake a claim.[2]

The trails between Dawson and the heavily worked areas on Bonanza and adjoining creeks were by then well established. The main trail started on the south side of the Klondike River and kept well up on the steep bank. About one mile upstream a V-shaped trench intersects from the south. This is the valley of Bonanza Creek. From there the sled trail followed the windings of the creek some thirteen miles to the discovery claim. But a person on foot could cut the meanders. The more direct route involved more changes in elevation but shortened the distance to eleven miles (Adney, 253–54).

7.1. The trail from Dawson to Bonanza and Eldorado Creeks, along the north bank of the Klondike River. *(UW, A. Curtis photog., 46170)*

Following custom, all claims on Bonanza were numbered from the discovery claim. Those upstream from discovery were "1 Above," "2 Above," and so forth, while those downstream were "1 Below," "2 Below," and so on. When Klondike gold was first discovered, each claim was allowed five hundred feet, following the valley of the creek. But none of the early stampeders carried surveyor's gear. And often the line of the valley was hard to follow as the creek twisted through woods and brush. As a result, there was considerable confusion about claim boundaries, and disputes were inevitable. Consequently, when William Ogilvie, Dominion Surveyor, came to plat Dawson townsite in January 1897 the miners begged him to survey Bonanza and Eldorado creeks as well (Ogilvie, 164).

Ogilvie's survey revealed that while some claims were too short, others were too long. Short claims remained short. Long claims were divided into a regulation claim and a "fraction," designated by the same number as the original, with a letter added. For example, the survey of John J. A. Dusel's 2 Above Bonanza, found the claim too long. The extra land, cutting a little wedge out of the

Bonanza valley eighty-six feet at its widest, was numbered 2A Above Bonanza. It was claimed by Dick Lowe, who before the Klondike discovery had been prospecting at Circle City but at the time was working as one of Ogilvie's chainmen.[3] Although the fractional claim might have looked inconsequential when Dick Lowe somewhat reluctantly staked it, 2A Above Bonanza later proved to be some of the richest ground in the Klondike, yielding half a million dollars in gold.[4]

Proceeding up the Bonanza valley in the summer of 1897, Belinda would have seen little activity at the mouth, but by the 60 Belows there was more evidence of mining—digging, sluice boxes, flumes to carry water to the sluices, and cabins.[5] The density of equipment and the pitch of activity increased with proximity to the discovery claim.

Seven claims above Bonanza discovery, Eldorado Creek enters from the south, the miners referring to the junction as "The Forks." Since Eldorado was considered a tributary or "pup" of Bonanza, its claims were numbered from the mouth. In the summer of 1897 a person standing at The Forks could see vigorous efforts on many rich diggings well up the Eldorado valley as well as in both directions on Bonanza Creek.

Belinda did not stake a mining claim on her first trip to the creeks in July. But her experience in Dawson suggested a possibility for another kind of gold mine. On the north side of Bonanza Creek, across from the junction with Eldorado, where Belinda saw a relatively flat, open wedge of land with a few tents and a cabin or two, she recognized a perfect spot for a roadhouse or hotel. Technically, the wedge of land was part of the Bonanza claims 7 and 8 Above. But a mining claim grant includes surface rights only to the extent they are necessary for the mining operations. With no one actually mining on the land, if Belinda were bold enough and not too concerned about deeds, she could build on it. Here is one man's humorous account of what happened.

> When Miss Mulrooney came up to The Forks . . . she appreciated the mathematical advantage of the situation at once, and acted upon her perception with such decision that the news of her wonderful undertaking went up and down the creeks that very day.
>
> "Boys," said the heralds to the scoffers, "there's a new woman up to The Forks with a bit of an Irish brogue and the tongue of a lawyer, that's goin' to show us old moss-backs how to get rich. Hanged if she ain't got so much money to lose that she's goin' to build a two-story hotel bigger'n any in Dawson right up here on the creeks."

7.2. An early photo of George Carmack's discovery claim on Bonanza Creek, taken in the summer of 1897. *(UW, Sether photog., from Adney,* Klondike Stampede, *285; 17735)*

"Strange things was to be expected from the Cheechawkos [newcomers] once the news of a strike got into the newspapers all over the States," said the scoffers; while the saloon keepers, being specialists on the subject, appreciated with professional disdain that Miss Mulrooney might as well start a hotel at the head of the Stewart [River] or at the North Pole.

The next installment of news related that Miss Mulrooney was up on the hillside superintending the labors of the one lone mule surviving of those brought down the river on rafts in the summer, which she had hired for $20 a day to drag logs to the site of her building. That class of women who are too common in the Klondyke are not given to this sort of thing. And, moreover, they wear bloomers, while Miss Mulrooney wore long skirts. A new woman deserved punishment for such folly, but a good woman who wore long skirts was entitled to the friendly advice which one of the leading claim owners undertook to supply.

"I've been in the country some time," he told Miss Mulrooney, "and I don't mind telling you for your own interest that Dawson's the place, not The Forks, for a hotel."

"Now, that's kind of you," assented Miss Mulrooney. "And may I ask if you would like something to drink?"

"Er-r-r, well," stuttered the Committee-of-One, as he tried to get his bearings, "well, I admit I sometimes do, like the most of the boys—but I didn't know as you'd be mentionin' that."

"Oh, I'm not, and I'm not likely to," with a toss of her head, "when I know there's no chance of your accepting. Of course, if you or any of the other boys was hungry or thirsty, you wouldn't think of buying a drink or a meal up here. You'd walk sixteen miles to Dawson and back for it, wouldn't you? And the boys going over the divide to Dominion or Sulphur, when they break the journey at The Forks would hang up in a tree over night before they'd sleep in a hotel, wouldn't they, now?"

A light burst upon the Committee-of-One. "You'll pass, Miss Mulrooney, you'll pass," he said. "You kin take care o' yourself all right. With that head of yours, you'll own the Klondyke by the time you've been in the country as long as I have." (Palmer, *In the Klondyke,* 141–43)

While the miner attributed everything to Belinda's brains and quick acquisition of know-how, she was more modest about her abilities: "The miners never knew how little I knew, and I never got close enough for them to find out. I was the only one who knew how little I knew, and that was why I was credited with being so devilish smart and was expected to solve every problem" (NW 10:3).

Despite her lack of particular knowledge of the region, Belinda knew from her experience in Chicago, San Francisco, Juneau, and Dawson that building and running a roadhouse were well within her abilities. Although running a hotel was an accepted occupation for a woman, owning the bar inside was not only rarer but was considered by many to be inappropriate for a woman.[6] Because she had enough faith in herself to analyze the situation quickly, take some calculated risks, and act decisively, no one ever guessed that she had anything but the utmost confidence. Psychologists would say Belinda had great ego strength, and as Jill Ker Conway has noted in *True North,* largeness of ego, not humility and self-abrogation, usually accompanies great accomplishments (161).

Belinda worked hard to get the hotel ready for customers as soon as possible. According to her contemporary, Frederick Palmer, there was also another reason for her haste—her mule Gerry.

. . . She expected that every day would be the lone mule's last. There was neither hay nor oats in the country. As the story was told to me, he held body and soul together on birch bark and willow sprouts until the final log was dragged to the foundations, and then promptly expired.

"He had nothing to live on," as Miss Mulrooney expressed it, "and nothing to live for. And I'm thinkin' the poor fellow was so slow because he just knew that

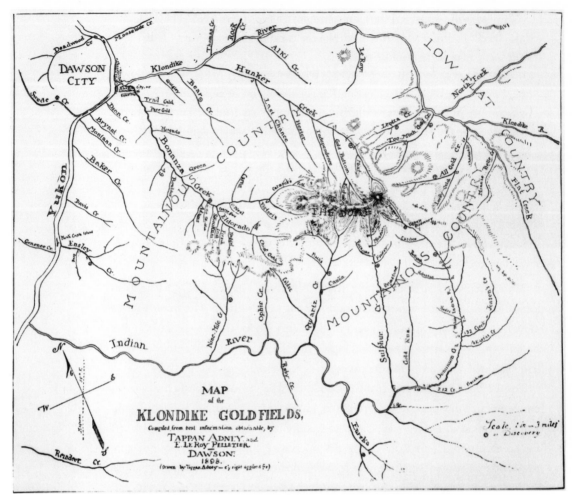

7.3. An early map of the Klondike mining district. Dawson is at upper left, where the Klondike River enters the Yukon River, flowing roughly northward. Grand Forks, not marked yet on the map, would grow at the intersection of Eldorado Creek with Bonanza Creek, shown somewhat left of center. The discovery claim on each creek is designated with a ⊕. *(UW, Adney and Pelletier, 1898. 16621)*

his interest in the enterprise was all that kept him up. And, like the rest of us, he wanted to postpone the last hour as long as he could." (*In the Klondyke*, 144)

It must have been hard for Belinda, loving animals as she did, to have to work poor Gerry under those conditions. Perhaps the only consolation was that he would have received no more humane treatment anywhere else in the Klondike.

Belinda finished her hotel in about mid-August[7] and named it The Grand Forks Hotel. According to one Dawson newspaper, it was the first business erected at the Forks.[8] It was a two-story, rectangular log structure, about 16 by

32 feet,[9] its longer dimension divided by a log partition. Like all her construction projects to come, the rustic Grand Forks Hotel showed Belinda's appreciation for good natural lighting. The long south-facing front of the hotel looking up Eldorado Creek had on the ground floor four relatively large, six-paned windows, even though glass was hard to come by and expensive in 1897.[10] These windows were further enlarged in a subsequent remodeling. The front of the hotel, approximately three hundred feet from Bonanza Creek, paralleled the trail to Dawson and upper Bonanza. Belinda was especially proud of the kennels in the back for dogs (Franklin, 23). Dogs were one of the major modes of transportation during the winter months, and taking good care of them was important.

Palmer described the accommodations offered at the Grand Forks Hotel.

> The ground floor of the hotel was divided into the bar room and the dining room. Cards were permitted, but no gaming tables were maintained. Upstairs was a tier of bunks running along the wall with a passageway between them. The blankets seemed cleaner than elsewhere—no hotel had sheets—and the bunks had curtains. Either a nice sense of individuality or sheer fatigue restrained the guests from removing their socks. And I have known miners who were over-tired by a long tramp not to remove their boots. They had enough respect for Miss Mulrooney to hang the soles of them over the edge of the bunk, however; though, if in their dreams they should participate in a stampede to some new creek, their good intentions were sadly belied.
>
> The sole occupant of a lower bunk, which was supposed to accommodate two in case of necessity, might be awakened at any hour by a nudge, and "Pardner, sorry to trouble you, but I guess you'll have to move over a bit to make room for me." (*In the Klondyke*, 146–47)

The Grand Forks Hotel was a hit from the day it opened. It became Belinda's "cash cow," providing the capital she needed for nearly all of her future business ventures. As other entrepreneurs realized the benefits of being out at the creeks, other businesses—mainly hotels, bars, and transportation companies—opened nearby, first in tents, but then in other buildings that appeared adhering to the Grand Forks Hotel's alignment. Soon the trail began to look like a street of sorts and the area came to be called by the name of Belinda's hotel, Grand Forks.[11] Unlike Joseph Ladue, Belinda had not claimed a townsite, so the only benefit she derived from the growth of the little settlement was the pride she could take in knowing she had estimated its potential correctly.

One of Belinda's first employees at the Grand Forks Hotel was a young man who tended the bar. Palmer describes him as follows:

7.4. The town of Grand Forks and Belinda's hotel, after additions and renovations. Bonanza Creek is in the foreground. (*UW, Child photog., 3*)

Andrew, a quiet, soft-voiced, obliging young man, who wore a white shirt and was solicitous about keeping his tie straight, had charge of the bar. According to all the traditions of new placer mining camps he was as much out of place as the average bartender would be in a chair of moral philosophy. He was so essentially lacking in combativeness that no one ever thought of picking a quarrel with him. (*In the Klondyke*, 148)

Belinda also asked Sadie O'Hara to come out to help her at Grand Forks. All supplies for the hotel had to be brought from Dawson, and it was while Belinda and Sadie were hauling goods on the trail that they met Belinda's next employee.

On our second trip up to Grand Forks, Sadie and I were freighting from Dawson. . . . Walker [Gilmer, who had leased a claim on the creek] when we first saw him was frail looking and was winding a windlass over the shaft. . . . [This would hoist a bucket from the hole in the ground where his partner was digging in search of the pay streak.] It was all he could do to make it. We watched him and saw him barely able to slide the board over the opening after the bucket was hoisted up. . . . He didn't want to hurt [his partner in the shaft]. The board was hardly in place before Walker fell over in a faint and rolled down the hill.

"Sadie," I said, "it looks as if we've had a man wished on us at last, even if

7.5. A windlass being operated on Skookum Jim's claim, 1 Above Discovery Bonanza, in about 1897. The man at left may be Skookum Jim Mason. *(UCB, Prather photog.,* Midnight Sun. *F909, L23, x)*

he may be a dead one." . . . We put him on our sled and took him into Grand Forks. We put him to bed and sent for his stuff. Dr. McLeod said he'd wrenched his back and shouldn't do any hard work. When he got well, we put him in charge of the hotel.

He was a refined, cultured gentleman from Boston who had left a trusted position with [a company] in Seattle to come North. He had a good knowledge of business and stood for all the better things of life. (NW 10:3)[12]

From the beginning the Grand Forks Hotel was so popular that Belinda found she couldn't live there and still have the privacy and order that she needed. So she built a cabin behind the hotel, further up the hill, where she, Sadie, and Nero lived.[13]

Belinda had been among the first to reach Dawson once news of the strike had trickled out to Juneau. The next wave of the Klondike gold rush was made up of tens of thousands of Outsiders, bedazzled by the arrival of the Klondike miners' treasure ships on the west coast in July of 1897, who set off for the Yukon to get some gold for themselves. Some of the earliest of these stampeders made it to Dawson that fall. But by then the surface of the ground was frozen and the Klondike once again was beginning to feel the grip of winter closing around it.

By September it also was becoming clear that even with the supplies already in transit to Dawson, there would not be enough food for all the people then working in the district, let alone any stampeders who managed to make it In before the Yukon froze. When some of the anxiously awaited supply boats were frozen into the Yukon River before reaching Dawson, a panic developed. People began hoarding food. Authorities advised all those without supplies on hand sufficient for the entire winter to leave while they still could get out. Many did leave, but Belinda was not intimidated.

A town meeting was held in a Dawson street in October for all of those who were staying. Those with extra provisions were urged to share them.

> I had an enormous accumulation of food stuffs from purchasing outfits all summer and was spotted as one who had too much. After taking out enough for myself, I was willing and did divide the balance of what I had. Here I was at the beginning of winter with a perfectly good hotel at Grand Forks, my great big Saint Bernard pup, and Sadie O'Hara on my hands![14]
>
> At first we couldn't run our hotel on account of the shortage of provisions, but we managed. . . . When anyone wanted to stay there, we had him put in his provisions with ours. All we needed were staple goods. There was plenty of meat game and everything else.
>
> . . . After thirty days food stuff loosened up and the hotel was running full blast. In no time we had a lot of people living with us. They got tired of individual cooking and turned in their provisions. We had a fair supply of waiters and cooks from the steam boats. They had gone gold crazy, left their jobs, gone up to the mines to find pick and shovel mining too hard for them. (NW 10:1–2)

The Grand Forks Hotel survived, but the food shortage forced the closing of Belinda's restaurant in Dawson.[15]

Scarce supplies that fall were also to blame for a drastic change in Belinda's relationship with one of her friends from Grand Forks, Alexander McDonald. Though not much older than Belinda, Alex was counted among the "Old Timers," having come into the Yukon basin in 1895.[16] He had been working a claim on a tributary of Sixtymile River when he heard of the Klondike strike and rushed to the new ground. He reached Grand Forks in September of 1896, only to learn the nearby creeks were already staked. But Alex began investing what money he had in buying out those who wanted to sell. Now, one year later, he was the owner of a number of very rich claims.[17]

Belinda and Sadie were in Dawson, preparing their sleds for a trip to Grand

7.6. Alex McDonald, Belinda's friend and rival. *(Anchorage Museum of History and Art, B74.1.25)*

Forks, when Belinda noticed two men poling a small boat upstream. She quietly met them as they landed and learned that one of the men owned a small steamboat that had run aground just around the bend below Dawson, after nothing but trouble on their way In. Now the crew was revolting and refusing to float the boat again without full payment of their wages. But the owner did not have the money.

The cargo had lots of provisions in it. He had $50,000 worth of stuff on the boat, and I told him then and there I could close the deal if he'd give me an option for a few hours. "I can't handle it myself, but I can get people to go in it with me."

. . . I sent Sadie to find Alex McDonald. Alex, big Honest Alex. He was a blacksmith from Nova Scotia, tall—over six feet, with hands—well his fingers were as big as sausages. He was so tall he always stooped over when he talked to you and always in a low voice. He was so deeply saturated in religion that everyone looked forward to doing what he did, he was held so high as an example. I heard he was paying $100 for a sack of flour. I knew that he wanted to do a lot of prospecting that winter.

Alex . . . returned with Sadie. [He was] quite excited. I told him I thought conditions were adjusted now and that what we purchased now, we would probably be allowed to keep. I told him I needed stuff badly to run the Grand Forks Hotel, explaining, "The public needs the hotel as there is going to be an immense quantity of freight run up from Dawson to the mines."

"Yes, yes," Alex said, "What have you got?"

"A little steamboat with lots of provisions on it. I'll take a third. I can't handle all of it, so we'll divide it. You stay right here and I'll go up and get the currency for the owner."

. . . Alex, [Lafe] Hamilton, and Tom Chisholm[18] were there. I made out a crude document to cover the thing with a side agreement. The captain was to sell me the mattresses. "I'll get you enough passengers goin' out to fill the boat, and they'll have their own bedding," I told him.

[To my partners I said,] "I'll leave you two men to help you unload, and we'll put . . . all the provisions in one warehouse and divide when I come back from the hotel, where I'll be getting ready for the mattresses."

"All right," they said.

So I left it to them with just two men to pick up my part of the labor of unloading. When I returned to Dawson I was very happy. On the trail I had met one string of men after another freighting in flour and provisions, all for Alex McDonald. Imagine what I felt when I got back and found in my warehouse there were no food stuffs! I needed staples, was absolutely short of them. None had been left for me. Oh yes, there were a couple of sacks of flour!

They had loaded off the boat for my share cases of gum boots, . . . tobacco, underwear, socks, dried onions, and hardware. Also all the candles in the world and fifty barrels of liquor. . . . There were a couple of sacks of beans that had fallen in the river and swelled up and had busted themselves all over, and a couple of sacks of wet rice. Honest Alex! At first I took it as another . . . joke.

. . . I caught Alex and asked, " . . . Where's my part of the provisions?"

"You have one outfit allowed, and Sadie has one outfit, and there are a couple of sacks of flour. Of course, if you run short I'll provide for you, but I have so many men to feed."

I told him I wanted to supply my hotel.

"Hotel? You couldn't run a hotel."

"Alex, do you seriously intend to gyp me out of that stuff? Is that final?"

"My stuff is all moved up to the mines," he said.

Then I knew what I hadn't had the slightest idea of before. All that flour and stuff I had seen going to Grand Forks was from shipments off the boat.

. . . "You're not mad at me?" asked Alex, stooping and whispering as usual.

"No, only you better not let me meet you anywhere after dark."

Then I went back to that place, that long cold warehouse, and I blew up. I had kept myself to myself pretty thoroughly before, but I walked up and down and was saying, "You great big driveling idiot! To let a big stiff of a Nova Scotian cod fish put something over on you."

Sadie came in and saw me. She was shocked. "What has happened?"

"Sadie," I told her, "I guess my guardian angel let go my hand for five minutes, and look what's happened." I showed her (all the stuff.) "I feel as if I had been caught swimming without my clothes on." (NW 11a:6–9)

Belinda was both angry and hurt. Her friend Alex not only cheated her out of the supplies she needed, but implicitly was saying he didn't think her work was as important as what he was doing. Belinda vowed to get even with Alex McDonald, however long it might take.

LIFE AT THE GRAND FORKS HOTEL settled into a routine that winter. Nero, Belinda's St. Bernard, became her almost constant companion. He had filled out and matured under Belinda's care and now was very big and very strong. Belinda trained him to pull a sled, and their trips into Dawson were noted in the *Klondike News* of 1 April 1898:

Miss Mulrooney is a modest, refined and prepossessing young woman, a brilliant conversationalist, and a bright business woman. She makes the 18 mile trip to Dawson in a basket sleigh drawn by her faithful dog Nero, a noble animal of the St. Bernard breed and the largest dog in the Northwest. The trip is made in less than three hours.

As Belinda had predicted, those on the trail to other locations made a point of stopping at Grand Forks to rest and eat. "All the freight hauled in passed our place, all the stampeders from all over the world that came in." And one traveler noted, "Meals could be had there, served on a clean table cloth with china dishes, for $3.50 each, or $12 a day for meals and bed" (Adney, 258). But the hotel's main customers were the miners with nearby claims who lived, took meals, or just socialized there. The Grand Forks Hotel's reputation for good and ample meals spread to Dawson, for when Grand Forks miners went into town, they compared the restaurants there to the standard they had come to enjoy at Belinda's hotel.

7.7. Belinda with her dog Nero. (*UW, Palmer, In the Klondyke, 142+1. 17736*)

"I don't mind paying double," said the Committee-of-One to a Dawson waiter, "s'long 's I get sumthin' to eat. Just bring that dinner over again. Then I'll have only half a square meal for $5, not to mention that no fixin's go with it. Miss Mulrooney charges $3.50 for a square, but she gives you canned beef, canned mutton, and ham, and fixin's, and keeps askin' you if you won't have more, and you keep acceptin' till you have to send for a drink 'fore you're strong enough to get up from the table. Jumpin' John Rogers! How you fellers must suffer when you pass out a bean and a rind and think of what a woman is doin' up there to The Forks!"

If you want to reach a man's heart through his stomach in a scurvy-stricken country, feed him, if it is the best you have, with sauce made of dried apples. Miss Mulrooney kept a great bowl full of this on her table. The transient ate of its contents with the ravenousness of the thirsty traveler drinking from a spring of cold water. No sooner was it emptied—I know by actual observation of a quart of applesauce having been eaten by two persons—than it was filled again by the cook, rapid if rough in his movements, who picked it up and put it down as if it were a red-hot ingot. (Palmer, *In the Klondyke*, 145–46)

Belinda's reputation also grew from her handling of difficult situations. Her approach was a psychological one.

Miss Mulrooney did not depend for purposes of pacification upon a huge St. Bernard who was always at her side when he was not drawing her upon her sled up and down the creeks in winter, but rather upon her blarney. She knew when, where, and just how much to apply.

"I always appeal to their best instincts," she said. "It's easy to lead and hard to drive. That's what you men don't understand. You try to drive."

I saw her theory put to the test. . . . A giant who was so well on in his cups that he could scarcely walk, concluded, only half an hour after he had finished one, that he wanted another meal. When it was placed before him he seemed to think that the cook was trying to hurt his feelings by making him eat twice, and with an oath he threw a dish of stew on the floor.

Miss Mulrooney happened to be passing through the room at the time. She stepped over to him and told him in her pleasantest tone that accidents would happen.

" Accident?" he asked, dazedly.

"Of course," she said. "I know you're too much of a gentleman to do such a thing purposely."

"Coursh! Coursh it was!" he kept repeating, as he dropped down onto his knees and tried to scrape the stew up into a little pile, despite her protests.

Then out of the maze of his crippled memory another horror presented itself suddenly and prompted him to arise. "Miss Mulrooney," he asked, his face very red, "did you hear me swear?"

"A little one—a slip," she replied.

He told her that it was only a real lady who would put so liberal a construction on what he called a breach of "ettykit." Fearful, nevertheless, that she might secretly think ill of him, he followed her about the hotel with apologies and dripping hands while he kept repeating how a poor devil might be a little weak, so rarely did a good bench claim fall to a poor devil's lot, until the inner workings of his conscience culminated in a full confession that the plate had not been broken by accident but intentionally. She forgave him even this, and then he went upstairs and to sleep. (Palmer, *In the Klondyke*, 148–50)

While the Grand Forks Hotel built a strong reputation as one of the best of its kind, it also was more than an inn. At the end of a hard day of work, with temperatures well below freezing and long hours of darkness stretching ahead, there was warmth and light and companionship to be found at the hotel. Furthermore, with candles and stove fuel in short supply, an evening spent reading in the dining room was more economical and more comfortable than in one's own cabin. The hotel also served as a community meeting hall and a church for the people on the creeks.[19]

The Grand Forks Hotel also became a focal point for other businesses. Walker Gilmer, Belinda's trusted manager, became known for his skills as an accountant. Anyone on the creeks who got his reckonings confused would go the hotel to ask Walker to help straighten them out; Walker soon was earning quite a bit of money on the side for these services. Many of the miners found it convenient to use the hotel as a bank, leaving their gold there for safekeeping until it could be transported to Dawson. Walker recalled: "We had no safes, nor any place but the floor to put it. In that [roadhouse the miners] threw on the floor $50,000 in gold dust or $100,000, according to the season. . . . The gold was tied in . . . pokes, the buckskin and moose hide sacks the native women made, or was packed in tin cans."[20]

A natural extension of Belinda's rudimentary banking and her acquisition of mining properties for herself was her brokering exchanges of claims, as described by one early Klondiker.

> Miss Mulroney [sic] also ran a mining brokerage business, and her turnover was huge. I remember a young fellow who sold his one hundred-foot-square claim on Gold Hill, which was within hailing distance of the hotel. He made the sale through Miss Mulroney and received the thirty thousand dollars in cash, over the hotel bar. Just twenty-four hours later, he went back to work for the fellow to whom he had sold the claim. In the interval he had lost the entire amount at faro. (Pitcher, 26)

At least once, for Yola Grignon, Belinda represented the legal interests of a Klondiker who was going Outside.[21] Whether this was an act of friendship or strictly a business arrangement is not known. Other businesses Belinda managed from the hotel were freighting and milling lumber. Flumes and sluice boxes were constructed with the lumber, as well as other buildings for the town of Grand Forks.

> Lumber was the main thing [the miners wanted]. The small saw mill I had brought from Circle City was a great help. I had a good freight outfit and dogs and delivered them lumber wherever they were—Dominion or Sulphur. I

could always supply the men I staked. It gave me a chance to get in as a partner reasonably.

I spent the time looking around the country getting fuel, logs out for cabins. Dog houses chiefly were my occupation.

Belinda also ran a rudimentary trading post out of the hotel, as can be seen in the following story, which moreover tells us how Belinda patiently waited and schemed all through the winter to even the score with Alex McDonald. Though she hired out twenty-eight members of her own mining crew to work for him, Belinda would not forgive his betrayal. Whenever an opportunity presented itself, she made his life uncomfortable.

One afternoon . . . I came into the Grand Forks and found . . . Tom Chisholm at the good stove we'd taken such pains to make, cooking dog food for his team. "Where did you get the idea you can use my place like that?" I wanted to know.

"Why I thought it was all right. I'm in charge of Alex's freighting," Tom tried to explain.

"I don't care who you are engaged by. You can't use my place for yourself, your dogs, or Alex either. You can finish this mess and stay this once, but don't come back."

The next day Alex himself came down. "What will you take for your hotel?" he wanted to know. "I'm trying to buy it for Tom Chisholm, not myself."

"Tom Chisholm, no nor you either, won't have it. And tell your Tom Chisholm to keep away from here. He is so coarse and rough, he has too many dogs, and is too dirty. I don't want him."

"I'll give you $10,000 for the hotel," Alex offered.

"If you get it you'll pay more than ten times $10,000 to me."

Alex was puzzled. "Good God! I got to use this place for distributing up Eldorado and Bonanza. Couldn't I make some arrangements with you to use this for my headquarters and my freight?"

"No, you can't use this place for your headquarters or your freight. This is our home, and we have not enough provisions for a hotel. If you want to provide for your immense amount of freight, mess, . . . dogs, and men, you'll have to build yourself a place. You are not going to use my house."

"Why," Alex said, "it's only a shack, just some logs!"

"Yes, but it's worth $100,000 to me. It may be just logs, but what are your claims? Just dust. It's only a state of mind anyway."

"You're not mad at me?" Alex asked, bending down and whispering as usual. (NW 11b:1–3)

Belinda, mad? Yes, and she was letting Alex know she hadn't forgotten what he had done by making sure he didn't take advantage of her again. As the winter began to give way to spring and water began to flow again in the creeks and down into mining shafts, Belinda finally saw her chance to make Alex McDonald pay his dues.

Alex had a lot of unfinished business around Grand Forks Hotel that winter. That was what made the Pioneers say he wanted to marry me. Besides, he was afraid to tell the truth about the food deal. If they had known it, I believe the Pioneers would have killed him.

However, I had my own ideas of getting even. Gum boots. You see, the miners have to have gum boots in the spring. They can't stand in melting ice water in their shoes and socks. They would freeze their feet.

So around towards spring I outfitted my own crew who were working for Alex with new socks and underwear and everything I could get. I told them to trade anything they had for gum boots.

Walker wondered why I wanted so many old gum boots. "Because they are the best things in the world, Walker," I told him, trying not to grin, "to use to start a fire. In the woods if you have just a five inch square of rubber, they make the best fire starter." He just looked at me.

The men suspected something, but they didn't know what. Before long I had every boot in Alex McDonald's outfit. When the men began to wonder about boots, Alex told them, "Don't worry. There's lots of boots. I'll get them when they're needed."

He didn't know that I'd gone to the trading post at Dawson, found out how many boots they had, bought them, and freighted them up to Grand Forks.

Candles began to give out too. There were all (of) mine from the boat, and I bought all the trading post had too. I controlled the candles.

When Alex went down to Dawson and asked the trading companies for boots, there were no boots. "Miss Mulrooney has some at Grand Forks," they informed him. He had to come to me.

I'd sold gum boots before that at $15 a pair to other miners when they came in. "What will you charge for a pair of gum boots?" Alex whispered to me.

Then I told him, "Thirty dollars, and if you take one pair you take cases and cases of those boots." Honest Alex McDonald, the Nova Scotian cod fish, had to buy every one. (NW 11b:3–5)

Belinda's imagination, beyond competitive game playing and schemes to make a profit, also extended to community developments that improved life at Grand Forks for everyone. She was among the founders of the Yukon Telegraph and Telephone Syndicate, which brought better and more efficient communication to the Klondike region as a whole. Eventually it connected Dawson with not only Grand Forks but other outlying communities as well.[22]

I'd always been crazy to have a telephone. "What the hell do you want a phone for, Girl?" the men asked me.

"To save time," I said. "The number of trips I have to make with Nero between Grand Forks and Dawson wastes too much time."

I suggested that we have [a fellow who was going Outside during the winter] get us the equipment for the telephone and get it onto the Summit. I could supply the poles myself. Clarence Berry[23] agreed. "Why yes we could. We could get twenty of the mine owners to put in $1000 a piece." So we made a list.

The first man to put his name down on that fool list was Alex McDonald. He flops his name down for $5000. "Nothing doing Alex," I said to him. "That's putting this business off with a wrong start. It's a thousand dollars each. Besides, I'd rather see you out of it." Yes I was still mad at him about that [boat cargo]. "I don't believe you and I can do business." But I let it go with $1000 from him.

7.8. Belinda's hotel and the main street of Grand Forks in about 1898. *(UW, Cantwell photog., 54)*

[A man] went out with money enough for one hundred phones and equipment and was to bring it back with a man to put the system up and work it. When he came In, we sent a crew with an outfit and dogs to meet him, fixing up boats at Bennett and meeting him at Sheep Camp.

When the stuff got in at Dawson, we found Tom O'Brien[24] had been out in San Francisco with an order for phones, and he'd come back too late. He was boiling mad. I told him there was plenty of room for both of us and bought the equipment at its value. I told him, "You can run the company."[25]

BELINDA'S EARLIEST BUSINESSES in Dawson and Grand Forks all were natural outgrowths of her previous experience Outside—importing clothing and soft goods; retail sales; running a restaurant; construction contracting; running a hotel, restaurant, and bar at the roadhouse; and buying and selling property. Other businesses, such as banking and the telephone company, evolved because she was at the center of economic activity and seemed to know how to get things done right. People came to trust her judgment and reliable action.

If Belinda had confined herself to her support businesses and continued with them in the manner in which she started out, she would have been financially successful beyond most people's wildest dreams. But now that she was on the creeks, she was eager to try the occupation that most stampeders imagined was the way to make money in the Klondike—gold mining.

8

Mining in the Winter of 1897–98

T HE GRAND FORKS HOTEL, like Belinda's Dawson restaurant, was an ideal spot for learning where gold had been located, how much pay dirt was taken out, who was getting rich, and who was feeling discouraged. When claims became available, Belinda was in a good position to buy them outright or to help finance the owner in exchange for a share of the output.

> You happened to be in place, and the men were going to stake, a stampede was on. They wanted to exchange an outfit for an interest. They needed something, provisions or money or something. They had no hesitancy in coming to me because I was always around. I got to the state where I'd say "Yes" to everything. "Yes, boys, we'll do the best we can." (NW 58:2–3[299–300])

By grubstaking prospectors, Belinda became what today would be termed a venture capitalist. Not all the resulting claims proved valuable, but enough of them paid dividends to keep Belinda encouraged.

> During the winter I secured knocking around and by purchase, about three claims on Eldorado, [and] about ten claims from [new strikes]. I bought them but I didn't pay much for them except for the Eldorado one, as its value was established.

I think in the shuffle of that winter I got four good claims. Buying from the miners was better than staking claims. Or I grubstaked them to outfits they couldn't get and a little cash. They didn't care enough for the money. What they wanted was things with which to prospect—axes, shovels, picks, clothing and whipsaws.[1]

Belinda also enjoyed the excitement of competing with others to do her own staking on a newly discovered creek. The Grand Forks Hotel was often ahead of Dawson in learning of new strikes. This was the case with Dominion Creek, a tributary of the Indian River, located across the hills to the east and south of Grand Forks. (See map, Figure 7.3.) Shortly after Belinda and Sadie arrived at Grand Forks, the freeze set in and miners could begin prospecting.

When . . . gold was discovered there'd be an immense stampede. At the hotel there would be dogs, people, all going mad, staking everything, everywhere in the district.

Sadie and I joined one stampede to Dominion, took dog teams and staked claims.[2] We came back that night exhausted and slept in the hotel. That was our one night in the hotel. The place, except for the little room for women, was filled with miners, tired from their long round trip to Dominion and back again. We went in because we didn't want to warm up our own cabin. (Hawkins)

The lumber of the hotel had shrunk. There were wide cracks everywhere so you could hear everything. (At) night there was such snoring, . . . belching, . . . moaning, and . . . talking in their sleep from the miners, the whole place rocked with the noise. I stood it as long as I could. In the middle of the night I got up and said to Sadie, "This is surely a man's hotel."

Sadie sat up and started laughing and then began to cry. It was real hysterics this time. I finally had to get water and throw it at her to get her out of them." (NW 10:6)

Nearly all of the early mines in the Klondike region were placer claims, where the gold had been freed from its rock matrix by the action of natural forces—freezing, tumbling, and washing by water. The loose placer gold was usually washed downslope, where it would be found lodged in what was referred to as "bedrock"—between stones in the bed of a creek.

On Bonanza and Eldorado Creeks, the main concentrations of free gold were several feet below current stream levels, apparently in older beds of the creeks. Consequently, the first challenge was to dig down through the permanently frozen overburden to reach bedrock, and then try to locate where within that layer the gold had been deposited. In the earliest days this digging was done by hand during the cold months of the year so surface water would not flood the tunnels. The following description of the process, from a solicitation to buy shares in a mining company, emphasizes the expense involved.

> The first thing necessary is to thaw the ground. The only present means of doing this is by burning wood on the ground. Wood costs $25 per cord and labor $15 per day. Only 6 to 8 inches can be thawed out at one burning. Hence, a shaft to bed rock 3-½ x 6 feet and 14 feet deep costs about $400.

> After bed rock is reached [and if gold is actually located] every inch of the pay streak must be thawed out by this slow and expensive method. . . . Only about 25 feet of drifting [from the shaft] can be done owing to want of air, until another shaft is sunk and connected with the first in order to create a current of air.

> . . . During the frozen season no water can be had for washing out gold. During the thawing season mining can not be done without pumps to keep out water. During the mining or frozen season the days are only from four to six hours in length. Artificial light in the shafts is therefore necessary. The only artificial lights at present are candles, [costing] from $1 to $1.50 each.[3]

Missing from this description is the miner doing all the work down in the cold, dark holes. He worked with pick and shovel, with no room to stand straight; shoveled the muck into buckets; then hauled them to the vertical shafts to be hoisted by windlass to the surface for dumping. Placer mining in the Klondike took a lot of hard work under very stressful conditions, and doing it efficiently took capital.

By early December of 1897 new ground very close to Grand Forks was coming into its own. This was on the hillsides above Bonanza and Eldorado Creeks where, contrary to conventional wisdom, rich deposits of gold were found. Belinda was on the spot to stake her own placer claim on what became known as Gold Hill. Seven months later she also would purchase for $250 another placer claim on the adjoining Cheechako Hill.[4] A photograph taken in about 1898 (fig. 8.1) shows Gold Hill covered by mounds of dug-out dirt. Cheechako Hill is out of the frame to the right of this photo.

In the earth's crust, gold is often found enveloped in quartz. Speculators guessed that the source of all the placer gold in the streambeds of the Klondike, the "mother lode," was in the quartz in the hillsides above the creeks. Quartz or lode claims required a different type of mining than the placer claims. The rock had to be blasted and dug out. If it contained gold, it had to be crushed by large, heavy, expensive machinery. The gold could then be extracted with washing and chemicals. But as the *Kansas City Star* (7 April 1898) pointed out, "There

8.1. Gold Hill, looking southwest across the Bonanza and Eldorado Creek beds. The back of the Grand Forks Hotel is at the center bottom. Props sticking up from the roof are to support the "GRAND FORKS HOTEL" sign seen in Figs. 7.4 and 7.8. *(UW, A. Curtis photog., 46149)*

are no drills, sledge-hammers, powder, dynamite, stamp mills or machinery of any kind in the Northwest Territory. . . . Quartz mines can not be worked without all these" (4).

Buying the equipment for hard rock mining was more of an investment than the typical Klondike miner was ready or able to make. To get capital to search the hillsides for the mother lode required Outside investors. In December of 1897, the Eldorado-Bonanza Quartz and Placer Mining Company was organized for that purpose. Belinda Mulrooney was one of six original claim owners whose combined properties formed the company. Who took the initiative for organizing the business is uncertain, but the fact that claims were put into the name of Michael J. McNeil just prior to being transferred to the company[5] suggests he was the promoter. Also listed among the officers and directors were Old-Timer placer miners such as Alex McDonald and the Berry Brothers— Clarence, Fred, Henry, and Frank—along with Dr. P. D. Carper, a geologist, and Dr. C. C. Savage.[6] The company was organized some time before 26 December 1897, because on that date two of its officers, McNeil and Savage, left Dawson for the Outside to find investors.[7]

According to newspaper accounts, the company was incorporated in Mis-

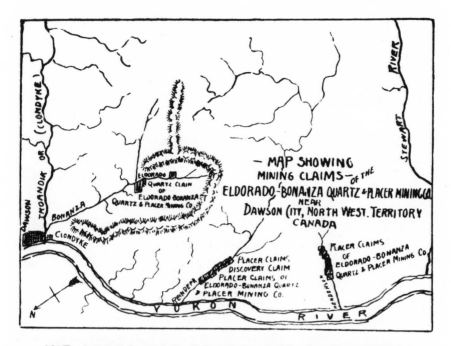

8.2. This map appeared in the *Kansas City Star,* 7 April 1898, to show the location of claims that were part of the Eldorado-Bonanza Quartz and Placer Mining Company. Note that north is down and to the left. *(Mayer Collection)*

souri, with its general office and many of its directors in Kansas City.[8] Its holdings included nine quartz as well as twelve placer claims.

The nine quartz claims of the company were located on the hillsides above Eldorado and Bonanza Creeks. Six of them "at the junction of Eldorado and Bonanza creeks, [cover] the entire mountain from Eldorado Creek to Skookum Gulch and extend north[east] to Bonanza Creek on either side of this mountain."[9] This was the area that would become known as Gold Hill, and it simultaneously was completely covered by placer claims. The three quartz claims on the northeast side of Eldorado Creek were opposite placer creek claims 44, 45, and 46.

The placer claims of the company were numbers 60 through 65 Below Discovery on Henderson Creek and numbers 1 through 4 Above and 1 through 3 Below on Reindeer Creek, according to the *Klondike News.*[10]

Publicity announced that the company was capitalized for $1,500,000, with $100,000 of stock offered for sale to the public and $500,000 held in reserve. The original six owners received paid-up stock of $150,000 each in exchange for their claims.[11] An advertisement in the *Kansas City Star* on 7 April of 1898 offered stock in the company for $10 per share, the proceeds to be used for the purchase of machinery and supplies. The large, half-page ad also explained the expense of quartz mining and the improvements in both quartz and placer mining that the new company would finance.

> What can be done with [the proper] machinery on the quartz claims of this Company can be readily ascertained from a simple inspection of the stupendously rich specimens chipped off with a pick and always on exhibit at the offices of this Company [in Kansas City, Missouri].
>
> OUR PLAN. For our quartz claims we will purchase sledges, drills, blasting powder and a stamp mill. For our placers we will purchase steam engines, dredges, pumps, electric light plant and saw-mill. We will make a shipment of pumps, not only for our own use, but for sale or lease. From the sale and lease of pumps we will make a profit in excess of the cost of our own pumps. With a saw-mill we will not only save $250 per thousand on our own lumber, but make an immense profit by supplying lumber for all demands. We will also take a dredge into the Klondyke to operate on gravel bars carrying very rich deposits of gold in the Klondyke and Stewart Rivers, which will be a source of great profit to the Company. Our electric light plant will have a capacity in excess of our own requirements—by the sale of light we shall make a handsome profit. We will also take with us a large stock of general merchandise. (4)

That sawmill mentioned in the plan may actually have been the one Belinda said she brought to Grand Forks from Circle City. Another portion of the advertisement explained the advantages of the mill. "Lumber is necessary for sluice boxes and other mining purposes, but lumber costs $360 per thousand, while logs can be had for $30 per thousand. The necessity, economy and profit of a saw-mill is obvious."[12]

Also included in the plans was the purchase of a boat to operate on the Yukon River. Thus the company could give priority to transporting its own goods and equipment. Stock in the Eldorado-Bonanza Quartz and Placer Mining Company was to be sold only until May 1. On June 1 M. J. McNeil, who was then in Kansas City, having bought the needed machinery and supplies, would start back to the Klondike, presumably using the company's own boat for the final leg of the trip.[13]

In retrospect, knowing the proven richness of the Klondike region, it is easy to forget the uncertainty of nearly every new mining operation in the area during the winter of 1897–98. Many placer claims on Bonanza, Eldorado, Sulphur, and Dominion were, of course, very rich. But many others, on different creeks or even on the proven creeks in different locations, had little or no gold. Likewise, quartz mining, though common in other parts of the world, was unheard of in the far northwest.[14] The Old Timers thought so little of the hillside claims, placer or quartz, that most just scoffed at the cheechakos (newcomers) who explored the possibilities there. Consequently, the Eldorado-Bonanza Quartz and Placer Mining Company's proposal to undertake quartz mining in the Yukon district was highly speculative. It would take organization, engineering, determination, and luck to make it a successful operation. On the other hand, the company did have a powerful argument to balance the risk in the eyes of potential investors. Compared with the risks and expense people accepted to get to the Klondike, the company's proposal was reasonable, though the "certainty" of success the company promised investors was a gross overstatement. "Thousands of dollars are being spent in sending inexperienced men to Klondyke to find gold," read the advertisement. "We have found the gold. Why spend money on uncertainty when with us your investment is a certainty?"

By March 1898, work on the quartz mining operations on Bonanza Creek was underway. The *Klondike News* of 1 April 1898 reported the progress.

> Development of the quartz claims is being pushed forward as fast as conditions permit. A tunnel is being driven through the mountain from the Bonanza side, about fifty feet above the creek bank; the work is progressing at the rate of about three feet per day. At this writing one hundred and fifty feet distance has been gained. This tunnel will diagonally cross-cut the vein at a distance of about two hundred and fifty feet from the entrance, and at a depth of about five hundred feet from the surface. (36)

According to this same article, work on the Eldorado quartz claims would await arrival of blasting powder and other materials when the steamers were once again able to get to Dawson.

As it turned out, Gold Hill did not have much quartz gold. Instead it was again free gold that was found lying in ancient, now elevated creek beds. But lode claims had no right to placer gold found in the same ground. Consequently, it was the hillside placer claims that took precedence on Gold Hill and made it famous.

Despite the thought and effort that went into its planning and organization, the considerable publicity it generated, and the expertise of its officers, it is not clear that anything ever came of the Eldorado-Bonanza Quartz and Placer Mining Company. The state of Missouri has no record of the company's incorporation there,[15] and we have been unable to locate any further reference to it in public records or through surviving members of the principals' families. Therefore we do not know how many people actually bought stock in the company, nor whether they saw any return on their investment.

If the Eldorado-Bonanza Quartz and Placer Mining Company was a poor investment, it was no different than many others that came out of the Klondike. The company's organization was typical in involving two levels—the promoter and the original mining property owners. The owners transferred their property to the promoter in exchange for stock in the company. The promoter then tried to sell the stock to Outsiders. Having well-known names associated with the company was key to successful sales. The Berrys were reputed as being among the wealthiest Klondikers when they arrived in Seattle on the "Ton of Gold!" ship the previous summer. And Alex McDonald and Belinda Mulrooney were beginning to make their reputations in the Klondike, for anyone who cared to check further. These were the names that might lead investors to buy Eldorado-Bonanza Quartz and Placer Mining Company stock and to run up its price. Then both the promoter and the original owners stood to gain purely from the sale of their stock. If the ground also had potential and the stock proceeds were used to develop it, then the company could earn enough money to pay dividends to all stockholders.

But often only the most unpromising claims were put into an investment company, so only the promoter and the original owners ever benefited. According to the *New York Times* correspondent in Dawson, E. LeRoy Pelletier, by early 1898 Dawson had already made the transition from mining camp to speculative center. Pelletier warned *Times* readers (8 May) that none of the really good properties were ever included in the Outside investment schemes. Since Pelletier was also doing business as a mine broker, he presumably was in a position to know. According to William F. Berry, grandson of Fred Berry, president of the Eldorado-Bonanza Quartz and Place Mining Company, the claims put into this company by the Berrys were basically worthless.[16] Lewis Green, former resident geologist for the Geological Survey of Canada at Whitehorse, Yukon, reports, "Over the years there have been many attempts to develop lode or quartz properties in the Klondike, but to date none have been successful and the gold production from them is insignificant."[17] It seems likely that the Eldorado-Bonanza Quartz and Placer Mining Company ended up more a promotion than a successful mining company.

Whether legitimate or not, the Eldorado-Bonanza Quartz and Placer Mining Company represented another step in the development of Belinda's business acumen. It was the first time she operated in an extended partnership or got involved in starting a business that she did not manage herself. Finally, if the company was a scam, then it is the first example we have found of her implication in fraud, whether knowing or not. Her previous below-board activities, such as selling liquor, though illegal, had no innocent direct victims.

Another aspect of Belinda's experience that first winter in the Klondike remains a mystery. How did she contend with the stresses of that long, harsh season? By late December temperatures were routinely near minus thirty degrees Fahrenheit. For six weeks the sun did not appear above the horizon. Only for a couple of hours at noon was there a kind of twilight. Adding to the otherworldly gloom of winter was the fog that blanketed the ground. The mining area around Ground Forks resembled a scene from hell. Smoke rose from hundreds of holes being burned through the permafrost, with those nearer the surface casting an eerie red glow. The fumes climbed only a short distance before being pressed down by the cold air, then settled and mingled with the fog, adding to the gloom. With no electricity, few oil lamps, no magazines or newspapers and few books, it is easy to see why many people would welcome the stimulation and warmth of public places, such as the Grand Forks Hotel, rather than stay in their small cabins in the winter.

In January and February, even as the light began to increase, the temperatures dropped still lower, sometimes reaching minus sixty to minus seventy degrees. Then to go outdoors was to risk frozen lungs with each breath and almost instant frostbite of unprotected skin. But staying indoors was not all that comfortable either. The uninsulated buildings in those early years in the Klondike were only crude protection from the bitter cold. Heavy clothing was still needed indoors. The fire in the stove had to be kept going constantly. Even then water in a bucket on the floor only a few feet away would freeze, while cabin walls turned white with rime. The lowest temperatures would be signaled by loud cracks like pistol shots from brittle nails popping under tension in the walls. As the winter wore on, the olfactory atmosphere in community gathering places grew redolent with smoke, thawing hair and fur, and unwashable bodies and clothes.

Most pioneers and stampeders comment on what it was like to stay In during a Klondike winter, but from Belinda's recollections we hear only of adventures, planning and organizing, routine activities, and sometimes mishaps. Perhaps her restless activity insulated her from the cold and the darkness. In any case, Belinda was not a person to grouse about hardships.

By late March of 1898 spring had come to the Klondike. Snow melted from the hillsides and streams began to flow. The muck that had been hauled from mining shafts to the surface, where it promptly refroze into the mass of the dump, also began to loosen. It was time to sluice the dumps to recover the gold and to see what profit, if any, the long, hard winter's digging had yielded. For miners in the Klondike, spring was like harvest time in more temperate, agrarian regions. At the Grand Forks Hotel Belinda prepared for the heightened activity.

> Walker, Sadie and I planned for the spring. I needed more building space, sleeping quarters for the public. We decided to build two more buildings as an annex to the Grand Forks Hotel.
>
> "Build some counters," I said. "Put some scales on them so the miners can divide and weigh their own gold dust."
>
> . . . I told Walker, "You must work some plan where you and Sadie will make some money. Get an assistant. For heaven's sake get someone who hasn't the gold fever. Tons of gold will go through this place in less than a month and we mustn't let anything disagreeable happen."

As usual, Belinda accurately gauged what would be needed as the cleanup proceeded.

> The miners were all excited about the cleanup of '98. I was invited to cleanup on Clarence Berry's[18] claim on Eldorado where the sluice boxes were yellow with gold. . . . They were scooping the gold up in copper scoops, something like a fire shovel. All the tin cans [and] pails around the place were filled with gold lying around the cabin floor.
>
> They were wondering who had the richest ground. We all had to agree that Dick Lowe's fraction at the junction of Eldorado and Bonanza was by far the richest. I saw him take a pan of dirt from bed rock, almost solid gold, only a little dirt mixed with it. The sluice boxes were a sight. They had to clean them every day. All the Indian women in the country were busy making gold sacks out of moose skin. The miners all had to have sacks to empty the tin cans in so they could have the cans for the next cleanup. The tin cans were almost as valuable as the gold!

8.3. Cleanup on the Berry claims on Eldorado Creek in 1898. Clarence J. Berry holds a gold pan filled with pay dirt from the sluice box he leans against. Edna "Tot" Bush stands at left in the black dress, next to Henry Berry, C. J.'s brother, whom she will eventually marry. Ethel Bush Berry, Tot's sister and C. J.'s wife, stands with folded arms in a printed-leaf dress. The tall man behind her is Fred Otis, who worked on the claim, like the unidentified others. *(Berry Collection)*.

Belinda was in a position to know just how well everyone near Grand Forks was doing not only because they were neighbors, but also because her hotel had taken on another role. In addition to serving as an informal bank, the Grand Forks Hotel had become a collection center for mining royalties.

The Canadian government worried that the mineral resources of its newly developing territory would be carted off by the predominantly American miners in the Klondike. Therefore, Ottawa instituted royalties in August 1897 to raise revenue to support administration of the territory. But the distant government acted with little understanding of the conditions prevailing in the Klondike. The royalty rate was set at 10 percent on the gross output, or 20 percent on claims producing more than five hundred dollars per day,[19] levels even the Canadian miners greatly resented as unreasonable given the expenses of mining under the Yukon's isolation and extreme weather conditions. When government officials arrived in February 1898 to begin collecting the royalty, there was widespread discontent and such deception in keeping records that one miner estimated that no more than one-tenth of the correct tax was ever collected. For this he did not blame the miners.[20] According to Belinda,

> [The gold] all went through the Grand Forks Hotel for royalties. They left it there for the purpose of shipping it all together. It was hard to handle. Those gold pokes were the worry of Walker's life. He refused to take them unless the miners put their names on so he could tell them apart.
>
> . . . There seemed to be a steady stream of miners coming into Grand Forks with dust to haul. I got sick of the dust—would rather see a pile of cord wood than sacks of gold dust. They were mean to handle—heavy and hard to pack. They were like a piece of lead when you put 'em on your back—would work into your backbone and shoulder.
>
> Alex [McDonald] had mules to haul his. He certainly took out a lot of gold dust that spring.

Belinda had the proceeds from her own claims and shares in claims coming in as well. Like the rest, she turned over most of her dust to Walker Gilmer for safekeeping. Eventually it had to be taken into Dawson where it would be held by one of the trading companies until the Yukon River ice broke and transportation to the Outside was re-established. Until the Bank of British North America and the Canadian Bank of Commerce arrived in the early summer of 1898, the Alaska Commercial Company and the North American Trading and Transportation Company provided rudimentary banking services for the Klondike area. They were, of course, also the main suppliers of goods, and Belinda often refers to them as the "trading posts."

The creeks were kind of high that year. We threw logs across for bridges. One trip to town I had my dog Nero loaded up with two sacks of gold dust, a poke on each side, and one on my back. When we came to this log it was wet and slippery. I was walking ahead and forgot all about Nero. He was such a big clumsy thing, and the log was so slippery. His paws went out from under him. One big splash! There was Nero in the creek, gold dust and all.

The water was deep and he so heavy with gold dust! I dropped my pack as fast as I could and went to help him. He went right down with his heavy load. When he came up again I couldn't reach him. The only way I could get him was to climb out on a limb of a small willow thing. I got to the end. It dropped with my weight down far enough so I got Nero by the collar. There we were, that God damn gold dust making the dog so heavy I couldn't lift him.

I couldn't get out, but I could keep his poor head out of the water. I just could, that was all.

Some men came along. Nero's eyes were sticking out. I was holding him by the collar so tight he was choking. "For God's sake, help us," I said. "Cut that darned gold dust off the dog and let it sink into the river, but get the dog out."

It sounded easier than it [was to do]. One took his belt and tied me to the limb. "Got to tie you or you'll fall in," he insisted.

He started out on the limb. I told him the poor dog was dying, but his mind was on me, and darned if the limb didn't break and there was I in the ice cold water, dirty mud and everything. Gee, it was cold. That fool dog. He was a monster and so hard to lift him, with the weight of the gold dust, out of the mess.

Nero's gold off, he shook. One man came along and wanted to put his coat on me. "Don't I weigh enough now?" I was like a ton.

DIVERSIFYING INTO MINING seemed a very natural way for Belinda to try to in-crease her fortune, and in the Klondike at that time there was nothing to stop her. Though many people in the late 1890s thought women were legally excluded from mine ownership, in fact, this was open to interpretation. Any adult, male or female, could buy a mine. There was some uncertainty about who was eli-gible to stake and work a claim, however. For example, in November of 1896, Surveyor William Ogilvie noted that in British Columbia "every person over but not under 18 years of age" was permitted to take out a mining license, a pre-requisite to staking and working a claim. That sounds fair enough, but under English Common Law tradition, "person" often meant only males,[21] and min-ing was one of the traditionally exclusively male industries. Therefore, Ogilvie recommended for the Yukon basin that only males over 18 be allowed to take out a license.[22] However, the government in Ottawa in January of 1898 made the code for mining in the Yukon quite specific: " 'Free miner' shall mean a male or female over the age of 18, but not under that age."[23]

Between the discovery of gold in August of 1896 and these new, clearer regulations in January of 1898, there seems to have been no *consistent* official effort to prevent women from staking claims. But it did happen. We know of one early incident where staking on Bonanza in the name of absentee women was not recognized. Here the situation was complicated by questions of the legitimacy of the proxy staking. Still, the fact that similar claims for males were recognized suggests bias.[24] One of these dispossessed women, Bella (Mrs. John J.) Healy, protested and maneuvered to secure a claim, eliciting disparaging comments from at least one male government official.[25] Nevertheless, it may have been Bella Healy who, through her powerful friends in Ottawa, influenced the non-biased wording of the January 1898 mining law.

To maintain harmony and avoid ruffling feathers, some women undoubtedly simply acquiesced to the social prejudice restricting their mining. Belinda was not one of these. To the resentment of some and the admiration of others, she took advantage of the ill-defined legal situation, followed her own inclinations, and acquired a large number of claims by staking and purchase.

As in her days of hoarding money in Pennsylvania, Belinda spent little of her income on anything other than necessities and business. She conserved funds partly because she was simply frugal. But in addition there really was not much else in the Klondike on which to spend her money. Like most successful entrepreneurs, Belinda did not take uncalculated risks, and her taste for gambling apparently was satisfied by her business ventures. The other usual excuses for extravagant spending in the region—liquor and women—did not affect Belinda, although she undoubtedly drank liquor moderately in private if not in public. By the spring of 1898 Belinda Mulrooney was almost certainly the wealthiest woman in the Klondike and was considered to be one of the leading citizens of the area.

9

Winds of Change

SPRING IN THE NEAR-Arctic zone of North America is a blithe time. After the cold, long, dark hours of winter, lengthening days boost everyone's spirits. Small creeks appear and begin to burble, harmonizing with the hums and drones of insects. Vegetation springs into action—buds pop and lush foliage unfurls within a matter of days. The spring of 1898 in Dawson occasioned even more excitement. Once sluicing was underway on the creeks, gold shipments began to arrive in town in a steady stream. And once again the Klondike's fabulous richness became evident—a cause for celebration.

The thaw also reminded Dawson's inhabitants that the town indeed was built upon a swamp. Poor drainage soon turned lower-lying areas into barely passable quagmires. All the sewage and refuse that had lay frozen on the ground now melted and oozed with the mud. Something had to be done about the unhealthy mess.

By the time the big rivers began to flow in late May and early June, there was even more widespread flooding from ice jams damming the waters behind them. Then, according to Tappan Adney, "Enterprising boatmen were carrying passengers along the main street, charging 50 cents a head" (372). One jam with icebergs as big as small cabins also took out the stout piers of a new bridge near the mouth of the Klondike River (367).

9.1. Dawson streets turned to mud in the spring of 1898, leading to spectacles such as this one on the east side of Front Street between Second (Queen) and Third (King) Streets. *(UAF, Hegg photog. probably, Mackay Collection, 70–58–258)*

In March, all of this was just a whisper in the first trickling water, loud enough only for those with imagination and foresight to hear. A more tangible message arrived with the travelers from the Outside who made their way in over the trail from the coast. They warned that tens of thousands of stampeders were poised at Bennett Lake and would be arriving in Dawson as soon as the Yukon flowed.

> After reading and discussing the news the pioneers called a meeting in the A. C. [Alaska Commercial Company] warehouse to see what to do about receiving the newcomers. They found it necessary to drain Dawson, which was on swampy ground, and to build more cabins. I made the suggestion that all business houses on Front Street add another story to the buildings and put bunks in. They all laughed and said, "Alright, but you couldn't heat over one story." I thought you could. Of course my idea was ridiculed.
>
> I hadn't taken much action in a meeting before then. It was the first meeting where I broke in as a Pioneer. I felt by then I had been accepted.

Of course Belinda felt humiliated that her first venture into public life had met with rejection. One of the most vociferous critics of Belinda's ideas was a miner by the name of Bill Leggett. He mined successfully in the Fortymile area as early as 1894 and therefore was considered one of the Old Timers. Now he owned a rich claim on Eldorado Creek, and so knew Belinda from Grand Forks.[1]

> I was peeved. It seemed everywhere I went Bill Leggett stuck pins in me. . . . [So] I said I intended to build a three-story hotel, more in a spirit of getting even just then. That caused an uproar. They all just screamed. I was boiling. I made up my mind to make the bluff good.
>
> Then Big Bill yelled, "The camp will be worked out before you get that three story building built. If you ever did get it built, you couldn't get it heated afterwards."
>
> "Bill, old man, if I was as rusty as you are, I never'd get it built."
>
> "Bet you five thousand dollars you won't have that three story building built this summer," Bill taunted.
>
> "I'm not much on betting, Bill," I said. "Besides, that looks like easy money."
>
> "Knew darn well you'd crawfish," old Bill yells.
>
> Alex McDonald leans over and whispers in my ear, "I'll pay that bet for you."
>
> "Alex," I told him, "you got me dead wrong. No man is paying my bets, and I don't intend to lose this one. The man that will pay will be Bill Leggett."[2]
>
> "You don't mean . . . to say you're going to build the hotel?" Alex asked.
>
> "I do mean it."
>
> "For pity's sake now," murmured Alex.
>
> Our scrap put some pep into the meeting. Somebody got us down to business. All wanted to do something. The miners all agreed to help in a wagon road between Dawson and Grand Forks, each grading in front of his mine. Each agreed to build extra cabins and help drain the town site in Dawson, find better drinking water, enlarge the hospital, and to assist Father [William] Judge, Rev. Dr. [sic] Hall Young, and Bishop [P. T.] Rowe to get what was needed to improve social conditions.

The ambitious plans were not all about work. To support the hospital established by Father William Judge, a benefit was organized at the Pioneer's Hall.[3] The entire community had benefited from the medical care available at the new hospital, so all the Old Timers enthusiastically supported the fund-raiser.

> Looking back on the money we made that night always makes the pickings of the usual church fair on the Outside somehow seem small to me. . . . They had dancing, with Bill McPhee as judge. Bill with his white hair made a good looking judge, and he certainly did a lot of business. If the miners danced too much, he'd fine them.

Now some newcomers, there were a great many in the country by then, objected to Bill's methods and left the hall to complain to poor Father Judge, who from the top of the hill where he lived, came waddling down to look at us. Also Dr. [*sic*] Young came from the other direction, down by the barracks, to see for himself what we were doing.

. . . Just about the time they both came in, the president of the Order of Yukon Pioneers was roasting Bill McPhee. He didn't mean anything—it was just talking. Bill fined him so much for talking, and they were having a lot of fun out of it. Father Judge understood. "Children, children. Just children," he said, "but you mustn't make people give money."

"That's the miner's only amusement," I told him. "They can't dance, a lot of them, can't take any part, so they argue."

Dr. [*sic*] Young wanted to know what it was all about. We just told him to beat it, run away home. "If any newcomers don't like it or don't understand us, let them go home to bed too. This is the Pioneers' show. They like to stand up and argue when their cases are tried. That's what they go up there for, to be fined." (NW 42:1–2[226–27])

It is in association with this fair that Belinda first acknowledges any direct connections with the dance hall women and prostitutes in Dawson. Of course her friend, Esther Duffie, has been identified by others as a prostitute in Circle City.[4] Esther apparently continued this practice in Dawson, for she was among the large group of women arrested and fined for prostitution in September of 1898.[5] However, Belinda never admits this,[6] though she undoubtedly knew it. Esther's association with the prostitutes is only hinted at when Belinda relates that the dance hall workers and prostitutes wanted to contribute to the hospital fund. Esther collected the money and then gave it to Belinda's friend, Joe Barrette, who then took it to Belinda. Regardless of her show of bravado, Belinda was already a little intimidated after the encounter with the church men over McPhee's money-raising tactics.

"Good God, Joe!" I said. "I was razzed pretty strong for a little innocent fun. What will I do with this? I can't account for this." I went into a little corner of the kitchen of Pioneer Hall. "Joe, you better give the stuff back. They'll think it dirty money."

. . . Joe thought maybe they thought the money was physically dirty. "Maybe we fix 'em," he said. "Get all gold dust. That's clean enough."

"It's not that," I explained. " . . . It's where it comes from. You take it back."

"No, I can't do that." Joe was serious. "Fine women! Give for churches! Good as anyone! I know it! You know it! Make the rest know it!"

So we turned the $20,000 in as "A Gift." That was all the information they could get out of Joe or me. (NW 42:3–4[226–29])

The finale for the fair was a raffle. One of the donations was a pillow Sadie O'Hara had made of leather and stuffed with moss.

My Lord! The bidding was a scream. Alex McDonald certainly spread himself that night. I think it was the first time in his life he'd ever had a good time.

When Sadie's pillow went up—of course every miner in the country loved her—they bid and bid. Finally Jim McNamee and Alex got into a death struggle over the pillow. Yes, this was the same Jim McNamee I threw out of the restaurant. The one who wanted to come back and hear Sadie laugh.

. . . During the bidding I was getting afraid the damn bit of moss and leather would go to $100,000, or we'd have to pull it apart. It sounds too much, but you can safely put its final price up to $5,000. Alex got it. We made between $50,000 and $60,000 as the result of our effort at that fair. (NW 42:4[227])[7]

Another celebration that spring was set for St. Patrick's Day, 17 March. For this gathering, the A. C. warehouse was volunteered.

The ladies of the camp were to take care of the eats. The men were to decorate the building, plane the floor, and furnish music.

The seventeenth was beautiful weather—the sun shining, the snow still on the ground, and the air crisp. Everybody, including the dogs, looked happy and free. But somewhere, someone had found a bunch of summer hats. God only knows of what vintage! Some with the streamers down the back were meant for children. Every woman in camp had one of those foolish hats. With winter footwear, mukaluks of hair seal to the knees, fur coats or parkees, and those blessed silly hats stuck on top of their heads, they were a scream.

. . . We sensed something, as if we were about to lose something near and dear. We were all happy and overexcited. George Burns,[8] George Noble,[9] and [Edgar A.] Mizner,[10] [manager] of the A. C. Company, were blessed with the most wonderful voices. What pleasure it was to hear those fellows sing, especially when they were as happy as on that seventeenth of March.

All at once someone hollered, "My God, a dog race!"

"Clear the way and clear it quick," everybody yelled.

"Whose teams? Whose teams?" Gordon Battles[11] called out.

"The Mounted Police crack team, Corporal Owens driving, and Joe Barrette's huskies, Joe driving."

We all crouched down on the ground, afraid to miss any part of it. We all got down so we could watch the dog's little feet. My God! How they would fight for space. The lead dogs would watch each other to take advantage of everything.

The Dawson people yelled, "Come on, you Corporal!"

The miners, "My God, Joe! Don't let him win."

It was just splendid to watch those magnificent animals strain all their muscles and fight with all their might for every inch of ground. Up to the finish none of us could name the winner—they were neck and neck. When Joe's leader stuck his head over the line, those miners all just went wild.

It was good to see how much they thought of Joe Barrette. He surely had crawled through their hides and reached their hearts. The women were petting and hugging the dog teams and making a fuss over the Corporal. Sadie, next to me let out a deep sigh. I turned around, "Sadie, darn it, you got me crying too. What in heck are we crying about?"

. . . After the excitement we left for the warehouse to enjoy the big feed, to dance square dances, waltzes and jigs. There was an undercurrent of feeling like a big family that dreaded some unknown danger. I think it was covered by an old timer who couldn't sing or dance, but had to make a speech. He asked us all to have a good time while the country still belonged to us. He hoped to the Lord that the mosquitoes would chase the new arrivals back to where they came from, so we could live our own lives and be happy in God's country.

We danced and played until daylight. Then we had a big breakfast of hot cakes, coffee, fed our dogs, and started back to the mines.

After the party Belinda returned to Grand Forks, where she had a conference with Walker Gilmer. She told him she would be spending more time in Dawson because she was going to build a hotel there, and because the telephone equipment would be arriving soon as well. She also needed him to check her accounts to see how much capital she had to spend in building the new hotel.

"Alex and . . . Joe Barrette don't want you to try and build that hotel. They don't feel you can make a go of it," Walker said.

"I guess that's just why I'm going to build it. If they didn't say that, I wouldn't think of it."

"By gosh," Walker said, "I don't want to see you lose that bet. If you do start, I'll do everything I can to help it along. Sadie and I'll pray for you with all our might, won't we Sadie?"

"Bet your life we will," said Sadie.

"That settles it," I told them. "With you and Sadie praying for me, I can't fail. The lot is about two blocks from the saloons, and I'll be able to run a clean, decent place."

"Good Lord! You've bought that lot already?" said Sadie.

9.2. Sadie O'Hara on Belinda Mulrooney's dogsled in Dawson, with an early view of
the north side of King Street between Front and Second Avenue. Others in the photograph are not identified. *(UCB, Hawkins Collection, 77/81)*

"Yes," I told her, "I bought it while old man Ladue and I were dancing the
Virginia Reel on Patrick's day. Didn't you think we were a kittenish pair of little
devils?"

She pictured us flouncing around. I knew as much about dancing as a pet
bear, and old man Ladue knew less.[12]

Another harbinger of the changes coming to the Klondike was the arrival in
February 1898 of government officials to oversee the administration of mining
regulations in the "Provisional District of the Yukon." These were Thomas H.
McGuire, judge of the Supreme Court of the Northwest Territories; Frederick
Coate Wade, Lands Agent; and Henry H. Norwood and James McGregor, Min-
ing Inspectors.[13]

The miners of the district had been dissatisfied since the summer of 1897
with the inept performance of the Gold Commissioner, Thomas Fawcett. They
had raised even stronger protests when royalties of 20 percent on the gross over
$500 per day were imposed on each claim. On 18 January 1898, royalties were
finally reduced to 10 percent of gross less $2,500 for the cost of working the
claim, but even this amount seemed too high, and there was still much resentment (Adney, 435).

By late 1897 the government in Ottawa realized the potential for the situation in their fast-growing territory to get out of hand if a strong official presence were not maintained. It is estimated that in the winter of 1897–98, 90 percent of the miners in the district were not Canadian citizens,[14] and with no legal outlet to vent their opinions, they might resort to other means. Therefore, administrators were appointed and dispatched to Dawson. They were backed up by an armed militia, the Yukon Field Force, to act as a deterrent to any pro-American coup and to help maintain law and order whenever necessary (Greenhous, 20–21). But the government officials sent In in early 1898 were also inexperienced and soon generated even more heat by their errors. For example, as Tappan Adney pointed out, "The mining inspectors had only such previous experience in mining as they may have acquired as a horse dealer [McGregor] and an uncertified master of a whaling vessel [Norwood]" (439).

Henry Havelock Norwood was originally from Nova Scotia, the son of a Baptist preacher. He had dark eyes that often twinkled with mirth, and he stood well over six feet tall and was massively built (Dill, 227). Since Captain Norwood was assigned to the mines around Grand Forks, he was the one Belinda got to know first.

[The Canadian officials] were in an embarrassing position. The government at Ottawa didn't know conditions in the Klondike and left it all to them. The miners didn't see any use of government. They were used to conducting their own affairs at miners' meetings and naturally didn't receive the officials very kindly.

. . . I don't think that any of those men weighed less than 250 pounds. They were dubbed "The Big Four." The miners thought the government had sent them in to scare them.

. . . Captain Norwood, being one of the bunch with a great deal of experience with Americans in his sea faring life out of San Francisco, was picked to move up from Dawson to the mines to see what he could do with the miners.

There were rumors good and bad. The miners didn't know what they were going to do with the Canadian, and he didn't know what he would do with us.

Captain Norwood arrived [at Grand Forks] and arranged with Walker to live at the hotel. . . . At the hotel we had a large table where the regular family group ate. Skipper Norwood began at me one day there.

"Well, I hear there's been another miners' meeting. The damn Irish are always starting something against the government. Wherever you find the Irish you find trouble."

Inasmuch as there were no Irish miners I knew except Jim McNamee, I knew all this was directed at me.

The Skipper looked up at Sadie one day later at the table, "Have the miners decided to hang the Canadian officials yet?"

Sadie told him, "I don't know, Skipper. It looks pretty serious."

"Wait until us fellows start in doing business," he puffed. "You'll find 'em pretty tame."

"Captain," I told him, "the Canadian government used poor judgment and are not at all entitled to succeed. One little Irish man with a little sense already would have collected last year's royalty and be all set for next year's."

"What's your exception to us?" he wanted to know.

"I think the government sent in too much tonnage."

"What do you mean?"

9.3. Captain H. H. Norwood in the Klondike in the summer of 1903. (UW, McLain, Alaska and the Klondike, 65. 17734)

"It's very costly to send freight over the Summit. You fellows must weigh tons. That was their first stroke of bad business. The less weight the more sense." (NW 12:2–5)

Belinda had won the first verbal battle. In subsequent days she gave no ground.

One day outside the hotel he came waddling along. "Say, young woman, I want to talk to you," he said. "Let's cut this Big stuff out. The first thing you know it will be all over the camp. I want to know how to get next to the miners, how to collect royalties, and what is fair."

"Yes," I agreed, "we don't hide anything. The miners object to you fellows. They are not used to government, as they are used to adjusting their own affairs."

"Well," he wanted my opinion, "just how can we get at the thing and have a peaceful adjustment?"

"It's your job, Captain," I told him, "but if it were mine, this is what I'd do. I'd attend one of those miners' meetings and ask for their view point. Ask what [royalty] they think would be fair. Your government is here. You have to perform your duties, but you don't want to work hardships. You want to get acquainted with a few of them first." (NW 12:6)

Captain Norwood took Belinda's advice and met with several of the miners one evening to discuss the royalty rate and how to best collect it fairly. The conversation was eased by liberal doses of good whiskey.

The Skipper came home next morning just waddling. Do you know, I always found a childish side to a big man. When they are pleased, they are as happy as children. Of course Skipper's head was splitting in the morning, but he came in with a smile.

"I like those old brutes," he said. "They are damn fine fellows."

"Yes, Skipper," I said, "a good barrel of Scotch makes fellows seem different."

"Oh go to hell!" he said. When Skipper was pleased with me he always said, "Go to hell," and I always came back with "I am going but I'm not ready to start right now." (NW 12:8)

THE SPRING OF 1898 marked a kind of initiation for Belinda and a transition for the Klondike gold fields as well. Those who were already in the area of the Klondike when the discovery was made and who had established the earliest claims formed the nucleus of a loose community, the Old Timers. They were used to the wild beauty of the north, the rigorous physical demands of the climate and of mining, and the largely unfettered expression of their inclinations. The newcomers of 1897 were Outsiders who, nevertheless, shared many of the values of the Old Timers. Belinda was among these, and by the spring of 1898 she had tested her mettle and demonstrated her worthiness to be included into the community.

The soon-to-arrive stampeders of 1898 would be like the peak wave of a tsunami, drastically altering the landscape that lay within its wash. And the Old Timers in Dawson in the spring of 1898 had heard the warning sirens—the on-slaught would arrive with the thaw. There was an inkling that these newcomers would be a different breed—more cautious, more comfortable with the con-straints of civilization, less accustomed to independent living. The Klondike Old Timers sensed that life in Dawson and on the creeks would never be the same. But to those who were willing and able to adapt, the new boom would present even more opportunities for building personal and community fortunes.

10

A Fair View in Dawson

B ELINDA'S AMBITION in spring of 1898 was to build the finest hotel in Dawson, and she drew on her knowledge of grand hotels in Chicago, San Francisco, and Seattle for inspiration. First she looked up Harry Cribb, who had supervised so reliably the construction of her cabins the previous year. She knew that getting the hotel built would take even more effort than usual because nails as well as lumber were in such short supply. Because of these deficiencies, *New York Times* correspondent E. LeRoy Pelletier had informed the world (29 May 1898, p. 13) that little building would be done in Dawson that spring. Such pronouncements from her neighbors—Pelletier's office was only two buildings away from the new hotel site—did not stop Belinda. She knew Harry Cribb would work with her to get the job done if it were at all possible.

Belinda asked Harry to get some of the old crew together and to take them up the Yukon to cut some large logs. Once the river opened, the logs could be floated down to town where they would be sawn at a local mill.

> Harry Cribb said, "It'll be pretty green lumber."
>
> "I know, Harry," I said, "but we might be able to keep it . . . from shrinking by building two walls, sixteen to eighteen inches apart, and packing . . . saw dust in between and wetting it down well."

"How about nails?" Harry wanted to know.

"We'll have to put a good man to rustling nails, pulling boats and scows apart. Saw the lumber too. Beside," I told him, never cracking a smile, "you can get lots of nails from the miners' pants. They use 'em to hold up their suspenders where the buttons used to be." (NW 14:1–2[103–4])

Belinda also used a little psychology to spark additional interest in the project from her workers. It came in the form of a suggestion to Harry Cribb.

"Now Harry, if we can keep our plans to ourselves, I'll show you and your men how they can make some easy money. Those miners are aching to find something to bet on, and I'd give a good deal to take some of the noise out of that big bull moose Bill Leggett. He seems to spend most of his idle moments beefing about what I can't do and how crazy I am. I want all your crew in on this so they'll work with me and keep quiet about it. Now Harry, what do you think?"

"I'll give you my answer right now," he told me. "I'll put that blame hotel up if I have to tie it together with wooden pegs."

I was pleased. "I thought I could count on you." I told him to go to Mack at Bill McPhee's. Mack had been my selling agent for the cabins, you remember. "Tell him here's $10,000 to bet on this hotel. Also I think it will be good business for you and your men to pledge all your wages. I can see where Dawson is going to have a new hotel, and where we are going to have a lot of fun.

. . . "Get Mack specially to get as much of Bill Leggett's money as he can," I insisted.

"A few other rich sports will separate from their money too," Harry said. He must have been sore at somebody. (NW 14:2–3[104–5])

Once Belinda had determined to do something, she usually got it done. Even the sawmill operator got sucked in, placing a bet and then diverting lumber originally cut for other customers to Belinda's project.

Heating a three-story building in the Klondike had not yet been attempted and was the aspect of the new hotel about which Old Timers were the most skeptical. Belinda, however, was undaunted and had some ideas about how to accomplish it. She went to her friend the metal worker, Julius Geise, and asked him to make a heating plant for the hotel out of a coal oil tank.[1]

Belinda's crew worked hard and for long hours, motivated not only by side bets, but also by their wages, which were riding on finishing the hotel during the summer. As they worked, the melting streams of the countryside funneled into the still-frozen Yukon River. Between 28 May and 5 June, Dawson was in-

10.1. The intersection of Princess Street looking north along Front Street on 1 June 1898, during the flood. The building with the "Wanted! Quartz and Placer Claims" sign became the post office. The Nelson and Soggs building was on the northeast corner of the intersection, and Belinda's Fairview Hotel was being built at this time on the southeast corner, just out of view to the right. Note the one remaining, strange tree at center, and the dirt covering the roofs of several of the log buildings. *(UCB, Prather photog.* Midnight Sun. *F909, L23, x)*

undated by floodwaters from an ice jam just below town. But construction of the hotel continued.

Belinda won her bet. The hotel was officially opened on 27 July 1898.[2] On that day, Belinda presented to Dawson not just a hotel, but a wonder to those who could remember the tent-lined streets of only a year earlier. It set the tone for Dawson's growth from a mining camp into a city. It was a monument to Belinda's imagination and determination, a tribute to her tough, competitive spirit, and a triumph for the hard work and ingenuity of her crew. And for all of them, it was also an instant financial success. After the final reckoning, Belinda found that nearly $100,000 had been bet on successful completion of the hotel, explaining that "The miners liked to bet with each other against each other's judgment. The Old Timers, the mine owners, cared as little for money as they did for sawdust. It didn't mean anything to them" (NW 15:5–6[110–11]).

10.2. By early July 1898, Front Street had recovered from the flood, and construction of the three-story Fairview Hotel, near the center background, was well along. Note the stud-wall construction, in which planks of inner walls were applied first, probably so sawdust insulation could be poured between the studs from the outside as the outer walls were applied. Also note stumps in middle of street. The strangely bent tree still stands at center. The buildings in left background are the same as those in the fore-ground of Fig. 10.1. *(UW, Hegg photog., 456)*

Belinda called her hotel the Fairview (also spelled Fair View). It was located on the southeast corner of Front at Princess Street.[3] Because there were no buildings on the west side of Front Street this far south, the hotel had a clear view of the flowing Yukon River—this was a fair view indeed. And the facade of the hotel was itself pleasing, offering a well-composed, finished look in contrast with the rough-hewn appearance of most of the rest of Dawson. Large windows at the front of the hotel on the ground floor provided a river view as well as natural lighting, and all of the upstairs rooms featured large, double-hung windows. The main entrance was set on an angle at the northwest corner, facilitating traffic on both thoroughfares.

There were actually two grand openings for the Fairview. The first was a party thrown for the workers. A second the following night was for everyone else.

The opening of the Fairview was an immense thing. For the boys who had built the hotel in such a short time it was one big potlatch. They had the biggest blow I could give them [and] a special barbecue across the river—I thought that was the safest place—[with] a scow to carry them over.

Bill Leggett was pretty sore. It took him until about 12 o'clock to loosen up. The men [gibed] him and teased and showed him all over the place, including the telephone [and] the electric lights. The lights we had from a steamboat which was tied up in front of the Fairview. The telephone men fixed them. There were lights on the porch, the second floor porch, and in the center of each big room. . . . The blamed daylight . . . [of] the Arctic summer stuck so long we prayed it would rain, so it would get dark enough to use the fancy lights.

"Those were not in the contract, Bill," the miners would tease. . . . "Aren't they pretty?"

Julius Geise was yanked down to the basement all evening for them to see the heating plant. "Get Bill to see the heating plant," they'd say. "Where's the place for the dogs?"

The miners always had to dry their feet, change their socks and shoes when they came in from the trail. We had around the fire in the basement a wire to hang their socks on. There were shelves where they could leave their shoes. That was great too they thought.

The miners felt they owned the place as much as anybody, but they'd be damned if they would dress like the dudes from the Outside. So I took the partitions out of the third floor for pioneer headquarters. The second floor was given to Society. (NW 15:1–2[106–7])

Mary E. Hitchcock was a visitor to Dawson who arrived on 27 July, the day of the Fairview's more public opening. She took a tour of the new hotel before the evening's festivities. Her description is from the eyes of a sophisticated, somewhat demanding traveler, used to the amenities then available in finer establishments in the Eastern United States. Hitchcock's observations tell us about Belinda's sense of style, as well as the incongruities that the exigencies of living on the frontier produced.

The house, built of wood and three stories high, quite towered above the tents and cabins of its neighbors. The only entrance that was finished was through the new and elaborately furnished barroom, within whose walls many a sad history will probably be recorded during the coming year, as we are told that "the liquor business here is bigger pay than the richest mine," and that "even the smallest barroom realizes between five hundred and a thousand dollars a night."

10.3. The Fairview Hotel bar. Painted canvases, such as the one behind the bar, were featured throughout the hotel. Note also the gold scales at center and the wallpapering. The people in the photo are not identified, although there is a notation, "Tom McCowan." *(ASL, Hegg photog., Wickersham Collection, 277–1–102)*

Separated by a hallway from this saloon is the dining-room, beautifully clean, table covered with damask, and even napkins (something unusual for this part of the world) at each place. The menu, beginning with "oyster cocktails," caused us to open our eyes wide with astonishment, after all that the papers have told us of the starvation about Dawson. We next visited the kitchen adjoining, where there was a stove that would have gladdened the heart of any cook at home. The chef was said to be from Marchand's of San Francisco. The proprietress explained to us that she had sent for chairs, which had arrived without legs, they having been left on the dock at St. Michaels, one of the inconveniences that one has to bear through the negligence of transportation companies, so she had carpenters at fifteen dollars a day manufacturing new legs.

On the second floor, a long, narrow hall separated rooms that were about double the size of an ordinary cabin on shipboard.[4] Each room contained a primitive wooden bedstead, but there was no space for wardrobe, closet or dressing table. Evidently the pride of the hostess's heart was centered in Brussels carpets and lace curtains, to which she called attention as having been in-

10.4. The chef at the Fairview Hotel and his staff in the kitchen. The sign on the post at left says, "Notice to Employees. ??day 5th of each month. Bellboys, waiters and porters will take their meals in the kitchen and will please inform the chef when ordering for themselves." *(UW, Larss & Duclos photog., 22)*

troduced into Dawson for the first time. The price of one of these tiny rooms was six dollars and a half a day, food five dollars extra, or two dollars a meal.

On the third floor the carpenters were busy preparing for the evening dance, after which the large hall was to be partitioned off into small rooms, at five dollars a day each, providing that the sojourns of the guest should be at least of one month's duration, otherwise terms to be increased accordingly.

We were cordially invited to return for the dinner at 10 P.M., and also for the dance. Noticing that there were no panes of glass in the windows, which were simply covered with cheese-cloth, we asked what happened in case of rain, and were told that it very rarely rained, but that when it did there would probably not be sufficient to do any damage. Glass also had been ordered, but, as usual, it was impossible to tell when or by what steamer it would arrive. (Hitchcock, 100–102)

A glowing report of the new hotel also appeared in the 27 July edition of the new Dawson newspaper, the *Klondike Nugget*. Here it was announced that the hotel would be managed by J. K. Leaming on both the American and European plan, and that it was "by far the most pretentious structure now in Dawson." The next edition of the *Nugget* (30 July) described the official opening festivities.

A very large crowd had gathered by 9 o'clock, when Captain Norwood, mining inspector, stationed at the forks of Bonanza and Eldorado, through the telephone declared the hotel open. Seven receivers had been arranged at the hotel and each individual at a receiver tried to repeat the captain's neat little speech. Then, when the ice was well broken, all proceeded to the dining hall. The spread would make your mouth water to give an account of it in detail. Suffice to say that the menu was equal to anything produced in the center of a more pretentious civilization, while the wine list was an eye opener to those who suppose the principle convivial drink of Dawson to be "hootchinoo." Mumm's extra dry flowed freely in the heat of conversation, and Col. Domville's[5] speech of welcome was declared the very best thing of its kind in Dawson. (4)

Belinda's account of the opening gives more of the behind-the-scenes details of the extravaganza.

. . . The wives were there and their doll rags were all new to us and brought a touch of the Outside. Colonel Bonneville [Domville] was there with his decoration from the Queen, his ribbon across his breast, the gayest and gallantest. [Land Commissioner and Queen's Counsel in Dawson, F. C.] Wade was a good second. The boys from the bank helped. The puzzle was how to please the miners and how to please the rest at the same time. For dancing I had one perfectly equipped orchestra.

Walker and Sadie were helping. Sadie took care of the women's wraps in the society room on the second floor. I gave most of my time to the Pioneers and the kitchen. Murray King decorated the dining room, using boughs of spruce and pine made into wreaths. Esther had rustled every place where she could get a knife and fork. She didn't join the party, just helped with the cooking.

Bill McPhee got all the dishes he could. Several saloon keepers brought me stuff we needed in glass and silverware. I remember Jim Kerry bringing me some of his really fine glasses. When I told him the stuff was too good, that it would get broken and I couldn't keep track of it, Jim told me not to worry, "I've got five times more out of this opening than these are worth." By that time I knew Jim was pretty well heeled from his bets too.

For drinks we had a shipment that had been assigned to [David Doig, Dawson branch manager] of the British Bank of North America. An assistant in the bank we called Satan brought it in. I'd told him to hang onto the whole business for me. There was Murray King in charge of the bar. He was clever and never drank anything. That night I told the boys, the bartenders . . . , "For the love of God, no one on the job must touch a drop of likker." They certainly hung onto themselves, cooks and all. There was not a jar to the whole thing.

There was $6,000 due on the likker, and I told the bank to take it out of my account. There were eighteen cases of champagne in the lot. In the dining room was a horse-shoe table piled with sandwiches and lots to drink.

A lot of workmen didn't feel they could come in. We couldn't get them in, but they came to town for the opening just the same. They stayed out on the porch, a regular mob. I sent them out a wash tub full of punch with a dipper in it, sandwiches and cake. When the punch was getting low my boys would take a big bucket of the stuff from the kitchen and pour it into the tub.

I wanted the opening free. . . . My friends said it would cost too much—$10,000 at least. "What of it?" I said. They finally let me give everything free for the first two hours.

Do you know during the first two hours it was hard to get those fool miners to help themselves? They waited for the time to be up so they could spend their money. They had so few places to spend it, they wanted to wait for a chance to make a noise like a man.

The outside mob was having most of the fun. Anyone with a partner knew he was welcome, and after they got warmed up with punch, the outside bunch got more courage and wanted to see what was going on inside. The miners dug up their own favorite musicians, grabbed them and kept them on the third floor. They had fiddlers, an accordion, and a mouth organ. It was regular music and they hoed it down.

Harry Cribb came over. . . . "God," he said, "I hope the place (doesn't) fall down." The chaps downstairs were scared stiff, the floor looked like it was coming down any minute.

. . . The celebration lasted until morning, . . . until 6 or 7 o'clock. They couldn't leave. They kept coming back to say what a wonderful time they'd had. Everybody when they left said, "Put up another hotel and make it six stories next time." (NW 15:2–5[107–10])

The Fairview was a great success from the beginning. It was, of course, the place to stay for anyone wanting a better hotel in Dawson, despite its missing furnishings. Competing establishments typically offered one common sleeping room filled with tiers of double-decked bunks, accommodating twenty to thirty sleepers. The bedding was rough blankets and a small pillow. There would be no ventilation except that offered by cracks and one small window at the end of the room. In winter, the room would be heated very hot, so the stench from unwashed bodies and feet was almost unbearable, and the bedding was alive with vermin (Adney, 349). The Fairview was way ahead of its competition.

Tappan Adney, a particularly observant chronicler of the Klondike in 1897–98, described the Fairview as

> . . . the handsomest building in town. . . . Although the inevitable bar occupied the front, the Fairview could lay claim to being a respectable hotel, as there was a side entrance for ladies, who might not like to pass through the bar-room. One of the best chefs was employed, and meals were served on linen-covered tables, with sliver and china. The price of a meal—considered by some the best in Dawson—was $2. Board, with a 10 x 12-foot room, was $125 to $250 a month, according to location, and for transients $6.50 a day. Board without room was at first $25 a week, but was afterwards raised to $35 a week. (392–93)

Belinda's hotel soon became a popular location for social gatherings. Private parties were given on the second floor, and the dining room was a comfortable place to entertain a guest. The dining room had a stage as well, where acts arriving to play at the theaters in town would often give a performance to the society of Dawson (NW 17:1[117]). For example, the popular Newman children —Margie, Willie, and George—who are seen advertising their opening at the Mascot Theater in figure 10.2, sang and performed various sketches at the Fairview on the evening of 12 August. "After the performance, Miss Mulrooney will tender her usual Friday evening social hop," announced the *Klondike Nugget* (10 August).

The Fairview also was a communication center: it housed the telephone switchboard that connected all the phones in town with those at Grand Forks and the creeks. Near the hotel was another Belinda Mulrooney enterprise—a bathhouse.

> One day a man and his wife—she was a big Swedish woman—came to me. They wanted work. I asked them what they were doing before they came north. They told me they'd been running a bathhouse in Tacoma.
>
> "See you don't wander away," I told them. "I need you."
>
> The worry of my life was finding a place where people could bathe. So I anchored two scows in front of the Fairview, built up a bathhouse. Harry [Cribb] and the building crew fixed it up. We got the water from the river.
>
> We were quite a distance from the saloons and if any of my friends would wander down, full as a Lord, the help at the hotel had orders to stick 'em in the bathhouse. (NW 16:3–4[115–16])

Dawson was hit by two floods in the early summer of 1898—one of water, the other of stampeders arriving from all over the world. Although many Americans were diverted by the outbreak of war with Spain on 25 April 1898, there were still many thousands who continued their rush to Dawson. Population estimates ranged from about 16,000 at midsummer[6] in Dawson proper to nearly 60,000 having passed through by the fall. The new arrivals came from all walks of life. Though some were able to stake or buy claims, and some were hired to work on the claims of others, most found little to do in Dawson or the Klondike District.

> After the ice broke up in the Yukon, it became a floating mass of people. The banks were lined with boats and scows. There was just about standing room on the streets of Dawson. All wanted a gold mine and wanted us to show them where they could find one right away.
>
> We thought we had a foolish mob, but it was nothing to the mess that came up the river [i.e., those who came by river boat from the lower Yukon.] All they had to do was pay their passage, ride along until they arrived, and take it easy. They didn't have the hardships of the pass or trail.
>
> We had plenty of dance hall women and pasty looking men. They didn't look good to us or to the Mounted Police either, who kept a constant watch, day and night, on the slippery artists. There were all kinds of schemes to separate the miner from his money. . . . We didn't realize then, and some never will, what protection the Mounted Police gave us. Colonel Steele[7] had a splendid bunch of men. I don't believe there were any better men of the corps anywhere in Canada. . . . There were not very many in Colonel [Steele's] force, but he knew every pioneer woman and man in the north was back of him, and the decent citizens among the newcomers. They left it up to the crook to get religion or move on.

With so many of the newcomers looking for work, Belinda found a ready supply of educated and talented people to staff her hotel and bathhouse.

> The help of the hotel was made up of lawyers, doctors, and druggists. Had one in particular, LeRoy Tozier,[8] a young attorney from Portland, and one particular nice fellow, Murray King of San Francisco, a young druggist. Nine of them were bartenders.(Hawkins)
>
> A young Austrian of a noble family and a young German were in Dawson. After college in their own country they were making a trip through the United States. They got the gold fever, landed in Alaska, and once there didn't know what to do next.

They dropped in to see me and asked for work. They couldn't speak English well enough to work in the hotel, but I thought they'd be wonderful around the bathhouse. They knew all about how a fellow should take a bath. The miners . . . used to follow them around . . . , asking them over and over, "Where do you work?" just to hear the boys answer, "In de bad house." (NW 16:4[116])

COMPLETION OF THE FAIRVIEW HOTEL was a landmark in Belinda Mulrooney's career. She was only twenty-six years old and had been in the Klondike a little over a year. And yet in that time she had parlayed her nest egg, built up from her merchandising business on Alaska's southeast coast, into a considerable fortune.

One component of Belinda's success was diversification. She generated new business ideas seemingly effortlessly, and she had nearly boundless energy to bring many of these ideas to fruition. Belinda sometimes repeated her own previously successful patterns: investing in merchandise she could readily sell at higher prices to an isolated but affluent clientele; opening restaurants; and constructing her own business buildings. In the Klondike she also expanded into new areas, such as contracting buildings for immediate resale. As with any real estate development, the most important feature was location, and Belinda had a knack for recognizing what was needed where. She had the background to make decisions about all aspects of the construction—from lumbering to final decoration. At the same time, she knew how to delegate responsibilities, to recognize others' talents, and to motivate those who worked for her. So she could manage many projects at one time while keeping close control of all of them.

Belinda's hotels were also a venture into new territory, starting with the small but highly functional roadhouse at Grand Forks and soon expanding to the elegant Fairview in Dawson. To boost profits, both included popular barrooms that were a cut above those of the saloons and of the gambling and dance halls. Furthermore, both hotels housed services that were important for the community as a whole, such as banking, fee collection, brokering, and telephone communication. The hotels, with their facilities for socializing and community events along with their accompanying businesses, not only were immediately profitable, but also had the potential to be steady sources of income so long as Dawson and Grand Forks were viable towns. Likewise, Belinda's many mining claims and interests in claims had immediate as well as potentially long-term payoffs.

By July of 1898 Belinda had hit her stride. There was joy and exuberance in her work. The Klondike was her playground, and she had become an acknowledged winner. The teenage misfit had found her niche.

11

The Skagway Caper

Like many building projects, the Fairview was not completed by the time it opened. Belinda continued to make additions and improvements throughout the following year. The most pressing need was for the furnishings Mary Hitchcock had noticed were missing, such as windows, bedding, dishes, and furniture. In addition, staple foods were needed to feed the increasing clientele and to last through the coming winter.

Belinda was most concerned to get windows in place before the colder weather set in. Given her experiences with the transportation companies, she didn't trust such an essential order to anyone else. And so, soon after the Fairview opened, Belinda left on her first trip Outside since her arrival in Dawson in June of 1897.[1] She carried with her $30,000 for the needed supplies, plus mail for her friends and from Colonel Steele of the Mounted Police in Dawson to Major Zachary Taylor Wood, who headed the post at Bennett.[2]

Belinda steamed up the Yukon River on a small, makeshift boat that could barely make way against the current.[3] Unlike the larger transportation companies, who had contracts with wood cutters along the route to supply fuel, the little steamboat's owner depended on his passengers to gather, cut, and load wood. After reaching the town of Whitehorse at the bottom of White Horse

Rapids on the steamboat, Belinda set out poling and paddling a canoe with the help of two Native American employees. Their real names have been lost, but Belinda referred to them as Jenny and her husband Jack.

> They were decent, clean, healthy looking Indians. Jenny used to do wonderful work with furs, make capes and gloves of coon and beaver, mink and marten. . . . [Their little boy] was always hanging around the Fairview when it was being built. I first got interested in him one day when I found him drawing a fish on a board. It was quite good. After that I found little jobs for him, and through him I got his mother and father. (NW 18:2[122b])

When they reached the head of Lake Bennett, Belinda was amazed to see the shores still cluttered with tents and crowds of people so late in the season.

> There were mobs around watching us, hanging around to get news from Dawson. The contrast from my first stop at Bennett! I couldn't believe my eyes. It discouraged me to see them. I wondered what would happen to them in Dawson. The food there was used up as it came in. At Bennett was a dissatisfied, restless bunch of people, heart sick, no harmony or friendliness like there was in our party when we went in. (NW 19:1[126])

In the excitement and confusion of landing at Bennett, Belinda's canoe tipped, throwing her, Jenny, and Jack into the water.

> I picked out two old men, very old, who were standing on the edge of things and who hadn't said a word. I [told] them if we could use their tent to dry off in, we would pay for any damage done. They said we were perfectly welcome, and I asked them if they could take care of the Indians too.
> "Yes."
> And I said, "After we are changed let them cook up your food. I know good meals have been scarce while you boys have been so busy packing."
> One of the old men grinned, "It's been a long time since we were boys."
> They showed us where we could find food. I asked them if we could buy it, and they said, "No, use ours." We took off our clothes and hung them by the fire and one of the old men had some extra underwear which he gave to me, and the squaw wrapped herself up in the blanket. (NW 19:1–2[126–27])

Belinda chose the old men to talk with because they seemed safer than the others who were pressing her for information about Dawson and mining. They were California miners lured by the prospect of gold in Alaska. They had with them a younger man, George, who had lost all of his money in a shell game in Skagway[4] and was packing for fifty cents a pound per crossing to make up the thousand dollars he needed for another outfit. His earnings were being held for him by two brothers who shared the adjacent tent.

Later that day, when George returned from his latest trip, Belinda heard him talking excitedly to the two old men.

> Someone . . . had knocked the fellow in the next tent on the head and had taken the money, all of George's money cached there. He told how hard he'd worked. He just sat right on the ground, his head on his hands. "God, such luck!" he said. "My mother thinks I'm in Dawson right now making a fortune."
>
> "Never mind," I told him. "You join my outfit and I'll guarantee you'll get food." He was in condition, that youngster, I tell you. He had the finest physique I ever laid my eyes on.
>
> I was pretty darned curious about the stealing business. Personally I had a lot of money on me. I inquired. Yes, there were a lot of professional thieves. The man in the next tent was in terrible shape. His brother was nursing him. He couldn't talk, his head was so bandaged up.
>
> I told the boy George . . . I needed him as I had no knowledge of the [White Pass] trail. "I'll have to see the Mounted Police boys, and I'll guarantee your outfit." He felt good about getting through, but not about losing the money. (NW 19:4[129])

Belinda left her mail and money with Major Wood at the Mounted Police headquarters. She respected the Mounties and knew everything would be safe with them. Later a Mountie came to the old men's tent to invite Belinda to dinner. Shortly after the policeman left, Belinda noticed something unusual in the adjoining tent.

> It seemed to have a damned busy look about it for the home of a man not able to move. I could see, the tent was open, that the wounded man . . . was pretty active and kept a close watch on the Mounted Police. . . . When his brother came back later with water, the injured one called the police "dirty yellow legs." It was then I decided if the money had been stolen, that bird had it.
>
> I went right away to Major Wood and told him I thought the fellow a thief. "He was such a busy sport when he saw your boys I don't believe he's hurt at all." Major [Wood] was for sending the boys back with me. I said, "Send someone in civilian clothes. Let them play doctor, if you like, and take the bandages off."
>
> So Major Wood had a perfectly good doctor call on the sick man, and when the doctor took off the bandages there was not a damn scratch on the brute. The envelope with the money in it was under the pillow.

Later there was a terrible stink about the theft at a [camp] meeting. There
are always agitators in such places who want to hang somebody. I left them in
that mess. The kid had his money. It had been a gol darn easy crime. I had
George hand his money to the Police. "Now," I said, "you can go on alright or
work with me."

He said, "I'll work with you." (NW 19:6–7[131–32])

And thus Belinda had another loyal employee. She asked George to locate a
campsite away from the crowd. She put Jack and Jenny in charge of the camp,
and got money orders and some cash from her stash with Major Wood. She
arranged with a boat builder to have fourteen scows ready for her return.[5] Then
Belinda, Jack, Jenny, and George headed for Skagway.

Skagway had a reputation for being a tough, lawless town. But everyone
Belinda met there seemed to be a fine person in her estimation. Among them
was Michael J. Heney, who was supervising the railroad being built over White
Pass.

I never knew a more decent fellow than Heney, or one more gallant.[6] Not
only I found him that, but the world outside did. I told him I had a lot of stuff
to get and needed a lot of men. He told me there was quite an order on the
next ship, some already delivered and some coming for a hotel in Skagway.
Maybe the owner of the hotel would sell [to] me. [But] Heney needed the
hotel for his men.

"It won't hurt you to wait," I explained to him. "You will be able to send
back on the next boat a load of supplies from either Portland or Seattle."

I showed him how impossible it would be for me to go Outside and get
back before the river would be frozen.

. . . Getting the hotel materials was not so easy. . . . [Miss Burke[7] was evidently back of the hotel, but I was dealing with her agent or partner.] His stuff
was exactly what I wanted—windows and doors. I didn't like his price. He was
the only one in Skagway trying to hold me up, trying to make a year's profit
out of me.

So I turned his proposition down cold. I'd give a reasonable profit, but no
more. Then I played my last bluff. "I'll stay here and build a hotel myself," I
threatened.

Heney got an awful kick out of it. The bluff worked. The agent agreed
to sell me what I wanted—windows, doors and furniture—but it was on my
part to tear out of the building the materials I bought and pack them up.
(NW 20:2–3[134–35])

11.1. Michael J. Heney, contractor for the White Pass and Yukon Railroad, stands at far right. He and other railroad officials look over the route through Rocky Point, 18 September 1898, a few miles outside of Skagway. The Skagway River flows in the background. *(Yukon Archives, Barley photog., 5406)*

Belinda was also able to buy the other furnishings she needed from a man named Peoples.[8] "Peoples was certainly a prize—a fine cultured fellow lost in Skagway where he didn't know what to do next. I found him putting up his store with supplies from off Captain Moore's[9] boat. I bought his outfit just as it was" (NW 20:3[135]).

With the supplies and building materials secured, Belinda had to arrange to get them to Bennett and load them onto her newly built scows. She also needed to hire trustworthy men to pilot the scows. And all this had to happen before the river froze. The *Skaguay News* of 16 September 1898 tells a somewhat garbled account of Belinda's progress.

A few days ago Miss Maloney [*sic*], landlady of the Fairview Hotel in Dawson City, and called by the residents of that place the "Dawson Queen," arrived in Skaguay on her way out from Dawson to purchase supplies for the winter. In addition to her hotel in Dawson, Miss Mahoney has recently completed, at a cost of $70,000, a hotel at a point called "The Forks," a few miles out from

Dawson, on the river, and it was for these two hostleries [*sic*] that she desired supplies.

As time to her is very valuable, owing to the approaching end of the "open" season, she began, on her arrival in Skaguay, to inquire around among our big stores here, thinking at the same time, however, that she would be compelled to journey on to the Sound in order to procure what she wanted. Imagine her surprise when, after a short conversation with Mr. W. F. Lokowitz, of Burkhard & Co.'s big store, she found that by purchasing her outfit here she could not only save two weeks time, but also a large sum of money. The result was that Mr. Lokowitz put on his most pleasant smile, the one he had saved up for Sunday, and sold the Dawson lady goods amounting to nearly $2000.

Then Miss Mahoney hunted up J. H. Brooks, the packer. She contracted with him at a big price, but in the contract was this clause: "The goods must be at Bennett within three days, or no pay, see?" Brooks took the contract, and ere this the goods are at Bennett and will be half way to Dawson by the time the lady would have reached Seattle had she not been able to make her purchases in Skaguay. (p. 2, cols. a–b)

Belinda agreed to pay Joe Brooks forty cents a pound to pack her goods to Bennett. The clause guaranteeing delivery within three days was apparently the suggestion of Michael Heney, who worried that Brooks was unreliable because he spent too much time gambling (NW 22:1[141]). Belinda was able to hire some additional people to help pack her outfit over the trail. One of these was a former gambler by the name of Broad, who actually had been the shell game operator who first had cheated her foreman, George, out of his money. Needless to say, George was not too happy to see Broad. But Belinda reasoned that the experience had been valuable for George, since he never gambled again. Moreover, if Broad was determined to go straight, as he claimed, and if he was wise to the ways of the con artists, then he would be just the person to protect her outfit. Besides, she explained, she liked his wit and quickness:"I picked Broad for his light line of talk. In all the hardships, a light character would help lift the load. Oh gee! Broad proved himself to be a wonder. He had a brain like chain lightning. He saw everything coming before it arrived" (NW 21:3[159]).

Belinda stayed in Skagway long enough to send letters and money to her family in Pennsylvania[10] and to see the first load of goods packed onto Brooks's twenty-two mules. She then went ahead to Bennett to make sure the scows she had contracted for were ready. Broad joined her at the camp in Bennett with the scarcely believable news that Brooks had dumped the first load at the head of the Summit and gone off on another contract (NW 22:4[144]). Broad explained

that Brooks had been offered more money to transport a load of whiskey headed
for Dawson.[11] This was intolerable to Belinda. Not only was she pressed to get
her goods to Dawson before winter set in, but her reputation for accomplishing
what she set out to do was at stake. Belinda was at her ruthless, calculating best
to meet the challenge.

> We borrowed two horses. The gambler Broad went with me, and I went to
> [the Summit] to see what I could do about the thing. I was getting pretty sore
> on the way back. The stuff must be brought over if humanly possible. I had to
> have it for the Fairview Hotel, which was running full blast . . . . The miners, I
> knew, would be laughing their heads off, especially Bill Leggett. I could see
> him laughing every time I thought of failing.
>
> We got to the Summit and saw the mess. "Get packers in," I told my crew,
> "men on the trail. I'm going to take the stuff over. Show your mettle. I have a
> clause in the contract that I can take possession of the mules."
>
> Then I told Broad to get a bunch of toughs, "Pay them anything they ask
> for until we get possession of the mules. This isn't your old game of three little
> silly shells. You got to use your head and muscle too before you get through
> this stuff."
>
> Broad told me how tough Brooks's foreman was. "Hire some men just as
> tough," I told him. "There are not many men with the mules. If Brooks is
> what you say, the men can't have much respect for him. The boys will be glad
> of a chance for a rest. We'll take good care of them if they want to give up the
> mules easily."
>
> . . . We hired anything or anybody that looked tough enough. There were
> desperate looking fellows on that trail, hard as iron. The men we hired were
> packing for people going over the trail. They were dead tired, all in. They'd do
> anything for a change, especially as we'd promised to take their packs over to
> Bennett for them. So they'd put their loads down at our camp and do as they
> were told.
>
> I don't know what Broad said to them, but I told them, "We have a dirty job
> on hand. I will take the lead and won't ask you to do anything I wouldn't do.
> I'll pay you well. All you have to do is to stand by and not change your mind in
> the middle of it."
>
> We planned to meet Brooks's men a mile over the Summit on the American
> side where the contract had been made. We didn't want the Mounted Police
> mixed up in it as they had enough to do. Besides, they wouldn't have let us pull
> off the work we wanted to do.
>
> . . . After lunch, around two o'clock, . . . we saw Brooks's pack train, the

foreman in the lead, coming around a bend of the narrow trail that broadened out in places. I rode out to meet him, my chaps behind me standing along the wider part of the road. When the foreman saw me he kicked his spurs into his horse to have him go faster. I put my horse across the trail to stop him. There was a big string of mules behind him. "Is that my stuff you are packing?" I asked him.

"No. Get out of the way in a hurry."

I told him I wouldn't move until he had read one clause of my contract with Brooks. "Read it carefully."

"We're not bothered with a contract, woman," the foreman threatened. "Get out of my way. This is no place to talk paper. I have no truck with that sort of business anyway."

"You'll study this for a minute," I said. "It is just as well to take the time to let this seep through your head. We mean business."

"Don't give a damn what your business is. Mine's packing, and I'm going through with this pack train."

"All right," I said, "if you won't respect contract rights, I've got to take care of ours. In that contract there is a clause saying we can take possession of your pack train."

"Well, you'll have a hell of a chance taking this pack train."

My men standing around were tickled to death. Anything for excitement, anything new. They had such hard work, so drab, they'd follow a leader into any deviltry. "Well, old man," I told the foreman, "I hate to do it, but I must. You better get off."

I had a [gun] under his belt by that time. Yes, I was the same girl who had rattled a pistol against the glass door of a Chicago bakery. . . . Did you think I was going to take that mule train with a bunch of roses?

. . . Brooks's foreman didn't have a weapon, and I only pulled that gun on him to give him a decent excuse for giving up the mules. A man had to have a decent excuse in Skagway. Of course my men took the foreman and messed him up enough to make him feel it was a real hold up.

We took possession of the mules, unloaded the other outfit's stuff, and took the foreman, Al was his name, to our camp. To the rest of Brooks's boys we offered jobs, told them to see George for orders. We'd treat 'em well and pay 'em well. If they didn't want to join us, they could stay in our camp with their boss.

My men started loading my stuff, taking it from our Skagway camps to the Summit. Believe me, they didn't waste much time. When we did get our stuff dumped near the Mounted Police, it seemed like home.

11.2. Packer Joe Brooks on his pinto horse, with the coastal mountains behind Skagway in the background. *(UW, Larson Collection, 9080)*

. . . Brooks's crew thought it was all a wonderful joke on him. One of his men brought me Brooks's wonderful saddle horse. Everyone on the trail knew Brooks's pinto. Said I might as well have it. That horse was the swellest little animal I ever knew. (NW 23:1–4; 24:1–2[145–50])

Belinda did not have time to gloat over her victory. She had to get back to Dawson. But her progress was blocked again by trouble from a new direction.[12]

12

Racing with Winter

CONDITIONS ON THE White Pass trail were already deteriorating, warning of winter's approach. The packers in Belinda's party had to protect themselves as well as their mules from onslaughts of driving sleet sharp enough to cut exposed skin. In mid-September of 1898 there seemed to be only a short time before the lakes of the upper Yukon River would begin to freeze,[1] blocking passage until the ice was strong enough to bear the weight of heavily loaded sleds. Belinda had to get into the flowing waters of the Yukon before the lake ice trapped her scows. Loading the fourteen boats at Bennett with her goods as they were delivered from Skagway, she hired a steamer, captained by an Old Timer, to tow the skows down to the outlet of Lake Bennett.

But she was not fast enough. The doctor assigned to the Mounted Police at Bennett had heard of her imminent departure. "His scheme was to quarantine for imaginary diseases rich Alaskans who were in a hurry. He'd hold them until he got a lot of money from them, to make him let them go" (NW 25:1[153]). Major and Mrs. Wood had warned Belinda of this doctor; they could do nothing to stop his racket, because he came under the control of another department. When the doctor found Belinda at her camp, he declared her sick with a fever. There was fear of typhoid at Bennett. Perhaps Belinda was carrying it. Furthermore, typhoid had been responsible for several deaths in Dawson before Belinda left there at the end of August, so it was not completely far-fetched for the doctor to propose such a diagnosis. He quarantined Belinda in a little cabin he had under his control.

Belinda knew she had no fever, and she felt completely well. So she did not hesitate to subvert the doctor's plans. Before leaving her boats, Belinda secretly asked the towboat captain to find Broad and to finish loading the scows. When all was ready, they were to figure out some way to distract the doctor and to give her some signal. In the meantime Belinda went along to her confinement, confident that she could out-fox the doctor.

> The doctor locked me up, gave me some pills and told me I had a serious case of something or other. . . . I asked him how often I was to take the pills and told him I thought I'd spend the winter with him as I needed rest. I palmed myself right off on him. He had expected a big argument and was disappointed, but he put a sign or something on the door of the cabin and went away.
>
> . . . The first thing I knew of the crew's plan . . . was when one morning the door of the cabin was busted in and the men of my crew were saying, "Run quick! We've got him out [of here]."
>
> They had reported to the doctor that a rich outfit had had an accident out in the canyon. . . . They were all yelling at him to hurry up and had a horse ready for him to grab to get there.
>
> When the cabin door was broken in, I had to run like a thief, hop on the boat and pull out of Bennett. However, the doctor found out the plan and was back at the shore as we were going down the lake. . . . The men saw him and as we pulled out they were all laughing and throwing him kisses and hollering, "Good-bye, Piggy Dear."
>
> Later in Dawson Colonel Steele was really angry at me because I wouldn't make out affidavits against the doctor. He had a lot of other affidavits [complaining about the doctor], but I wouldn't sign. I had a horror of lawsuits. In Ireland they were the same as a disgrace, like murder in the family. (NW 25:2–4[154–56])

Belinda had triumphed over the doctor. Now the only contest was with the approaching winter. Once Belinda's party was on the flowing Yukon, they used the sweeps on the bow and stern of the scows to keep them in the current. They floated along the river from dawn until dark, then found a place on the bank to camp overnight. But when they reached Miles Canyon rapids, Belinda had to show her tough leadership once again.

The Miles Canyon rapids, followed almost immediately by the feisty White Horse rapids, were the most hazardous on the Yukon. Here the water from all of the surrounding lakes funneled through high granite walls. The water surged through a hundred-foot-wide channel, swirling around and over boulders and digging souse holes as it sought its way to lower levels to the north. Many outfits had been lost in Miles Canyon. The lower water levels of autumn made the rocks of White Horse rapids an even greater danger. Belinda had been through the rapids on her first trip In, and possibly she had seen them again when she, Jenny, and Jack portaged around them on the trip Out. Belinda knew what lay ahead, and she knew that with some skill and some luck, the hazards could be negotiated.

One of Belinda's crew, a man by the name of Lake who professed knowing a lot about handling boats, took a close look at Miles Canyon and proclaimed that going through the canyon was suicidal. He refused to do it. Other members of the crew seemed inclined to follow Lake's example.

> "Here," said George, "we got to get through."
>
> "Sure," I told them, "anyone who is yellow here and walks around the Canyon will have to walk the rest of the way to Dawson, and they won't go at my expense."
>
> Lake spoke up. "Bet you won't risk your precious life in it. I don't see why you should ask the rest of us to do it."
>
> It took Broad to promise, "I'll go through once, but if I drown don't ask me to take another scow down for you." (NW 26:3–4[159–60])

Fortunately Belinda's crew included an experienced river man by the name of Thompson, whose skill Belinda trusted. While Lake was betting that no one could take even a canoe through the rapids, let alone the unwieldy scows, Thompson was sizing up the canoe Belinda had used on her trip upstream.

> Coming back to me he said in a low voice, "Take him up. If you'll sit still, I'll take you through."
>
> I had confidence in Thompson and knew he wouldn't risk his life if he thought he couldn't make it. Up to this time Lake had been a perfect nuisance. Some of the fellows believed him too. I was in it, worked up to the point where I had to put some stuff in the men.
>
> "Alright Lake, if you got any money I'll go through. I don't want you to bet your useless life. I don't want it. But if you do have any worldly chattels, put them up among the boys. Thompson and I will come and tell you what it's like." (NW 26:4–5[160–61])

12.1. A raft goes through the White Horse rapids. *(UW, A. Curtis photog., 46062)*

Off Belinda went, with Thompson piloting the canoe. Again he warned her not to move, for timing of his maneuvering of the canoe would be critical. Belinda went through the rapids almost holding her breath.

> The only way I can describe it is like being shot through. Those three quarter miles of walls went by like a streak of granite. I was praying. I didn't know anything [until] I got through to the eddy below the canyon. . . . When we could open our eyes and breathe naturally, I [could hardly believe what I saw.]
>
> . . . Thompson was staring at the bank, and then he stared at me. He said, "Do you see anything there?"
>
> I asked him, "Do you?"
>
> What we saw on the bank were gol darn alarm clocks, ever so many of them. I don't know how many dozens and the lot were going tick-ticking to beat anything. We pulled up to feel them before I was sure. Then we laughed like two fools. (NW 26:5–6[161–62])

Belinda and Thompson were looking at the remains of a peddler's box of clocks. His scow had wrecked in the rapids, but he had managed to rescue the clocks and was now drying them on the bank.

12.2. Ella Card, pregnant with her son Freddy, carries her infant daughter at the beginning of Chilkoot trail in April of 1897. It is this infant daughter who later died on the trail. *(ASL, Winter and Pond photog., PCA 21–13)*

When they got back to the top of Miles Canyon rapids, Belinda found Lake rather shame-faced, and the rest of her crew ready to move on.

> We took the boats three at a time through to the foot of the canyon until we got them all down. Then we shot them down three at a time to below White Horse where we made our camp.
>
> It was a beautiful sight to see those men on White Horse rapids, every muscle in their arms showing, stripped down to undershirts and pants, managing those long sweeps, which were clumsy to handle because of the danger of breaking them [on the rocks in the low water.]
>
> Yet the men managed their scows so wonderfully. (NW 27:1–2[163–64])

Once through the White Horse rapids safely, Belinda kept a promise to a friend back in Dawson, Ella (Mrs. Fred) Card, who had lost a child coming through the rapids in 1897. She and her husband had not been able to bury the body deeply because the ground had been frozen. Now Ella was tormented by an image of the grave being disturbed by animals. Belinda was a great admirer of Ella Card, whom she considered one of the bravest women in the North. Before leaving Dawson, Belinda had promised to try to find the grave. When she

did locate it, she had her crew help roll heavy rocks over the site. "I was thinking of that mother and her baby," she said. "It kind of hurt me."[2]

At Whitehorse, with the worst of the trip over, Belinda boarded the little
steamboat *Ora* with some of the supplies and left the rest to be brought down
by the scows. Belinda was back to Dawson on September 27,[3] to the amaze-
ment of everyone who had expected her to go all the way Out to Seattle.

Belinda was quick to enjoy the luxuries offered by her bathhouse. Then
she took a refreshed look at her town. By October of 1898 Dawson had four
churches, two hospitals, two banks, three newspapers, and a number of variety
theaters. From the time of Dawson's founding, there were two major transportation and supply companies trading goods for gold and furs and running
steamboats on the Yukon. But now there were a number of independents as
well. Belinda was surprised to see how many improvements had been made in
Dawson in just the four weeks she had been gone.

Before she left, she had already started a two-story addition to the Fairview
that would extend it to the full 160-foot depth of the lot.[4] Now expansion projects on other buildings were being completed, perhaps influenced by Belinda's
success with the multi-storied Fairview. The *Klondike Nugget* announced it had
become the rage in Dawson to tear off roofs of existing buildings so that one or
two stories could be added.[5] Less substantial but with strong visual impact were
the decorative facades added to many of the older log buildings. The Dawson
waterfront was beginning to look more imposing, and Front Street, newly improved with layers of sawdust, was the promenade for the crowds.

On October 17 the little *Ora* arrived from another round trip to Whitehorse.
There was some question whether it would be her last for the season because
the Yukon River was getting shallower and in places was beginning to freeze.
The *Ora* had to force her way through chunks of ice and a more continuous sheet
forming along the shore to land Belinda's last scow in front of the Fairview.[6]
The steamer had rescued the scow after it had run onto a rock and punched a
hole below the water line. Nearly a thousand dollars worth of "choice groceries
and wall paper"[7] had been lost, but the rest of the load was safe. Belinda had
gotten her supplies and furnishings to Dawson before the freeze-up, as she had
intended.

As they secured the scow to shore, Belinda's triumphant crew were met by
crowds of well-wishers and the curious. Front Street over the summer had become like a circus midway with milling crowds of unemployed newcomers taking in the sights as they tried to decide between weathering a Klondike winter

or facing the embarrassment of returning to the Outside no richer than when they left. The crowds had thinned with each outgoing steamer, but the arrival of Belinda's outfit was as good as any carnival attraction. And some of Belinda's crew rose to the occasion.

> Broad got on top of a scow and took off his hat. He made a speech as only Broad could, thanking them for the warm reception.
>
> It was such a pleasure to have them looking forward to his arrival with such excitement. He thought it was great to be popular. He thanked them. As he said that, he stood beside me and thanked them all on behalf of his brothers and sister. I ducked as someone stuck my squaw cook Jenny under his arm. Everybody screamed.
>
> . . . The hotel people were glad to see [the scow]. They'd been worried about their windows and were shivering around. There [were . . .] heads sticking out of every window [of the Fairview].
>
> . . . I had a very nice woman from San Francisco keeping house for me [at the Fairview]—Kitty Pilkington. When she heard [the boat] coming, she dropped everything and ran down to us. Of course, as housekeeper she had had all the brunt of the troubles.
>
> Sadie was at Grand Forks, but she came the next day. Everybody was curious to see what was in the boxes. Sadie had her hands out for the Grand Forks and Kitty Pilkington for the Fairview.[8]

On the evening of her return to Dawson, Belinda had been plunged into the politics of the growing territory. A public meeting was held at the Fairview to discuss how to get a more representative government to replace the appointees from Ottawa. After much discussion, those assembled voted to have the Miners' Association take up the matter at once. Belinda was one of only two women at the meeting. The other was Faith Fenton, a reporter for the Toronto *Globe*, who had arrived in Dawson in mid-September.[9]

Belinda also found a more personal debate going on at the Fairview. A rivalry had started between three of the government men—Queen's Council F. C. Wade and Mining Inspectors Jim McGregor and Captain Norwood—over the use of her office while she was away.

> Right at the head of the stairs on the first floor of the Fairview I had an office. It had a desk and some large chairs from the Transportation Company. On the floor was a big white polar bear rug. Moose horns—everybody had 'em—and some wonderful skins of animals were on the walls. . . . [It] was rather a big room as I had a large number of men to pay off. (NW 32:1[180])

Before she left for Skagway, all three government officials had asked to use her office. Wade wanted it for court business. Captain Norwood, whenever he came to town, would try to displace him, for there was a shortage of rooms in Dawson. As a bluff, Norwood claimed he had an interest in the hotel and was, therefore, entitled to the office. Belinda heard of this upon her return and decided to teach Norwood a lesson.

> Skipper and I always understood each other, always liked the same things, were the same kind of people, and were always having some sort of a fight. After I had cleaned up from my trip from Skagway, a very important chap, a Mr. Davis,[10] a new Custom's officer, came to see me. The town's business people had appointed him to solicit money for some fire protection. (NW 32:2[181])

Fire was a constant worry in the Yukon, where candles, lanterns, and metal stoves could easily ignite the tinder-dry buildings. Dawson newspapers in September and October reported a number of barely averted disasters. Belinda's Grand Forks Hotel was almost destroyed when a hanging lantern was accidentally knocked to the floor.[11] But the worst fears were realized with the fire that broke out in Dawson on the morning of 14 October 1898. The Fairview was spared, but forty other buildings in the central business district, many of them only recently constructed or remodeled, were burned to the ground. The loss was estimated at $503,000. Ironically, new firefighting equipment had been delivered to Dawson by that time, but it lay still packed at the North American Trading and Transportation Company warehouse, for the money to pay for it had not yet been raised.[12]

D. W. Davis had been appointed Fire Commissioner shortly after the October disaster, and his first mission was to get the fire equipment out of hock.

> . . . The Fairview was down for $500, and I gave it. Then I noticed Skipper was in my office behind the counter putting papers in the safe. I pointed him out to Davis. "There's the new owner in the office," I said. "Put him down for $500 too."
>
> "Well Captain," Davis said as he walked over to Skipper, "I understand you claim an interest in the Fairview."
>
> "I am the owner," said Skipper. "Anything I can do for you?"
>
> "Yes," said Davis, "the new owner is down for $500."
>
> "Are you taking names or cash?" the Captain asked.
>
> Davis told him cash . . . . So Skipper took $500 from his box and said, "I hope you are not starting another fire company right away. This hits us pretty hard."

Davis, as he slid out into the hall, said to me, "If you pay back the $500, I'll murder you."

"I will not. It will cost that old sport that much for his bragging." [Then] I went to Skipper.

"Glad to see you," he said. "I just paid out $500 of my money for you to Davis, for the fire department. The hotel was down for $500."

"You didn't anything of the kind," I said. "You did it for yourself."

"It was for the Fairview," he insisted.

"It must be worth $500 for the ownership," I told him. . . . "That'll teach you to claim interests you haven't got."

Davis got all the officials into the joke. They would give a list to the Captain and say, "As owner of the Fairview, we want your name on this for so much." It nearly got him crazy.

After it came, the fire department turned out to be a couple of dog trains and a donkey engine. It was all about as good as a bucket of water. You would dip a bucket into the river and the bucket would be full of ice by the time it was passed on and had reached the fire. Fire in Alaska was a marvelous thing to put out. (NW 32:2–4[181–83])

Despite Belinda's skepticism, the new fire equipment in the hands of a more tightly organized volunteer fire department soon proved its worth. In fact, the Fairview was one of its early beneficiaries when, on the night of 3 November, a blaze on the roof of the hotel was quickly extinguished before doing much damage.[13]

13

Charles Eugene Carbonneau

Shortly before Belinda went Out in late August of 1898 to get supplies and furnishings for her hotels, there appeared among the tens of thousands of new arrivals in Dawson an unusual-looking man. Rather than the cotton shirt with suspendered pants and muddy boots of the stampeder, this man was dressed in tailored clothes, with spats over patent leather shoes. At five feet, ten inches in height, his 210-pound weight suggested a life tending to indulgence rather than athletic exertion. Still, a dispassionate observer of this dark-haired man called him "handsome and well-dressed."[1] He wore cream-colored kid gloves and carried a cane as he strolled down the streets and boardwalks. Though he spoke only when directly addressed, he replied with dignity, politeness, and a cultured French accent.

The newcomer and his valet registered in the best hotel in town, the Fairview, and his scrawled signature in the hotel's register looked like "Count C. E. Carboman"[2] to a *Klondike Nugget* reporter. But the man's real name was Charles Eugene Carbonneau. His calling card identified him as the representative of a well-known French wine merchandiser, Messrs Pierre Legasse, Frères et Cie, of Bordeaux, Paris, and New York,[3] but Charles had other business in mind as well.

Though he lacked apparent prior experience with the Yukon or with mining,

13.1. Men checking the flumes of Eldorado 3A, the claim that Charles Carbonneau purchased in 1898 and that Belinda Mulrooney worked extensively. *(Yukon Archives, McLennon Collection, 6501)*

Charles while in London had interested a group of investors in acquiring and mining Klondike claims. They then had dispatched him to the Klondike to look for likely prospects.[4] Charles arrived in Dawson in the company of Thomas Pelkey, an early staker on Bonanza Creek.[5] As a well-known Old Timer, Pelkey introduced Carbonneau to Dawson mining and miners. Carbonneau in turn, who had connections in Ottawa, impressed Pelkey with his political acumen. Soon after coming to Dawson both Pelkey and Carbonneau attended a large dinner party at the Fairview hosted by locals in honor of Colonel James Domville, a visiting member of the Canadian Parliament.[6] Nine days after the party, Carbonneau purchased four of Pelkey's claims—41 A/D on Bonanza, the fraction 3A on Eldorado, and two on Lucky Gulch of All Gold Creek, a tributary of the Klondike flowing down the east side of the Dome.[7] (See fig. 7.3.) The Eldorado claim was only 131 feet 6 inches long,[8] but it was adjacent to the discovery claim, No. 3 Eldorado. It and the Bonanza claim were already considered to be good producers,[9] while the Lucky Gulch claims were more speculative.

It was about this time that Charles Eugene Carbonneau first met Belinda.[10]

> I came into the hotel office after a tiresome day and heard the manager of the Fairview,[11] who was awfully over-bearing, arguing with a man. "What's the matter?" I asked the manager. "It seems most of the time you spend quarreling with the guests."
>
> "This man is kicking about the price of wine," the manager explained.
>
> . . . Mr. Carbonneau insisted, "I'm not kicking. I want to know if this is the usual price."
>
> The manager told me, "I had to get it for him specially."
>
> "What's wine?" I was tired and disgusted. "Let him have it. Charge the bottle to me. But after this if he wants wine he can get it by the case."
>
> Mr. Carbonneau objected. "I don't intend to let you give me wine."
>
> . . . I looked at Pelkey during this argument, and Pelkey said, "You try to tell Carbonneau anything! He wants to be boss. He wants his wine with every meal." (NW 45:1–2[233–34])

Charles was embarrassed by this encounter. Appearances were important to him. He liked to be noticed wherever he went, but he did not want to appear in a bad light. He was very particular about his meals and wanted to have good wine and mineral water with them if it was at all possible. But he did not want to make a bad impression on anyone who might really count. The next night he was waiting for Belinda when she returned to the hotel.

> "I want to explain to you about that wine," he said. "I won't have you paying for it."
>
> "Oh write it. I'm busy."
>
> He insisted, "I must adjust it."
>
> "Do it at the office. Let's forget about it."
>
> So he sat down at my table in the dining room and talked. He had his card in his hand. He told me he'd just arrived from London, with an option on Pelkey's mine for a large company in England which wanted more mines. Even if he didn't want to be over-charged for wine, he wasn't cheap, he wanted me to understand.
>
> "Do you know," he said, holding his card out towards me a little further, "there are two Lords in the hotel?"
>
> "I'm more accustomed," I told him, "to recognize only One."
>
> "They are big game hunters," he gossiped, "and came in over the Summit."
>
> "Why did they pack in their title?" I asked. "It was foolish. They should have left it over the other side of the Summit, traded it for two yards of mosquito

netting or something useful. But as long as they don't tell anybody, they may get by."

Carbonneau's own card with his title of "Count" on it was already lying by my plate on the table. He reached for it and snatched it away. (NW 45:2–3 [234–35])

Charles, despite his best intentions, had managed to irritate Belinda yet again. She, like most Old Timers, had little use for titles and putting on airs. Still, she did notice Charles. "His eyes were large with a sort of sleepy, gentle look some Frenchmen have, and he had a heavy mustache. A dashing short of chap in his good clothes." And although he was just one more guest kicking about the service, "he interested me because he was so persistent in paying for that darn little bottle of wine. That's all he meant to me" (NW 45:2, 4[234, 236]).

Belinda left soon after these first encounters to get the supplies needed for her hotels. By the time she returned on 27 September, Carbonneau and Pelkey had left for Europe,[12] where Charles would proceed with arrangements for a company and would interest other investors in the Klondike gold mines. He needed more money to buy the claims and to hire the men to work them. A genuine Old Timer like Pelkey would help to authenticate Charles's descriptions of the riches to be gained.

The Anglo-French Klondyke Syndicate, Ltd. was capitalized for £50,000 (about $241,550)[13] and incorporated in London on 10 November 1898, with wide-ranging objectives. Besides gold mining in the Klondike, the company was set up to mine any ores; explore anywhere in Canada; acquire and develop land, transportation facilities, and utilities; carry out a wide range of businesses, including services, export/import, retailing, and banking; as well as acquire and sell other companies.[14] It seems that the means to accomplish all these goals was to be Charles E. Carbonneau.[15] He agreed to transfer the claims on Bonanza, Eldorado, and Lucky Creek to the company for £44,000 (approximately $212,564), with £14,000 to be paid in cash and the rest in 30,000 paid-up shares of the company.[16] It was also agreed that Charles would be manager of the company's interests in the Klondyke, receiving 10 percent of the net proceeds from the mines plus reimbursement for reasonable and necessary expenses in connection with representing the company.[17] Having organized the syndicate and having received £2,500 and 500 shares as down payment until all titles could be transferred to the company,[18] Charles was then ready to return to Dawson by way of Paris.

In early December he was back in Vancouver, where he took out a Free

Miners Certificate in the name of his new company.[19] Several days later he arrived in Skagway, where he was referred to in a newspaper article as "Count de Carbonneau" and was described as a "French mining expert,"[20] though there is no other indication that he had ever had any experience in mining. "Promoter" would have been a better description of Charles's business. He put schemes for making money together with investors, and the nature of the venture always varied. Now he was trading in mines, and as was his wont, he operated in a grand style.

Charles brought with him several men, a team of thirty-three dogs, and 7.5 tons of supplies as he started for the interior.[21] He is recorded twice in the Royal Canadian Mounted Police border crossings registers for 22 December 1898. In one place he is listed as Vice-Count Carbonneau from Paris, France, in the second as C. E. Carbonneau from London, England.[22] Apparently he was being more selective now about when he used a title.

When Charles arrived back in Dawson on 9 January 1899, he again registered at the Fairview and created quite a sensation throughout the town. First, not many travelers braved the winter trails. Temperatures in Dawson during the previous week had been cold, with lows of minus-40 and highs in the minus-20 degrees Fahrenheit range. Any arrival in these severe conditions, when just breathing could freeze air passages, was likely to be noticed. What's more, Charles brought with him accounts of recent political events in Europe and the United States—war between Norway and Sweden; breaking of the "Triple Alliance" between Germany, Austria, and Italy; terms of the peace settlement of the Spanish-American war; strains in relations between France and England; results of the recent elections in the United States; how reports of misgovernment in the Yukon were weakening investor interest; and near completion of the Paris world's fair buildings. With no regular means of getting Outside information, Dawson's news-hungry citizens eagerly read the local newspapers to learn what Charles had to report.[23]

Charles also told of the difficulties of his journey, which took twenty-three days from Skagway.[24] Many of his dogs had died on the trail. This he attributed to the fact that they had come from the Hudson Bay Company's McKenzie River country stock. According to Charles they simply were not acclimated to the conditions of the Klondike. At Lake Bennett and on the lakes and rivers of the upper Yukon, the water was still open; consequently, Carbonneau's party could travel by boat, presumably commercial steamers. But as he progressed north, Charles met with more and more ice, so that for the last several days of his journey he was traveling by sled. When he arrived at Dawson, most of his outfit was still behind him. But he reported himself glad to be back and ready to start 100 to 150 men at work on the claims of the Anglo-French Klondike Syndicate,[25] to whose name Charles had just transferred title.[26]

In addition to the excitement of Charles's arrival with all the news, people in Dawson also were much impressed by his remaining dogs. Especially alerted was Mike Mahoney, who was an expert musher and carried mail between Dawson and Skagway that winter. He remembered that Carbonneau's team included a number of champion Siberian huskies brought in from Russia (Denison, 226). The San Francisco *Examiner* had offered a prize of a thousand dollars for the fastest time from Dawson to the Outside that winter,[27] and Mahoney held the record to date with a fourteen-day trip in December. Charles boasted that with his superior team he would beat Mahoney's time to Skagway. But Mahoney considered Carbonneau a four-flusher and a phony, and was determined not to let him win. In February 1899, Mike made the trip in ten days and eight hours, a record that Charles never challenged (Denison, 222–29).

Belinda, who was always keen on animals, thought Charles's dog team was the best she had ever seen. He knew from observing her with Nero that Belinda loved dogs and would take good care of them, so he made a point of boarding his team with her (NW 45:4[236]). And it probably impressed Belinda that Charles was one of the few people Nero seemed to like. There is even a certain resonance in Belinda's descriptions of Nero and of Charles: "[Nero] was fond of Carbonneau, liked him better than anyone else excepting me. He liked people while they were admiring him, but he didn't want to stay with anyone else or do anything for anyone else. He tolerated them and looked pleasant."

But there was another side to Charles that Belinda did not see at that time. We learn of it from a newspaper story about another traveler on the Skagway-Dawson trail who was headed Out at the same time Charles was coming In.

CRUEL TO HIS DOGS

Accusation Made Against Count Carbonneau—Making a Record

There came down from Skagway on the steamship DIRIGO from Dawson several passengers who tell a story of cruelty to dogs on the Yukon trail.

"When we were at Steamboat slough coming out," said W. C. Watrous,[28] one of the proprietors of the Dawson Nugget, "we ran across Count C. E. Carbonneau, whom we understood had some connection with the French Exploration Company.

"He and two Indians with him would be heard coming down the trail a half mile away yelling at their dogs like madmen, with whips in their hands. And the dogs, frightened and wan, tore along with their tongues hanging out of their mouths. He was then twelve days from Skagway, and would reach Dawson possibly in three more.

"He had left dead and dying dogs behind him at various points on the river. We found a dog near Little Salmon, beaten up, with blood all over him. There must have been a half dozen dogs in all that he left behind almost dead from exhaustion, left alone to freeze or starve. One of them which we ran across could not walk more than ten feet without falling. It seems that he would beat a dog to death and then leave him behind. We didn't stop to talk to this fellow. We heard simply that he was a French count trying to beat the record. Someone on the trail said that he was really a cook from Montreal."[29]

What Belinda was aware of was that Charles was not widely liked by the Old Timers. She thought it was because he was just not one of them.

Carbonneau's manners were very different from those of the men I'd been used to. And in contrast to the rough looking and sometimes not bathed miners, he was always particular about his person.

. . . Carbonneau fitted in with the Canadian officials like Wade and the others, but not very well with the miners.

"I like the officials and the business men," he'd say, "but the miners don't like me, and I don't like them. I wish they'd shave once in a while."

Little things, cheap things, ordinary things never appealed to him. The very best of life, especially when it applied to his own living, was never too good for him. He wasted no time transacting business in a small way. . . . He was immaculate in dress, appearance and table manners. (NW 45:6–7[238–39a]; 56:1[291])

The *Dawson Daily News* observed, "The count is active and affable in his address and bearing, and is fond of club life and the comforts of luxurious living and surroundings."[30] Charles's investors might have been less than reassured had they seen what their funds were supporting. By mid-March about a hundred men and women from England, Scotland, and Ireland had bought a total of 15,000 shares in lots of 8 to 1,000 at £1 each.[31] Charles also was presumably marketing his own 30,000 shares by this time. The £15,000 ($72,465) raised from the company's stock would pay for the claims and laborers. The capital also would finance Charles's "necessaries." On his return to Dawson in January of 1899, "He left nothing behind, had magnificent furs and other equipment—

tents, spirit lamps, steaks and fine food stuffs. The ordinary tent wasn't good enough for him. He had to have silk tents. His cot—you know the rest of us put down pine boughs and would think them a great luxury, but he had some blessed thing that knocked down and was padded especially with curly hair" (NW 56:2–3[292–93]).

It is perhaps surprising that Belinda would be taken with such a dandy. But there were other aspects of Charles's character that appealed to her: she "found his conversation restful and interesting, especially his description of life in Europe," and she was interested in his discussions of business conditions (NW 5:6–7[238–39]).

In fact, Belinda and Charles were quite similar in their entrepeneurial attitudes. They both were far-thinking, independent opportunists; moderate risk-takers; confident, goal-oriented, and enthusiastic competitive game players. But they did approach their businesses differently. Belinda specialized in starting with her own resources businesses that would supply a product or service she judged was needed or desired. Charles was more a promoter of ideas, an organizer of capital to be applied to some venture which he felt appealed to people, even though he might have no direct knowledge of the business.

Furthermore, Belinda and Charles highlight an interesting ambiguity about entrepreneurship. While entrepreneurial activity is endorsed in a capitalistic economy, it also can be exploitative, with criminal disregard for the welfare of others. With any given business it is sometimes very difficult to judge what aspect of entrepreneurism—the light, creative side, or the dark, exploitative side—is in ascendance. And even the entrepreneur, blinded by ambition and her own image of the possibilities of the situation, may be unable to discriminate where on this continuum her own activities lie.

Belinda saw many new and interesting perspectives on the world through Charles's eyes.

> Carbonneau didn't stay in Dawson long for any one time, but he always showed up again. He was always leaving for Canada or Europe, purchasing some mine. He always took some of the miners with him and was full of interesting things to tell about the miners and what they thought of France and London.
>
> He used to speak to me of his family from Bordeaux. They went to Canada when he was quite a little boy. His father had died and his mother was living with his sister in Ottawa.[32] The sister had married a government official, and they had seven children, six boys and a girl. The father's government position

13.2. Charles E. Carbonneau, far right in back row, with Yukon Territory officials in Ottawa. James McGregor, Mining Inspector, in the center of the back row, is the only other person identified. *(Yakima Valley Museum, Carbonneau Collection, 6115)*

didn't yield much, and Mr. Carbonneau provided the funds for their children, for their higher education at least.

He seemed to have a good deal of influence with the officials at Ottawa. It was easy for him to acquire concessions, [and] while it was difficult for others, he rarely had any trouble. In Dawson, three of the government appointees were French—The Honorable F. D. Juiard, Xavier Gosselyn, and Judge Dugas.[33] . . . Those men knew him from early business in Canada. (NW 46:1[239a])

Belinda obviously enjoyed knowing someone whose interests were wide-reaching and international. She appreciated Charles's complexity—here was a man who was a challenge for her intellectually, psychologically, socially, and culturally. At the same time, she admired his softer side too, such as his nurturing of his sister's children. As they got to know each other better during the winter of 1898–99, sharing meals whenever Charles was in town, Belinda found her interest in him growing. He also began demonstrating his regard for her by regularly giving her flowers,[34] and Belinda was impressed by the gesture. Charles also started bringing her presents from his trips Outside. While Belinda appreciated his generosity, some of the gifts were awkward because they did not suit Belinda's taste.

[The North] was the only country where I took great pains to have proper clothes. Then I had useful things, well made by a tailor. They were what I felt were right for the country—riding skirts, silk shirts, top boots. I paid $37 for my boots. They were like a cowboy's, made to order by Slater's, New York, two pairs every year. I wore a Stetson hat in summer and silk shirts of pongee or white silk, with a tie and with . . . little jackets made of kid, the finest kid. You could wipe them off with a cloth with a little oil on it. I had some clothes for dinner, but I didn't dress often, only for special occasions. I was on the trail all the time, and there a clean shirt was dressing up enough.

On one of Carbonneau's trips In, he brought me a trunk full of clothes. He had the clothes he got for me brought into the country without attracting too much attention, as he bought for Wade and all his family every time he went out.

But I was furious! The trunk was full of the most beautiful gowns, but I blew up like a balloon. He thought I'd be tickled to death with them. He thought he'd done something wonderful for me when he opened the trunk and showed me those clothes. I was shocked. I felt I'd seen too much of him and the reaction might set in.

Good Lord, he just slumped when I wouldn't take them. . . . " What have I done now? What have I done to cause this?" was his . . . cry. He was fifteen years older than I was, but he seemed to be a small kid in nature—just bubbling over or all in, over nothing.

Those clothes caused a perfectly good quarrel. He'd had the trunk put in my room when I was at the mines. "Let's give them to Sadie," I suggested. But no. The trunk stayed there quite a while. I wouldn't wear the things, but they were tempting enough at that—the feel of them was, I admit that. It was fun to feel the silks and satins, the beautiful hose. (NW 46:2–4[240–42])

WHILE BELINDA'S INTEREST in Carbonneau grew, her own projects also demanded her attention and her time. Her businesses were flourishing, and she was actively involved with her several mining claims. The year 1899 was to become one of Belinda Mulrooney's most successful.

14

Belinda at Her Peak

By THE WINTER OF 1898–99 Belinda Mulrooney was one of the Klondike's central figures. She owned two hotels—the Fairview in Dawson and the Grand Forks at the junction of Eldorado and Bonanza Creeks—along with the restaurants and barrooms connected with both hotels. The Grand Forks Hotel served as her center for trading goods and supplies, rudimentary banking, and land brokering. She was a principal in the local telephone company—the Yukon Telegraph and Telephone Syndicate—and in the Eldorado-Bonanza Quartz and Placer Mining Company. She had extensive mine holdings, most of which she managed by hiring a foreman and workmen, although in some she involved herself more actively. Although women were not allowed to join the Yukon Order of Pioneers, she was accepted as one of a very few honorary members.[1] Tending to all her businesses filled her days, and she traveled regularly between Dawson, Grand Forks, and the creeks of the district. Though not particularly interested in the trappings and traditions of society, Belinda nevertheless regularly participated in the civic and social life of Dawson and the Creeks.

Dawson in the winter of 1898–99 supported an active social calendar that relieved the tedium of the dark winter days and nights. As one of Dawson's more prominent citizens, Belinda joined in when she was in town, enjoying dancing

and entertaining. Social events in this stage of Dawson's history were more em-
bellished than the impromptu affairs prior to the summer of 1898, now that some
people had the time and inclination for the longer-term planning required by
costumes and performances. For example, in mid-October "families and the
upper social set of the community" gathered in Pioneer Hall for a production
of "Three Hats," a social drama. According to newspaper coverage of the event,
the costumes and sets for the play were impressively elaborate. Among the performers, "Miss B. A. Mulroney took the part of Grace, the daughter, and acquitted herself with much credit."[2] A month later a large segment of Dawson
turned out for a masquerade ball to benefit the Dawson Fire Department. For
this event Belinda teamed up with her housekeeper at the Fairview, Kitty
Pilkington, dressing as a bride and groom (and carrying as one of their props a
"baby"). The *Klondike Nugget* of 26 November reported that "Miss Mulroney
made a dapper little husband, in regulation broadcloth and silk hat" (p. 3,
cols. a–b).

In addition to supporting more frequent and elaborate social events, the pop-
Despite Belinda's reputation for seriousness, she was persuaded to partici-
pate in a benefit minstrel show. On 5 January 1899 she appeared on stage in
black face and, with the nineteen other Dawson women in the show, raised
$1,100 for St. Mary's hospital. Belinda also is listed as one of seventeen women
who contributed to the success of the children's Christmas party at St. Paul's
Episcopal church.[3]

In addition to supporting more frequent and elaborate social events, the population of Dawson was becoming more stratified. The Elks' benefit for the hospital and burial fund on 25 October 1898 signaled the shift in moral and social
sensibilities. For this event the most popular performers in the vaudeville acts
around town combined with local talent to put on a show for a general audience
at the Tivoli Theater.[4] Belinda was in the "brilliant assemblage" of spectators
and watched the show from her box overlooking the stage.[5] The concluding act
was a newly arrived professional performer, Cad Wilson, advertised as adding
"new ginger" to her performances at the Tivoli Theater.[6] For the Elks benefit,
Cad sang some of her usual repertoire and was enthusiastically applauded by
many. But apparently her performance was too spicy for others in the audience.
The *Klondike Nugget* on 29 October scolded her in an editorial.

> The Elks benefit performance . . . was an unqualified success but for one
> thing. It is doubtful if the ladies would attend a second one. At least a hundred
> ladies were present in the body of the house and many more upstairs. . . . The

last act caused ladies to reach for their wraps, and many and severe were the comments at the conclusion.

. . . Cad Wilson is undoubtedly popular, her repertoire extensive, and there can be no excuse at all for her breaking faith with the public who had been assured . . . that there would be nothing but what a gentleman might take his wife and family to hear and see with perfect safety to their sense of propriety. . . . Words are hardly strong enough to express our condemnation of anyone who deliberately and premeditatively insults the better part of an audience. (p. 2, col. a)

This incident reveals at least one effect of the influx of women into Dawson in the summer of 1898. Among the newcomers were businesswomen, nurses, professionals, reporters, and socially conscious wives and would-be wives interested in imposing "standards" on the loose women and "entertainers" taking advantage of the freewheeling atmosphere of the mining camp. Now there were debates about who was "good" and what was appropriate for the "good" women to see and do. Many newcomers assumed that most women who had been in the area prior to 1898 were less than respectable. And some suspected that very few of the women remaining in Dawson during the winter of 1898–99 were of the "good" type. One Dawson newspaper, the *Yukon Miner*, even printed an opinion that there were only four good and pure women to be found in Dawson (30 December 1898). A rival newspaper, the *Klondike Nugget*, took the assertion seriously enough to debate it (4 January 1899, p. 2).

Belinda was among those who resisted the stereotypes and stoutly defended the character of women in the Klondike. According to her, even among the dance hall girls were to be found many respectable women.

As for dance hall girls—those women were there to dance with the miners, much as the women danced with the soldiers in the First World War. They didn't have to be bad. Several lawyers married those women, and they never made a mistake. After life in a dance hall, those women appreciated a good home, and you can be darn sure they never tried to break up any other woman's. Of course, they had to put up with a lot in the North. (NW 33:3[187])

Whether Belinda was offended by Cad's performance is not known. It is possible that her feelings were somewhat mixed. Though Belinda was seen as straight-laced and businesslike and seldom if ever visited the saloons or dance halls, she also enjoyed the rough play of her fellow miners. And on other occasions she expressed dismay over the airs put on by newcomers who saw wrong in everything (NW 42:3[226]; Hawkins).

14.1. The Yukon Order of Pioneers Christmas dinner at the Fairview Hotel dining room, 1898. *(Yakima Valley Museum, Carbonneau Collection)*

Besides the larger, community-wide events and organizations, Belinda was at the center of the social scene of Dawson simply because of the Fairview. Her telephone company's switchboard on the first floor of the hotel was the hub of local communications within town and to the creeks. The hotel dining room was popular for entertaining because of its good food as well as the performances offered on its stage. Organizations such as the Dawson Club, whose members included the "most prominent citizens representing the government, legal, medical, and other professions,"[7] and the Yukon Order of Pioneers held their special celebrations in the Fairview dining room. Here they knew they might find "the best public dinner ever served on the Yukon."[8] In addition, the hotel bar served as an informal gathering place for many, which put Belinda into the midst of another contentious social debate.

There was considerable ambivalence about the public use of liquor in Dawson, as there was in the rest of North America. The temperance movement had been a factor throughout the nineteenth century, but by the 1890s it was gaining enough strength that strict regulation if not prohibition of all liquor was the object of international agitation. In Canada, one of the earliest governmental disputes concerning the Yukon was about who had jurisdiction over the liquor trade—the Northwest Territories, in which the Yukon was a district until it became a territory itself, or the government in Ottawa. In the Yukon itself, regulation of liquor was an issue throughout Dawson's early history. Saloons were among the earliest and most central buildings constructed in town. And although the quality of liquor served was often abominable, the saloons were widely patronized because they provided not only drinks but also warmth and social contacts. Bars operated relatively freely in Dawson through the summer of 1898, before the new Yukon government, under pressure from Ottawa, imposed restrictions.[9]

The citizens of the Klondike represented the full spectrum of opinion and behavior concerning liquor. Some abused it routinely, others used it occasionally, and still others abstained and tried to persuade others to do the same. The pressure on women to abstain was particularly strong, both socially and legally. By social convention, "good" women did not drink. By 1901, in order to control the "bad" women who hustled drinks in saloons, the Yukon council passed ordinances prohibiting women from consuming alcohol in saloons or theaters (Guest, *History*, 207).

Belinda's contradictory statements about use of alcohol in the Klondike probably reflect the conflicting pressures she faced. She undoubtedly did drink moderately herself, but she disapproved of drunkenness and the havoc alcohol could wreak on people's lives. And yet, she saw humor in some of the antics performed during occasional drinking sprees, which she felt were just a part of life in the mining camp. Because she was careful not to give the impression that she was a "loose" woman, Belinda appeared straight-laced enough that some thought she was a teetotaler. One visitor to the Forks recorded in his diary that "the women of Dawson have a saying about Miss Mulroonay [*sic*]. While they wore bloomers, Miss Mulroonay wore long skirts. She has been known as the committee of one against drinking" (Nelson, 26 November 1898). Given that Belinda owned the bars in her hotels, it seems incongruous now that she might be identified as running a campaign against alcohol.

Belinda said that drinking was not a big part of the scene either in Dawson or at the creeks for the people who were actually working, and that later, when she saw films portraying Alaskan men and women as drunk all the time, she wanted to get up and walk out. On one occasion she even implied that the primary use of alcohol in the Klondike was for medicinal purposes.

> I always kept a case of assorted likkers in every one of my camps. Also some red pepper and glycerin for cramps. Once Dr. McLeod showed us how to fix the stuff up. Whether for a horse or a man, I forget which. But I always

kept a supply at each camp. It was the exception if anyone ever took away any of the whiskey. When guests stopped to eat, they liked something to drink because if the meal wasn't so good, it helped.

When they were at work the men had no hankering for the stuff. On the job and on the trail there was no demand for it. If they could get a hot cup of coffee they were blessed.

An assistant to the cook stole some likker once and Nels the cook threw him into the flume and nearly drowned him. I ask you, where in the U.S.A., even in a church lot, could you hide likker and not have it stolen? In Alaska we had no hiding place for the stuff. Put it in with the groceries and the meats. (NW 33:2–3[186–87])

On the other hand, according to sister-in-law Betty Mulrooney, keeping the cooks at her hotels sober was an ongoing problem for Belinda. Furthermore, she often told stories of various associates under the influence of alcohol (e.g., NW 30:1–3[172–74]). And she mentions that her friend Esther Duffie was known to go on drinking sprees.

One of the best old hearts God ever put on the face of the earth! Esther! Yet when drunk she was a holy terror. In later years I got to know her well, but I never lost respect and liking for her. She could get stewed as much as she wanted to and blow up the town. I always liked her. Both my eyes went shut when she went on a spree. When she wanted to celebrate she would treat everybody everywhere. I've known her to go to every saloon in Dawson with her gang, spending fifteen thousand at a crack. Old Timers tried to protect her, but they couldn't stop Esther. (NW 1:3–4)

DURING THE WINTER of 1898–99, Belinda started yet another business. This was in response to the unhealthy conditions prevailing in Dawson during the preceding summer and fall, when a number of people had died from typhoid fever and dysentery. It was in everybody's best interests to establish a clean water supply, uncontaminated by sewage, mining operations, and germ-laden dust, before the next warm season arrived.

By December 1898, Belinda was forming the Yukon Hygeia Water Supply Company. The company issued stock valued at eight thousand dollars, divided into three equal shares. Belinda's partners in the enterprise were J. B. Ogilvie and J. J. Mulroney.[10] As far as we have been able to determine, the latter person was not directly related to her. If J. J. Mulroney were her brother or father, one might wonder why his address was given as Ottawa, when her father and brother were still residents of Pennsylvania.[11] It seems more likely that Ogilvie and J. J.

Mulroney, both Canadians, were simply important partners for Belinda, the American, because they were needed to counteract the anti-alien sentiment in certain areas of Canadian government at the time. For example, British Columbia had recently passed a law excluding aliens from placer mining in that province, and there was feeling in Dawson that the Yukon government had similar protectionist intentions.[12] With the Yukon nearly overrun by Americans and with many Americans believing that Dawson was actually in American territory (Ogilvie, 219–20), it is easy to understand why the Canadians would be sensitive to the influence of aliens (Morrison, 11). It was important for the Yukon Hygeia Water Supply Company to be seen as legitimately Canadian because its owners intended to avail themselves of one of the advantages being offered by the Yukon Council to developing businesses.

The Yukon Council was now the governing body of the territory, and its actions marked a new era of more controlled management. While the new order was generally welcomed as an antidote to alleged misconduct by early officials in the Klondike, the actions of the Council did not always bring about the desired results. For example, concessions were given to some businesses to operate as monopolies, as an incentive for enterprises requiring large capital outlay that would benefit the general populace. One such proposal—to build a tramway along the trail leading up Bonanza Creek to Grand Forks—would facilitate shipping to and from the mines; however, the concessionaires promptly set up toll booths at regular intervals along the trail before any tramway was built, so everyone was required to pay for using the existing trail. Dawson citizens and miners raised an outcry about this arrangement, and the *Klondike Nugget* quickly took up the campaign against the "tramway without a tram."[13]

Once the water company was formed, Belinda and her partners decided to try to protect their interests by eliminating competition. In early January they applied to the Yukon Council for an exclusive concession to purify and deliver water in Dawson. The Yukon Council referred the matter to its chief counsel, Judge Dugas. At the same time, the council asked three local doctors for advice on the company's concept of purified water.[14]

By April others were trying to capitalize on the profit to be made in providing safe drinking water. At the 7 April Yukon Council meeting, three others proposed schemes for bringing water to Dawson. All were referred to the commissioner.[15] But by 20 April the Yukon Council was ready to grant to Belinda's company the rights for exclusive sale of boiled and filtered water. According to the *Klondike Nugget* of 26 April,

The petition of the Yukon Hygeia Water Supply Company was presented for the exclusive privilege and right, during a term of two years, to manufacture and sell in Dawson, filtered, boiled and germless water. The rate at which the water shall be sold shall not exceed ten cents per gallon delivered, and any person not employed by the company who shall sell in the city water purified by filtering and boiling shall be fined $50 and costs for each offense. (p. 4, col. a)

Although the idea of an exclusive concession was not new, the *Klondike Nugget* on 29 April strongly criticized the Yukon Council for granting the Hygeia Water Company these rights.

The fifty dollar fine imposed upon anyone who shall infringe upon the council-given rights and prerogatives is a fitting monument to the insincerity of whoever framed the resolutions appearing upon the minutes of the council but a few short weeks ago that "A discussion ensued and the council expressed itself as strongly opposed to the granting of exclusive privileges." There is yet time for the council to grant the exclusive privilege of selling ice, and we suggest this as another means of demonstrating that it is not so much the principle of the thing as the persons desiring a given exclusive franchise which carries weight. (p. 2, col. b)

The editorial continued sarcastically with the suggestion that Commissioner William Ogilvie was granting money-making monopolies to increase the number of his supporters. Although the editorial was directed primarily against the Yukon government, it also indicates that Belinda had by this time become a person whose support was to be courted.

The Yukon Hygeia Water Supply Company originally planned to draw water from the Yukon or Klondike Rivers.[16] And in fact the *Nugget* announced that the purification plant was located on the banks of the Klondike River, just below a sawmill.[17] One might wonder about the quality of water in the Klondike River with all the mining going on along its tributary creeks. The location downstream from a sawmill would hardly improve matters. But as Belinda later explained, the water for her company actually came from a spring on the opposite side of the Yukon from Dawson. "We had to run a cable across the river and ferried the water over in barrels loaded on a scow. On the Dawson side I sold it for twenty-five cents a pail."[18]

The business was scheduled to open 1 May 1899, under the management of F. E. Manchester. Dawson's citizens were advised that they could leave orders at any time at Bill McPhee's Pioneer Saloon or at the Fairview Hotel.

14.2. The first White Pass and Yukon Railroad train to the summit in February 1899 stopped on what had been a cliff on White Pass trail, Porcupine Hill. Belinda is second from right, and Michael Heney, contractor for the railroad, is fourth from right. While Heney wears an informal coat with turned-up collar and a warm cap, Belinda is among the more elegantly dressed. Her well-tailored outfit has an ankle-length skirt trimmed with an elaborate piping pattern and a hip-length jacket with a wide cape-collar of dark fur. Her hat is trimmed with feathers, fastened at their bases with a shining buckle-like pin. *(UW, Hegg photog., 663)*

They will have several delivery wagons, and will make daily deliveries to stores, offices, saloons or residences, and will deliver any amount from a gallon up, and at such a low rate that every one may have pure water this summer.

The treatment of this water makes it absolutely free of all disease germs, and the plant and water are subject at all times to a rigid inspection by the health officers.[19]

Somehow in her busy schedule of business, mining, and socializing, Belinda found time to make another quick trip to Skagway in February 1899. She made the long journey over the snow because contractor Michael J. Heney invited her to join in celebrating the opening of the White Pass and Yukon Railroad

14.3. One part of Porcupine Hill on the White Pass trail as it appeared to packers in 1897. *(UW, Curtis photog., 214)*

across the most difficult portion of the trail, from Skagway to the summit of White Pass. The ceremonial passenger train made the historic first round trip on 20 February and stopped several times en route for photographs. Belinda appears prominently in many of these photographs, although her name is not included in the Skagway newspapers' coverage of the guests at the celebration.[20]

One of the ceremonial stops was at Porcupine Hill, a section of the White Pass trail that had been particularly difficult. For Old Timers, it was a moment for sentimental reflection as they remembered their struggles at this spot and what it had meant to them to have made it through. Perhaps Belinda smiled recalling the excitement of hijacking Joe Brooks's pack train and hauling her hotel goods across this trail just a few months earlier.

Soon anyone would be able to travel between Skagway and the headwaters of the Yukon River simply by boarding a train. The White Pass and Yukon Railroad meant unprecedented access to the Yukon basin. Dawson was no longer so isolated an outpost.

Mining, Maiden, and Mouse

While socializing and business in Dawson were engrossing, Belinda also was happy with a simpler life. Consequently she used the need for supervising her mines as an excuse for a respite from town. One of her potentially most valuable claims was on Cheechako or Adams Hill. The original discovery on Bonanza Creek had been close to the mouth of a stream entering from the west, later named Little Skookum Creek. The hillside between Little Skookum and Adams Creek, the next downstream tributary, was sometimes called Adams Hill, but became known as Cheechako Hill because the gold was found there by newcomers.[21] Many thought that Cheechako Hill was the source for all the gold in Bonanza Creek. Belinda's claim there was next to O. B. Millett's discovery claim and was in the center of the rich pay streak that gradually was uncovered in the summer of 1898.[22]

In October [1898], for a vacation, I made a round of my claims. We had interests in all the good claims, either I had or my partners. Skipper [Captain Norwood] was always in with me on most of them. Frank Larson[23] or Skiff Mitchell[24] were partners too. (NW 37:1[202])

The claim on Cheechako Hill was discovered by Maiden,[25] who was an old man even in [1898]. He spent his time prospecting or tinkering around for others, or sometimes for me getting out wood. When the water in the spring at the top of the hill showed some colors of gold dust, the old man, who was a good miner, came down and told us about it. He and another fellow . . . went back up the hill with me. As I had used up my rights for staking, they did the staking for me. Afterwards I bought them out.[26]

Maiden was a character, really like a child. Over eighty years old, he had forgotten his age. His cheeks were pink, not a wrinkle, like a young person. He had perfect teeth. . . . Even his hair was alright. He was so unusual the doctors used to look him over. But his body was no older than his mind. He was really childish, as simple as a baby. The harder you worked to protect him, the harder he'd work to see he wasn't protected. . . . For instance, I tried my darndest to make him keep his interest in the Cheechako Hill claim, when he wanted to sell it to somebody else. As I already had an interest in it, I had to buy Maiden's to protect both of us.

The other fellow who had an interest had typhoid fever and was homesick. I told him I'd work his interest for him or give him cash. He wanted cash, so I bought him out too. (NW 37:2[203])

14.4. Mining on Cheechako Hill on the southwest side of Bonanza Creek. The Klondike discovery claim was on the creek, out of view at left. The tier organization of hillside claims is clear. Wooden flumes snake down the hillside, and a huge pile of firewood is at creek level in the center foreground. *(UW, Cantwell photog., 21)*

However, even on the claims, socializing was a regular part of the routine, as seen in the following incident from the summer of 1898.

> . . . I went up to Cheechako (that means Newcomer) Hill where I established a camp. Me, the cook and her husband were hardly settled there when people started visiting me.
>
> . . . I managed always to have a case of whiskey about. Drinking water was hard to get clean. We had to go to the head of Adams' Gulch for it, and even then it was mixed with moss and little pieces of wood. So we always hung a small strainer up alongside the dipper and water bucket.
>
> Quite a party came one morning—Captain Norwood and big Government officials, Colonel Domville, Warren Wilkinson, a New York newspaper man, Joaquin Miller, and a mining engineer from the Government. (NW 17:4–5 [120–21])

Joaquin Miller was a writer and performer who came to the Klondike as a correspondent for the *San Francisco Chronicle*. *New York Times* correspondent

E. LeRoy Pelletier cited Miller as "the most prominent of those whose exaggerations and imaginary statements inspire . . . wonderment."[27] John Muir described him thus:

> He may be a great poet and is, but he is utterly unfit for a job like that, and the editors know it. Miller's disability is this—he cannot tell the truth or distinguish between truth and falsehood. His imagination is always running away with him. The pictures flashed on the screen of his fancy are more real to him than every-day facts. He will tell tremendous stories and describe imaginary events most enchantingly, but the papers and the public want facts about the Klondike rush—statistics, data on which to build their stories. That Miller cannot and will not give.[28]

Muir's assessment of the intensity of Miller's imagination is humorously born out in Belinda's description of his visit to her camp on Cheechako Hill.

> There was only one bottle of whiskey left in the cache. I showed them the water and told them they'd better strain it. The men had a drink, all but Joaquin, who was watching himself in the glass, arranging his hair. The rest of them were admiring the scenery. The trail was just on the edge of the hill. Joaquin, looking down, saw an athletic, beautiful woman coming up, hat in hand, her hair red.
>
> Joaquin was particularly fond of his drink, but he liked a pretty woman. When he saw her he had the bottle in one hand, and he reached for the dipper but got the strainer. He was looking at the woman all the time and started to make a poem about her beautiful hair with the sun shining on it. It was impressive, that poem. . . . It was all about sunshine on her glorious auburn locks or something like that. He was in raptures, pouring, without looking, the drink into the strainer. It was running down his trousers when the men caught him. "Joaquin, you fool," they yelled at him, "that's the last drink." Joaquin looked at the drink dribbling down him and he looked at the woman. "Damn her red hair," he said. (NW 14:5[121])

Of course Belinda's main objective for going to the creeks in the winter of 1898–99 was to mine. Even within the short time she had been in the Klondike, she had seen great changes in techniques. Prior to the Klondike strike the earliest mining in the Yukon had been of gravel and sand bars in and around the streams. A single person could prospect and excavate the bars with only a shovel and a pan. If the placer gold was buried but near the surface, it could be reached by first stripping off the overlying soil as it was melted by the summer sun or running water. One or two people could manage it.

14.5. Several miners use steam points to thaw ground in an adit of a hillside mine, this one on the fourth tier of Gold Hill. Steam is generated by a boiler outside the mine and distributed by pipes and hoses to an array of sharpened, hollow rods. The top of one of these is being maneuvered at left. The points are driven into the frozen ground. When defrosted, the ground is shoveled into buckets or tram cars. Note the cramped space and that candles are still the source of light in this mine. (UW, Hegg photog., 776)

But in the Klondike, gold was often ten to thirty feet below the surface and required the labor-intensive method described in chapter 8—burning through permafrost to dig vertical shafts and then horizontal tunnels (drifts or adits) in search of the deposits. This kind of mining was most efficient with at least two people—one digging in the hole and one hoisting and dumping the dirt. And at least one other person could be fully occupied getting the wood needed to fuel the defrosting fires, to timber the excavations, and to build flumes to carry water and sluice boxes to wash gold-bearing soil.

But soon mining in the Klondike became so concentrated that larger operations made sense. With the high density of mining, there was intense competition for resources. And with the influx of stampeders in 1897 and 1898, the only resource not in short supply was men. Consequently it became more common to see greater numbers of people working a claim either on payroll or on lay. A

14.6. A closer look at one of the tiers on Cheechako/Adams Hill. Tram cars move dirt from the mine adit (out of view to the left) to the dump at the rim of the tier. A wooden drum for winding cable is partially shown at left. Note the signs of domestic activity as well, such as the wash hanging out to dry. Piles of lumber and wood are stored at the ready on the hillside above the tier. *(UW, Larss and Duclos photog., 66)*

lay agreement was a kind of lease: a miner was given exclusive access to some ground for a specified amount of time, agreeing to split whatever gold he found with the owner, usually 50–50, and paying any expenses out of his portion.

There were also new ideas about how to make operations more efficient. Steam engines were introduced to run hoists, conveyor belts, and pumps, and to generate electricity. Then someone realized that the steam also could be used to thaw the ground by injecting it through pointed pipes driven into the permafrost.[29] This yielded more controlled and efficient melting, reducing the amount of wood required for thawing as well as for timbering. After coal deposits were found near the Klondike, the boilers could be fueled with coal and the need for wood was reduced further.

For the hillside mining such as Belinda was doing, obtaining sufficient water was even more of a problem than on creek claims. It had to be pumped up to the workings, or the gold-laden dirt had to be taken down to the creeks for processing. Belinda, having seen tram cars used by her father in coal mining in Pennsylvania, tried various adaptations of them in 1898–99 to haul pay dirt through long adits and down to the water.

French Hill[30] was the first mine I worked summer and winter, where we could get water. We could melt snow in barrels under a log shelter. It was my own first actual mining of placer dirt. Also it was the first mining done with a tram in all Alaska. We made a tunnel clear through the hill working back to the mouth, used cars running them down low enough to pick up water. We thawed the dirt by steam with the first upright boiler, driving the tunnel 1200 feet clear through the mountain. It wasn't hard after we got the steam points. It was just fun. In removing dirt into the cars, we'd just shovel it in, load one car, take up another.

The carpenter built a big drum for the cable. We had wooden rails with sheet iron, cut in little strips and put on the rails to save them. The wheels we found somewhere and had perfectly good cars when we got through. I saw the idea worked in coal mining in [the Scranton, Pennsylvania, area] when I was a kid.

The carpenter had some knowledge of plumbing, so we got the boiler from a little saw mill. The original ones had smaller boilers. I thought we could improve on the little tin cans they'd been using. Skipper, myself, and Larson [used this method of tunneling] on Adams [Cheechako] Hill. . . . It was economical, and I acquired the reputation of being a brilliant miner on account of it.

In the winter of 1898 I spent most of the time on Cheechako Hill. I got a lot of money out of that mine, worked it continuously '98, '99, 1900, '01, '03. The discovery claim and the adjacent ones were 1200 feet. I took out $150,000 a year (gross).[31]

Belinda enjoyed mining and spent a good part of her time doing it. But she also was aware of whispers and even resentment stirred by her activity. More than one man voiced complaints about her. Pierre Berton reports that one sourdough, C. W. Hamilton, recalled her as a holy terror: "The morally severe Belinda would allow no smoking on the job. Hamilton tried to break this edict, but before he had a match lit Belinda gave a low whistle, crooked her finger, and said sharply: 'Get off this claim before nightfall.' Hamilton obeyed" (426).

Here is another example, this from the Englishman Neville Armstrong.

As her name implies, Miss Mulrooney was Irish—distinctly so—short, dark, angular, masculine, could swear like a trooper on occasion and was, generally speaking, "hard boiled." . . . Belinda owned a fraction of a bench claim on Cheechako Hill, close to our ground. She came up and took charge of it herself and could be seen standing about in a short skirt[32] and knee-boots, direct-ing operations and swearing at her employees. I don't think she made much out of her holding. (49–50)

There is no doubt that feminine charm had little to do with running a mining operation successfully. Belinda's toughness was well known by her colleagues. A story passed on from a miner who was a contemporary of Belinda's to his son shows Belinda's hardness in action as well as crudeness in language.

> Belinda went to one of her mines and was standing on the bank watching the men work. When one of the men came out of the bushes, she asked him where he had been and what he was doing. He replied, "A man has to relieve himself once in a while." Her response was, "You have been there long enough to jerk off. Get your pay and get out of here."[33]

In a somewhat muddled report in which Belinda's name is reported as "Kate," a disgruntled miner analyzes Belinda and tries to imagine what a husband might see in her.

> Kate, with the continued growth of her holdings, became a rather hard taskmaster to those she employed. Henry F. Woods recalled working for her as a miner at the Cheechako Hill claim and being paid $1 a day. Even at that in-significant pay scale, Woods was fired by the now imperious Kate because the shovel he was using was too small, in her opinion. [Her husband], Woods said, "has always had my sympathy for I am certain that if, indeed, he was a drone, Kate took it out of his hide."[34]

Belinda was not deterred by the feelings against her, though she did take them into account. To a newspaper reporter she confessed, "I like mining. I only hired a foreman because it looks better to have it said that a man is running the mine, but the truth is that I look after the management myself."[35]

While Belinda could be as tough as she needed to be in running her mining operations, it was out on her claims, away from the social whirl of Dawson and after a hard day of mining, that Belinda also had time to feel lonely.

> I had friends and partners, was running two hotels, but I was [an] unmar-ried woman, still Miss Mulrooney to everyone, and I hate to admit it, must have been lonesome when I was alone in my cabin after work was over on the claim.
> One day in my cabin when I opened a box of provisions from the Outside, I found in it a mouse! He was as fat as could be as there'd been plenty in the gro-cery box for him to eat, but his tail was cut off. It must have been lost when it

had been caught in a crack of the packing box somewhere. The only thing I hadn't liked about mice was their long tails. I guess I remembered the long tail of that rat in Chicago, but this mouse was trimmed to suit my fancy.

I kept this mouse in my cabin and made a little box for him, putting it against the side of the wall so he could go behind it and feel protected. For his nest I use the stuff they have for packing. The whole thing was his own little house, and before long he was the boss of the cabin.

On this account I ordered my meals to be brought there, although the cook didn't like it very well and didn't know the sudden change in my habits was because I wanted to feed my mouse and get him to eat like a gentleman. I finally tamed him so he would come out of his house and eat, not from my hand, but he would come right up on the table. He'd keep going around in circles, his eyes on me all the time, while he was eating his little food. We got to be good friends, and he was lots of fun.

. . . Now if Maiden didn't get a certain amount of attention, he'd get to whimpering about it being time for him to go prospecting. "I guess you don't need me any more," he'd say. Then I'd have to tell him I wouldn't feel protected unless I had him and his old gun Betsy around. He'd had Betsy ever since he was a boy, I suppose. And I knew if it ever did go off it would probably make a noise like a cannon. So Maiden was pleased when I told him I had to leave for Dawson for a few days, and that he'd have to live in my cabin and look after the gold dust there until I got back. But I forgot in my instructions to tell him about my friend the mouse.

When I returned from Dawson I asked him how everything was at the mine and the cabin. I told him I hadn't worried, everything must have been alright if he'd been there.

"Yes," Maiden bragged. "Everything was alright. I slept on the cabin floor. I guarded the gold dust. . . . But the first night you were gone I had to just take out my Betsy and shoot a gol darn mouse. I got rid of him for you."

"Good Lord, Maiden!" I was almost crying. "You didn't kill my pet?"

Maiden was so sorry. "Don't feel too bad. I'll get you another one." But we both knew there wasn't another one this side of Seattle. (NW 38:1–3[209–11])

15

Spring 1899, and Carbonneau A-Courting

BESIDES TWINGES OF LONELINESS, thoughts about marriage had also begun to prod twenty-seven-year-old Belinda (NW 45:1[233]). Having a family rather than marriage *per se* seems to have been what Belinda really wanted, so if she hoped to have children, getting started sooner rather than later was probably a good idea.

Sweetening the prospect of marriage for Belinda was the good example of her friends F. C. and Edith Wade. After being appointed Registrar of Lands in August of 1897, Frederick Coate Wade had managed to get to Dawson by dogsled in February of 1898,[1] assuming the role of Ottawa's man-on-the-spot in Dawson. He apparently was on good terms with Minister of the Interior Clifford Sifton, for his correspondence with Sifton reporting on conditions in the Yukon and its officers was often critical and far exceeded his official capacity. By the time Major James Morrow Walsh, the new Chief Executive Officer of the (then nonexistent) Yukon Territory, finally got to Dawson in May of 1898, the government in Ottawa was already reorganizing the Yukon.

On 27 May 1898 the Yukon was made a separate territory with a full complement of appointed officials. With the new appointments, Wade first became

15.1. Yukon officials soon after the final contingent arrived, in about June 1898. They are in a tent on the hill at the north end of Dawson. The waterfront is in the background at left. (*L. to r.:*) Captain H. A. Bliss, accountant; Dufferin Pattullo, secretary to CEO Walsh; Major James Morrow Walsh, chief executive officer of the Yukon; Registrar of Lands Frederick C. Wade; Mining Inspectors James D. McGregor and Captain Henry H. Norwood. (*Dawson City Museum, B. Carbonneau Collection, 984R.153.1*)

legal adviser to the Executive Council, a post he held until October 1898. By February 1899, he was appointed Crown Prosecutor.[2]

Very early on F. C. and Belinda had become business partners. For example, Belinda said they owned coal mines together near Five Fingers rapids on the Yukon River (NW 58:2[300]). Wade was also Belinda's legal adviser. When Edith Wade joined her husband in Dawson, she and Belinda became friends too.

> Mrs. Wade was a wonderful woman, and just to look at the Wade home made you want one of your own. . . . The love and affection of children and parents were pouring out there, it seemed. In Alaska then, children were so scarce they were like a zoo or a regular work of art. It was a privilege to get to see them. Every miner wanted to give them some gift, a dog or a pet. F. C.

15.2. Frederick C. and Edith Wade in about 1900. (*Yukon Sun Special Edition, September 1900. Mayer Collection*)

would take . . . a half dozen miners to see the children when they first arrived. One look made a man want a home. The Wade home was ideal to me. (NW 45:1, 4–5[233, 242–43])

Confirming Belinda's good opinion of the Wade's relationship is a letter F. C. wrote to Edith a couple of months after his arrival in Dawson. The tone of the letter is obviously warm, considerate, and loving toward his family.[3]

To encourage Belinda's romantic thoughts in the spring of 1899, there was Charles Eugene Carbonneau, who had been patiently wooing her since they first met in the fall of 1898. Charles had been to Europe and back in the meantime, and like Belinda, was frequently traveling back and forth between Dawson and the creeks. They had often shared meals at the Fairview whenever Carbonneau was in town. They also sometimes accompanied each other on trips to their mining interests.

> I was on the trail with Carbonneau . . . in March [1899]. He'd been paying me compliments before, if he only had a chance, but at last this day he said to me, "For God's sake, stand still long enough. I want to talk to you." Riding up [to] Grand Forks we had quite a serious talk. He'd been asked to take a government position. I asked him, "Why don't you take it?"
>
> "A man loses his influence if he takes a job. I make more money as it is now. Besides, I feel as if I'd have to be a miner or a sourdough to get you interested in me, and I want to get married."

Well, I knew long before that I was interested, but I didn't see how I could get married. I couldn't think of it. His wife[4] had died five or six years before, . . . and he was anxious to have a home and wanted to make it quick. I told him I had no knowledge of a home, or of caring for a house. He told me he would never think of his wife doing house keeping. I told him, "That suits me."

I had so many partners, I had to dissolve so much before I ever thought of marrying anyone. There was my duty to be discharged to my family, which I wanted to do. Finally we decided to be married in the fall of 1900 and go abroad after that. But as for our engagement, he promised not to let anyone know it. (NW 46:5–6[243–44])

Belinda needed to dissolve her partnerships because she was still affected by the traditional disabilities placed on married women by the English Common Law's legacy in Canada. Under the common law, a married woman's property became her husband's, over which he had exclusive control (Blackstone, 16). By the middle of the nineteenth century, coverture had been modified so that a woman could hold property in her own name, but still her husband controlled it, and she could not sell it without his consent. Also, married women could be restricted in entrepreneurial powers such as the right to contract, sue, and conduct business. In the last quarter of the nineteenth century, most of the Canadian provinces were gradually adopting more egalitarian legislation.[5] However, legal interpretations would continue to be conservative, and the exact rights of an entrepreneurial married woman in the newly formed Yukon Territory were probably hard to determine.

As her attorney, F. C. Wade, may have explained to her, legally it was important to distinguish between personal and real property. Personal property consisted of money, goods, apparel, promissory notes, stocks and bonds—that is, anything movable. Real property was permanent, fixed, immovable things, such as land and buildings. Wade also may have advised that until the Yukon enacted its own ordinances, those of the Northwest Territories applied. In 1886 the Northwest Territories passed an ordinance allowing a married woman to convey her real estate on her own.[6] Unfortunately this law was repealed within two years, and in 1899 only an ordinance removing disabilities with respect to personal property was in effect.[7] Depending upon the political climate, even that might be revised again.

In any case, real property was still under the influence of a married woman's husband. Therefore, it was prudent for Belinda and her partners to dissolve any arrangements that might be compromised by her new status. Furthermore,

Belinda's partners might not have favored being so closely associated with Charles, who was not generally well liked.

Until Belinda could inform her partners personally, and so that the need for liquidation would not devalue the properties involved, it probably was best to keep the reason for her divestitures confidential. As in any small town, maintaining secrecy in Dawson would be difficult. Nevertheless, Belinda and Charles managed it for a while. They occasionally held hands at the dinner table. But when Belinda rode Charles's horse and sparked comments such as, "It's getting pretty thick. Miss Mulrooney is riding Carbonneau's thoroughbred" (NW 46:6 [244]), she immediately returned the horse to the stable.

Belinda continued with her mining and business operations. In April her water company was getting under way, so there was much to do with its organization. And then there was the usual socializing. On 7 April she hosted a dinner party at the Fairview to welcome back F. C. Wade and Captain Norwood, who had just returned with some of the other government officials over the ice, having been Outside during the winter months. Skipper Norwood told stories of their adventures and trials on the trail. A mule they were bringing In had disappeared, apparently into the stomachs of their sled dogs. Then, a few days later a great commotion was heard in the stable area of the roadhouse where they had stopped for the night. This time the men dashed to the stable soon enough to prevent the dogs from devouring their poor horse. Skipper also told of being sick, apparently with pneumonia, and how the loyalty of his friends who would not leave him behind resulted in some delay in their return to Dawson.[8]

On 9 April another traveler from the Outside, Ronald Morrison, brought news that Alex McDonald, who had gone Out the previous October, had married a woman he met in London, Margaret Chisholm.[9] Perhaps this information also influenced Belinda's acceptance of Carbonneau's proposal.

Belinda and Alex had been both rivals and friends. When Tappan Adney, the *Harper's Weekly* correspondent, wrote of the Fairview Hotel in his description of burgeoning Dawson of the summer of 1898, he thought Alex was part owner of the establishment (392). There is no evidence of this, and there is much to suggest the contrary. However, Belinda and Alex were partners in mining interests. And both were adept at business, though with very different styles. Alex seemed simply to want to acquire as many claims as possible. At first he undertook only what other enterprises were necessary to support the mining operations, though eventually he invested in several properties and businesses in

Dawson. He seemed to care little for the gold itself, was generous, and was un-comfortable in social situations.

Alex's moniker was "King of the Klondike,"[10] and if Alex were "King," then for many Belinda was its "Queen."[11] But Belinda was more sophisticated than Alex. She had more of an eye for style, an ear for conversation, and a mind for the adept strategic thinking needed in the entrepreneurial game. Although Belinda's schooling had been disrupted early, she was probably more educated and certainly more clever with figuring as well. W. D. Johns related that on Alex's trip to London, during which he was trying to sell some of his claims, he asked 25 million pounds, or nearly 125 million dollars,[12] for them, having no clear con-ception of the true value of the claims, nor of the pound with respect to the dollar. Johns also recalled that Alex did not realize his one-half interest in a claim was equivalent to a three-sixth interest (250–51).

To many, including their friends, Belinda and Alex seemed a good match. But while Belinda said they were the best of friends (NW 58:3[301]), she denied there was any romance involved. Nevertheless, years later there was gossip that when Belinda married Carbonneau, Alex sued her for breaches of trust and promise and for the return of $200,000.[13] Given that Alex married first, even before the secret engagement of Belinda and Charles, it is unlikely Alex sued Belinda over broken matrimonial promises. Nor is there official evidence of a suit over any other issue between them. Belinda and Alex, like most Old Timers, were more likely to settle disputes through direct, personal confrontation than through the courts.

By MID-APRIL, longer days and occasional warm spells signaled that spring was once again pushing ahead. All mine operators on the creeks waited eagerly for the water to start flowing so that the winter's dumps could be washed.[14] But then disaster struck Dawson.

Smoke was detected at about 7:30 P.M. on 26 April in the Bodega Saloon at 223 First Avenue (Front Street). Within minutes, a southerly wind fanned the fire to a blaze and carried it to the Northern Restaurant on the south. On the north side of the Bodega, the Tivoli Theatre caught, and its owner, George Noble, had time to haul out only three recently installed large mirrors from the smoking building before the theater was completely engulfed.[15] The Tivoli generated such intense heat that the Rutledge building on the river side of the street ignited. Volunteer firemen, who responded within minutes of the first alarm, dragged a new fire engine a half mile through the frozen accumulation of garbage in Dawson's streets to where it could pump water from the Yukon River.[16] But their efforts were frustrated when the pump failed to operate properly, and for twenty-five minutes the only source of water was the bucket brigade.

In the meantime, with the fire now raging on both sides of Front Street, it became obvious that the one little engine would not be able to keep up, even if it were working as it should. The scene was that of a dreaded nightmare.

Dark figures silhouetted by the red glare of the flames scrambled along rooftops, trying to prevent flying sparks from lighting the tinder-dry shingles of adjacent buildings. Cries of alarm went up as the next structure nevertheless burst into flame from the intense radiated heat. People climbed the sides and roofs of buildings further down the street, draping them with wet blankets in an effort to keep them from igniting. Teams of men, led by the Northwest Mounted Police, frantically tore down some structures and dynamited others, sacrificing some to prevent their fueling and spreading the flames to all the rest of the town. Residents and business owners desperately rescued what furnishings and goods they could before buildings were engulfed, while the accumulation in the streets blocked firefighting efforts. Bottles, kegs, and barrels of whiskey lay in heaps in the streets and proved too much of a temptation for some, so that more reasoned firefighting was hampered by the drunken citizen volunteers. The injured and homeless, in shock or in tears, were conducted to safer places.

> . . . We went down the line to rescue the gold dust and money in the different buildings. Everything we got of value, we put in charge of the Mounted Police boys, who were doing what they could.
>
> We got into old Bill McPhee's [Pioneer Saloon] and busted open the wooden box that looked like a safe. You remember I started that darn idea. Those safes were just a place to keep gold dust. We busted Bill's open though it was red hot.
>
> When Bill came along we called to him, "For heaven's sake, Bill, help us with the gold, to get it down to the Fairview."
>
> "To hell with the gold dust," Old Bill said. "Save my moose horns." He looked up at them as wistful as could be. They spread right across the bar and were the pride of his life.[17]

Bill McPhee was another admirer of Belinda. That their relationship was a close one is suggested by the fact that Belinda owned the horse Bill had brought In across Chilkoot Pass in 1893, an accomplishment Bill considered his proudest moment in the Yukon.[18] And he and Belinda had been on good enough terms to be business partners in a small cabin behind the Grand Forks Hotel.[19] When

15.3. The conflagration on Front Street in April 1899, viewed from the banks of the frozen Yukon River. *(UW, Cantwell photog., 57)*

Bill was going on a trip Outside in the late fall of 1898, Belinda hosted a farewell banquet in his honor at the Fairview.[20] This dinner may also have been a way of declaring a truce, for Belinda and Bill enjoyed a good deal of competition. One source says it was Bill McPhee who had convinced Joe Brooks in Skagway to take his whiskey over White Pass trail instead of Belinda's supplies (Berton, 312). Therefore, it would have been Bill's liquor that Belinda off-loaded when she took over the pack train. Consistent with this scenario is the fact that Bill came down the Yukon with a scow of goods soon after Belinda's last scow got to Dawson.[21] But in the fire, Belinda was glad to help her friend Bill McPhee if she could.

The fire continued to extend further on both sides of Front Street. At the same time, buildings in the 200 block on the west side of Second Avenue were set afire from the blaze behind them. The flames jumped Second (Queen) Street and started down the next block of Front Street. Belinda had some tense moments as the fire progressed toward the Fairview at the southwest corner of Front and First (Princess) Streets. But it seems she was so busy taking in and caring for burned and half-frozen refugees at the hotel and fortifying firefighters, she hardly had time to think about it.

> We had an enormous arrangement of copper used for coffee in the kitchen at the Fairview. It was filled with coffee that night, and I dumped into it a lot of rum or brandy or something. . . . When I took a cup myself, it nearly knocked me silly.
>
> . . . After the men who were fighting the fire tasted that coffee, they all wanted to save the Fairview. The place had caught fire a couple of times on the roof. After the coffee the men stood around all night and threw buckets of muck at the hotel where it didn't need it. We had to ask them to stop. (NW 41:3[223])

As it turned out, the progress of the fire down the east side of Front Street was stopped before it got to the corner opposite the Fairview by demolishing and removing some small buildings that had been under construction.

By 2:30 A.M. the fire was contained, but there were still hot spots to be fought. One hundred and eleven buildings in the heart of Dawson's business district had burned and another fifteen were torn down in the efforts to stop the spread of the blaze. Many of the goods and furnishings rescued from the flames were subsequently ruined in the mud and water. Almost miraculously, no one died in the conflagration, though several were injured. Losses were estimated to exceed one million dollars.[22]

As dawn broke the next day, a strange sight was seen amidst the smoldering ruins—men, blackened from head to toe, crouched with pans in hand to wash gold from the ashes. And the exhausted residents of Dawson began to mend their lives and their town.

> For a few days after [the fire], we served meals in the Fairview from a long table in front of the kitchen stove. People just took food up in their hands.
>
> . . . The hotel was crowded. . . . After a few hours of sleeping, someone else would turn you out and take your place in bed. In my office and my room, all you could see was bare feet sticking out. The place was lined with mattresses. (NW 41:4[224])

An investigation into the cause of the fire produced a reprise of the "good women vs. bad women" debate. The blaze had started in the room of Helen Holden on the second story of the Bodega Saloon. Holden was identified at that time as a dance hall woman, but people in Dawson knew her in other contexts as well. The previous fall she had opened the Opera House Hotel. She had gained less favorable public notice when she faked an attempt at suicide in early 1899.[23] Holden, who was out of her room when smoke was first detected, was suspected of having been careless with the fire in her stove, or of having left a lamp or a cigarette burning. However, after carefully questioning witnesses, the inquest jury was unable to identify the cause of the fire. Nevertheless, the jury of six men saw an opportunity to reinforce an earlier decision to eliminate from the business area those considered undesirables by morality monitors.

A couple of weeks earlier, government authorities, yielding to "the demands of progress," had notified occupants of Dawson's "tenderloin" area on Second Avenue that they would have to move from the central business district by 1 May. The *Nugget* estimated the number of "women in scarlet" affected as three hundred,[24] though it is not clear whether all of these were actually prostitutes. In fact, others have estimated that the number of prostitutes in Dawson was less than half that.[25]

The jury investigating the fire used it as an excuse to further the growing social conservatism: "It is recommended that all women of the town be excluded from public buildings other than licensed hotels."[26] By the phrase "all women of the town" the jury meant only the prostitutes or those suspected of prostitution. But the ambiguous phrase hints at the tension of the controversy.

In this context, it is understandable why Belinda took such pains to maintain respectability. But Belinda's later account of her response to the fire's female victims makes clear that, at least by 1928, when she told the story of the fire, she felt that her own reputation was unassailable. And she would not be bullied by the innuendo.

> Now the poor dance hall women all had their cabins back of Second Street, the first cabins I had built back of the saloons, and of course they caught fire right away. That set the women to running in every direction, looking crazy in their light pink silk underclothes, some in bare feet, some in slippers with not enough clothes on to wad a shotgun. "Boys," I said, "I think we've got a new job—rescuing those women."
>
> So we lined the girls up and dragged them off the snow as fast as we could. We'd stop and take the coats off any man we passed, and wrapped them around the poor freezing women. Then we carried them to the Fairview Hotel dining room and put them on the tables. [Louis F.] Cooke, the manager, was crazy. "What the hell . . . are we going to do with that bunch?" [he asked me].
>
> "This is where they stay, Cooke," I told him. "I'll be boss of this hotel tonight anyway."

Dr. Simpson[27] took charge and got all the other doctors he could to help. You couldn't tell a doctor from a wood chopper that night. The women's feet were frozen, and I think they were a little crazy by the way they were screaming and yelling. There were fifty of them, their cabins burned, they'd lost everything. That night we got mattresses and bedding for them.

. . . All the attention and luxury there was around the place was given these girls. God knows they needed it. Poor things.

. . . The Mounted Police [later] relieved the Fairview by putting the dance hall girls in barracks. (NW 41:2–4[222–24])

Despite censure from some Dawsonites, Belinda defended the dance hall girls. She stoutly denied that there was any problem.

Did the fire reform the dance hall girls? To tell you God's truth, many were reformed before coming in. Many who got caught in the mess in the trail changed their names, and when they got to Dawson started to swing men around in the dance hall. Some never took a drink. Maybe you don't know it, but some of the best women in the Northwest today have been in those Klondike dance halls. (NW 41:2–4[224–25])

By her own account Belinda was not particularly sophisticated when it came to the affairs between women and men. She told of an incident in the summer of 1898 when she had been trying to assure good care for the child of a miner who drank too much and whose wife had died. She thought she could easily convince him to sell a claim to support the child.

"He can't object to taking care of his own child," I said.

Esther [Duffie] suggested, "Suppose it isn't his own child."

"Then why didn't [his wife] tell me something about her first husband's people and get them to help invest in [the child]?" I was provoked.

Esther smiled a bit. Wade said, "There may not have been a husband."

I couldn't sabe that. "There's got to be a husband, and he had to die before she could marry again."

You see, I never bothered with such things. My Grandmother had told me that God sent children to married people for them to take care of, and that was all. . . .

"Where did you come from?" Wade asked.

"Ireland," I told him.

"That explains it," he said.

I got hopping mad. "You think we don't know about such things in Ireland?"

Esther let one big howl out of her. Wade laughed just as loud. I walked around from the table, ready to quit them, I was so furious. (NW 31:2–3[177–78])

AFTER THE FIRE, there was even more to be done in Dawson. Almost immediately, people began to rebuild the town, this time imposing some of the order and improvements that had been wanting earlier, such as wooden sidewalks and restrictions on buildings on the waterfront. An editorial in the *Klondike Nugget* remarked on the resilience of Dawsonites. Though the newspaper refers only to men, women, of course, were also of the tough pioneer stock.

That the people of the Yukon are the picked men of the continent for fortitude and indomitable energy and pluck was never so well exemplified as on Thursday morning on the site of the four burned blocks. Smoldering ruins on every hand, without a dollar of insurance, the smoking ashes representing in many cases the accumulations of years, and on every hand the cheery sound of the hammer and saw, and new white lumber gradually taking away the everlasting blackness of the scene.

. . . The fact is that Dawson is peopled with the six thousand people who alone of a half million . . . who left their homes in the states or provinces, overcame a thousand and one reverses and obstacles, overcame shipwrecks and disaster, scaled the passes, shot the rapids, and in spite of everything succeeded in reaching the point of destination at last. Such men are simply unconquerable and unconquered, and the sudden loss of a year's or ten years' work is but something to be forgotten as quickly as possible and a new start made.[28]

The Fairview was undamaged, but Belinda probably helped her friends, such as Bill McPhee, who had lost so much. A couple of weeks after the fire, Bill and Belinda announced a consolidation of telephone companies, possibly in connection with repairing the poles and lines consumed by the fire. Bill McPhee became president of the new company, Belinda became vice president, and N. A. Fuller[29] served as general manager, secretary, and treasurer. Belinda's Yukon Telegraph and Telephone Syndicate, founded in late 1897, was one of the principal contributors to the new organization, which now would be able to furnish service not only to Dawson, but also to Klondike City (or Lousetown), Bonanza and Eldorado Creeks, Grand Forks, the Dome which formed the headwaters of many of the gold-bearing creeks of the region, and Sulphur and Dominion Creeks.[30] (See map, fig. 7.3.)

As part of the general rebuilding of Dawson's business district and possibly because she was thinking about selling the hotel, Belinda planted some young evergreen trees around the Fairview. She also decided to put a second-story porch on the street sides of the hotel, this, she declared, so that her guests could see the river break up to the best advantage and without getting their feet wet.

15.4. A young woman washes a pan of enriched gravel from the sluice box of 7 A/D Bonanza while four men look on. This view shows in the background how the town of Grand Forks was laid out on the claim. The Grand Forks Hotel is the large, two-story building partly obscured by the man at the left. *(ASL, Wickersham Collection, PCA 277-1-134)*

On a more utilitarian front, she had a canal dug to drain into the Yukon the pool of water that had accumulated at the back of her hotel. Belinda was not able to arrange a satisfactory sale at this time, so she leased the Fairview to Fred Kammueler for three years at $1,200 per month.[31]

Belinda was beginning to put her business affairs in better order in preparation for her eventual marriage to Carbonneau. One goal, of course, was to minimize her partnerships held with so many other men. But there were other complications looming at the time.

At Grand Forks, the town along with Belinda's hotel was situated on parts of claims 6, 7, and 8 above discovery, Bonanza Creek. A survey on 31 May 1899 by the Crown Timber and Land Office identified the existing townsite with respect to the boundaries of these claims. A list of the locators and present owners of the claims was prepared. Belinda was not on the list because, of course, she did not own the claim on which her hotel was built.

The survey was completed under the direction of the Crown Timber and Land Agent, F. X. Gosselin, who had arrived in Dawson in January 1899,[32] and who was one of the three French officials with whom Belinda said Charles had a good deal of influence (NW 46:1[239]). Therefore, it is likely that Belinda, through Charles, had advance warning that there might be entanglements once the survey was completed. Charles's alerting Belinda would have served his own self-interest as well as Belinda's, for according to an unregistered agreement, dated 15 March 1899, Belinda and Charles had become equal partners as hotel keepers and general traders at Grand Forks. The agreement specified the following:

> B. A. M. brings into the partnership a property situated at the said forks of Bonanza and Eldorado Creeks known as the Grand Forks Hotel, together with the License already granted for the said premises, fixtures, furniture, ustensil [sic] [and] as everything now stand.
>
> C. E. C. brings into the partnership a property now being erected as an annex to the said property known as the Grand Forks Hotel, being understood that the said C. E. C. will pay all bills for the construction of said annex building excepting the Bar Equipment.
>
> An inventory will be taken of the present stock of provisions and liquors and the said C. E. C. agrees to pay the cost of the half of said inventory to the said B. A. M.[33]

Although Charles's contribution seems less substantial than Belinda's, there is no indication in the agreement that Belinda received any money. It could be that no money did change hands. Or it may be simply that the agreement concerned the operation of the partnership rather than the deal that set it up.

From property records we see that by 3 May Belinda, who was still the only officially listed owner, had arranged to sell Grand Forks Hotel, for on that date she transferred ownership to Anton F. Stander[34] and his wife, Violet Raymond.

Anton Stander was one of the original locators on Eldorado, claiming No. 6. He traded Clarence Berry half of No. 6 Eldorado for supplies and half of No. 40 above discovery on Bonanza, which at that time was supposed to be of little value. Later Berry and Stander bought controlling interests in Nos. 4 and 5 Eldorado as well. All of these claims proved very valuable. Violet Raymond was an actress and vaudeville performer who with her sister Maud came to Dawson

15.5. Violet Raymond and her husband Anton F. Stander in front of their cabin on Number 3 Eldorado. The logs are chinked with moss, dirt covers the roof for insulation, and glass windows capture precious light on the sunny side. What little we can see of the interior seems to be well finished and nicely furnished. Note that the cabins are located in the midst of the mining operations. *(Yukon Archives, Gillis Collection, 4470)*

from Juneau in 1897 with a troupe accompanying the impresario Max Endelman.[35] Before her marriage to Anton Stander, Violet had lent him twenty thousand dollars, taking a mortgage on the upper half of 40 A/D Bonanza as security.[36]

For the Grand Forks Hotel the Standers paid Belinda with cash and their one-half interest in 40 A/D Bonanza. Apparently in acknowledgment of Charles's interest in the hotel, his name appeared with Belinda's on the deed to the claim.[37] Whether he also received part of the cash is not known. Belinda recalled getting about forty to fifty thousand dollars for the hotel and surrounding property, including cabins, a butcher shop, and freighting business.[38] After the sale of the Grand Forks Hotel, it was remodeled and expanded. Its name was changed to the New Gold or Gold Hill Hotel. It reopened on 18 May with William Emerson, Bert Schuler, and Max Endelman as proprietors, Endelman apparently having bought it from the Standers.[39]

Since mining claims carried rights only for the material under the surface of the ground, Max Endelman proceeded to obtain grants from the Crown for the Grand Forks townsite. But the government granted the surface rights only on the condition that Endelman agreed to sell lots with existing buildings to the owners for designated prices. That is, Endelman's surface rights did not include improvements, and any lot with existing buildings would have to be offered to the building owner at a fixed price. Therefore, Endelman did not have automatic rights to the Grand Forks Hotel. He would have to "sell" the land to the owner at the official price or purchase the building at whatever price was agreed upon. In buying it from the Standers he may not have had to pay as much as the Standers had paid Belinda for it. Since Endelman and the Standers were friends, however, the complicated transactions may have turned out to everyone's satisfaction.

Charles was also at this time acquiring another mining claim in his own name. This one was on a tributary of Dominion Creek, on the south side of the Dome, south of Grand Forks. (See map, fig. 7.3.) The new creek was called Gold Run, and although claims had been filed on it since March of 1898, none were heavily mined as yet. Charles bought the lower half of No. 12 Gold Run for $1,200 on 9 May.[40]

The first week of June 1899 was a hectic one for Belinda and Charles, as he was preparing to go Outside. The upper half of No. 40 A/D Bonanza, which they had acquired from the Standers, adjoined claim 41 A/D, already held by the Anglo-French Klondike Syndicate, C. E. Carbonneau, manager. Charles and Belinda now began a series of transactions shuffling money and title to their new fraction. On 7 June Belinda transferred her half of the half claim to Charles. This apparently was to cover the sale Charles had made the previous day of the entire upper half to E. Servais, that sale not being recorded until over a month later. Later that summer, Servais would sell the fraction back to Carbonneau.[41] What was behind these transactions is not clear.

The following day, 8 June, continued at the high-energy pace. Between the business dealings, Charles was called into court to answer a charge by Alex Milner of assault. Milner was one of the employees working on Eldorado 3A. Testimony showed that Charles had taken Milner by the shoulders and ejected him from the Fairview Hotel. Perhaps this was a show of gallantry for Belinda's benefit. In any case, the presiding judge apparently decided Carbonneau's actions were justified, even in orderly Dawson, for the complaint was dismissed.[42]

On this same day, as manager of the Anglo-French Klondike syndicate,

Charles mortgaged both 41 A/D Bonanza and 3A Eldorado. Among the mortgage holders on the two claims was Belinda, who was down for $10,026.86, with first and second mortgages to two other lenders for $5,050 and $2,834.04.[43] The interest rate for the loans past the maturity date was to be 24 percent per annum, and repayment was due on 2 October, by which time the cleanup should be over. While the interest rate may seem high now, it was not necessarily so in Dawson. The previous year, for example, the interest for loans, even with "gilt edge security," was 10 percent per month.[44] The Toronto *Globe* correspondent in Dawson reported on 14 January 1899, "Money is remarkably tight, and ten per cent per month is quite a common rate of interest, as high as 15 per cent being freely offered."[45] By June the pressure for funds had eased somewhat. As claims were sluiced and more regular communication with the Outside was reestablished, money became more readily available. Consequently interest rates decreased.

These mortgages are an interesting turn of events. It is surprising that Charles needed to borrow money, for certainly Eldorado 3A was rich, and by June, when sluicing is typically at its peak, plenty of gold should have been recovered.[46] We can take Charles's actions on face value: Assume he needed some cash; therefore, he set up a favorable, though not out-of-the-ordinary, business arrangement with his wife-to-be in order to get the money. But knowing as we do that he eventually would be called to account for a series of alleged fraudulent promotions, it seems reasonable to ask what Charles, if he were a con artist, had to gain from the transactions besides some ready cash. First, as Belinda's eventual husband, whatever Belinda gained would also become his. And then, he also could have been working at least two long-term confidence games—an investment scam with the Anglo-French Klondyke Syndicate, and the romance and marriage con with Belinda.[47]

The investment scam is often hard to distinguish from a speculative though legitimate business. Charles's role in either case would be the same—he was both the promoter and the manager of the company. Legitimately, as promoter he would convince other people to invest in the business. As manager he could then use the money not only to buy and operate claims, but also to pay his own expenses along with a salary. For a confidence game, it is most convenient if the manager's operations are far away and inaccessible to close scrutiny by investors. Then who can say whether the expenses and salary are overly-generous given the conditions in the country? If the manager borrows money on the company property, he stands to gain in two other ways: he has the immediate benefit of the ready cash; and if the mortgage is not repaid, the possibility of gaining private control over the now-proven property through a back-door deal with the mortgage holder.

According to one source, Charles Carbonneau was operating a scam, and he took advantage of the April fire in Dawson to help pull it off.

> . . . Carbonneau's power of attorney specifically and absolutely prohibited him from granting . . . a mortgage or in any other way encumbering the company's title to the claims, and this would, to the ordinary individual, no doubt, have presented an insuperable difficulty to carrying through his scheme. Here accident, however, came to his aid, and his power of attorney was burned while in the custody of the bank, during the fire which occurred in Dawson in the spring of 1899. This cleared the way for Carbonneau, who thereupon proceeded upon his scheme by swearing an affidavit that his power of attorney gave him power to grant such a mortgage, which he thereupon granted.[48]

If Charles was working a scam, he was careful enough not to make it too obvious, for Belinda's mortgage was the third in precedence, although it was the largest.

The typical mark or victim for a romance and marriage con is a well-to-do but lonely woman. Belinda obviously fit these characteristics. By June she had already agreed to marry Charles, but her feelings were ambivalent. As a con artist, Charles would recognize this and would attempt to weave Belinda's ties to him more tightly, but only gradually. If the mark can be induced to take small steps at first, the larger leaps of faith eventually will follow. If played right, the mark will provide her own rationale to reduce any dissonance between her actions and what her own conscience, common sense, or friends might advise.

In this context, taking Charles into partnership in the Grand Forks Hotel and subsequently in the upper half of Bonanza 40 A/D can be seen as Belinda's first step down the garden path. The risk did not seem that great to her, and the payoff for Belinda was to have Charles help her make a good sale while getting out of a business that was potentially legally encumbered. The mortgage on the Anglo-French Klondyke Syndicate claims might be seen as the next step. To Belinda the loans must have looked like a good business bet, even though her mortgage was the largest and even though it was behind two others in priority. The claims were obviously valuable, and the interest was good.

As it turned out, the loans were not repaid and both claims were tied up in foreclosure proceedings the following year.[49] These events eventually led to Charles's and Belinda's recovering the claims in their own names after their marriage. They also led to bankruptcy for the Anglo-French Klondyke Syndicate, Ltd.[50] It is not clear whether Belinda in June of 1899 realized that Charles might be involving her in an investment scam. In any case, by borrowing money from her and perhaps implicating her in fraud, Charles also could have been furthering his marriage scheme. Belinda had taken another step toward binding herself more closely to Charles.

For his final actions in Dawson in June 1899, Charles put Edmund Letourneau in charge as manager of the Anglo-French Klondyke Syndicate claims (NW 46:6[244]), and had at least $18,819 in gold taken out of the Eldorado 3A sluice boxes.[51] Charles then got ready to leave Dawson on the steamer *Victorian*, headed for Ottawa, where he hoped to arrange for some concessions from the government.[52]

> There was quite a party. . . . H. T. "Chief" Wills[53] . . . was going out on bank business. I went to the boat to forward some money to my family Outside and incidentally to say good-bye to Mr. Carbonneau. Half the town was down at the steamboat as usual, and that man, like a Frenchman—Carbonneau—grabbed me and kissed me good-bye before them all.
>
> I was stunned, gasping. It was a good thing the boat was ready to pull out. I was never so embarrassed in my life. (NW 46:7–47:1(248–49)

Charles had left his mark.

16

The Klondike Rush Is Over

Belinda would have the whole summer to sort out her feelings about Carbonneau's impulsive display, for Charles was not expected back until early fall. In the meantime, she was left to deal with the more immediate repercussions of the revelation of her relationship with Carbonneau. Reactions from her friends were mixed.

> Wade was there [at the boat] with a damn fool grin as wide as his ears. Chief Wills was grinning. Joe Barrette said, "By gar, that's alright with me." Joe liked Carbonneau.[1] "Fine! Carbonneau by gosh, is a fine fellow."
>
> As we walked back from the boat, I didn't give Wade any chance for questions. "We're engaged to be married," I told him.
>
> Wade said, "That's alright, but I wish it was Alex." (NW 7:1[249])

Belinda was having her own doubts about her decision.

> By the way, I was mad at Carbonneau. I was not sure it was ever going to happen. If I hadn't explained to him so thoroughly why we had to keep our engagement a secret! I had so many mining interests with so many people. We'd had lots of rows about that.
>
> . . . But Wade in my office was saying, "He seems a nice fellow, but he is a

16.1. Belinda Mulrooney in a studio portrait taken about 1899. She wears a tailored dress, offset with a nugget-studded belt and a jeweled pin at the collar.
(UCB, Hawkins Collection, 77/81)

man of the world. There isn't much in common between you. You are North and he is Europe."

" . . . F. C., don't get alarmed or worried. It may never happen, and if it does, it won't happen soon. . . . I'm sorry he did what he did at the boat. It will disturb the peace of mind of my partners."

Wade said, "I think that's what he did it for. At any rate, as your lawyer I'll find out just exactly what he stands for. He is pretty well known by the three Frenchmen here. But I'm going farther to Ottawa and Montreal. You will not marry for a year anyway." (47:2–3[250–51])

Wade's concern perhaps arose partly from the fuss over Carbonneau's use of the title "Count." Justice C. A. Dugas had met Carbonneau in Montreal in 1898 when he was applying for a saloon license. Encountering Carbonneau again in Dawson, Dugas revealed that Carbonneau was not a French count, but a French-Canadian.[2] Others in camp reported that he had been a barber on Rue St. Denis in Montreal,[3] and the French consul in Vancouver emphatically repudiated Charles's right to call himself "Count."[4] In Dawson the *Klondike Nugget* expressed the opinion that he should stop using the phony title: "It is just as well that the title of Count be dropped from C. E. Carbonneau's name. Mr. Carbonneau is a French-Canadian of Montreal antecedents, and should himself have stopped the use of the title."[5]

Wade also may have worried for Belinda because of his greater familiarity with the vicissitudes of questionable business practices. Himself a controversial figure in Dawson, by most accounts F. C. Wade was proficient in exploiting political influence. For example, an early Presbyterian missionary, Reverend S. Hall Young, accused Wade of graft in his assessments as land commissioner and said Wade was recalled from that job after only four months because of flagrant dishonesty. Young also reported Wade as saying, "I don't mind a thing like that, for I have cleared four hundred thousand dollars in the time I have been here" (371). A confidential letter from F. C. to his wife Edith,[6] written a couple of months after he arrived in Dawson, certainly suggests he was doing well for himself, though it isn't clear he was actually doing anything illegal. He catalogued a number of mines, town properties, and franchises in which he held interests. He also listed an additional $27,000 in yearly retainers he received for his private legal work, with more expected. When Wade was later appointed Crown Attorney, both Young and Tappan Adney accused him of carrying out controversial practices in that office as well.[7] However, Wade had higher political aspirations.[8] He could not afford to be too outrageous. And in fact, after an official investigation of the charges brought against him, he was cleared of any wrongdoing.[9]

As a lawyer, Wade had seen many examples of unscrupulous business practices. Perhaps he suspected that Charles was not all that he claimed to be. Perhaps Wade also suspected from "man-to-man" conversations with Charles that he was not likely to be a reliable husband for Belinda.

What neither Belinda nor F. C. knew at that time was how Charles was revealing himself on his way Outside. In Vancouver, with money in his pocket and perhaps thinking that Belinda was in the bag as well, he felt like celebrating. After a night of revelry, the local newspaper noted, "the rich and titled Frenchman, whose prodigious spending proclivities, likewise his convivial habits are well known," reported in the morning that his $3,300 was missing, as was the woman he had spent the night with, May Evans.[10] When May was arrested without protest the next day, she admitted to having taken only $650, and the evidence seemed to substantiate her claim. By that time, the editor of the *Province* was taking a dim view of the carrying on.

The case of "Count" Carbonneau which has been reported in the city papers lately is one which may well cause thoughtful men to wonder how far the law should go towards protecting a fool from the results of his folly. The trouble into which he fell is not particularly interesting in itself, but the legal proceedings which are even now continuing are food for fair moralizing.

According to this alleged count's own story he is a debauchee and a libertine. So far from denying this he appears rather to glory in it. The blind goddess of Fortune appears to have been kind to him for he has certainly traveled about with more money than he should be permitted to have, but when the inexorable rule of fate decreed that a young person of the "count's" own class should relieve him of a portion of his wealth, the law must needs step in and protect him.

Stealing is stealing under all circumstances and it is not for a moment to be understood that there is by this comment any wish to palliate the offense of the woman who stole or of the men who possibly assisted her, but it does seem odd that the affairs of such a person as this fake count should be allowed to take up public attention for even a small space of time. If the charges against the accused persons are proved, due punishment will unquestionably follow, but despite existing laws the average good citizen will say that any man with $3,500 in his pocket who deliberately seeks the kind of society which "Count" Carbonneau enjoys is entitled to little sympathy when his money disappears.[11]

Punishment was indeed exacted from May Evans, who fainted when she learned she would be in prison for eighteen months, while her three children were left without support in Seattle. May's alleged accomplice got off. Nor was Charles prosecuted for filing a false report.[12]

Back in Dawson, unaware of the events in Vancouver, Belinda was continuing to divest herself of her partnerships. Probably Belinda's most difficult conversation about her plans to marry Charles was with Captain Norwood.

"My God!" Skipper almost jumped. "If you want a husband, why not take me?"

Skipper had held off from any talk of marrying, I found out later, because he'd married a native woman when he was on one of his first voyages North and had a daughter that was half Eskimo. She grew up to be a fine woman.

We were always scrapping. I told him, "I don't want a husband that bad." . . .

I had my doubts if it would happen. I was still angry about the boat. I could have killed that Frenchman. At that time, if I could have had him on a shore somewhere, I would have gladly pushed him in the ocean.

Skipper was saying, "Our business is badly mixed up, you know."
(NW 47:3–4[251–52])

Belinda knew it only too well. She had been fronting ownership of mining interests for Norwood, because at various times the Canadian officials were not allowed to own claims (NW 13:1–4). Eventually, when Norwood could hold claims in his own name, Belinda may have been a silent partner with him in some of these as well.

> The officials were square shooters. Lots of the property they picked up was worthless, but they picked up enough good ones to make it worthwhile. Skipper owned most of Adams Hill and sold it for an enormous amount, almost a million. He lived on his property there—had a fine cabin and entertained very well.[13]

Nevertheless, mining officials holding their own claims raised questions of conflict of interest, and there was always the possibility of graft. Norwood was not immune from such suspicions, no matter how square a shooter Belinda thought he was. In one episode that spring, Belinda may have run interference for him on a potentially shady deal involving a claim of Nellie Cashman, who was a long-time miner as well as a restaurateur.

On the surface, it might seem that Nellie and Belinda naturally would be friends. They were both independent, active women, used to looking after their own affairs. Nellie was in her fifties and, like Belinda, had immigrated to the United States from Ireland, though Nellie had arrived thirty-some years ahead of Belinda.[14] When Nellie arrived in Dawson in late spring or early June of 1898,[15] she opened a grocery store and restaurant while she acquired and managed claims on the surrounding creeks. It was at Nellie's restaurant that Belinda usually ate that summer until her own dining room was operating at the Fairview.[16] And apparently Nellie was pleased to get to know someone with Belinda's experience in mining in the Yukon.

In the fall of 1898 various complaints arose about allegedly illegal conduct of the Yukon officials, and Nellie Cashman was one of those to bring charges. She said that Captain Norwood had accepted a bribe of a quarter of her claim on Skookum Hill in order to settle a boundary dispute, and that Belinda Mulrooney had been the means for transacting the bribe. The government in Ottawa appointed a Royal Commission to investigate the charges, headed by William Ogilvie, but because of delays in communication, the inquiry did not take place until May of 1899. For a time, there was considerable confusion surrounding the investigation of Nellie's complaint. When on 9 May the Royal Commission searched for her to testify, she was reported to be out on the creeks. A summons was issued, and Nellie was then found to be sick in bed at the house of a friend. Resolutely, the commission went to her bedside to take her testimony. By this time Nellie recanted all she had charged and said she had been entirely mistaken in the matter.[17]

Nellie explained she had given a one-fourth interest in the claim to Belinda (intending it to be a bribe), but she had no knowledge that Captain Norwood ever knew of it, or that the gift profited herself except in having Miss Mulrooney as a partner. Nellie's other partners in the claim, T. H. Crowey and T. G. Cunningham, testified they had turned over an interest with the understanding it would help resolve the boundary dispute, but they had had no dealings with Captain Norwood.[18] Belinda then was given her turn to explain the strange affair. In her account, Nellie had come to her with a deed to a quarter interest, which she threw in the safe and never even recorded. As reported by the *Klondike Nugget,* "Witness never spoke to Norwood or anyone else about it, and produced the unrecorded deed from [Cashman] to show that only half of the writing was her own."[19]

It seems obvious that Belinda was tempted by the proposition, though her better judgment won out. Why Belinda would want then to keep up the pretense of bribery is not so apparent. Nellie explained she should have known better,[20] because Belinda had a tendency to play practical jokes and to make fun of her. According to Nellie, Belinda "was well capable in making transactions of that sort."[21] Furthermore, Nellie confirmed Captain Norwood's testimony that he had had nothing to do with any transfer of the property. Norwood was acquitted of any wrongdoing.[22]

THE SUMMER OF 1899 was pivotal for the Klondike. The spring cleanup had yielded another impressive mound of gold, estimated to be worth from $7.5 million to $16 million,[23] most of which would be transported out of the North and into the United States and Canada. The Dawson banks were prepared to handle it in a methodical way, melting it into bricks for more convenient shipment. Wealthy Klondikers could still be seen carrying pokes of gold dust as they headed for the outgoing steamers. But now they were just as likely to be carrying bank drafts for the major portion of their mining fortune.

Dawson itself was no longer the fast-growing, gangly adolescent of the previous two years. New buildings replaced those that burned during the winter.

16.2. A gold brick is poured in Dawson. The photo was probably taken in 1898. On-lookers include H. H. Norwood, seated second from right; F. C. Wade, standing right; and Duff Pattullo, standing third from right. *(Vancouver Public Library, 32864)*

Wooden sidewalks, more or less uniform, lined the major streets, which were now surfaced with planks and slabs of wood so the mud in the wet season was only a few inches deep instead of to the knees. Service from government offices, such as the mining recorder and postal service, was more reliable and less time-consuming. Sanitation was under tighter control, with privies more organized and water supplies better isolated from the contamination of civilization as well as of mining. In fact, the water supply situation changed so quickly that Belinda's Hygeia Water Company probably never did much business hauling water. By August two other companies were battling over providing running water to Dawson—not a trivial undertaking considering winter temperatures and the permanently frozen subsurface ground. One company had a pipeline using gravity flow to all parts of town and was supplied from a spring-fed reservoir on the hill to the east of town. The other system was supplied by a well on the banks of the Klondike River. Its pipeline ran across the flats into town, and plans called for steam heating it to prevent freezing during the winter.[24] Either of these systems to supply running water would make Belinda's hauling operation obsolete.

Dawson had become one of the major cities of the west, it seemed. And travel to and from the Klondike was getting easier every day. The railroad from Skagway to White Pass summit, in full operation since February, essentially put packing out of business on both the White Pass and Chilkoot trails. By July, the railroad was completed to Lake Bennett. The line extended to Whitehorse by the following summer, thereby eliminating the threat of Miles Canyon and White Horse rapids. Between Whitehorse and Dawson, plans were under way to remove the remaining dangerous mid-channel rocks so that steamers could ply the river safely and on regular summer schedules. Sled-stages took the place of the steamers during the winter.

Social standards were also changing as Dawson became more settled and concern grew for a family-oriented atmosphere in town. The changes were not welcomed by all, however, especially the Old Timers. Belinda recalled that "by now Society had hold of Dawson very strong. The ladies were dressing elaborately and there was a different atmosphere. The amusements had changed. Dawson was absolutely in the hands of the Outside" (NW 48:3[256]).

Even the *Nugget* commented ruefully on the social transformations in a front-page story concerning a suit for breach of promise.

> That the Klondike is rapidly taking on the airs and mannerisms of the effete East no one needs be told who is half observant, but that the stage of breaches of promise had been reached and a full-fledged suit of that order sprung upon the unsuspecting public is a fact just a trifle startling.[25]

Nevertheless, the dance halls, gambling houses, saloons, and vaudeville theater performances were still a big attraction for "the boys."[26]

Ironically, just as the Klondike seemed to be getting it all together, a "new act" was appearing on the horizon, two thousand miles downstream, near the mouth of the Yukon River. As early as November 1898, gold had been found in the sands on the north shore of Norton Sound. As in the Klondike, at first there was only a local rush. But when spring arrived and travel became feasible again, word reached the Outside of what appeared to be another fabulous strike. By 10 June,[27] when the news of Nome reached Dawson, the rush from the Outside to the new ground in Alaska was already well under way, usurping the Klondike as the preferred destination for individual gold seekers. That summer many of the Klondike's disaffected as well as those who simply wanted more excitement also left for the new goldfields.

Yet life in Dawson went on in a grand style. If there were not so many stampeders, then there were still tourists to be entertained. And of course, there was
plenty of gold left to be extracted in the Klondike region. So it was by no means
the end of the district's business and commerce. And because the social order
was becoming more defined and better organized, more elaborate events and
programs could be planned and carried out.

The first boat from the Outside for the season was the steamer *Flora,* arriving through the chunks of ice from the foot of Lake Laberge on 23 May.[28] The
Nugget reported that the banks of the Yukon were black with people cheering
the little boat that afternoon. The festive spirit continued throughout the following day, the celebration of Queen Victoria's eightieth birthday in the sixty-
second year of her reign. Feelings ran high, buoyed not only by patriotism but
also by release from the grips of winter and by word from the creeks that the
cleanup from the winter's mining was looking very rich indeed.

The Queen's birthday celebration featured a full day of athletic events. There
were races between the fire brigades; Caledonian games such as tossing the
caber and putting the shot; foot races; competitions for the Sword dance, Scot-
tish reel, and Highland fling; canoe races; a tug-of-war; climbing a greased pole;
chopping wood; and races for packers carrying varying weights. Bands played
and large crowds gathered along Front Street to cheer the contestants, standing
in the street, or seated on newly erected bleachers, or observing from the upper
windows and rooftops of buildings. The crowds were undaunted by an afternoon rainstorm, and enthusiastic hurrahs accompanied the award of cash prizes
donated by Dawson citizens and businesses. Belinda fulfilled her civic responsibility with a fifty-dollar contribution in the name of the Fairview.[29] The finale
was a ball in the evening at the Alaska Commercial Company's warehouse, last-
ing late into the night.[30]

But as Belinda noted, the ill effects of the changing social climate could be
felt that year even in the queen's birthday celebrations, for the dance at the AC
warehouse became the scene of acrimonious strife.

> The Outsiders wanted to take hold. We didn't know anything, they thought.
> We were in hall the twenty-fourth of May when a devil of a storm came on—
> two women, a Canadian . . . and an American. . . . The Canadian woman tore
> down the American flag and the American woman tore down the Canadian
> flag. There was an awful mess as the husbands took sides and everything. The
> churches were practically in the hands of the same people. It shows the state of
> mind people can get into over nothing.

16.3. Crowds line Front Street to watch the hundred-yard foot race in the Fourth of July celebration, 1899. *(UW, Hegg photog., 2345)*

Thanks to the efforts of Edith Wade and Judge Dugas's wife, tempers were soothed and a truce was declared. By the Fourth of July, people were feeling like celebrating again. To outward appearances at least the tolerance and friendly rivalry typical of the early days seemed to be restored. First Avenue was again the scene of a day of athletic contests, accompanied by parades and music and speeches.

Belinda sponsored a tug-of-war in front of the Fairview between a team of married men and a team of single men. The marrieds won and voted to give the medal to their captain, "Uncle Andy" Young, salesman for the *Klondike Nugget*. The medal was one Belinda had cast from gold and was particularly impressive.[31]

About this time prominent Klondike citizens began to organize a Klondike exhibit for the world exposition to be held in Paris in 1900. Plans were made to show gold dust and mining techniques. There was to be a glass showcase containing one cubic foot of pay dirt from each of the major creeks. Next to each sample would be displayed a pile of gold illustrating the results of washing out an adjacent cubic foot. Also to be shown were specimens of Indian crafts, agricultural products, game and fish, and timber. These exhibits were to be supplemented with photographs of the Yukon district.[32]

Even more exciting was the arrival in July of Thomas Edison's representatives to take kinetoscope pictures of the mining, transportation, and living conditions in the Klondike. Edison's crew had already re-enacted scenes of stampeders climbing the (now obsolete) Chilkoot trail, and shooting the Miles Canyon and Whitehorse rapids (as few would ever do again). They also had footage of the new railway lines and the "palatial" river steamers.[33] Their filming in and about Dawson would furnish the scenes necessary for documentation of the saga of the fabulous Klondike gold fields at the Paris exposition.

There was another important transition during the summer of 1899. Throughout the summer, work progressed on stringing a telegraph line from Skagway to Dawson. Completion of the telegraph line at the end of September[34] meant that the Klondike would no longer be isolated from communication with the rest of the world, even in the winter.

But the boom times were now over in the Klondike. The *Nugget,* despite denying the importance of the new Nome fields, was worrying about the declining population of Dawson.[35]

Belinda too was entering a new phase of her life. Her forte was entrepreneurship—being at the right place and at the right time with products and services customers needed, and catalyzing new developments. The new-growth opportunities of the Chicago World's Fair, shipping in the expanding northwest, and the Klondike boom had been ideal for her. Her talents were for quick assessment, confident decision making, marshaling resources and workers for development ahead of any competition, and then capitalizing on her investment or turning over the business to managers. By the summer of 1899, opportunities in the Klondike were of a different sort, and it seemed that Belinda was ready to make the transition. First, she was ready to think of getting married. Second, she began to concentrate more on macro-management of her various businesses than on developing new ones.

> I began to mine extensively. I had sold my smaller interests, stuff that wasn't paying. My idea was to get as much ground as possible together that had not been spoiled by primitive ways of working. The miners too were beginning to change their methods. There was more profit to mining in summer and doing the preparatory work in winter. They drove tunnels and cross [cut], got out wood for fuel for the steam engines and washed the dirt in the summer. That left them free with plenty of money to visit the states in the Fall.

I think I enjoyed mining most of anything. I felt I had conquered it, especially when experienced engineers adopted my system. I felt rather good about it.

. . . The clean-ups were enormous that year. It was about then I remember Chief Wills of the Canadian Bank of Commerce coming to me and telling me, whispering, that my credit was good at the Bank if I wanted to do any buying.

I knew what it meant to have my credit good at a store, but what could you buy at a bank? When I talked to Wade about it, "Good God," he said, "I wish Chief Wills would say that to me!" I thought a bank all right to put money in, but I didn't know you could take any out. (NW 48:1–3[254–56])

Belinda was not in the mood to be borrowing money, however. Why should she pay to use other people's money when she had plenty of income from her own claims? In the summer of 1899 these included partnerships in 57 B/D Bonanza (renumbered to 53 B/D), 47 B/D and 210 B/L/D Dominion, the Cheechako Hill claim, three bench claims on Gold Hill, a bench on No. 31 RL Eldorado, and a bench at No. 26 RL, right tier Hunker, plus a lay on 26A A/D Bonanza.[36] She also would realize a good profit from her mortgages on the Anglo-French Klondike Syndicate claims, Bonanza 41 A/D and the Eldorado fraction, 3A. These mortgages were not satisfied by their October due dates and so were returning 24 percent per annum on the investment.[37] Belinda by this time also had decided to liquidate most of her other business holdings. She had already sold the Grand Forks Hotel. Now she began looking for a buyer for the Fairview.

After a lot of deals for selling the hotel fell through, I rented the place to a man named Kamila [Fred Kammueler] at $1200 a month for three years. My own quarters and living I reserved there, including my meals when I'd be at the hotel. Later I cut the meals out as I was always having guests and didn't feel comfortable taking something for nothing. Mr. and Mrs. Cooke, who had been in charge of the hotel, left, as they'd refused the offer I made them for first chance to buy the hotel. (NW 48:2[255])

The Fairview ad listing "B. A. Mulroney, Prop. and L. F. Cooke, Mgr." appeared in every edition of the *Nugget* in the spring of 1899 through June 28. At the same time Henry Cox, formerly of the Monte Carlo Theater, became proprietor and manager of the Fairview restaurant.[38] Thus Belinda had probably relinquished control of the Fairview by mid-June 1899. With the change in management, Kitty Pilkington, the Fairview's housekeeper, decided to join the migration to the new goldfields at Nome.[39]

By the time Carbonneau returned to Dawson 27 August,[40] Belinda had arranged her affairs well enough to be ready for her own trip to the Outside.

> Walker sent his wife Out and took charge of my business as general manager. Sadie decided to sell out her interests, take a vacation and go out that fall with me. I didn't take the matter of Carbonneau up with her, as I was a little janey about discussing my private affairs.
>
> . . . I got Walker to check up my money and get all he could for the full lot, as I was going to look up my family when I went Out. I'd written my mother to find a place where I could send the children [Belinda's younger brother and sisters] to boarding school.
>
> . . . I had written my grandmother regularly. Her influence was with me all the time. . . . I promised my Grandmother a visit. (NW 48:2–4[255–57]; 48:3–4[256–57])

Belinda also had some gifts made from her mining claims to take Outside.

> I had Peterson, the goldsmith who made things so well, hammer . . . solid gold out of my claim into small cigar cases. Six small ones. I had initials put on in emeralds and diamonds. I got the idea of it at first to make my peace with Skipper and keep him in good humor. I gave him one just before I left for the Outside. I knew it made him feel very bad to see the old gang breaking up.
>
> With Skipper, you never knew what to expect. He'd grunt you know, "Gee, that's pretty!" He thought a lot of that case and showed it around like a baby. It was classy.
>
> . . . I [gave] one to Mrs. Wade to give F. C. for Christmas after I was gone. (NW 47:4–5[252–53]; 51:5[272])

Belinda left Dawson on 5 October 1899 for her triumphant tour Outside. This time she rode in style on the reliable little steamer *Flora*,[41] once more heading up the Yukon River toward Whitehorse and Skagway, and then on to Seattle.

17

Belinda's Triumphal Tour

THERE WERE A NUMBER of people leaving Dawson at the same time as Belinda, hoping to get out before the river and lakes began to freeze. Accompanying Belinda and sharing her cabin on the *Flora* was Sadie O'Hara, her friend and loyal employee. However, Belinda's faithful dog Nero had to be left in Dawson. She tied him in the Fairview Hotel basement, where he was accustomed to sleeping. But though she tried to behave toward him as usual, he nevertheless seemed to sense that something was wrong.

> All of Dawson was on the bank calling "Good Bye!" to us. . . . The Fairview crowd was on the porches and on the bank shouting "Good Bye." All of a sudden Nero bolted into sight and dashed through the crowd for the river.
>
> I was in a mess. How [did he know] I was going when I did everything in my power to deceive him? The crowd was cheering Nero, "Don't let her go, Nero."
>
> It was very cold in the water by then, the current mighty swift, but he was in it, going for all that was in him, heading for the boat. I asked the captain to let me off. He stopped the engine and let the boat drift, as the current was taking Nero down stream.
>
> There was a place on the boat where the crew could take on wood, a low, large sliding door, level with the engine room. I didn't know what to do, but the Captain said, "Take him on board," and opened the engine room door.

I said, "I can't take him with me!"

The gang of miners on board were calling, "We'll take you, Nero!"

There was a piece of the rope he'd been tied with floating from his neck in the water. They grabbed that as he went by and pulled him into the engine room.

Sadie had the blanket off her bed, ready to dry him. He was awfully cold. But Nero just lay and whined, licking my hand and pleading and begging. He didn't know whether he'd be spanked or not. He was quite a problem for me. For the rest it was all right. The miners insisted he had to come. "Any dog . . . who wanted to go Outside that bad, that had to risk his life to get Out, should have a trip." (NW 49:1–2[258–59])

So Nero too was on his way Outside for the winter with the rest of Dawson's pioneers. The Old Timers on board the *Flora* were not necessarily old. Belinda was only twenty-seven at the time, for example. But they had come into the country across the trails, when the going had been rough and when traveling between Dawson and Skagway was not undertaken lightly. These pioneers possessed a wealth of experience in the North, if not of gold dust, and the Old Timers could fully appreciate the journey they were now taking in ways that Cheechakos could only guess. Now they could ride a steamboat upriver in relative luxury and comfort to Whitehorse without having to paddle a boat or help cut and haul wood to fire the engine. At Whitehorse a tram took them around the Whitehorse and Miles Canyon rapids that had intimidated all comers and had crushed so many outfits in their wild waters. Beyond the rapids the Old Timers boarded another steamer that deposited them at the head of Lake Bennett. At Bennett they climbed aboard the new passenger cars of the White Pass and Yukon Railroad to enjoy the ride to Skagway as though it were a scenic tour. Anyone who had endured the struggles of coming in over the trails had to be a bit awestruck by the engineering of the railroad, the ease of the current journey, and the realization that all of this meant a new era was upon the North. "We . . . stuck to each other like a lot of scared children," Belinda recalled (NW 49:2[259]).

At Skagway one steamer was in port, but Belinda decided to wait for the *City of Topeka*, the ship on which she had been a stewardess. Many of her old friends from the Klondike agreed to do the same. Belinda waited not only out of nostalgia, but also out of concern for Nero. She felt she'd be better able to take care of him on a boat with people she knew. When the Old Timers with their bags of gold began to board the steamship, they found the crew of the *City of Topeka* lined up at the gangplank and ready to help.

On the gangplank there was a little devil, a member of the crew whom I hardly knew or noticed, who threw his arms around me and kissed me when I went aboard. Old [Captain] Wallace's face was beaming, his gold teeth shining in his smile.

That ship was turned over to us. Every place they stopped, the Steward sent out to find anything fresh in vegetables and fruit, things we couldn't have up North.

. . . It was like getting home to see that great big family of a crew. The best state room was saved for Sadie and me. Funny, but not one man on board told anyone I'd worked there. They'd back me up, and "Don't be a simp and tell the Pioneers," they'd say. A loyal bunch of rascals.

The Old Timers would ask, "How'd you happen to wait for the *City of Topeka*? How'd you get this stand in?"

"I've always been famous, boys," I told them, "but you didn't know it."[1]

When the Klondikers reached Seattle, it seemed the whole town was aware of their arrival. Belinda and Sadie loaded their bags and Nero onto an express wagon and headed for the Rainier Grand Hotel. Since it was run by an Alaskan, all the Old Timers wanted to go there, thinking they would be more comfortable.

We were trailed by great mobs of people who met every Alaskan boat. We looked and felt like a circus, and I felt it was too bad we hadn't brought our bears out with Nero.

When we arrived at the hotel, it was interesting to see Taggart's, the manager's, face. We looked like a mob coming to take possession. However, Taggart was game. (NW 50:1)

The hotel was the same one where George and Kate Carmack, the original discoverers of the Klondike gold, were staying along with many other members of their large extended family. Belinda and her friends plus the Carmacks' party filled the whole hotel.

The first thing Belinda and Sadie did was to get cleaned up at a Turkish bath. They took Nero too, who was bathed, combed, and then blown dry with an electric dryer. Afterwards, as they paraded down the streets with him, he looked proud and interested in everything about the town. Back at the hotel, Belinda arranged to have him stay in the baggage room tied to a gate while she and Sadie went shopping for necessities.

After we went upstairs we heard the most terrible racket and a lot of people were shouting, "Go it, Nero!"

We looked and that dog was coming upstairs dragging that gate after him. And the miners were saying, "Don't let a little thing like that stop you Nero. You'll find her on the next floor."

We could hear the porters and the miners arguing. "Oh the devil with your little old gate. We'll buy a new one." The hotel people sent Mr. Taggart up in the elevator to our floor.

"Let Nero stay up here," he ordered. "The miners want him, and he is at home." So I had to get a room next to ours for Nero and put a little rug in it for him to sleep on.

Nero knew all the miners. They'd trot down Second Avenue with him, but he wouldn't let an Outsider touch him. He'd take a short walk with any of the Alaskans, but when he'd make up his mind to find me, back he'd come. (NW 50:3–4[265–66])

For their new clothes, Sadie and Belinda went to McDougall and Southwick, who had been Belinda's wholesale supplier just three years before. They got the best of service there, as well as advice on what was now in fashion.

Bicycle and horseback riding were popular then, and the store had some corsets for riding purposes. I didn't mind pulling in my stomach a bit, but those big high corsets! The woman who sold us our dresses said she couldn't fit a dress without them. I told her that was just a state of mind.

Sadie picked riding corsets too. She was tall, her flesh solid and strong, and she was graceful and very good looking.

We bought everything, the best they had. I was getting a good tailored suit, and we got some particularly good fur coats, found some that nearly fit us, also some pretty nice luggage. We were prouder of that luggage than anything else.

Laugh! Sadie and I just screamed about everything all day long. (NW 50:4–5 [266–67])

After a couple of weeks in Seattle, Belinda and Sadie were ready to head East. Sadie was returning to Toronto, and Belinda was going to Pennsylvania and New York, so they continued to travel together. But again Nero presented a problem. There really was no way to take him along. And even though Belinda arranged for his care in a roomy stable, it was obvious that he was no more resigned to being left behind now than he had been in Dawson. "He nearly spoiled my trip, he made me feel so bad," Belinda recalled.

Belinda and Sadie traveled by train to Chicago, where they bought some more clothes before taking an extensive side trip to Arkansas Hot Springs to sample the spa, the sporting events, and the food. The people at the spa, used to visits by invalids, were impressed to see such sturdy young women. Then Belinda and Sadie parted ways as they each went to their family homes.

All of Belinda's family still lived on Salem Street in Archbald, Pennsylvania. Besides her mother, Maria, and her father, John, there were her siblings—Patrick Joseph, 20 years; Helen "Nell," 15; Margaret, 13; Agnes, 12; and Jim, 7.[2]

Before leaving the North, Belinda had asked her friend Michael J. Heney, who had supervised construction of the White Pass railroad, for recommendations on schooling for her sisters and younger brother. In Pennsylvania Belinda talked over Heney's suggestions with her parents, and they agreed to send the younger children to boarding schools in Ottawa at the start of the next term. The girls were enrolled at Rideau Street Convent, while Jim entered another private school there.[3]

After a brief visit and having finished with various financial arrangements, Belinda was ready to start for Ireland. Although she invited her mother to accompany her, Maria declined and instead decided to go to Ottawa with the children because she felt Jim was too young to be in the unfamiliar city without nearby family. But Belinda did take all of her family with her as far as New York City, where she shopped for all of them and placed $16,000 in a bank for them; later she added to that fund for the children's education (NW 51:4[271]).

While in a furrier's in New York, arranging to have some of her fox skins made into clothing, Belinda was surprised by the sound of a familiar voice. It was Belle Cummings exclaiming to her partially deaf mother, Mrs. J. G. Brown.

> "Mother, look who is here!" They grabbed me and took me to 250 West 42nd Street to get me to tell my news. I know they doubted some of my story.
>
> I spent a week in New York, and J. G. Brown was in his studio, and he'd say, "Belle, bring her down. I want to listen to her." The old man was kind of stunned and would say, "Tell me some more about it." (NW 51:5[272])

Fortunately, Belinda was able to illustrate her stories with the various treasures she had brought with her. Jack, her former charge, was now about nine years old and was away at boarding school, but Belle Cummings arranged an impromptu holiday so Jack and Belinda could be reacquainted. Belinda gave Jack some raw nuggets from her claims. At Tiffany's she had some smooth gold made into cufflinks, with little stones in them and with his name on one side. She also gave Belle Cummings one of the little gold cigar boxes she had had made in Dawson, to use as a vanity case, or to give to her husband, or to save for Jack until he was of age. To both Mrs. Brown and Belle, Belinda presented a luxurious silver-tipped fox skin (NW 51:5–6[272–73]). It felt good to be able to give beautiful gifts to this family who had been so supportive and understanding at a critical time in her life, and who had helped her to imagine a life in America she could be happy working toward.

Belinda sailed for England on the *Kaiser Wilhelm der Grosse*,[4] an express luxury liner. With its twin propellers it could cross the Atlantic in about seven days.[5] In the dining room on the second day, Belinda was delighted to discover her friend Michael J. Heney, along with several other men associated with the Northwest. She joined their party and spent the Atlantic crossing engaged in lively conversation with them.

From England, Belinda went to Dublin, then on to Ballina at the head of Killala Bay, near the Mayo-Sligo County border. At last she was back in her beloved Ireland, and she was returning in style. At a hotel in Ballina, she cleaned up, put on one of her new riding habits, and hired a horse to ride to Carns.

> I was trying to time myself so I would arrive in Carns in the evening when my uncle George [Connor, her mother's brother] would be milking the cows. As a boy, you remember, I told you now he had had the habit of getting hold of my neck and pushing my nose good and hard with his other hand. I always promised him I would do the same to him when I grew up. . . . So I rode in the back way, [slunk] around the hay stacks, hid the horse and waited.
>
> . . . Finally George came sauntering along with the milk pail, whistling. When there were a few inches of milk in the pail, I sneaked up behind him and got his neck right in the bend of my arm and began to rub his nose for him. When I got through, we were all over milk, the pair of us. His curly hair had lots of milk in it. (NW 52:1–2[275–76])

The merry pair went to the Connor cottage, where Belinda was surprised to find her grandmother all dressed up, as though she were waiting for her.

> "Somebody told you I was coming."
> "No, nobody told me," she insisted. "I dreamed it."[6]
> My grandmother got young right off at the sight of me. I was sorry that my grandfather, aged 102, had just died a little while before I got there.
> As a matter of fact, they had had everything slicked up around that village for two weeks. There was quite a lot of excitement as all the village was in to see us. I don't know who milked. The cows had to take care of themselves that night. (NW 52:2[276])

Belinda's return to Carns was a cause for great celebration. Her parents had been desperately poor when they emigrated, leaving the infant Belinda in the care of her grandmother. Belinda herself had been only a child when she left Ireland for the United States. Now she was a successful young woman, returning from the fabulous golden country of the Yukon! People from all around the countryside began to arrive to hear her stories and to celebrate with dancing, games, and feasting.

> Grandmother started killing geese, ducks and chickens to feed us. "If they don't quit coming," I said, "you'll start killing the beef."
> Every neighbor took something home and cooked it. One would have geese, some more would be cooking bread or cake. You could smell chickens cooking all over the neighborhood as the houses were close together. There was always tea. . . . I didn't think they would ever go home, any of them, that night. (NW 52:3[277])

High on Belinda's list of priorities while she was in Carns was to make life a little easier for her grandmother. This she did by arranging for improvements on the Connor cottage. Then, while the work was going on, she took her grandmother and Uncle George for a horse-drawn buggy tour of the countryside, exploring Sligo County and the lake region, and visiting other relatives.

Next Belinda took her grandmother to Dublin and London. While in London they stayed at the Cecil Hotel, which had become a favorite of the Klondikers.[7] One day at lunch there, Belinda was startled to espy Carbonneau across the dining room.

> "Aren't you lost?" I said, coming up behind him.
> "My God!" he said, jumping up. "It is just like you. Why didn't you tell me you were here?" . . . He started to kiss me.
> "Don't pull that stuff you pulled in Dawson," I warned him. "If you do, there'll be a dead Frenchman." (NW 53:1[279])

Despite the stern talk, Belinda was glad to see Carbonneau and to introduce him to her grandmother. They arranged to go to the theater that evening and to have supper together after the show.

> I put myself in the hands of a woman in a shop and she outfitted me for that dinner. They were beginning to use the marcel wave[8] then. I had my very first one in the Cecil hotel. The hair dresser, after experimenting, made a rather good job of it. He dressed my grandmother's hair very well too. Hers was white as snow.
> She was one of the those young old ladies with lots of pep. For that night, I bought her lots of Irish lace, which made her happy. Although she couldn't un-

derstand how you could get such good Irish lace in England. Her slippers bothered her, so I got her some that were nice and soft, of regular kid with a little strap. I took the strap off, put little ribbons on and made a bow of them. She was the cutest thing with her new slippers.

"These are better," she said. She wanted to wear lots of petticoats with laces and frills. . . . I told her she did not need so many. . . . I had some fox fur boas she could wear around the hotel, but when she went out, she needed a fur coat. At Peter Robinson's [I bought her a nice chinchilla], one she liked, after looking at the whole bunch. . . .

I wore that night a kind of purple evening gown with an opera coat made with . . . the only six orange marten skins ever found in the North. They made a beautiful trimming. Also I had to wear a pretty good string of pearls I'd bought at Tiffany's. For my nice appearance, I had to thank the head lady in Robinson's.[9]

The chance meeting with Carbonneau in London proved to be an important one. Before, Belinda had seen him only in the context of the rough world of Yukon mining, where his habits were considered foppish by many. Here she could observe him in a milieu more to his style, for Carbonneau enjoyed luxury, good food and wine, socializing, and the theater, along with the excitement of working a lucrative business deal. And she was impressed with his charming attitude toward people who were important to her. "I liked him better every time I saw him, especially his manner with young and old. He was as kind to the people he met through me as he was to me" (NW 53:3[281]).

Carbonneau was eager to have Belinda join him on his business trip to France. He wanted to show her Paris and to introduce her to his uncle in Bordeaux.[10] However, Belinda says she refused his invitations because she had too many other responsibilities.

I had to go back to Ireland to see about the contractors and [to] take Grandmother back home. Then I had to go to Pennsylvania and Ontario.[11]

There was an appointment in Seattle I couldn't miss. I was obliged to be in Seattle at a certain date to get my freight on the *City of Topeka*. I had to spend two weeks there as I was sending up some heavy stuff by Captain O'Brien by way of Nome. Besides, our group of Alaskans had our space reserved on the *City of Topeka*, and due to the rush up North [to Nome], it was important because otherwise we couldn't get any space. (NW 53:1–3[279–81])

Nevertheless, it seems strange that Belinda would not accept Charles's invitations. They were, after all, engaged to be married, even though Belinda was ambivalent. So perhaps the *Klondike Nugget*'s report that Belinda visited France and saw the exposition buildings in Paris before they were opened gives a truer account of events. Of course, the newspaper does not say whether she toured France on her own or in the company of Carbonneau. In any case, Belinda did return with her grandmother to Carns, and after another round of parties, left for the United States, perhaps by way of France. She sailed for New York from Cobh, Ireland on 14 April.[12]

When she got back to Seattle, Belinda was heartsick to learn that Nero was gone. He had run away from the livery stable when let out for a little exercise, dashing first to the Rainier Grand Hotel, looking for Belinda, but then disappearing entirely. Belinda immediately started searching for him and spent the whole day talking to everyone she met and offering a reward for his return. On her second day in town, she continued her inquiries.

> Next morning, early at 4 o'clock, I got up and went down to the wharf where we had got off. I went under the wharves calling his name. That was how I found him.
>
> When he first saw me he raised his head and looked as if he were saying, "I knew you would come." He was dirty, almost dead from watching the boats. He cried and cried and whined and whined when he first saw me. I thought he'd cry himself to death. I guess I cried too.[13]

Belinda took Nero back to the livery stable to be checked by a veterinarian. Other than being starved, there seemed to be nothing else wrong with him. So Belinda fed him buckets of warmed milk and beef broth until he recovered. After another shampoo at the Turkish bath, Nero was welcomed back to the Rainier Grand Hotel.

Belinda finished her business in Seattle in good time. She saw to the equipment and goods she was having shipped north, then she sailed for Skagway. This time her brother, Patrick Joseph or "Paddy," who was then about twenty-one years old, came with her.[14]

As SHE SAILED NORTH AGAIN, she must have felt satisfied. Her tour Outside had been a great success. She was admired by people she cared for, and she was able to bestow beautiful gifts upon her family and loyal friends. She was recognized as a woman of means who had earned her wealth in the fabulous Yukon goldfields by her own hard work and business sagacity. She now saw Carbonneau in a new light and liked what she saw. She had done right by her family and had been able to improve her grandmother's circumstances substantially. She had returned to Ireland, as she had been so determined to do when she was younger. But now she also knew that her future was not there. Now she was truly a North American.

The tour also marked a shift in Belinda's ongoing relations with her parents and siblings, perhaps because she was now sure of her independence. After the spring of 1900, Belinda communicated with them more frequently, and they began to spend time with her. She could take this as an acknowledgment that what she had discovered and created, as well as who she was herself, was valuable for them to know.

18

A Wedding

BELINDA AND HER BROTHER Paddy arrived at Dawson in the early morning of 18 May 1900.[1] They apparently traveled by train between Skagway and Lake Bennett, but from there to the foot of Lake Laberge they were obliged to use the trail, because ice made the lakes impassable yet for boats.

At the foot of Lake Laberge the water was open again, so the rest of the trip to Dawson was by the sturdy little steamer *Ora*.[2] Rumors had been circulating in Dawson that Belinda and Charles were coming In together. For example, more than six weeks earlier the *Klondike Nugget* had reported, "Miss Mulrooney is on the trail between Bennett and Dawson. She is accompanied by Count(?) Carbonneau." Another notice in the *Nugget*, dated 29 March from Skagway, announced that Charles had arrived on 28 March and was planning to leave the following day for Dawson, thence to Nome. However, on 13 April Charles was still in Skagway, having returned to Victoria for more money to carry out his plans.[3] Perhaps he was also waiting for Belinda. Nevertheless, Charles was not with her when she arrived in Dawson on May 18, but in Vancouver, where on the following day he took out a Free Miners Certificate.[4] Charles did not get to Dawson until June 6, when he arrived on the steamer *Ora* from Whitehorse, and for some reason he was traveling incognito as "Mr. Des Long Champs."

Whether this was an effort to foil the gossip or because financial trouble was brewing in Dawson is not clear.[5]

Belinda's first priority in Dawson was a visit to Good Samaritan Hospital, where her good friend H. H. Norwood was convalescing from an illness.[6] Then Belinda got to work, for there were a number of problems needing her attention.

The first was at the Fairview Hotel. After Belinda had leased it for three years and had left in the fall, the Fairview had undergone renovations. The bar was removed and replaced by some large, comfortable offices; and electric lights were installed in every room. In January 1900, the Fairview reopened under the management of Mrs. Bertha H. Purdy,[7] who continued as manager until Belinda returned. Apparently something had happened to the original lessee, Kammueler, for when Belinda returned she signed a new contract to lease the Fairview to Julian Blaker for two years. Mrs. Purdy was replaced by E. H. Port, formerly employed at the Palace Grand Theater, who assumed control 1 June. Mrs. Purdy was not happy with this new arrangement and took Belinda to court to plead her case. But Belinda's wishes prevailed, for an announcement appeared within a couple of weeks that Blaker was in charge and had reinstated the Fairview bar.[8]

With the Fairview under control, Belinda headed out to the creeks to survey

18.1. A later view of the Fairview Hotel, now painted a light color with contrasting dark trim. *(UW, Ellingsen photog., 41)*

the work carried out on her claims during the winter.[9] The same warm weather that had allowed the river boats to get to Dawson a week earlier than they had the previous year also had melted the snow on the land at a more rapid than normal rate. For a short time, there was so much water coming off the hillsides that many of the dumps were washed away by floodwaters rather than through sluice boxes. Fortunately, the flooding was short lived, and Belinda found the dumps on her own claims were not threatened. Within a week or two the new worry was whether there would be enough water to continue sluicing operations through the summer.[10]

Besides the usual vagaries of weather in the Klondike, Belinda found she had other troubles to sort out. She had a lay agreement to work one of Jim McNamee's claims over the winter, so she needed to check on the progress of her crew there. Jim was the miner she had bodily thrown out of her first restaurant when he hinted that she might be cheating with her gold scales. But she and Jim eventually had made up their differences. When Jim's bride arrived in Dawson, Belinda was among those celebrating with a banquet at the Fairview. It was also reported that Jim was presently in league with Charles Carbonneau, among others, on two Eldorado claims, Nos. 14 and 15.[11] Here is the *Nugget*'s report on Belinda's examination of her crew's work on McNamee's rich claim.

"THE NEW WOMAN."

James McNamee is the owner of claim No. 26B above on Bonanza, and Miss Mulrooney has a lay on it. This being the season of the cleanup, Mr. McNamee's interests on the claim are being looked after by J. B. Fields. In some way or other, Fields has not endeared himself to the men employed by Miss Mulrooney, neither has he endeared himself to that lady herself. Last Friday morning [June 1] Miss Mulrooney and Fields had a dispute which ended in the latter being utterly vanquished for the time, the woman striking him over the head with a club, knocking him out in the first round and causing bright red blood to freely flow.[12]

Mr. Field may not have gotten the better of Belinda, but once again her own temper had. Perhaps Belinda was already on edge because other problems had just surfaced concerning the 3A Eldorado and 41 A/D Bonanza claims, on which she held mortgages. One of the other mortgage holders, A. G. Cunningham of Parsons Produce Company, had signed over his interests late in 1899 to David Doig, manager of the Bank of British North America.[13] The mortgage was unsatisfied, so Doig initiated foreclosure on the Anglo-French Klondike Syndicate.[14] After several postponements of hearing the suit, the territorial court had ruled that the foreclosure could proceed on the first of June, the day Belinda went to visit the McNamee claim.[15] This foreclosure put all of Belinda's investments in the two claims at risk. Even though she had not risked a large portion of her assets in them, she had worked hard on Eldorado 3A and she knew the potential for future production was considerable. She did not take these losses, either actual or potential, lightly.

So by the time Charles arrived in Dawson incognito, Belinda's financial interests in Charles's company's mining claims were looking very muddled. In this context, perhaps Belinda's emphasis on getting her business affairs in order seems all the more understandable. She didn't like losing control of a situation. Furthermore, even though she had decided to marry Charles, Belinda was aware that their differences could be a source of friction. But it is not clear whether she realized at this point how profound the gulf between them was.

The following somewhat confused description perhaps reflects some of her ambivalence. She understood at least part of what Charles needed. She wanted to accommodate herself to those needs, and at the same time she knew she was denying a fundamental part of herself—her love of nature and of simplicity without pretense.

> Carbonneau came In the last of June [actually 6 June] by boat. Like some of the others, he brought in some fine horses.
>
> I had to get rid of the pest somehow, so we were going to get married in October, 1900. About my trousseau? I wasn't anxious to get at it, as I was too busy thinking how I could postpone the wedding until we could get affairs straightened up, clean up, and buy a place somewhere and retire. I wanted to be through with Alaska, as I knew Carbonneau was desperately anxious for a home. Staying in a cabin alone used to bother him a lot. His mining was not a success, as he wanted his whole crew waiting on him, or to be ready for his guests to hold their horses for them, or fetch a bottle of wine. His hospitality was different from mine.
>
> For my guests I had a couple of beds, soap, water and a towel. The cooks had instructions to cook them a meal any time. My friends knew where the things were they liked, where to find them. With the officials, a drink was the first thing. After tramping over the hills, they usually had sore feet and were tired. After they were rested and had had food, they would come to the mine, where I was, and thank me. (NW 57:3–4[296–97])

The differences between Belinda and Charles certainly were more far-reaching than this short passage describes. Charles was routinely running on the thin edge between imaginative speculation and graft, while Belinda had been basically honest in her business dealings. Belinda wanted to marry because she was interested in raising a family and in having a stable, happy home, like her friends the Wades. Charles seemed most interested in Belinda's money and the high living it would support. To Belinda's priest the differences between Belinda and Charles seemed problematic enough that he advised against their marriage.[16] And when Belinda describes the reactions of her miner friends to Charles, one might wonder if she isn't speaking for a part of herself as well.

> Of course, they were nervous about my marrying someone they didn't know, like Carbonneau. You can see how they would distrust the owner of a silk tent and a title. They didn't want to lose one of their gang. I had built boats at Bennett, had got along as well as they had on beans and bacon. They resented my marrying a man who carried his steaks in a portable ice box and had his own brand of toilet water. (NW 57:4–5[297–98])

Perhaps to calm her misgivings, Belinda threw herself into her work. She bought Charles's lower half of claim No. 12 over the Dome on Gold Run Creek,[17] which was beginning to look like the most promising new ground in the district. But she devoted her efforts mainly to Eldorado 3A, on which she still held a substantial mortgage. For some reason the Eldorado claim was seen as Belinda's, both by herself and by others in the area. Whether Belinda had some unrecorded agreement with Charles to this effect is not known. Negotiations were under way with bank manager Doig and attorneys Tabor and Hulme to clear the title for the Eldorado 3A and Bonanza 41 A/D claims, but officially the titles were still in the name of the Anglo-French Klondike Syndicate.

> I was working with Nels Peterson,[18] my foreman on Three A Eldorado, a fraction. . . . I was standing on an incline watching the cars come out when I noticed some blue clay much like the formation on Cheechako Hill, different from the rest of the gravel, darker stuff. Do you know, I lifted the nuggets out by the hand full. Some of them were as large as my finger.
>
> "We've run into something, Nels," I said.
>
> "I'll say we've run into something!" He took his pick and dug it into a slab he was standing on. The slab broke. He took up half of it.
>
> "Yaysus! My God!" He held a chunk of something flat, almost as large as a medium sized plate. It looked like a piece of large liver. The whole nugget had been broken, but this part we took to the office, washed and dried it. It was solid gold. When we took the other piece and put them together, they were

worth near fifteen hundred [dollars]. The weight was—figure it out for yourself, at seventeen dollars an ounce—over 90 ounces, over seven pounds.[19]

While Belinda concentrated on mining, Charles was focusing on the businesses he enjoyed. Late in June he sold the upper half of 40 A/D Bonanza, the
claim he and Belinda had received from the Standers in trade for the Grand
Forks Hotel, to T. McMullen for six thousand dollars.[20] In July he was making
arrangements for importing a thousand gallons of liquor into the Yukon. There
had been official sentiment for some time that there was too much liquor flowing in the territory.[21] Nevertheless, permits continued to be issued, and on 27 July
Charles paid the two-dollar-per-gallon fee required for his imports.[22]

The social and political high point of the summer for Dawson was the arrival
on 14 August of Lord and Lady Minto. Gilbert John Murray Kynynmond Elliot,
the fourth Earl of Minto, had been appointed Great Britain's Governor General
of Canada. This was the first time in three years that any central government
officer had visited the Yukon; therefore, most Yukon residents felt it was an ideal
opportunity to present their complaints directly to Governor General Minto.
They hoped that at last their voices, unfiltered by the appointed local officials,
would be heard and their recommendations acted upon.

Official descriptions of the three-day visit tell of the elaborate preparations,
the ceremonies and parades, the various meetings and tours, and the grievances
presented by citizens concerning Yukon governance. But Belinda's recollection
is from a more personal, subjective perspective.

Lord Minto didn't know if his dignity would allow him to mix or no, so he
stuck to the Officials closely. And he was kept busy by them, asking favors for
themselves or their friends. That monkey husband of Lady Minto treated us
miners like we had the small pox. Believe me we treated him the same way.
. . . But Lady Minto [Mary Grey Minto] fell for us! Her heart was with the
miners. They stayed at the Governor's House,[23] but Lady Minto was on the
hike all the time, taking a look on the life of the North. She was interested,
was rather a thoroughbred of the best English type. She dressed appropriately,
was always cheerful. She was interested in our rotten roads,[24] went into the
mines. She went right through the tunnel of my mine. . . . Didn't want to be
waited on and could tramp like anyone. She kept up with me, and I was pretty
good at that time. She shook hands with every miner and made him feel at
ease.
. . . Returning from Grand Forks with Lady Minto, who was driving one of
my horses to a buggy, we met a six-horse team pulling a heavy load of freight.

18.2. Lord and Lady Minto, standing at center of the photo, visit Dan McGillivray's mine on King Solomon's Hill, above Bonanza Creek at about 23 B/D, August 1900. *(UW, Larss and Duclos photog., 30)*

The road with everybody freighting up, was cut up badly, and the teamster trying to get out of the way with his six horses, went a little too close to the edge and one horse fell over.

Lady Minto jumped out of the buggy right away and tried to help. The horse had just rolled over, the poor thing! So I cut some of the harness, got him free and to his feet. They unhitched my buggy and led my horse around the freighting team. When we got Lady Minto all fixed up again, she said to the driver, "I'm going to promise you here and now that when I reach Ottawa our government will certainly have to build you a road. . . . It is a disgrace with the amount of revenue we have taken out of the Klondike that they have not even given you a road."[25]

By the time the Mintos were to leave Dawson, the miners were completely won over to Lady Minto. As a farewell gift they took gold from their claims and had goldsmiths Sales[26] and Peterson fashion it into a flower basket. Then the pioneers went through their collections of coarse gold and nuggets and threw in enough to fill the basket. "They didn't give a damn thing to the dinky dunk of a Lord," Belinda stated. "He was out of the picture as far as they were concerned."

Then came the decision of who was to present the gift to Lady Minto. Belinda suggested Alex McDonald, and everyone agreed. Lady Minto was invited to the Pioneers hall. F. C. Wade escorted her and made introductions. After refreshments it was time for Alex to present the basket.

> Alex got stage fright. "No, for pity's sake, let Jeremiah [Lynch] present the basket."
>
> "Never mind, Alex. We'll stand right back of you and will catch you if you fall."
>
> The rest of the yahoos of Pioneers were all gaping and guying him. They had more fun with Alex than they'd had for a long time. (NW 59:5[307])

The *Klondike Nugget* reported that for the presentation, Alex stated the basket "was in token of good will to their distinguished guest."[27] But Jeremiah Lynch quotes Alex as stammering, almost inaudibly, "Take it, take it, Mrs. Minto: it's only trash, to be sure—it's only trash . . ." (215). The latter version fits better with Alex McDonald's taciturn nature and his lack of enthusiasm for gold itself.

> I don't believe Lady Minto ever received a gift that affected her so much. All she could do was to look at that basket and feel of it. She shook hands, both hands, with every miner in the room, the everlasting friend of those miners.
>
> . . . Later she defended our interests and got the road for the miners. The road machines were In pretty quick after she left. As the [Governor General's] wife, she was there in Ottawa, always our friend, ready to fight the big interests reaching out for all of the Klondike. (NW 59:5–6[307–8])

The big interests Belinda refers to were not the independent miners, but the large companies that would undertake hydraulic mining and eventually dredging on the Yukon Territory's creeks.

By the time Lord and Lady Minto left Dawson, summer was almost over in the North. On the creeks the cleanups were coming to an end, and miners were beginning to think about preparing for the winter's work or going Outside. But there was still much to do before Belinda and Charles married on the first of October. Most of that Belinda left to Charles: "Carbonneau decided he and Mr. Wade would take on the duties of preparing for the wedding. He had made $6,500 on a trip Outside, and he insisted on spending it all on the wedding. I'd looked after the miners and his interests while he was making arrangements" (NW 60:2[310]).

Belinda also continued putting her business affairs in order. In late August she sold her Cheechako hillside claim to her former employees for $20,000.[28] In September, she sold her part interest in 53 B/D Bonanza.[29] At about this time

18.3. This photo was sent as a postcard to Nellie Mulrooney in August 1906 and is labeled "Glenside Home." It is apparently the home Belinda bought for her parents in Glenside, Pennsylvania. *(Waugaman Collection)*

she also bought a large, comfortable home for her parents in Glenside, Pennsylvania.[30] Belinda must have been proud to be able to provide the house for her family. She also probably was practical enough to realize that this investment was a good way to separate some of her assets from those of her husband-to-be.

Belinda did not want to fuss about her wedding, but she did need a dress. So she arranged with her dressmaker in Dawson to sew one while she finished her business out on the creeks.

> The dress was ready for me the last few days before the wedding when I came into Dawson. The woman had made it of heavy white . . . satin, and she had those full sleeves in it with a train on the blessed thing. I thought I'd try it on and see how it looked on me. . . . The general result was that I looked like one of those rubber dolls you blow up, a bump here and a bump there!
>
> Mrs. Wade nearly killed herself laughing, and I never knew Mr. Carbonneau to laugh so hard. Of course, I acted up to make it look worse, stood bow legged and everything else. I got it into my mind that I must be like that squaw going down the gang plank of the *City of Topeka* in her bridal outfit.
>
> Mr. Carbonneau had lots of stuff, family jewels, lockets and things with curls of hair in them. He had a dog collar of jewels he thought was wonderful, very heavy. "Stick 'em on," I said, "and I'll be finished." (NW 60:1–2(309–10)

The week before the wedding, Dawson began to take on a festive air. The Mulrooney / Carbonneau work crews were in town, having been given a week off with pay. However, not everyone was happy. Some of Belinda's friends, such as Bill McPhee, refused to attend the planned festivities.[31] Of course, Captain Norwood was not hiding his feelings either. He had resigned office and lived at the Fairview, home to most of the wealthy miners and officials able to afford it (NW 60:2[310]). "Skipper went around looking mean, with his lip lifted. There were rumors that something would happen and the wedding never take place. Mrs. Wade evidently was worried and was with me all the time" (NW 61:1[313]).

Belinda could reasonably account for Norwood's and McPhee's disapproval of Carbonneau as a combination of jealousy and prejudice against an Outsider. But she also was ignoring others' warnings that Charles might not make a good partner for her. If nothing else, her own observations of his liberal spending of investors' money for his own benefit should have given her pause. But she probably never imagined that he would do anything similar to her. Belinda went ahead with her modest contribution to the wedding plans.

F. C. Wade and Charles, on the other hand, were expansive in their planning. To begin, they arranged for a bachelor's dinner, with about fifty guests attending. The celebration was held in the dining room of the Fairview Hotel. "Everything was done in proper style and in a manner befitting the host's reputation for good fellowship," reported the *Nugget,* "and the champagne was forthcoming without stint, no one being permitted to harbor an empty or half filled glass."[32] Belinda's recollection of the pre-wedding celebration tells not only of the heavy drinking, but also more about how the elaborate affair was managed.

> Wade and Carbonneau had their evening clothes all pressed for the occasion, but as they were the only men in Dawson besides the waiters who had such things, they decided not to put them on.
>
> Wade was toastmaster. . . . The hotel had arranged for the regular waiters to stay up until one or two [in the morning]. But there wasn't anyone of the guests able to quit then, so we filled in with the mining crew. The boys in their laborers' clothes hopped in and did the best they could. Three cooks passed out on the job. They, the company, kept it up until 4 o'clock, everybody happy, the host the only sober one. He had bought wines for the supper wholesale,[33] which was very wise. Carbonneau didn't drink much himself, but the men saturated his suit with the stuff. (NW 60:3[311])

The wedding took place on the evening of the following day.

> As to the arrangements for the wedding, I just took pot luck. I was excited about things until everybody made it their party. After that I just let things hap-

18.4. Belinda in her wedding outfit. The description on back reads "Taken in Dawson City, 1900." *(Yakima Valley Museum, Carbonneau Collection)*

pen. I didn't have a blessed thing to do with the church decorations. All day long they were hauling in plants, ferns, and artificial flowers. It did me good to see some funeral things turned back. Mr. Carbonneau even installed electric lights.

. . . The funny white satin dress had been discarded for a silver gray Paris gown I had bought in London. They used lots of Irish lace draped over that, and Mrs. Wade had a wonderful bridal veil for me. My bouquet was of lilies of the valley, which Mr. Carbonneau had ordered months in advance to be grown especially for the wedding. (NW 61:1–2[313–14])

At 8 P.M. on 1 October 1900, F. C. and Mrs. Wade drove Belinda and Charles from the Fairview Hotel to the Catholic church in a sleigh pulled by four bell-studded horses.[34]

My crew were looking in the windows of the log church where 500 wedding guests were waiting. I remember the mob that was outside as we drove in.

. . . As I stepped in the church, the altar and the candles were the first thing I noticed. Carbonneau, with the Honorable [Girouard] and Xavier [Gosselyn], was waiting for me. In the excitement and confusion I just did not know what was what. But I remember we were going down the aisle when the lights went out!

F. C. Wade, [who was giving Belinda away], put his arm around me. He was a giant you remember. "That's not an accident," he whispered. "Stick close to me."

Someone had cut the wires. They kept playing the wedding march on the little organ just the same. Everybody was hollering, for "Candles, more candles." All I could do was giggle. It struck me how funny it must be for those outside who were looking in the windows.

Where was Skipper? Somewhere near the nippers, I guess.

Father Crimont[35] forgot his talk.

I was married with a wedding ring made from native gold from Forty One Bonanza, Carbonneau's claim. He had one big ring cut into two. He wore one, and I the other. (NW 61:3–4[315–16])

After the ceremony the new couple were driven back to the Fairview for the wedding dinner. For this the Fairview dining room was decorated with greens and Chinese lanterns. Nearly 250 people attended.[36]

. . . Mr. and Mrs. Julian Blaker received them in a manner never before equaled in Dawson. The dining room was a bower of loveliness, and the repast served was the acme of culinary skill and attainment. During the wedding feast, music was furnished by Warwick and Creuse's orchestra, and afterwards, the "light fantastic" was enjoyed to music from the same source.[37]

A red embossed leather book, prepared in Ottawa for each member of the wedding party, listed the menu and the attendants.[38] Each page was hand painted with cupids, fleur-de-lis and shamrocks, and outlined with intricate border patterns. The larger characters of the calligraphy were illuminated with gold. Besides F. X. Gosselyn, T. Girouard, and F. C. and Mrs. Wade, the wedding party consisted of Belinda's old friend Joseph Barrette, along with his brother Norbert[39] and his wife and daughters. Also present were Belinda's brother, Joseph Mulrooney, Canadian Bank of Commerce President H. T. Wills, and R. L. Cowan. The menu, all in French, listed several courses, including hors d'oeuvres of caviar, fruits, and mushrooms with oysters. These were followed by a Romaine salad, chicken cutlets, peas in cream, buttered carrots, filet mignon, potatoes, asparagus in mayonnaise sauce, with cheeses, and petits fours for dessert. Along with the dinner wines, champagne was served, followed by port and a liqueur.

Things weren't too stiff, however, because R. P. McClellan[40] had put those rubber things under the plates. When he pressed a bulb, the plates danced. Mine popped just as I sat down.

But it makes me tired just to remember. I had to sit in the dining room from eight until daylight. Carbonneau made a wonderful talk. . . . He told the guests he wanted to be a pioneer, a sourdough, and a family man. He had lots of things to say about the country, but I don't know whether he meant them or not. The company would interrupt him all the time with "For he's a jolly good fellow."

As it grew later, many families sneaked away. But the damn officials wouldn't leave. I just sat all dressed up with my bouquet and my head with all my hair and the wedding veil feeling heavier all the time. I was darned nervous, but I had to sit there. We ate a little and then mixed around. Mr. Carbonneau was as fresh as could be. I wondered at him. Up all night and all morning! I'd had a little sleep myself.

. . . The darned wedding supper lasted all night. For the last thing they made a circle and put Mr. Carbonneau and me in the center and danced around singing, "Auld Lang Syne. Should Auld acquaintance be forgot?"

I didn't cry. I just told them to sing their heads off. If I could have lain down some there and rested, I would have been happy.

After telling the guests we weren't going to the cabin that night, we went upstairs to wait until the last one left. Then I put on a fur coat and with my husband walked to Third Street where the stables were and where Mr. Carbonneau had a swell cutter and a good horse. There had been a snow the evening before, and there was good sleighing. We drove up to 41 [A/D Bonanza]. After all the excitement, the quiet and the snow were wonderful. I was outdoors in Alaska again, and it was my country.

. . . The Count's cabin at Forty One Bonanza was different from the first ones built by me when I came North. It had three rooms, a living room with a fireplace, two bed rooms and an office. It was lined and papered, beautifully decorated with rugs and furs. The cabin adjoining it had a large dining room, a big kitchen, servant's room, and a place to store food stuffs. There was silver and fine linen, and Mr. Carbonneau had brought from Europe the most marvelous bed. All the luxury of Europe was there. (NW 61:4–6[316–18])

These two influences—civilized Europe and the wilderness of Alaska—would hold Belinda's life in tension for the next five years.

19

Carbonneau and Carbonneau

AFTER THEIR WEDDING Belinda and Charles seem to have led a quiet life socially, for there is no mention in Dawson papers of either of them at public gatherings through the winter months. But they were not idle. Almost immediately they were attending to business matters. In this Belinda was once again atypical. Most American women in 1900 stopped working outside the home as soon as they married. While more than 70 percent of foreign-born single women had jobs, their participation in the labor force dropped to about 4 percent when they married. According to one analysis, marital status more than any other characteristic save race determined a woman's economic role at that time.[1] Belinda was different perhaps because, unlike most female workers, she was self-employed and in control of her work. Also, her identity, her sense of who she was as a person, was tied up with her being an entrepreneur. Furthermore, when it came to mining in the Klondike, Belinda rather than Charles was the expert—she was the one who really understood the details of how to operate a mine profitably.

A little more than a week after the Carbonneau wedding, action was under way to clear the titles to the Eldorado 3A and Bonanza 41 A/D claims. These were the two owned by the Anglo-French Klondike Syndicate that Charles had mortgaged before going Out in the summer of 1899. First the syndicate lost both claims by foreclosure proceedings initiated by Bank of British North America Manager Doig, who had acquired an interest when he assumed first mortgages on the properties. Then Doig sold both claims to Nels L. Peterson, Belinda's foreman on Eldorado, for $8,500. The following day, Peterson sold the claims back to Belinda and Charles for $10,000.[2] Thus the titles to these two claims were now clear and were in the Carbonneaus' names personally. The Anglo-French Klondike Syndicate's subscribers apparently realized no income from these transactions. By the following June, the company declared bankruptcy and was liquidated,[3] leading some to conclude the Charles had committed fraud and was an unscrupulous promoter.[4]

Shortly after acquiring Eldorado 3A and Bonanza 41 A/D, Charles and Belinda also bought back for a nominal $1.00 the claim they had sold to T. McMullen in June for $6,000, the upper half of Bonanza 40 A/D.[5] The Carbonneaus were now in a position to exploit these claims to their fullest potential, which they proceeded to do.

Although their attention was primarily upon their mining at the creeks, the Carbonneaus were drawn back to Dawson for one issue at the close of 1900. A move was under way to incorporate the city. However, 90 percent of taxable property owners in Dawson were afraid the incorporation would simply bring another layer of inefficient and costly bureaucracy to the city government. Another issue for many was that much of the business in Dawson was owned by aliens. What voice non-British residents would have in any local government was not resolved. Belinda could identify with this concern, even though now, having married Charles, she had become a British subject. In late December both Belinda and Charles, representing the Fairview Hotel, were among a long list of signers on a petition to the Yukon Council opposing incorporation of the city.[6] As a result of the protests, the incorporation drive was halted.

THROUGHOUT THE WINTER of 1900–1901, the Carbonneaus worked steadily at their mining. They hired about ninety-five men to excavate the Eldorado and Bonanza claims.[7] As before, Belinda concentrated her energy on operations at Eldorado 3A. While directing the large crew was not without its problems,[8] by late February she and her men had managed to get a tremendous amount of steam thawing and digging done.

> Mrs. C. E. Carbonneau of 3[A] Eldorado is conducting that famous claim with her accustomed business acumen. With the exception of Chute and

Wills' dump on Gold Run, Mrs. Carbonneau has moved more dirt than any other claim owner in the country and expects a big clean-up.[9]

Toward the end of March as the days began to get longer and warmer, Belinda was figuring out how to get enough precious water to sluice all the dirt: "Mrs. Carbonneau, on 3A Eldorado, has moved her boiler and engine house and is putting in a dam, preparatory to washing the immense dumps she had drifted out the past winter."[10] By early May, once there was sufficient water, Belinda was using a centrifugal pump to get enough pressure to wash all the dumps efficiently.[11]

In the meantime, location of new gold was creating a stir at Grand Forks. Most of the placer gold on Eldorado and Bonanza Creeks had been found in a layer thirty to forty feet under the surface, forming a more or less continuous layer that probably once had been the bed of an ancient creek. Belinda's crew had been following that streak, first identified in 1896 and 1897. Now a new layer of gold, fifteen feet deeper, was found on claims at the lower end of Eldorado Creek, including the claim adjacent to Belinda's.[12]

On the basis of these new discoveries, Belinda was able to let a lay with L. F. Protzman. Protzman planned to go back over the previously dug ground, looking for the deeper layer of gold. In most lay agreements the claim owner and the miner split whatever was found 50/50, with the miner paying for the cost of the work out of his share. So this was a way for Belinda to get the more speculative exploration done without having to invest further in the claim. Protzman, on the other hand, did not have to put his resources into buying the land, and he benefited from the work already done on adjacent claims to locate the new gold. He planned to sink a new shaft in hopes of finding the path of the deeper pay streak.[13]

So in the late spring of 1901, prospects on Eldorado 3A were golden for Belinda. She had a large and rich cleanup under way, with the possibility of even more paying dirt should the deeper gold streak be located. Then a fire started and threatened the buildings on the claim. The following article appeared under the headline, "A Family of Title Narrowly Escapes Loss of Property by Fire."

> Count and Countess Carboneau [sic] narrowly escaped the loss of their combined dwelling and mess house by fire on claim 3a Eldorado yesterday afternoon. As it was, the fire was put out before but a few hundred dollars damage had been done. Constable Shafer at the Forks was first to notice the fire and he is reported to have run [a] half mile to the scene of the conflagration in 49 ¼ seconds by a steam gauge. Several hundred miners formed a

bucket brigade, but by the time they were ready to begin passing water they found they had not water, and even had there been water in abundance, they had no buckets. The police then got in and clubbed out the fire. The count and his retinue were not at home at the time, but the countess was there and is said to have taken a lively interest in saving her property from destruction.[14]

The article suggests that at least Belinda may have been living at the Eldorado claim, rather than at Charles's plusher cabin on the Bonanza 41 A/D claim three miles distant.

Where was Charles when the fire broke out? He might have been on his way to Dawson, for he was reported as being in town on business shortly after.[15] Charles, unlike Belinda, had been bogged down for most of the spring with problems. A news story later that spring described his difficulties: "Count Carbonneau has his troubles along with the rest of us. He pumped water for a month or six weeks, trying to clean out an old drift and gave it up as a bad job. He sunk a new shaft on the right limit of 41 above Bonanza, getting good pay. A few days ago the water came in there, too, and he is apt to have more trouble and expense getting it in shape to work again."[16]

Then a few days later, on 11 March, disaster struck. One of Charles's workmen, Samuel Nelson, was killed. A coroner's inquest was held to determine the cause and whether there was negligence involved.

> We consider that the deceased came to his death from the falling of a quantity of frozen earth from the face of the drift and do not consider any responsibility is attached to the claim owner from the falling of this particular piece of earth, but we consider the mine at present, from what we have seen, in an unsafe condition and not fit for men to be working in. We recommend that work be at once stopped until a proper and competent man inspect the mine.[17]

Charles did stop all work immediately, and he paid the expenses of Nelson's burial. The mine was inspected and eventually was reopened, though it is not clear whether any alterations were required. Even a month later, Charles reported that water intrusion was still causing a great deal of trouble on his claim.[18]

Charles also had some business problems needing to be resolved in court. In April he was sued for "wrongful conversion of a quantity of wood," by which we can surmise that the wood had been used as fuel for the steam engines but had not been paid for. In this case, the plaintiff, Labbe, was awarded $291 and Charles was ordered to pay court costs of $100.[19] The next month Charles was in court again, though it is not clear whether he or the other party (McLennan) collected $260 and costs.[20]

19.1. The Carbonneaus' claim at Number 12 Gold Run Creek. *(Yakima Valley Museum, Carbonneau Collection)*

Late in March, Belinda added a new claim to her holdings, the upper half of No. 12 on Gold Run, which she bought for $20,000, having already bought the lower half of the claim from Charles the previous summer for $9,500.[21] On the map of the Klondike region (fig. 7.3), Gold Run Creek lies between Dominion and Sulphur Creeks, on the south side of the worn mountain known as the Dome. By 1901 the richness of the creek was beginning to be realized, and the new potential was reflected in the increased price Belinda paid for the second half of No. 12. Once the claims on Gold Run began to be heavily worked, the *Klondike Nugget* started running a new column titled "Over the Divide," telling the news of that mining district.

Belinda's "neighbors" on Gold Run were the partners J. A. Chute and Dr. A. E. Wills.[22] Jerome Amandren Chute was an Old Timer[23] and a practical miner, who acted as on-site manager of the partnership's claims. Dr. Alfred Ernest Wills had come to the North before the Klondike strike to serve as the chief surgeon for the Northwest Mounted Police at Forty Mile Post and then Dawson. In early 1898 he was selected as one of a committee of three to present a petition of the miners to the government in Ottawa protesting the reduction of claim size, the 20 percent royalty, and the reservation of every other claim for the crown. To carry out this charge, he resigned his post with the Mounties.[24] When he returned to Dawson in the fall of 1898, he apparently took up mining in earnest.[25] His brother, Henry Thomas Wills, was manager of the Canadian Bank of Commerce in Dawson and a good friend of Belinda and Charles.

The Chute and Wills partnership was by far the largest holder of property on Gold Run. Chute and Wills began acquiring claims, the right to operate claims, and mortgages on Gold Run in 1899 and as early as November 1899 they had a hundred men working on five claims.[26]

In late June Belinda welcomed her father, John, to Dawson.[27] This was John's first trip to the Klondike, and he would stay for a year or two before returning to Pennsylvania.[28] For some reason, Belinda used the occasion of her father's arrival to divest herself of her property in the Klondike. On 31 July, she signed over to John her whole No. 12 Gold Run claim and her half interests in Eldorado 3A, Bonanza 41 A/D, and the upper half of Bonanza 40. In order to carry out these transfers, she first had to make an affidavit that the claims were in fact her property, for she had mislaid all the grant deeds.[29] It is surprising that Belinda was able to make these transfers without needing her husband to co-sign, for there was as yet no married woman's property right law for real property in the Yukon. On 5 August Belinda also transferred title for her final large asset, the Fairview Hotel, to her father.[30]

It is not clear what motivated these transactions. Was there some trouble between Belinda and Charles? Or was there a potential legal action pending that would be better faced if Belinda, and thereby Charles, were not on the deeds? Another possible explanation is that between 20 July and 20 September Dawson was undergoing reassessment for taxation purposes. All real and personal property was to be assessed at its actual cash value.[31] Since Belinda sold her property to her father for $1.00, this may have been a way to reduce her taxes. Indeed, a number of property owners in Dawson protested their assessments, claiming their property had recently been sold for much less than the valuation. In one remarkable session of the Board of Equalization, lots assessed for $400 each were sold during the meeting when the owner declared them worth only $50, the price for which he was prepared to sell them. Taking the owner up on his statement, a real estate man in the audience immediately bought two, and the tax assessor himself bought the other two![32]

Avoidance of royalties rather than property tax may have been a factor in

transferring the mining claims. For example, royalties of $16,200 were paid for
Eldorado 3A on 15 June, and then $225 on 13 November for the period covering
31 August to 6 November. But apparently there was no royalty payment for
this claim during the intervening months from mid-June to late August, when
Belinda's father (with Charles Carbonneau) were the registered owners and
when the cleanup would have been substantial.[33] Whatever the reason for
the maneuver of assigning her property to her father, all titles were restored to
Belinda within a few weeks and with Charles witnessing the reconveyances. And
on 24 August, one day after getting her interest back from her father, Belinda
and Charles agreed to sell the Eldorado fraction for $15,000 to A. R. Thompson
and W. C. Granger. On that same date Belinda "sold" half of her No. 12 Gold
Run claim to Charles for $1.00.[34]

Besides the higher taxes, another signal of changing times in the Yukon came
in mid-July with word that the government in Ottawa had granted a concession
for water rights on several of the major creeks in the Klondike district. Because
of this grant, Eldorado and Bonanza creeks, among others, were closed to further claims.[35] Water, of course, was essential to placer mining, for it was the action of water running across the mined soil in the sluice boxes that sorted the
gold from its surrounding dirt. But these new concessions had been granted for
even bigger operations—hydraulic mining and dredging of the placer gold. With
high-pressure nozzles aimed directly at the ground, whole hillsides could be
washed away through giant riffles. With dredges, all the ground along the flat-
ter creek beds could be turned over and washed for the gold. Both large-scale
methods required huge volumes of water—hydraulic mining to erode the land;
dredges because they ran on electricity and hydroelectricity was the most economical to generate. Because water was in short supply for most of the season
on the Klondike's gold-bearing creeks, extensive and expensive systems of dams,
flumes, pipes, and siphons had to be built to get water to where it was needed
on a reliable basis.[36]

The principal interest in the new water concession was held by an Oxford-
educated Englishman, Arthur C. N. Treadgold, whom Belinda knew from
Cheechako Hill in 1898 or 1899.

> . . . Treadgold [was] then a young man around twenty eight or thirty years
> old. He was an odd sort of fellow, never mixed with anybody, didn't wear a
> hat, and was constantly moving from one hilltop to another making maps. The
> miners thought he was a little bit crazy, seeing him perched on top of a hill
> making maps, drawing plans.

19.2. Hydraulic mining in the Klondike. Streams of high-pressure water eat through the hillsides. Washed-out heavy gold sinks to the bottom of the drain channels. (UW, A. Curtis photog., 29105)

He was accustomed to living at the Fairview and the Grand Forks Hotels. He used my cabins for drawing his maps. He told me then that after the miners were through with their methods, he'd form a company and buy their claims cheap as he could and work them over with improved machinery. I was interested in some well-worked-out bench claims and would secure some for him, put a fair price on them and see he got them. I sold quite a number to him. The dirt at the mouth of the creeks was almost too low grade for the miners to handle by their methods. He thought he'd take up those. I sold him 47 below, Bonanza—the creek was wide there—and a few others. He always gave his check and it was always good. He bought quite a few low grade properties. He only figured then on Bonanza claims. After a trip to England he came back to Dawson, stayed a couple of months and left for Ottawa.[37]

It was in Ottawa that Treadgold secured the water concession, before returning to Dawson with one of his London financial backers, Sir Thomas Tancred.[38] Though Treadgold's grant was protested and eventually revoked,[39] the respite for the Klondike was only temporary. As Belinda explained, "Everything Treadgold planned in my cabin on Grand Forks, the Guggenheim interests carried out later over the entire Dawson district, operating the largest dredges in the world" (NW 39:2[213]), with Treadgold as managing director.

By the summer of 1901 Charles Carbonneau was also thinking about mining on a larger scale. It would be an idea he would develop while he and Belinda went Outside for their belated European honeymoon. Meanwhile, he placed a newspaper advertisement announcing that laymen with machinery were needed to work the Carbonneaus' claims on Eldorado, Bonanza, and Gold Run creeks.[40] The lay offer on the Eldorado fraction suggests that although the Carbonneaus had just agreed to sell the property, it was still under their control until the purchase was completed. On the very promising Gold Run claim the Carbonneaus were able to let three lays almost immediately. On the upper half were Edmund Letourneau and Joseph Bernier, who soon had thirty men at work.[41] The laymen were to pay all expenses of the mining, all shafts and drifts were to be cribbed (that is, reinforced with wood), and all dirt containing gold was to be taken out. All recovered gold as well as the royalty payments were to be shared 50/50 by the laymen and the Carbonneaus. Charles and Belinda also agreed to lend Letourneau and Bernier up to $20,000 for expenses, the loan to be repaid by May 1, 1902.[42] On a portion of the lower half of the claim were William Abbott and partners, who also were actively at work during the winter of 1901–2.[43] We do not know who held the third lay on No. 12 Gold Run that winter. We also do not know whether the Carbonneaus had any success in working out a lay agreement for the troublesome Bonanza claims.

Belinda and Charles celebrated their first wedding anniversary with a small dinner party at the Northern Cafe. Their guests were their neighbors on Gold Run, Mr. and Mrs. (Jerome) Chute and Dr. A. E. Wills, Belinda's longtime friend Joe Barrette, Canadian Bank of Commerce Manager H. T. Wills, Judge C. D. Macauley, Land Agent F. X. Gosselyn, and Mr. McLennan.[44]

Robert Purvis McLennan made an interesting political addition to the Carbonneaus' inner circle. A businessman in the firm of McLennan and McFeeley Company, he had attended the Carbonneaus' large wedding dinner.[45] In late 1901, when another push was under way for incorporation of Dawson, a legal means had been found to extend the franchise to non-Canadians. R. P. McLennan was the person most often mentioned to fill the position of mayor,[46] and in fact he was eventually elected in early 1903.[47] If the appointed officials were no longer to be in control of Dawson, it would be to the Carbonneaus' advantage to be on good terms with those elected to office.

Belinda and Charles left Dawson on their "honeymoon trip" soon after their

19.3. The Carbonneaus, apparently on their trip Outside in 1901. *(Bolotin Collection)*

19.4. The Carbonneaus' apartment in Paris was on the second floor of this building at 15 avenue d'Antin. *(UCB, Hawkins Collection, 77/81)*

first anniversary celebration.[48] They spent the winter in Europe, where they traveled extensively.[49] These winter trips Outside became a regular practice for them over the next few years, and their style of living in Europe was both elegant and expensive.

In Paris they rented the second floor of a large home in a socially prominent neighborhood near the Champs Elysées at 15 avenue d'Antin.[50] "We had some business to put over and wanted to have the right atmosphere. My husband said that people in hotels were considered fly-by-nights. What we wanted was a home. So we rented a house and began to entertain." The elegant neoclassical house belonged to a Mrs. Margot T. Jackson of Boston, and the other floors in the converted estate were rented by a Russian princess, the actress Madame Réjane,[51] and a French count. Living with Belinda and Charles were Belinda's younger siblings, Nell, Margaret, Agnes, and Jim, who attended school in Paris. According to Jim, their second floor alone was bigger than most houses. To run the apartment there were a number of employees. A concierge controlled access to the building. There was a housekeeper; a valet for Carbonneau; a butler and two maids; a chef and assistant chef along with various kitchen help; and a coachman and footman for the family carriage, which was drawn by two fine high-stepping horses, kept in stables to the back of the building.[52]

The children were closely supervised whenever they went out of the compound, but inside the high fence seven-year-old Jim on his tricycle always seemed to be getting in the way of the Russian princess, who had a fancy electric runabout. The Carbonneaus often went to the opera or the theater and afterwards dined at a fine restaurant. Occasionally the two older girls would accompany them, all decked out in designer clothes. According to Jim, the Carbonneaus also entertained frequently at the apartment, and often had visitors from Canada or the United States, as well as French aristocrats. On most evenings at home, twenty people sat down to a long, leisurely dinner, prepared by the Carbonneaus' very able chef, who had formerly worked for Edward VII of England.[53] Every two to three weeks, musicians or singers also were brought in to entertain the guests.

The charming Carbonneau was the arbiter of culture and manners for the family at the public occasions. Belinda was the first to admit she had much to learn about social manners. But she was smart and therefore quick to learn.

> . . . When I came out of Alaska, I thought only one kind of woman smoked [cigarettes]. When we went to Paris to a hotel recommended by some good friends, I was shocked to see the women smoking in the dining rooms or in the lounge. I hoped when we moved we'd get into a respectable place.
>
> We were going down to Nice, and I did trust the woman who recommended our hotel there. But the first afternoon I looked out of my window there was an elegant old lady, followed by four flunkies, going out to sit in the sun on the terrace. She lay back in her chair, and first . . . flunky brought her sewing and then another her tea things, and another whisky and soda. The last one of them lit a match for her cigarette!
>
> I called my husband. "We've had the wrong dope on this place," I said. "Look at that old lady. She's smoking and drinking out of doors."
>
> He looked and laughed. "That is Lady So-and-So," he said. "Her husband is a high government official in India. This is a fine hotel. What she does, she does openly."
>
> So I got my first shock over.
>
> . . . I'll never forget our first dinner party [in Paris]. I saw the ladies were all watching me and finally my husband whispered, "They are waiting for you to light a cigarette so they may smoke."
>
> I lit a cigarette, and I took a long breath and,—I choked, and—I coughed,—and—I sputtered,—but I smoked. One American girl there told me afterwards she would not have missed it for anything, I was so funny. After the party I said to my husband, "If I have to do this thing, I'm going off somewhere into the country for a week and get the habit."

While Belinda was a quick study on social manners, she was not one to stand on convention when her own straightforward, no-nonsense perspective suggested something else was called for. For example, in greeting royalty she might shake hands rather than curtsy, as demanded by protocol. Though Charles scolded Belinda for her faux pas,[54] each had to admit that the other's way had its advantages. Carbonneau's social graces meant they could easily associate with the powerful and wealthy potential investors whom Charles was courting for his various business ventures, and Belinda's honest approach often won the trust and admiration of many of these as well.

In the winter of 1901–2 in Paris, Charles was actively recruiting investors for another mining syndicate, this one based upon their Gold Run claim. When the Carbonneaus returned to Dawson in early April 1902 on one of two mail stages,[55] they were ready to begin a new era of their life, one engrossed in the fortunes of mining on Gold Run Creek.

20

Mining Gold Run

ALTHOUGH BELINDA AND CHARLES held other Klondike property, Gold Run Creek, on the Dominion Creek side of the Dome, was the focus of their attention in the spring of 1902 and for the following two years. Belinda and Charles had their own claim on Gold Run—Number 12. In addition Charles had begun working on reorganizing most of the rest of the productive claims in the valley. These were primarily on the lower end of the creek and most of them already had been consolidated under the ownership of Jerome Chute and Dr. Alfred E. Wills. Owning consecutive claims on a creek was a distinct advantage for intensive mining. Larger equipment could be used economically, and there were benefits of scale also in managing labor and supplies. Charles had learned that Chute and Wills were interested in selling their holdings on Gold Run,[1] and he had his own ideas about how the creek might best be exploited.

Gold Run Creek is about sixty-six miles by upstream navigation from Dawson (Allen, 15). (See map, fig. 7.3.) Because of its greater distance from the supply center, the creek's development and operations were more costly than for streams like Eldorado and Bonanza on the Klondike River side of the Dome. The Chute and Wills partnership had been acquiring and selectively mining claims for three years. They had found a good deal of gold, but they had also built up a tremendous debt. By the spring of 1902 the Canadian Bank of Commerce held mortgages on the property for more than $637,000.[2] Once the ready gold paid the debt, no one knew whether the gold remaining in the creek would be worth the intensive efforts needed to locate and extract it.

Charles's idea was to consolidate all of the Chute and Wills claims plus No. 12 on Gold Run into a mining company financed by outside investors. This would accomplish several goals. If the selling price were high enough, it would mean considerable income for Chute and Wills as well as for the Carbonneaus. Chute and Wills could use the money to pay off their debt and perhaps still show some profit. New capital would also help finance mining on a larger scale using heavy equipment rather than the labor of many individual miners. And if the former mine owners held stock in the company, they possibly still could profit from any rich stores of gold the creek might yet harbor.

When Charles and Belinda returned to Dawson from Europe in April of 1902, they brought with them Jean Marc Bel, a French mining engineer who had been hired by potential French investors to evaluate Gold Run Creek. Just what Engineer Bel reported back to his employers in Paris is not clear. When he left Dawson on 19 June M. Bel was predicting "a splendid future" for the Klondike, but he, understandably, would say nothing specific about what he would be recommending concerning a Gold Run Creek mining syndicate. The *Klondike Nugget* declared, "[T]here is no better placer ground in the Klondike than Gold Run property."[3] However, according to one source, Bel's report was not so glowing.

> Upon his arrival in Dawson he was for some time most assiduously "shepherded" by Carbonneau and his associates, in order that he might be prevented from seeing things otherwise than through their eyes, or from hearing stories of Carbonneau's character and career, which are, of course, common knowledge in Dawson. After some little time, however, M. Bel succeeded in evading the espionage of the would-be vendors, and, on being informed in reputable quarters regarding the true character of the business upon which he had to report and those associated with it, he became so convinced of the undesirability of his employers having anything further to do with it, that he at once returned to Paris, closely followed by the indefatigable Carbonneau.[4]

In fact, while Bel was inspecting Gold Run Creek, a messy dispute had erupted between the Carbonneaus and two of the men who had been working No. 12 Gold Run on a lay agreement during the preceding winter. According to Edmund Letourneau, layman on the upper half of the claim, the Carbonneaus were at first pleased with the amount of work that he and his partner and crew had done.[5] However, the Carbonneaus had a different version of the state of affairs.

While the basic issue seems to have been whether the lay work had been proceeding apace, the legal dispute focused on repayment of the money the Carbonneaus had lent to Letourneau and his partner Bernier the previous September for the purchase of equipment and supplies. The $20,000 loan was secured with a mortgage on the equipment and the dumps and was payable on or before 1 May 1902.[6] When the mortgage was not satisfied by that date, it seemed straightforward enough for the Carbonneaus to enforce the terms of the contract. However, the controversy that ensued turned into a veritable hornet's nest.

Soon after 1 May the Carbonneaus foreclosed the mortgage. The gold was still in the dump, and there was only beginning to be enough running water for a cleanup. The Carbonneaus claimed that Letourneau had been drinking heavily and was not attending to business, and that their representatives had been repeatedly refused access to the claim. In response to this complaint, a receiver, William Baptiste, was appointed by the court. And then on 19 June the *Klondike Nugget* announced liquidation of the foreclosed equipment.

> Notice of Public Auction, property of C. E. and Belinda A. Carbonneau, to be sold at the Court House in Dawson, on Monday, June 23, the property taken at #12 Gold Run in a mortgage foreclosure. It includes a boiler, hoist, pump, tools, two horses, two bobsleds, 1 wagon, cord wood, stores, etc.[7]

Letourneau and Bernier fought back, for they stood to lose all their winter's work. They got an injunction stopping the sale, claiming in their presentation to the court that they had recovered enough gold to reduce their debt to the Carbonneaus to $13,700.[8] In a later hearing Letourneau and Bernier further explained that they had not read the documents they had signed, but had relied on Carbonneau's assurance that the lease and the mortgage expired at the same time. According to the laymen, the primary reason they were not prepared to pay on 1 May was that they thought the mortgage was not due until 1 September.[9]

As the date for the auction of the seized material approached, and it became clearer to Letourneau and Bernier that they were about to lose their case, they escalated the mortgage battle by bringing far more serious counter-charges against Charles Carbonneau. Letourneau and Bernier each swore that while Engineer J. M. Bel was inspecting the No. 12 Gold Run property in May to determine its value, Carbonneau had tried to force the laymen to salt the claim, that is to inject additional gold into a sample of the dirt.

. . . J. M. Bell [sic] was rocking on the said above mentioned property and testing the dirt when the said plaintiff, C. E. Carbonneau, asked Joseph Bernier, the other defendant, and myself repeatedly to put gold in the rocker in order that the dirt said J. M Bell was testing would give $2 or $3 to the bucket.[10]

Letourneau and Bernier swore that when they refused to salt the rocker, the receiver, William Baptiste, began to harass them at their work. They were sluicing the dump to recover the gold, and the receiver rushed the work to the extent that the sluice boxes were choked and much of the gold was lost. Letourneau and Bernier sought to have the receiver removed from No. 12 Gold Run, but the motion was denied by the court. Instead, the judge ordered the receiver to post a bond of $10,000 and pay into the court the gold recovered in each week's wash-up. The two laymen were permitted to be present at each wash-up.[11]

The scandalous salting charges had been revealed just before Engineer Bel left Dawson to return to Paris, so he must have been aware of them. We do not know what effect they may have had on his report.

In the meanwhile, plans for the Gold Run Mining Company were moving along. First, Chute and Wills transferred all of their Gold Run claims, plus equipment, improvements, and some town property held by their partnership to the Canadian Bank of Commerce on 19 May 1902 for $1,500,000.[12] Next Belinda and Charles signed over No. 12 Gold Run to the bank for $1.00. Then on 23 June 1902 the bank gave C. E. Carbonneau an option to buy all of the Gold Run property formerly owned by Chute and Wills and the Carbonneaus for $1,750,000. The purchase price was to be paid $750,000 in cash, and $1,000,000 in paid-up stock of the company Charles would be setting up to mine the claims. The cash was to be divided $687,500 to Chute and Wills (a large portion of which would pay the mortgage obligation to the bank) and $62,500 to Belinda and Charles. In addition, any net profits from operating the mines in the meantime would go to the purchasers. Finally, the option was good only until 15 January 1903.[13]

On 24 June Dr. A. E. Wills and Carbonneau left Dawson en route to Paris to organize a company.[14] Dr. Wills carried papers conveying to him, as trustee for the bank, the claims, real estate, and personal property involved in the deal. These would allow him to complete the sale in Europe.[15] During the summer of 1902, pending the sale of their property, Chute supervised 250 men employed on four of the Chute and Wills claims on Gold Run. And immediately after the Carbonneaus' lay agreements expired, the *Dawson Daily News* of 5 September reported that "C. E. Carbonneau is working No. 12." As Charles was in Paris, London, or elsewhere, it was actually Belinda who was undoubtedly running

20.1. An idyllic pen-and-ink sketch of Belinda's cabin on No. 12 Gold Run Creek. A flume is shown in the left background and various mining implements appear in the foreground. A gold pan sitting on the ground underneath the middle window of the cabin contains actual gold dust. This sketch on birch bark and the newspaper clipping in the bottom right corner, dating from early 1899, were among the few mementos from the Klondike that Belinda had in later life. *(Bouillon Collection)*

the operation.[16] From time to time she registered at the Fairview Hotel "from Gold Run," as did her father, John Mulrooney, who no doubt was assisting her.[17]

As mining and cleanup continued during the summer, regular reports were telegraphed to A. E. Wills in Paris verifying funds being deposited at the Canadian Bank of Commerce in Dawson. These reports showed regular cleanups every two weeks of two thousand to three thousand ounces of gold, along with expenses during the same period. By the end of September, a net of $1,418,000 had been credited to the Chute and Wills Gold Run account. The net output for 15 September to 1 October on the Carbonneaus' No. 12 was reported as $7,000.[18] Gold Run Creek was living up to its promise, and these reports must have been reassuring to potential investors in Europe.

What was happening concerning investors in Paris, however, is not clear. It could be that J. M. Bel did not recommend the mines to his employers. Or perhaps some of the unsubstantiated[19] accusations of salting had made their way across a continent and an ocean to undermine Charles's efforts. In any case, the company that was eventually created, The Gold Run (Klondike) Mining Company, Ltd., was incorporated in London, not Paris. We assume that the magic word "Klondike" was plugged into the middle of the company name to attract investors.[20]

In September, H. T. Wills, local director of the Canadian Bank of Commerce, left Dawson for Europe, apparently to join his brother and Charles Carbonneau to work out the final transactions concerning the company. The Chute and Wills operations on Gold Run closed down for the winter in October.[21] Belinda's name appeared in the Fairview Hotel register for the last time that fall on 28 October. By that time, the court proceedings of the Carbonneaus against Letourneau and Bernier had been decided in favor of the Carbonneaus.[22] However, the laymen were not satisfied, and their appeal of the decision was then in process in the territorial court. Belinda put the case in the hands of their lawyers and apparently left Dawson in late October to join Charles in Europe.

The Gold Run (Klondike) Mining Company

The Gold Run (Klondike) Mining Company, Ltd., filed incorporation papers in London on 1 October 1902.[23] The nominal capital of the company was declared as an impressive £400,000 (approximately $2 million)[24] divided into 800,000 shares at 10 shillings each,[25] and seven subscribers were listed. Four of these were Englishmen,[26] each having bought one share. The other three subscribers were also directors of the company, each having bought one share and having received a thousand paid-up shares, apparently for their official role in the company.[27] They were Charles Carbonneau, A. E. Wills, and Francis Jules Marchand,[28] a Paris banker who was head of Le Crédit Canadien.[29] By the articles of association, Charles was to receive about £50,000 outright in stock at the completion of the acquisition of the mining property for his role in setting up the company and for bearing the expenses of the incorporation, this amount being the difference between the £400,000 valuation of the stocks and the $1.75 million purchase price of the property.[30] According to a further agreement between Charles and the company, he would receive 400,000 paid-up shares of the stock in the company worth $1 million, which would go to the Canadian Bank of Commerce as per the option. He would also get the rest of the shares fully paid up to be re-sold to raise the needed $750,000 cash plus his commission. Thus it seems that the only cash investment made by the original subscribers was ten shillings each. The rest of the assets of the company was stock to be used to raise cash and satisfy the terms of the sale from the Canadian Bank of Commerce. Furthermore, any net profit derived from the operations of the property (mines, hotels, stores) between 1 July 1902 and the closing of the deal would go to the new company.[31] Presumably this would be the approximately $1,418,000 on deposit at the Dawson bank, which could finance mining operations in the following year, pay the cash part of the option, and perhaps pay early dividends to stock holders.

To facilitate his selling of shares, Charles had issued 230,000 Share Warrants to Bearer.[32] These were printed in both English and French, and most of them in lots of ten shares to accommodate many small investors on both sides of the Channel. Because holders of these warrants were not registered unless the warrants were exchanged for stock certificates, we do not know how many of the warrants were actually sold. Apparently it was fewer than had been hoped, for what we do know is that by December, Charles was renegotiating the deal with the Canadian Bank of Commerce.

First, the cash amount to be paid apparently was reduced to $650,000, and that was offered as a mortgage on the property in favor of the Canadian Bank of Commerce. To secure the mortgage, another 300,000 shares of the company stock (in addition to the 400,000 already agreed upon) was to be deposited into a trust account, with any proceeds from sale of those shares after 1 April 1903 to be applied to the mortgage. Also, any dividends paid for these deposited shares after 5 October 1903 would be applied to the mortgage. In turn Charles agreed to indemnify the company and the property against the mortgage.[33]

Charles "negotiated" these changes with the board of directors—Carbonneau, A. E. Wills and Marchand—who had been given extensive powers to run the company, including the ability to determine what number of directors would be considered a quorum to conduct business. Unless otherwise specified, that number would usually be only two.[34] The renegotiated terms were signed for the company only by F. J. Marchand. Apparently the directors had also decided that little or no money from the summer of 1902 workings was to be used to complete the purchase. That both A. E. Wills and the Canadian Bank of Commerce under the directorship of H. T. "Chief" Wills agreed to these changes is indicated by the fact that A. E. Wills accepted the $650,000 mortgage in trust for the bank.[35] The terms of these changes would become known to other interested parties only later. A. E. Wills assigned the mortgage to the bank on 1 May 1903, after he returned to the Klondike and after all of the other papers completing the complicated deal were registered.[36]

By 31 December 1902, only fifteen days before his option expired, Charles was able to complete the mining company deal. A. E. Wills transferred all the property to Charles. Charles gave him the $650,000 mortgage, and transferred the property to the Gold Run (Klondike) Mining Company. The company transferred all the required stock to Charles, who paid 399,993 shares to the Canadian Bank of Commerce and put 300,000 shares into a trust account with the London office of the bank.[37] Charles was then named managing director.[38]

At the end of January 1903, the *Klondike Nugget* announced the sensational news in Dawson: "Chute & Wills have transferred 19 claims on Gold Run Creek to a Paris syndicate for a fabulous sum." On 3 March under another bold, front-page headline, the paper gave further details of the deal when the Wills brothers arrived back in Dawson on the stage from Whitehorse.

> [It is] the largest and most important flotation of Klondike mining properties yet consummated. . . . The official name of the new company is the Gold Run (Klondike) Mining Company. The capital stock . . . has been placed at 400,000 British pounds, which has been practically all subscribed. Dr. Wills is the general manager of the company and will be in charge of local operations.
> . . . The property involved in the flotation includes in all 27 claims on Gold Run, or about one and one-half miles of the richest section of that creek.[39]

Actually, formation of the new company was not so assured as implied by the newspaper coverage. The stock had been issued "fully paid up," but most of it was yet to be sold. In addition, controversy already brewed between the principals in the deal. According to Jerome Chute, the changes to the deal were made without his authorization, and in negotiating the mortgage, A. E. Wills had left him, as a partner of Chute and Wills, still liable for the money owed to the bank. This was particularly irksome because getting out from under that liability had been one of the chief reasons for entering into the deal in the first place. Furthermore, the stock Chute was to have received as his part of the transaction was now tied up with the mortgage and in the keeping of the Canadian Bank of Commerce. To make matters worse, Chute had understood that he would continue to act as manager of the operations in the Klondike, with full charge and authority. However, as soon as the deal was completed, he was notified that his services as manager were no longer needed.[40] Chute was not going to take this power-grab lying down.

On 29 January he sought and obtained a restraining order against the Canadian Bank of Commerce, Charles Carbonneau, and the Gold Run (Klondike) Mining Company, blocking all transactions executing the deal. Therefore, none of the necessary documents could be recorded and the company could not operate legally in the Yukon. As more details of the deal were revealed, Chute also learned that money taken out of the claims the previous year was being used to purchase new machinery. This made no sense to him as a practical miner. He had shown that the old tried and true methods with the currently-owned equipment would produce substantial profits. Therefore, he felt those methods should be continued so that all resources could first go into paying off the mortgage. Only then should there be more investment in equipment.

On 17 March 1903, a settlement was reached whereby the defendants agreed that no new machinery would be placed on the Gold Run claims before 1 September 1903, and that Chute would receive regular monthly statements as to the affairs of the company. Chute then discontinued his action for an injunction, and the documents for transferring the properties to the company along with the consequent agreements were registered on 19 March. We do not know what further concessions Chute may have received in exchange.[41]

As for not buying new equipment, the agreement with Chute seems to have had little effect, probably because machinery had already been ordered and was in the process of being shipped before the March settlement.[42] Men were put to work on Gold Run Creek under the direction of Doctor-now-Manager A. E. Wills, and heavy machinery began to arrive as soon as the river opened for the steamboats. In early July it was announced that the largest mining plant in the Yukon would be erected on No. 27 Gold Run. Immediately afterwards, Chute filed a lawsuit, seeking an injunction to restrain the company from installing any more machinery on the property.[43] His struggle now was primarily over principles, for obviously the money had already been spent for the machinery and there was little to gain by letting it sit unused.

Belinda returned to Dawson and into the middle of the fray on 8 July. She carried with her power of attorney to act concurrently with A. E. Wills as manager in the Yukon of the Gold Run (Klondike) Mining Company. Accompanying Belinda was her brother Jim, who would celebrate his eleventh birthday in the Klondike. She told the press that Charles would arrive in the fall, after which they would stay only a short time before returning to Paris.[44] In fact, Charles had taken Belinda's sisters—Nell, Margaret, and Agnes—with him to Europe under

20.2. The development on claim 27 of Gold Run, owned by the Gold Run (Klondike) Mining Company. This area became known as "No. 27 Town." *(Wolfe photog., Waugaman Collection)*

the supervision of a chaperone, his relative Madame Arcond.[45] As far as we have been able to determine, Charles never did return to the Klondike after 1902.[46]

Jim recalled his summer in the Klondike as one of the happiest in his life. He apparently was an active boy—more than his fifty-three-year-old mother could handle. So Belinda took him with her, got him a .22 rifle, and turned him loose to explore the creeks and the hills.[47] In the meantime, Belinda was hard at work with her mining business.

Belinda is credited with bringing order to the work force on the Gold Run company's property during the summer of 1903. By then there were hundreds of employees as well as an assortment of company stores, offices, gold-processing workrooms, hotels, a bathhouse, bunkhouses, eating facilities, and cabins. They were concentrated on claim No. 27 and therefore became referred to as "No. 27 Town"[48] and eventually as simply Gold Run. The *Dawson Daily News* declared on 5 August that gambling was now dead on Gold Run, and other accounts inform us that Belinda not only cleaned up gambling and drinking on the creek

20.3. Henry T. "Chief" Wills, manager of the Canadian Bank of Commerce, left, and an unidentified guard, with two weeks' output from the Gold Run (Klondike) Mining Company in the summer of 1903 or 1904. *(Yakima Valley Museum, Larss and Duclos photog., Carbonneau Collection, 2392)*

(Mackay), but carried out even more sweeping reform: "Her first move was to throw out the roulette wheel and replace it with a bridge table. Her second was to drive the female camp-followers from the property. As a foreman (or, more correctly, a forewoman) she was a holy terror" (Berton, 426).

For a while that summer there was reasonable production from the Gold Run claims. A photograph probably taken about this time shows on the left Manager H. T. Wills of the Canadian Bank of Commerce, with a pistol-toting guard on the right. Between them are two chests and several sausage-shaped bags that are presumably filled with the gold, for the caption reads "15 days clean up by the Gold Run (Klondyke) Mining Co., Gold Run Creek, Y. T." Belinda laughed when she explained that the gun was only for show and that the guard never in fact carried one.

Besides her activity on Gold Run Creek, Belinda also negotiated a deal to acquire mining property nearby. The Crueger concession for hydraulic mining was originally issued on 27 October 1900 to Arthur B. Crueger[49] and was one of

20.4. Belinda Mulrooney Carbonneau and unidentified staff members of the Gold Run (Klondike) Mining Company in front of the recently constructed company office on the creek. The photo was probably taken in the summer of 1903. *(UCB, Wolfe photog., Hawkins Collection, 77/81)*

several granted in the Dawson area by the Laurier administration in Ottawa to encourage large-scale development of the territory. The twelve-year lease covered two and one-quarter miles from the junction of Dominion and Sulphur Creeks down the Indian River. (See map, fig. 7.3.) Therefore, the upper end of the property was only a few miles downstream from the mouth of Gold Run Creek. Belinda bought the concession for $60,000,[50] probably for the Gold Run (Klondike) Mining Company, for the Crueger property eventually was consolidated with the mining company's holdings. Jim Mulrooney recalled that Charles had arranged a deal to purchase a dredge for the Crueger company but couldn't raise enough cash in France or England, so the deal fell through.[51] Since the Crueger company, presumably as a result, did not have enough money to exploit its concession, perhaps Charles saw purchase of the lease as a good fall-back position. We do not know how much the Crueger company had invested in the concession, so it is hard to estimate who benefited or lost in this transaction.

In August, a blow far greater than Chute's lawsuit struck the Gold Run

(Klondike) Mining Company as well as all other miners in the Indian River area. The rain stopped. "There is not more than a sluice head of water in Gold Run," said the *Dawson Daily News* on 6 August. With no water, gold could not be washed from the dumps. Operator after operator had to shut down.[52]

Unfortunately, the summer drought of 1903 failed to break, so that even with tighter management of the company property, production fell off. By fall the claims along Gold Run and neighboring creeks had shut down completely, ending a thoroughly unsatisfactory season. All in all, it was not a propitious beginning for the Gold Run (Klondike) Mining Company.

Following the 1903 season, Belinda simplified her position in the Yukon even further. The trend toward bigger mining operations replaced the individual mining at which she had succeeded before. She followed the trend, which she herself was helping to set, by divesting herself of more of her remaining individual, isolated claims. In the fall of 1903 she arranged to sell her and Charles's 41 A/D on Bonanza for $4,600. She also sold her own one-half interest in a Dominion Creek claim, 73D B/L/D, for $2,500.[53]

One piece of good news for the Carbonneaus that fall concerned the dispute over the mortgage with their former laymen on No. 12 Gold Run, Letourneau and Bernier. The original judgment in their favor had been upheld on appeal in the Territorial court.[54] But Letourneau and Bernier decided to appeal to the Supreme Court of Canada, so the action would grind through another round in the next year.

Belinda and Jim made ready to leave Dawson on 16 October, along with H. T. "Chief" Wills of the Canadian Bank of Commerce. But the Yukon began to freeze early and the boat they had planned to take, the *Prospector*, did not make it to Dawson because of the ice. The stage to Whitehorse began running at once, with Belinda's party among the first to get out across the trail.[55] Jim remembered the trip as terrible,[56] for the stage still had to run on wheels, and the four-hundred-mile trail was filled with hub-deep ruts, now frozen hard and slippery.

For Chief Wills the journey Out was made more bearable by pleasant anticipation, for he was to wed Mary McElroy in Seattle. Thirty-six-year-old Mary was from a prominent pioneering family in the Puget Sound area, her parents having arrived there in 1871. She may have become acquainted with H. T. Wills through her brother Matt, who had rushed to the Klondike in 1897 and stayed for about a year. The wedding ceremony in Seattle was a small, family affair,[57] but Belinda and Jim were part of the party. Following the ceremony the bride

20.5. A banquet given by Emile Loubet, president of France, for the Comité Français des Expositions à l'Etranger, Réunion des Jurys et Comités des Expositions Universelles. Charles Carbonneau sits at the second table from the front, at the far right edge of the photograph, looking over his left shoulder at the camera. *(Yakima Valley Museum, Carbonneau Collection)*

and groom, who were to honeymoon in France, traveled east on the same train as Belinda and Jim. They got as far as Spokane, Washington, where Mary became ill. The entire wedding party left the train while Mary was taken to a hospital. Tragically, the new bride died the next day. Belinda and Jim decided to continue their journey while the rest of the saddened party returned to Seattle.[58]

In Paris during the winter of 1903–4, the Carbonneaus continued to live well and entertain lavishly. Charles had become a member of the Comité Français des Expositions à l'Etranger, a national committee formed to protect the interest of French exhibitors at international expositions, and was among the honorees at a banquet on 23 November 1903 given by the president of France, Emile Loubet.

About this time Charles was beginning to work on another big business deal, organizing a shipping company to encourage emigration of French peasants to Canada.[59] This he was arranging under the patronage of Raymond

20.6. The Carbonneaus' rented villa in Nice, France, in about 1904. *(UCB, Hawkins Collection, 77/81)*

Préfontaine, whom he had known from Montreal and who had been appointed Minister of Marine and Fisheries of Canada in November 1902.[60] Charles was in the process of investing nearly all of what had been Belinda's money in two steamships for this company.[61] He also was putting together a promotion for an iron and steel business.[62]

Belinda's siblings were once again sent to fine schools, now in Paris or Switzerland. When the Carbonneaus closed their apartment in Paris, they went south to take up residence in a beautiful villa in Nice, from which they would go on occasional jaunts to Monte Carlo.

But in fact Belinda's and Charles's high-flying, complex world was beginning to unravel. The year-end report for the Gold Run (Klondike) Mining Company showed that the Canadian Bank of Commerce had managed to sell only 136,000 of their 700,000 shares from the original 800,000 shares of the company. This amounted to about $350,000, which did not yet cover the outstanding mortgage of $650,000. There had been at least three one-percent dividend payments to stockholders, which distributed about $60,000 of the company's money, presumably from the gold mined in 1902. But by the terms of Charles's agreement with the Company,[63] only half of that would have gone to the bank. Pressure was mounting over the outstanding debt and the prospects for paying it from the next season's production of the mines.

Back in the frigid Yukon Territory, in the hope of a better season in 1904, the Gold Run (Klondike) Mining Company had put men to work early in the new year. Eight or ten were running tunnels and doing other preliminary work underground, and ten teams were hauling wood for the boilers.[64] Then, during the first week of March, the men were laid off and the operation shut down, "on orders from Outside." The *Yukon World* of 5 March reported that "though it is not given out authoritatively, it is presumed that the action is taken because of 'Count' Carbonneau's being involved with the Parisian courts. The shut-down means the suspension of big operations as the company has been doing work with machinery hoists and self-dumpers this winter" (p. 1, col. d).

The next news of the "trouble" was reported by the *Montreal Star* in its edition of 14 May. It said that "the French company to which the Carbonneau, Chute and Wills interests were sold might be liquidated by Le Credit Canadien." This, the paper said, was a banking institution in Paris promoted by Carbonneau.[65]

In the meantime Charles, Belinda, and A. E. Wills were on their way back to the Klondike and embroiled in a power struggle. On their stop in New York City, Wills said that Charles tried to persuade him to convene a directors' meeting to award both Wills and Belinda annual salaries of $6,000 in addition to expenses as managers. Wills said later that he thought this a fraud on the stock holders and refused. And he claimed that since Belinda was present at the time, she too was involved in the fraud. Realizing that Wills was no longer his ally, Charles as chairman of the board of directors fired Wills on 28 June and appointed Belinda as sole manager. But the action was a covert one. He used a document he had signed and dated 15 February, presumably before questions about his leadership in the company had come into question. Perhaps more strange, Wills was not notified of his firing until 1 August.[66]

The Carbonneaus learned of another snag in their business affairs while on the east coast. In the appeal of laymen Letourneau and Bernier against Carbonneau and Carbonneau, the Supreme Court in Ottawa had reversed the previous decisions. Now Letourneau and Bernier prevailed. According to Belinda, the Carbonneaus were notified by their attorney that what they owed would be paid out of moneys already in the court, for they had posted a bond of $5,000 before going Outside the previous year.[67] She found out only later that the bond did not cover the costs.

All was not going smoothly between Charles and Belinda by this time either. Belinda, realizing belatedly that Charles had married her primarily for her money, began to take steps to protect what remained of her fortune from him. She put her furs in safekeeping with Revillon Frères and her jewelry with Tiffany and Company[68] before proceeding on her journey to Dawson.

Belinda arrived in Dawson on 14 July,[69] while Charles returned to Europe. Though she said nothing in public at the time, two years later Belinda would claim that Charles had deserted her in March with no support.[70] Given what we know of their business affairs, this may seem unlikely, since all indications are that Belinda was at least as much a breadwinner in the family as was Charles. Belinda probably had decided by that time that she needed to divorce Charles, and by law it was (and still is in many places) the husband's duty to provide for the wife. So Belinda was simply stating that Charles was not fulfilling his legal obligations.

Belinda, apparently strapped for cash when she got to Dawson in 1904, turned to her old friend Captain H. H. Norwood for a mortgage soon after she arrived. He lent her $9,000 for a year, secured by the deed to the upper 250 feet of 40 A/D Bonanza, as well as several hillside claims on Dominion Creek.[71] Belinda needed to use her power of attorney from Charles for this transaction, for the claims were also in Charles's name. Besides providing Belinda with ready cash, this may also have been a strategy for her to insulate at least part of these assets from other claims against Charles that were soon to surface—actions in which she was also a respondent but from which she wanted to separate herself.

Belinda also carried with her to Dawson powers of attorney issued by the Board of Directors of the Gold Run (Klondike) Mining Company. These appointed her and Dr. A. E. Wills the general managers of the company's property in the Yukon Territory, with the restriction that they could not dispose of the mining property or the equipment.[72] Belinda first asked her attorney, J. B. Pattullo, for a legal interpretation of the documents' provisions for her managership.[73] Armed with her power of attorney and her determination to get the mines paying again, Belinda went out to Gold Run Creek and took charge. Belinda's activities as manager prove her ability to set clear goals, with strict control but generous rewards. They also show her once again succeeding despite the prejudice against her.

Because of inefficient management, with scores of miners drinking and gambling on and off the job, the first year's results alarmed the Canadian Bank of Commerce heads in Toronto. They hurried a special investigator to Dawson.

In due course he returned an ominous report and [the bank] ordered him to install the "most efficient and responsible mine operator available" to take complete charge of Gold Run, including one third ownership, predicated on success. He answered that "the most efficient and successful operator in the Klondike and best account of (the bank) branch in Dawson is B. A. Mulrooney." Toronto assumed this was a man.

The next day [Dr.][74] Wills called graciously on Belinda at her Fairview Hotel. "I never dreamed I'd live to see the day, my dear, when I'd be ordered by the mighty to hire a woman to take my job," he said in high good humor. Wills retained his part ownership, along with Belinda, and later shared in the huge profits.

. . . Setting inflexible rules of conduct on and off the job, she also devised production quotas and $500 monthly bonuses, which quickly resulted in fevered efficiency. Most of the men won the bonuses regularly.[75]

This is a rosy picture of what really happened. Contemporary newspaper reports in 1904 expand on the story and give some different slants. The positive tone of an article appearing in the *Dawson Daily News* of 27 July 1904 suggests that Belinda probably had supporters in Dawson who were sympathetic to her situation and impressed by her gumption. It also hints that there may have been some favoritism in Belinda's management of the company.

Gold Run [is] booming. . . . Mrs. B. A. Carbonneau, the present manager, with her quiet, unassuming dignity, superintends and directs the making of all contracts, in which she is ably assisted by . . . Dave Curry, the former foreman of the Gold Run (Klondike) Mining Company. . . .

For the past three days there have been many lays let on the different properties belonging to the company. . . . None of the claims have been worked since last fall, and but very few people have been up on the creek . . . this summer. . . .

The writer understands most of the property has now been disposed of. . . . We note amongst the late arrivals on Gold Run . . . Joe Barrett, who has procured a lay on a very rich claim. (p. 2, col. f)

This story was accurate but incomplete. A lay agreement on No. 16 Gold Run between the Gold Run (Klondike) Mining Co. and Belinda's friend Joe Barrette was filed with the Gold Commissioner on 18 July. The lay was 60 percent to Barrette, 40 percent to the company. A second lay agreement was filed at the same time on the same terms, this one for No. 9 Gold Run and with George Whittemore as the layman.[76]

In addition to getting work under way with the lays, Belinda started to correct some of the problems she saw had developed over the winter. On 20 July, as manager of the company, she revoked the appointment of W. S. Waugh as its caretaker, saying that he had refused to obey her orders and had moved the company's and Belinda's machinery to his own property without authority.[77]

On this same day, however, an official declaration was filed in the office of the Gold Commissioner.

> NOTICE. Mrs. B. A. Carbonneau is hereby notified not to deal in any way with the properties or mining claims on Gold Run Creek and in particular to let no lay or lays to any person whatsoever on any of the claims.[78]

Either Belinda was not aware of that notice, or she chose to ignore it. The latter seems more likely. During the next three weeks she issued fifteen additional lay agreements, all on the same percentage basis as the first two. But in letting the lays, she was going against the philosophy of using larger-scale methods as instituted by A. E. Wills in the previous year, and she was offering more favorable terms than usual to the laymen.

Ever since Alex McDonald had initiated the system in the fall of 1896,[79] lays in the Klondike were usually let on a 50/50 split. But possibly no layman would work the Gold Run claims for less than 60 percent of the gold recovered. As early as 1897–98 some laymen were getting as high as 75 percent on poorer ground.[80] In 1900 there had been general discussion in Dawson that even on richer claims the 50-percent lay system was a failure, for when mining was less than optimal, as it had been in 1903, the laymen often would go without pay.[81] So there were precedents for awarding a larger percentage to the laymen. Also, by this time there was suspicion among Dawsonites that the previous work on Gold Run Creek had already removed the richest ground, and that the remaining value of the claims had been grossly overstated.

About that time reports of more trouble in London appeared in the local papers.

> At a meeting of the Gold Run (Klondike) Mining Co. there was a dispute over representation by the French shareholders and the Canadian Bank of Commerce. Mr. Carbonneau agreed not to preside at a meeting of the shareholders until July 22. The case is now in the chancery division of the High Court of Britain.[82]

Unfortunately, official company documents do not clarify the situation. One report shows the election of three new English directors on 25 July and claims that all three of the original directors—A. E. Wills, F. J. Marchand, and C. E. Carbonneau—vacated their offices by failing to hold the necessary 2,000 shares each of company stock as of December 1902. It is true that with the incorporation documents, the original directors are shown as having only 1001 shares. But by the next report of allotments, and all subsequent ones, they each have the required minimum of 2,000.[83] This suggests that someone had decided that the original directors were not acting in the best interests of the company and had seized upon a technicality to remove them. The report of the July meeting also informs us that while the new directors had appointed A. E. Wills as an additional director, Marchand had in fact resigned by letter, but Charles Carbonneau was protesting his removal. In the meantime he was being permitted to sit in on board meetings until his case in the courts was resolved.[84]

But now Belinda's managership was on shaky ground, for her power of attorney could be revoked by the new directors. In fact, she was notified that she had been removed on 1 August.[85] In a counter-move on the same day, she served A. E. Wills with the document executed by Charles and dated the previous February, removing Wills from office. Belinda thereby became sole manager and local administrator of the company property.[86] She had a great interest in making the company profitable and in realizing some compensation for her lost claim No. 12. She also apparently felt that until Charles's status with the company was clarified, she still had the authority to direct the mining operations.

Nevertheless, the controversially deposed Dr. A. E. Wills was still on site in Dawson. He secured an injunction from the Territorial Court prohibiting further activities by Mrs. Carbonneau with regard to company property. This action may have been in response to orders from London, or it may have been at Wills's own discretion—a reflection of the power struggle between him and Belinda. Also, Wills may have viewed Belinda, as a married woman, merely as an extension of Charles. However, even if it were granted that Belinda could still work in the best interests of the company, there was a real contradiction between her mining strategy and the approach taken by Wills. This disagreement was an echo of the earlier struggle between Chute and Wills.

When Wills had been sole manager the previous year, he had operated the claims generally by hiring large crews of workers and installing more powerful machinery.[87] This approach has potential for great profit if the ore is rich and the cleanup proceeds apace. But because the drought prevented most of the sluicing and possibly because of lax management of personnel, the company actually had lost money in 1903.

The lay arrangement was a different strategy, requiring little further investment. Given the indeterminacy of the weather, mining on lay agreements seemed the best approach to Belinda in July of 1904, even with the 60/40 split. They were getting a late start on the sluicing, and if water again proved scarce, at least the company would not go even further into the hole. Only time would tell which strategy would be more profitable.

Belinda sought to gain that time by petitioning for the injunction to be lifted, and the matter was argued in court. However, in a sense, the company had already lost greatly, for the internal struggles between the "warring factions of the Gold Run (Klondike) Company"[88] were dissipating its human and monetary resources, as well as the precious time during which sluicing was possible.

Justice James Craig rendered a preliminary decision on 23 August. A principal consideration in the case, he said, was the meaning of the term "dispose" in the instructions given to Dr. Wills and Mrs. Carbonneau by the board of directors. They were not permitted to dispose of the mining property or the equipment. Did Mrs. Carbonneau "dispose" of mining property when she let lays? Justice Craig was not yet ready to answer that question. In the meanwhile, however, he did issue the following ruling, which could allow work to proceed:

> Lays let by Mrs. Carbonneau prior to August 1 are recognized, under certain conditions. . . . The laymen are to receive but 40 per cent of the output instead of 60 per cent as is stipulated in their agreements. The remaining 20 per cent will remain in the courts until it is decided whether or not the percentage given by the lessor is excessive. . . . Should the final adjudication of the case determine that Mrs. Carbonneau had no right to let lays . . . , then the laymen will have to pay back into court the 40 per cent already advanced.[89]

The first of August was set as the critical date for recognizing lays because that was when Belinda had been notified that her authority as manager had been revoked. She had issued ten of the seventeen lay agreements prior to 1 August. Justice Craig, with the consent of both parties, appointed William Bradley inspector on the Gold Run (Klondike) Mining Company property, and mining operations continued under his direction, pending final settlement of the lawsuit. Then Dr. A. E. Wills, now described as Manager in Canada for the company, issued a notice that only he was authorized to transact any business.[90]

By October a further partial compromise had been worked out with the ten lay holders so that they received the 60 percent agreed upon for work done to that point, but their lays were then canceled. By 8 October work on all the claims had been stopped. Furthermore, the 40 percent of output that was to go to the Gold Run mining company was ordered held by the court. Both the Carbonneaus and the Canadian Bank of Commerce sought possession of this share, the Carbonneaus perhaps to satisfy European creditors and the bank to satisfy the mortgage it held.[91]

The lawsuits were not yet at an end. The mining company filed two suits—one against General Manager Charles Carbonneau, the second against Belinda. On the first suit the court again ruled that the question of the meaning of the word "dispose" had to be decided and that any claims for damages were premature until the legal question was resolved.[92] The suit against Belinda eventually was dismissed.

All of this wrangling exacted a heavy toll. It is probably safe to assume that by September 1904 Belinda was feeling desperate. Her story-book marriage to Carbonneau was in fact a shambles. She was financially broke, her great Klondike fortune largely dissipated. Her efforts to put the Gold Run (Klondike) Mining Company back on sound ground, which also would have given her some income, had been thwarted, and in the process her reputation as a successful miner and businesswoman was undermined. The lawsuits and financial maneuverings had not only stripped her of any management authority, but had tied up funds which she needed to meet other obligations. One of those was the $6,000 judgment against the Carbonneaus by the Canadian Supreme Court in the appeal brought by laymen Letourneau and Bernier,[93] and the Carbonneaus also now were required to pay the defendants' costs.

On 7 September action was taken to secure payment of $6,222.39 through appropriation of Belinda's beloved Fairview Hotel and whatever other lands, goods, and chattels the Carbonneaus still had in the Yukon. However, by that time Belinda had sold and transferred the Fairview to a company, the Klondike Gold Venture Company, Limited, which she said was set up in New York in June in a partnership between Charles Carbonneau and a man named Schneider. Belinda swore that this was done before she knew there was a judgment against her.[94] Then she and Charles entered an appeal of this decision against them. The subsequent court action would take another year to be settled.

But in the meantime, following their triumphs in the lower courts, Belinda mistakenly had been allowed to withdraw the money that had been put on deposit by the laymen in partial satisfaction of the mortgage, $3,182. Now Belinda was ordered to return that money by 21 September. But she had spent the money and had no way to replace it. Just how fragile Belinda was feeling at this time can be judged by the fact that she broke down in tears when called to account on 21 September.[95] Belinda took pride in being tough, and she was not the sort of woman who generally used tears to manipulate a situation to her advantage. She was given an extension until 1 October to return the money.

Belinda assessed her situation and her prospects for being able to recover in the Yukon. Winter was coming. But even in good weather the Klondike was no longer a booming district where an individual miner could hope to create a fortune. Belinda felt she needed to start clean, much as she had done when first arriving in Dawson seven years earlier; therefore, she decided to take drastic action. Belinda left the Yukon on 26 September for the flourishing mining camp of Fairbanks, Alaska, and she never returned to the Yukon,[96] though it is not clear whether that was her intention when she left.

One local newspaper saw fit to interpret Belinda's precipitous action as skipping town, reporting on 13 October that she had taken pains to conceal her leaving and made sure her name did not appear on the passenger list of the steamer *Monarch*. The *Yukon World* got the date of her departure correct, but there were two steamers on that day, and Belinda was on the *Tyrell*, not the *Monarch* as the paper reported. Other information suggests that her intention to leave was certainly not a secret to a large number of people in Dawson. She had been busy forming a partnership with two other Dawson women to do mining in the Fairbanks area. She assigned power of attorney to her attorney, J. B. Pattullo, to settle her affairs. And she was buying mining equipment and arranging for its shipment to Fairbanks for at least a couple of weeks before she left.[97] So she was hardly sneaking out of town. Nevertheless, she did leave with money still owing and with cases unsettled.

Belinda's departure was dramatically brought to general public awareness when she was subpoenaed by Justice C. A. Dugas to testify as a witness on 11 October in a suit the Canadian Bank of Commerce filed against A. R. Thompson.[98] She failed to appear 11 October or the following morning, when the case was again called. The *Dawson Daily News* (12 October 1904) thought she might be held in contempt of court, but it turned out that Belinda probably had not received the subpoena, and she was at that time out of jurisdiction of the court.

The death blow to the Gold Run (Klondike) Mining Company came in February 1905 when the Canadian Bank of Commerce filed a $560,000 lawsuit against Dr. A. E. Wills, C. E. Carbonneau, J. A. Chute, and the mining company itself to collect on the mortgage.[99] The action may have been precipitated by news from Paris concerning Charles's legal troubles there. A Montreal newspaper, *La Patrie*, carried a reprint of a sensational article from *Le Journal* of Paris. Through the florid prose of the French paper we get a sense of Charles's style and reputation by that time in France.

> Yesterday appeared—or rather didn't appear—before the eleventh correctional chamber, a crook of wide range. Charles Eugene Carbonneau, calling himself Canadian in France and French in Canada.
>
> The crafty man, exploiting French sympathies for our former colony, had had the bright idea to found in Paris a whole series of institutions destined, in appearance, to tighten our commercial ties with the land sprinkled with the blood of Montcalm and his compatriots.
>
> One remembers certainly, in the world of finance and affairs, the spreading in our wealthiest quarters, of an announcement as sudden as [it was] sensational and ephemeral, luxurious decor behind which Carbonneau organized bold strokes against public funds, so accessible to golden dreams in our country.
>
> Alas! after having handled millions, inhaled the incense of popularity, [and] launched resounding speculations, to the stupefaction of his compatriots amused by our credulity, the unfortunate Carbonneau [ran afoul of] the police court, along with habitual vagabonds, under the charge of abuse of confidence.[100]

Many charges were leveled against Charles, but few of these were actually tried. He was convicted in Paris for embezzling obligations deposited into Le Credit Canadien for a promotion of "The Iron and Steel Company." He was also convicted of swindling 75,000 francs from a contractor of public works in connection with a promotion involving management of a railroad line. Charles was sentenced to two years in prison, fined 500 francs, and required to return the money he had gotten under false pretense. At the time of the trial he was reported as living in London.[101] We have found no indication that he ever served his time, paid his fine, or returned the embezzled funds.

Dr. A. E. Wills tried to revive the mining company in 1905 by organizing Crueger-Gold Run Consolidated Limited, which took over the interests and debt of both the old Gold Run company and the Crueger concession, formerly acquired by Belinda. He returned to Dawson on 1 August 1905, bringing with him two directors of the new company.[102] The new company had no better success than the old one, and the claims were sold off one by one. In 1907 the National Trust Company Limited took over the property but sold it in 1911 to the Treadgold/Guggenheim Yukon Gold Company.[103] Although a dredge was moved in to scour the creek in 1913, it was not completely worked out. By 1966 when the company, then called Yukon Consolidated Gold Corporation, shut down, there was an estimated $3.7 million in gold still to be harvested.[104] But subsequent work beginning in 1987 by Teck Corporation using bulldozers and motorized scrapers has produced even greater riches. Through July 1996, Gold Run Creek had yielded another 67,008 ounces of gold, with No. 12, Belinda's former claim, still in the midst of the paying ground.[105]

However, back in 1904, Belinda was starting a new life in Fairbanks, Alaska.

21

Starting Over in Fairbanks

In July of 1902, deep in Alaskan territory, new gold deposits were discovered by Felix Pedro in the hills of a wide, fertile valley of the Tanana River. Word of the new strike reaching Dawson in 1903 was like a tonic to old-time prospectors and individual miners. As its high-grade gravels petered out, the Klondike region was being taken over by more efficient, large-scale operations. Now there was new territory to explore, and the reports from the Tanana, if short on facts, did sound promising. Miners and speculators rushed to the new ground from the Yukon as well as from other parts of the world.

Fairbanks, the supply center for the new diggings, was on the banks of the Chena River, a tributary of the Tanana. By the time Belinda arrived at Fairbanks in October 1904, it was already a lively commercial center for the surrounding mining areas, including the creeks called Cleary, Pedro, and the most recently discovered, Dome.

Although the reverses in her fortune in the Klondike and in her relationship with Charles were discouraging, Belinda was not one to give up. She saw the Fairbanks area as a fresh beginning and, if the fates smiled, as a place to rebuild her wealth. She had access to some funds she had set aside back east for her family. And before leaving Dawson on 26 September 1904, she had formed a

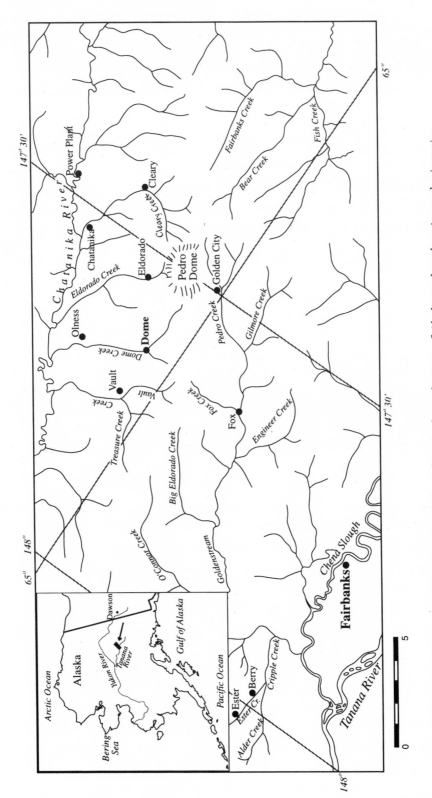

21.1. A detailed map of the Fairbanks area, with a darkened rectangle on the inset of Alaska to show location and orientation. (*Adapted from Prindle et al., Mineral Resources, 190+. Waugaman Collection.*)

partnership with two other women, Mabel Scouse[1] and Bessy (Lorene Elizabeth) Byrnes, to invest in mining property in the Tanana District.[2] According to a written agreement drawn up between them, each of the three invested $5,000 to acquire and operate mining claims. In addition, they split the cost of some machinery, worth $1,950, bought by Belinda to take with her to Fairbanks.

Mabel and Bessy had been in Dawson since 1899,[3] and in 1902 Mabel had married William Scouse, who with his brothers John and Thomas operated claims on Bonanza and Eldorado Creeks.[4] At the time of the formation of the Carbonneau-Scouse-Byrnes partnership, Bessy was running a business on Second Avenue selling ladies' goods, and all three were living at the Fairview,[5] though both Mabel's and Belinda's mining activities took them out to the creeks frequently.

According to Belinda, Mabel Scouse had talked with her in early September about a claim Mabel had optioned—No. 2 below, on the rich Cleary Creek, near Fairbanks. Belinda wanted to get in on it, and since she was going to the Tanana valley, she offered to exercise the option. The partnership was organized to raise the $15,000 to $17,000 needed for the purchase. Originally Mabel was to go to Fairbanks too, but she changed plans at the last minute, so Belinda was the only one of the three to be on the scene to carry out transactions for the partnership. Perhaps due to Mabel's change of plans, or maybe because she was more particular about such matters, or even perhaps because she knew of Belinda's legal difficulties in Dawson, a formal partnership agreement was drawn up and signed just before Belinda left Dawson. Apparently this document came as a surprise to Belinda, who was accustomed to making deals and agreements with a handshake. She said later that she saw the document only minutes before she had to sail. Among the provisions of the agreement was the requirement that Belinda give full accounts in writing of her activities on behalf of the partnership.[6]

Belinda did send a telegram to Bessy when she arrived in Fairbanks about three weeks later.[7] On 5 December 1904 Belinda wrote to J. B. Pattullo, her attorney in Dawson, reporting on her progress.

> I am working hard to get our little [company] off right. I realize that we are not rich and a false step would brake [sic] us all. I got options on three creeks—Cleary, Fairbanks, and Pedro. I have men prospecting those now. I'm down to [bedrock] on one hole [on] Pedro and found pay, but I must sink three others to see how wide it is. I have two claims tied up on this creek—sixty thousand, twenty cash if it is good. I must russel [sic] another five thousand some place.
> Mrs. Scouse owes seven hundred.[8] She must try and send me that. The bal-

ance I will pay out of the ground. I'll let some lays so to be sure to get enough out of the ground to pay the balance next summer. And I'll work myself like a trooper.[9]

Belinda asked Attorney Pattullo to show the letter to Bessy. When Pattullo wrote back to Belinda on 7 January 1905, he advised her to communicate directly with Mabel and Bessy, reminding her that she was to report regularly to them. Since Belinda was not inclined to write for any reason,[10] frequent written reports to the partners did not appear. However, when Bessy asked Belinda for an accounting that spring, Belinda did reply with a list of mining claims and some town property.[11]

What had happened to the original plan of buying No. 2 below on Cleary is not completely clear. Belinda said that when she was negotiating with Bill Gates for part of the claim, the price had already escalated to $80,000.[12] "Swiftwater" Bill Gates, the same egotistical miner who in 1897 had bought one of Belinda's painted canvas cabins on Second Street in Dawson, was one of the more colorful characters in the North. He commanded national headlines not by his mining, but by his outrageous antics wooing and wedding a string of young women, not always bothering to get divorces in between, while he charmed his way around irate mothers-in-law.[13]

Apparently Belinda never exercised the option on Gates's Cleary claim because it was just too expensive. Instead, she was looking at other claims more in the partnership's price range but still good prospects. She considered property on three creeks—Cleary, Fairbanks, and Pedro—all of which had their origins in Pedro Dome. (See map, fig. 21.1.) Speculators were hoping this area would be like the Dome of the Klondike, from which the best gold-bearing creeks radiated. In fact, time would show Cleary Creek to have the richest placer ground, but Fairbanks and Pedro would also make good showings. By late 1904, prices of claims on these creeks were beginning to climb as well. The option on Fairbanks was for No. 5, one of Felix Pedro's claims, at a price of $20,000. There also were two on Pedro Creek that included an option to buy for $60,000. But none of these deals went through, apparently because Belinda could not raise the necessary cash.[14]

Included in Belinda's letter of 5 December to Pattullo were warnings to her friends in Dawson about the conditions in Fairbanks.

> Bessy must not get the fever bad this winter as the Camp is terribly boomed. There is no money in circulation. There is not one business house in Fairbanks that's making money, and thousands of men without work or money. Men

who took out a little money last summer put it into machinery and property. Those who brought money into the country invested it in property, and the result is everybody is broke, and its a very lonesome town. You must tell Kummuller[15] that he could not make his board in Fairbanks this winter and not to get excited over the wild [stories] the Fairbanks people are liable to circulate as there [sic] life depends upon a boom next spring. The town is much two [sic] large.[16]

Although the Fairbanks area was terribly boomed, as Belinda put it, she still saw opportunities for investment. Throughout the spring and summer of 1905, she continued to acquire claims and property, both for herself and for the partnership. A list of the claims she said were taken up for the partnership included forty-two sites on creeks with names such as Tenderfoot, Delta, Fish, Sorrell, Elliot, Ophir, Kokomo, Rex, Sawyer, Iowa, Illinois, Baker, Gold, Portage, and—as in the Klondike—Bonanza and Eldorado. However, the listing did not say when these were acquired nor at exactly what cost.[17]

Not appearing on this list were other properties Belinda held in her own name. These included lots in Fairbanks, on one of which, on Third Avenue west of Lacey Street, Belinda built her house. Belinda declared the partnership had no interest in the lot with her residence but did in the three adjoining lots.[18] Belinda also may have invested in the Cecil Cafe, run by her long-time friend from Dawson, Ella Card, who had migrated to Fairbanks in February 1905.[19] Many of Belinda's other Klondike friends made their way to the Fairbanks area as well. Esther Duffie was associated with the California Hotel on nearby Ester Creek, named after her by her fiancé, George Haskins.[20] The Berry family was mining on Ester Creek. Bill McPhee was back in business with a bar in Fairbanks, first with the Nevada Saloon, and then The Washington.[21] In fact, estimates were that fully 90 percent of the residents of Fairbanks had been in Dawson.[22]

By late summer of 1905 Belinda had added to her investments by forming a partnership with Charles Robinson and James Kelly[23] to acquire a two-thirds interest in bench claim No. 3 A/D, first tier, right limit on Dome Creek.[24] Belinda claimed that the Dome Creek property was not part of the partnership with Scouse and Byrnes. The problem was that she did not keep her private funds separate from those of the partnership, nor, according to Mabel Scouse and Bessy Byrnes, did she give a full account to her partners of what she was doing on behalf of their company. To make matters even more confusing, Belinda had acquired interests for the company in her own name, as an addendum to the partnership agreement authorized her to do. So sorting out what was hers personally and what belonged to the partnership was open to wide interpretation.

When Mabel Scouse finally arrived in Fairbanks in early August 1905, the atmosphere was charged with tension. Mabel wanted a full accounting of the partnership money. Belinda was disgusted with the whole business. They agreed to dissolve their association on 7 August and drew up and signed papers to that effect.[25]

Belinda said that she gave a full accounting to Mabel and to Mabel's lawyer, LeRoy Tozier, at the dissolution. Tozier confirmed this. But upon further reflection and probably after asking around Fairbanks about Belinda's activities, Mabel was not satisfied with Belinda's account of what had happened to their money. Furthermore, she claimed later that going to Tozier had been Belinda's idea, and that Tozier had not represented Mabel's and Bessy's interests by urging her to settle.[26] Both Belinda and Mabel knew LeRoy Tozier from Dawson, so it is plausible that either could have thought of going to Tozier for the dissolution of the partnership. Tozier had been one of the young professional men who had worked for Belinda at the Fairview Hotel bar in its early days (see chapter 10), but he had left Dawson in 1904 for American territory, where he was qualified to practice law.[27]

Mabel had learned that Belinda had some apparently valuable property that had not been listed as belonging to the partnership. On the other hand, the claims made for the company looked worthless to Mabel. None of them had been well prospected; therefore, whatever value they had was speculative. Nevertheless, Mabel did see fit to keep some of the claims on Tenderfoot Creek represented.[28] The Tenderfoot district, about seventy-five miles southeast of Fairbanks, by the end of 1908 would produce one to two million dollars in gold (Stiles, 274). Other claims on Portage Creek were under option to be purchased,[29] which meant that someone else thought they might have some value.

In the meantime, Belinda, considering the partnership with Scouse and Byrnes ended, was carrying out some transactions that would further muddy the waters. She had probably gotten wind that Mabel was having second thoughts about the settlement. On 15 September 1905, four days before she left Fairbanks for a trip Outside for the winter, Belinda conveyed her interest in the option for the Dome Creek bench claim to A. Gowran for a recorded consideration of $1.00. Belinda explained that she actually sold her interest in the claim for $1,666.60, which was used to pay the second installment on the price of the claim, because she had insufficient funds to complete the purchase.[30] It may also be true, as

Scouse and Byrnes would contend, that this transfer was an attempt to isolate the Dome Creek property from any claim of Belinda's former partners.

The day before Belinda left Fairbanks, Mabel filed a lawsuit claiming that Belinda's share of the Dome Creek property belonged to the Carbonneau-Scouse-Byrnes partnership, and therefore any proceeds should be shared with her and Bessy.[31] Identifying "Mr. Gowran" would help substantiate Mabel's accusation that Belinda was trying to defraud them, because Mabel contended that A. Gowran was just a front for Belinda. Belinda denied this. She said the Gowran she sold the option to had the first name Andrew and was someone who had been in Fairbanks and whom she had known for years. John McGinn, Mabel Scouse's attorney, disputed this, saying Gowran had never been to Alaska and was a resident of New York City. The notarized transfer from Belinda to A. Gowran was dated 15 September, while Belinda was still in Fairbanks, but there is no indication on the document that A. Gowran was present, and it was not recorded until ten months later, on 21 July 1906.[32] Although "Mr. Gowran's" identity was not conclusively resolved at the time, it now seems likely that this was, in fact, Belinda's cousin, Alice Gowran, the daughter of Aunt Bridget and James Gowran,[33] with whom Belinda first stayed in Philadelphia after fleeing Archbald. In February 1906, while she was still in the East, Belinda would oversee the transfer from A. Gowran of her former interest in the Dome Creek claim to her mother, Mary Mulrooney.[34]

The timing of Belinda's leaving and her sale of the Dome Creek interest so close to the filing of the Scouse lawsuit may have been just coincidences, but Scouse and Byrnes took these facts as further evidence that Belinda was trying to defraud them of their interests. To make matters even more complicated, the attorney for Scouse and Byrnes, John McGinn, was also part owner of the other one-third of the Dome Creek claim, as well as the attorney for Belinda's partner, James Kelly.[35] McGinn may have supplied Scouse with fuel for her charges by revealing information that he knew as a result of his professional relationship with Kelly.

By this time Belinda probably felt justified in subverting Mabel's legal maneuverings. After all, Belinda had been doing all the work for the partnership, she had been sending back information to Dawson as she said she would, and when her partners had declined to invest the additional money needed for more expensive claims, Belinda had bought other property that might prove up. As far as she was concerned, the matter ended with the dissolution of the partnership in August. And Belinda may have thought it was a good joke that she left Fair-

21.2. This photo was taken at about the time Belinda visited her family in late 1905. Jim Mulrooney is in front. An unidentified, well-dressed woman is seated in the middle. From left to right behind her are Nell Mulrooney, an unidentified woman, Agnes Mulrooney, Belinda, and Margaret Mulrooney. (Identifications by Agnes's son, Charles Johnston to DeArmond, 24 January 1989.) One family member, who knew Belinda only as an older woman, commented, "I had never seen Belinda smile in the flesh." *(Johnston Collection)*

banks just as the angry Mabel thought she was delivering her best shot. But Mabel Scouse was a determined woman, not put off by Belinda's disappearing. The wrangling over who owned what and when, and what money, if any, was owed to whom would dog Belinda for the next eleven years.

WHEN BELINDA LEFT for the Outside in the fall of 1905, she went to the east coast to visit her family. While there she went into New York City to retrieve the jewelry and furs she had stored upon her return from Europe in the spring of 1904.[36] By that time Belinda's relationship with Charles already had been falling apart, and Belinda said he had deserted her without funds. Belinda had stored her valuables with reputable companies—Tiffany's and Revillon Frères—in order to keep them out of the hands of her free-spending husband. But when Belinda returned

21.3. Belinda is "on the beach" at Atlantic City, New Jersey, in her stylish bathing costume. The photograph is not dated, but we assume it was taken after her marriage in 1900 because of the rings on the third finger of her left hand.
(Waugaman Collection)

for her possessions in 1905, she found they had been released to Charles. Her sweet-talking spouse had charmed his way through even these well-established, conservative businesses. Belinda was furious. Tiffany's paid her the declared value for the jewels when they were deposited, $500. But Belinda knew they were worth much more and eventually sued the company for an additional $10,954. At the same time, she sued Revillon Frères $6,000 for the lost furs.[37] The litigation took some time to resolve. According to her attorney, she did secure a judgment or made a settlement and got a small amount out of the firms, as they had let the jewels and furs go without any authority from her.[38]

BELINDA'S FIRST YEAR in Fairbanks, 1905, was a mixed success. She re-established herself in the new territory that was full of many of her old friends from the Klondike. She freed herself of the legal entanglements with Charles Carbonneau in the Yukon, but he had continued to best her by absconding with her jewels and furs. The expansive boomtown atmosphere of Fairbanks was to Belinda's liking, for it allowed her to use her freewheeling style together with her mining and business know-how to start a financial recovery. But she also made enemies of two former friends who had trusted her—Mabel Scouse and Bessy Byrnes. The new year of 1906 would be burdened by repercussions from the unresolved disputes of their partnership. Now Belinda's business activities no longer had the sense of exuberance that characterized her earlier years in the Klondike. Her enthusiasm and joy for the entrepreneurial game was replaced by a more ruthless determination to succeed.

Belinda returned to Fairbanks in March, accompanied by two of her sisters —Margaret, or Meggie Ann to her family, almost twenty years old,[39] and Helen or Nellie, twenty-two years old.[40] Younger sister Agnes had stayed in Pennsylvania to attend school, while brother Jim went to Belgium to school.[41] Although Belinda obviously was taking her sisters under her wing, they may also have been providing support for her. They explained later that much of the money they brought back In with them was the result of liquidation of the many expensive gifts Belinda had given to the family, as well as proceeds of a family trust fund set up by Belinda at the turn of the century.[42] Belinda, no doubt, was glad for their emotional support as well.

Belinda, Margaret, and Nell came In over the trail from Valdez, Alaska.[43] The trip by sled stage line, with regular stops at rustic roadhouses, was far advanced over the Klondike trail of 1897–98. Still, the journey could be an arduous adventure in early spring, with high winds, minus-thirty-degree temperatures, unpredictable melting, and overcrowded inns.[44]

Back in Fairbanks, Belinda's inspiration was to do as she had done at Grand Forks. She moved away from the more developed town and out to a creek where mining was actually going on—to Dome, about eighteen miles from Fairbanks. There, with her sister Margaret, she took up a new line of business—banking.

22

The Dome City Bank

Business and Funny Business

D ome City was on the discovery claim of Dome Creek, and in the spring of 1906 it was the newest of the creek towns of the Tanana district.[1] It was some eighteen miles from Fairbanks by the government road and a mile from the nearest station on the Tanana Valley Railroad. The town was so new that it did not get a post office until October 1906, and by then it had several saloons, two or three general stores, a hotel, and two banks, one of which was Belinda's.

In the relatively unrestricted days before Alaska acquired a territorial government, the only legal requirement for starting a local bank was a $250 business license. There were no worries about regulation, examiners, reports, and other such impediments to progress. This fit Belinda's operating style. She had a building erected, announced that the Dome City Bank was open for business, and moved herself and her sisters into apartments above the bank, which were described as "finely furnished."[2] On 5 May 1906 Belinda began buying gold dust and sending it to Fairbanks for shipment to the U.S. Mint.[3] The difference between the price paid for the gold at the bank and what it sold for at the mint was one way the bank earned money. Its other main income was from interest charged on loans.

That the bank was profitable is attested to by the fact that within a year its

22.1. Dome City, Alaska, from a hill looking east in about 1907. The highest mountain in the distance is Pedro Dome. Dome Creek runs from right to left across the approximate middle of the photograph, just beyond the town buildings. Most gold was located roughly parallel to the stream, but further out in the valley where the dumps are visible in the photograph. *(UAF, Joslin Collection, 79–41–209N)*

assets, less that due depositors, were $81,676, with $50,000 of this from capital stock. By that time Belinda had organized the Dome City Bank as a corporation in the state of Washington, with herself and a partner, Jesse Noble, as the principal stockholders.[4] Noble, a rough-hewn miner thirty-five years of age, was a native of Indiana. He had first come north to Circle City in 1896 and had been successfully mining for gold since then in Dawson and Nome. In Fairbanks he was well known for having made good money from the discovery claim on the rich Cleary Creek, as well as from other valuable mining properties in the Tanana district.[5] Three others, all from Seattle, also were named as bank trustees—James F. McElroy,[6] C. E. Burnside, and Howard A. Hanson.

According to incorporation papers, Jesse Noble put $14,800 cash into the new bank and Belinda put in $14,900, for 248 and 249 shares of stock, respectively. Each subscribed an additional $10,000. Jesse became president of the corporation, Belinda was vice president and bank manager, and sister Margaret was secretary and cashier.

Margaret has been described as "a cheerful, vibrant extrovert, with a smile

22.2. Margaret Mulrooney in the early 1900s. One family member, who knew
Margaret only as an older woman, by which time she was quite heavy, declared
that this looks nothing like her. On the other hand, the photo is signed
"Margaret" in her verified handwriting *(Gauslin to Dougher, 8 December 1965,
Vitzthum Collection)*. Moreover, the photo is from the collection of Judge James
Wickersham, who knew Margaret well and supplied the note identifying the
subject as Jesse Noble's sister-in-law. *(ASL, Wickersham Collection, PCA 277–11–36)*

and a kind word for everybody."[7] She was clever academically and had attended business school before joining Belinda. As the glamorous photograph of her shows, she was a very attractive young woman as well. According to one family member, Margaret was the one in charge of the day-to-day operations of the bank.[8] Margaret's outgoing, charming ways of doing business were a contrast to Belinda's more sober, tough-minded approach.

The amount of cash either Jesse or Belinda actually put into the bank originally was probably minimal, according to John A. Clark, the bank's attorney during its first year: "At the end of the year I hastened to sever my connections with the bank, for during that time I had learned considerable about how a bank can be started without any capital and yet made to appear to have that which it does not possess."[9] While Clark's statement might seem scandalous, it coincides fairly well with what Belinda would contend as she fended off accusations from Mabel Scouse and Bessy Byrnes[10] that the bank was started with money from the Carbonneau-Scouse-Byrnes partnership. Belinda testified that she had very little money in late 1905, and that the bank was started with Margaret's money from the family trust.[11]

Once the bank was incorporated, Belinda first placed her shares in trust for her sisters Nellie and Agnes, but later put them in Margaret's name. That may have been because Scouse and Byrnes were taking action to claim nearly all of Belinda's assets, including the Dome Creek mine, the Carbonneau residence in Fairbanks, and the building on Cushman Street in Fairbanks occupied by Ella Card's Cecil Cafe.[12] Belinda's former partners would argue that since Belinda could not adequately account for the partnership assets, all of her property was to be considered derived from the partnership and subject to their settlement demands.

Mabel Scouse must have been angry to see Belinda apparently piling up assets while she and Bessy Byrnes had not recovered their investments. They filed an amended complaint in July, asking that a receiver be appointed for any gold that James Kelly had been taking from the Dome Creek claim. In response, Belinda filed a counter-complaint, saying she owed Scouse and Byrnes nothing because everything had been settled 7 August 1905. She then lodged her own accusation that Scouse and Byrnes had appropriated their jointly owned equipment and disposed of it without paying Belinda her share. The litigation would be muddled not only by charges and counter-charges, but also by obvious subterfuge by both parties. To make matters worse, many of the papers relevant to sorting out the partnership's holdings were burned in one of the ubiquitous fires that

22.3. Ella "Mother" Card and Margaret "Meg" Mulrooney stand in the door of Ella's Cecil Café at 63 Cushman Street in Fairbanks. This photo was taken in the spring of 1906, before the building was destroyed by fire in May. The young man at right is not identified. *(Waugaman Collection)*

plagued frontier towns. Attorney Leroy Tozier's office, with all his records, was consumed by the fire on 22 May 1906 that destroyed most of the central business district of Fairbanks.[13]

On 13 October 1906, James Kelly, who had been doing all the work on the Dome Creek bench claim, bought, along with partner Henry Broome, Mary Mulrooney's interest in the claim.[14] They were not able to pay cash, so they mortgaged the claim for $8,000 at 1 percent interest per month, payable after cleanup in May and June of 1907. Adding another twist to the tale, the mortgage was held by the Dome City Bank, so Belinda now held an interest again by way of her partnership in the bank. This fact would bring another barrage of actions from Scouse and Byrnes in an effort to get what they thought was their due.

In the meantime, the Mulrooney clan and the Dome City Bank prospered. In June the *Fairbanks Daily Times* noted that the bank was making a good showing and had been shipping many pounds of gold to Fairbanks. For example, a "very ordinary shipment" of 250 pounds had recently arrived.[15]

Belinda was becoming a celebrity, a person to be noted and quoted. In the following front-page story from the *Fairbanks Sunday Times* of 10 June 1906, written when the spring cleanup was at its peak, she is mistakenly identified as president of the bank; according to most documents, she was vice president and manager, while Jesse Noble was president.[16] For the informal interview, she appears to be avoiding publicity; nevertheless, she is so enthusiastic about the Dome City mining area that she is easily drawn into talking about it.

"Mrs. Carbonneau, I believe?"

"Yes."

"May I ask you a few questions?"

"Well, if it is an interview you want, I will have to decline," said Mrs. Carbonneau, laughing.

"Yes, but I want to interview the only lady president of a bank on the western slope of the continent."

"Well for goodness sake, what for?"

"Do you find, and you have had an extensive business career, that being president of a bank is more facinating [sic] than other lines of business?"

"Yes, indeed. It is a far more interesting business than one would suppose. Indeed, ordinary business pursuits do not have the same intense attraction as the banking business. Really there is more to it than appears on the surface. One gets interested so quickly in the surrounding community. And even tho it does not seem so, yet there are enough things to keep one's mind busy all day. What are you doing with that note book?"

"Just to get down what you have to say about Dome creek."

"Well, young man, you can fill that book of yours up with good things to say about Dome creek, and then you will not have done it justice. Deep tho it may be, difficult as the pay is to find on account of that, across the summit from the railroad and with a few other obstacles, yet it has got a goodly number of producing properties. And mind you this, Mr. Reporter, and remember it. Dome, from its very head to where it goes out on the Chataniki [sic] will be producing shortly. This is not boom talk. I have told what difficulties are to be encountered in the way of development on the creek, but we have men over there who have the energy and the confidence to demonstrate the prophecy I am making. But I told you I was not going to give you an interview."

"Just one more question."

"What is it?"

"Presidents of banks have some hobby. Many of them are interesting. Have you . . . "

"Yes, I know. Well, walking is mine, and I came over the new trail which comes out at 6 below on Pedro. The government has put it through and it will soon be used for wagons. The party with whom I traveled today came over in

40 minutes. It is a little less than three miles across the hill from Dome city to Pedro."

"Mrs. Car—"

"No, sir, not another word."

Belinda was now thirty-four years old and still hearty. Vigorous walking on well-traveled trails was fairly sedate for her. Prospecting was more to her liking.

We were going into the Mt. McKinley country one spring.[17] I was the only white woman in the party—Gordon Battles[18] and his [Native American] wife,[19] Gus Peterson, George Noble,[20] . . . Jim Cronister,[21] . . . myself, two French Canadians, and some men of my crew. I had the only horse—a great big black animal. I packed him and rode him both. . . . We wanted to prospect the creeks and water sheds of the Mt. McKinley district.

You see in spring the water and the melting snow cut the banks of those gullies. The frost goes out of the ground about six inches and after that it is solid ice. I had to get off my horse and lead him over some of those ravines, they were not so very deep, a natural incline say of four or five feet. But I got tired of leading and decided I'd put him over one of them, ride him over in a jump.

That horse's forefeet hit the opposite bank and struck the ice. He slid. His hind quarters went down, the saddle slipping over. He tried to kick the saddle loose, but he kicked me instead. His shoe hit me in the left side and shook every thing inside me, teeth and all. My hair pins scattered in every direction, and I lost my glasses.

I remember I told them to try and save that horse, not to let him hurt himself. We needed him badly on the trip. Battles and Mrs. Battles were trying to see if I was still there. Battles said, "My God! You must be bursted for good this time."

I was pretty fat then, but the print of the horse's shoe was here [on the left side], and he must have broken this rib. It still sticks out a little.

. . . The nearest hospital was in Fairbanks, 1,000 miles away the way we came, going down one river and poling up another.[22] We camped right there, the moss was good and soft, and I lay there for a day or two. The boys made a fire. Mrs. Battles fixed up herbs, a poultice of native stuff. She cooked it. I was interested in my glasses. When they found them hanging on a twig, I felt better.

After I was better, they boosted me on horseback again and held onto me, taking turns as we went along. Didn't get a doctor until we got to Seattle nine months later.[23]

22.4. The women strolling down an earthen street on the outskirts of Dome may be Mulrooney sisters, since the photo was in Margaret's collection. The roadway, bordered by telephone poles, has been improved with log underpinnings for firmer ground in the wet season. Numerous log cabins line the road, and there are at least a couple of buildings with sawn wood siding—both types of construction being notable developments from the sod structures on the creek two years earlier. *(Waugaman Collection)*

Belinda's social life in the Fairbanks area was probably even more active than it had been in Dawson, due to the influence of her lively, attractive sisters. Newspapers often report on their visiting in Dome, Cleary, and Fairbanks, and they likewise entertained many of their comrades in their quarters above the bank. Among Margaret's and Nellie's friends was Caro Clum, whose father, Major John P. Clum, was an Alaskan postal inspector and in charge of establishing U.S. post offices throughout the district. The *Fairbanks Evening News* for 9 August 1906 announced that "Miss Nellie Mulrooney, sister of Mrs. Carbonneau, has been appointed postmistress for Dome City by Major Clum and will at once assume the duties of the office. With her sister, Miss Margaret Mulrooney, cashier of the Dome City Bank, she has been in the city [Fairbanks] for several days. Both young ladies have been entertained by Mrs. John McGinn during their stay here."

Although it seems that everyone considered Nell to be Dome's postmaster that summer, the first to get official recognition was George Thomas, appointed on 26 October 1906.[24] Thomas was a friend of the Mulrooneys at Dome City who operated Thomas and Taylor, a mercantile firm; ran the Samuel Bonnifield bank; was agent for handling meats; and was U.S. Commissioner as well as postmaster.[25] Margaret and Nellie's hostess in Fairbanks was the wife of the same attorney John L. McGinn, of McGinn and Sullivan, who was representing Mabel Scouse and Bessy Byrnes in their suit against Belinda. Somehow, through it all, they continued to be friends.

BELINDA HAD OTHER serious business besides the Scouse and Byrnes lawsuit to attend to in the summer of 1906—initiating her divorce from Charles Carbonneau. The year before, Charles had been convicted in France of embezzling funds from the Crédit Canadien and of swindling 75,000 francs from a contractor of public works, supposedly for the management of railroad lines.[26] Among his other schemes, he had established a bureau to promote emigration of French peasants to Canada and a steamship line from Brest, France, to transport them to Quebec. After the steamship line failed, sinking Belinda's fortune with it,[27] Charles had deserted Belinda and stolen her jewelry and furs.[28] Adding to these crimes and disasters the domestic troubles that were probably a part of the story but for which we have no records, it is easy to see why Belinda had had enough of Charles Eugene Carbonneau.

The implications of Belinda's decision to divorce Charles were indeed sad for her. She had sincerely wanted children of her own and a happy family life like the Wades'. Having a child out of wedlock was out of the question; as unconventional as Belinda was in many respects, she was not prepared to choose that path. Nor was she likely to marry again. Though not a practicing Catholic, she knew the civil divorce would not be recognized by the Church, and to marry anyone else would be bigamous. The divorce truly signaled the end of Belinda's dream for a family.

The decision to divorce also was difficult simply because of the stigma it carried traditionally in Anglo-American society.[29] By 1900, while more couples were taking advantage of the increased availability of divorce, especially in the Western United States, still there was considerable uneasiness, apart from religious scruples, about its effect on the American family. According to one analysis, in freedom-loving America, marriage was the only institution that was accustomed to submerging crude individualism into broader social values (Lucie, 145). Therefore, American society could not afford to make divorce easy, and in fact a widespread backlash was already beginning to restrict it once again (May, 4).

In Canada the feeling against divorce was even stronger than in the United States,[30] and the restrictive laws made divorce nearly impossible. The English Matrimonial Causes Act of 1857 formed the basis for divorce laws in several Canadian provinces and territories, including the Yukon (Dranoff, 62). According to this act, a man could get a divorce on grounds of adultery, but a woman had to prove her husband guilty of "incestuous adultery, or bigamy with adultery, or of rape, or of sodomy or bestiality, or of adultery coupled with such cruelty as without adultery would have entitled her to a divorce à mensa et thoro, or adultery coupled with desertion without reasonable excuse for two years or upwards."[31]

In 1867, when Canada became a federal union, divorce became a federal issue in provinces and territories that did not have relevant codes of their own—a bill had to be introduced, debated, and voted on in the Parliament in Ottawa to resolve each petition for divorce. This was the procedure for the Yukon in the early 1900s.[32] Two trends became notable in the federal proceedings. First, there was a gradual move to eliminate the double standard of chastity, though it was not completely removed until 1925 (Zucker and Callwood, 55). Second, very few divorces were granted.[33] Another deterrent to a woman considering a divorce in the Yukon was that the petition had to be filed whereever the husband was domiciled. In Belinda's case, Charles had been reported in France, England, Belgium, Italy, Germany, Quebec, Pennsylvania, and New York; filing in his unknown domicile was impossible. In fact, the near impossibility of getting a divorce in the Yukon may have been one of the more compelling reasons Belinda left Dawson. Fairbanks was attractive not only because it was booming economically, but also because procedures for getting a divorce there were more lenient than in the Yukon.

On 30 July 1906 Belinda filed for dissolution of her marriage on the basis of desertion, and asked that any property she now held be declared her sole and separate estate.[34] An alias summons was published for nine weeks in the *Fairbanks Evening News*, and copies of the summons along with the complaint were sent to Charles's last known address at the Bristol Hotel, Berlin, Germany. Charles did not respond to the complaint. And in fact, one bizarre incident reveals he was in the United States during at least part of the fall, a circumstance of which Belinda surely must have been aware, for in early November, Charles kidnapped Belinda's sister Agnes. An article in the *Dawson Daily News* of 16 November 1906 was based on a story from Philadelphia with a dateline of 3 November.

With an automobile and two detectives Carbonneau on Friday night took away from the alleged machinations of Francis J. Crane, the sister of Belinda Mulrooney, whose toil in the mines of the Yukon and as woman Boniface of the roadhouse at the Forks of Eldorado and Bonanza gave him millions. It is said that Carbonneau, since his practical separation from the partner of his poorer days, took a great interest in her pretty sister, and the many persons who knew him in the club and financial life of New York, London and Paris believe the tale because of his past exploits.

Francis Crane, whose family owned the Crane Paper Company in Philadelphia, had been a suitor of Agnes's, according to a Mulrooney family member.[35] Exactly who stood to benefit from the kidnapping is not clear. Agnes was, at the time, attending a convent school at Chestnut Hill, near where Belinda had worked for the Cummings family fifteen years earlier. Charles said he seized Agnes and took her in his auto to his hotel, the Bellevue-Stratford, because he saw her in the arms of Crane. However, it was Crane who notified the police.[36] Those who knew Charles in Dawson assumed that his lust and jealousy was the motive, but a family member has speculated that it also may have been another way for Charles to hurt Belinda, for Belinda had been promoting the liaison with the Crane family.[37] In any case, apparently Charles presented evidence in court that provided a plausible excuse for his actions. Although Agnes testified that Charles had been living off of Belinda's money, he declared that he had his own funds and that he had been the one paying Agnes's tuition. Charles was declared not guilty of kidnapping on 2 November.[38]

In Fairbanks, after the appropriate waiting time, Belinda was granted her divorce on 10 December 1906. Thereafter, whenever she was asked about her marital status by those who were not in a position to know better, she described herself as a widow. Other embellishments would be added if it came to light that Charles was still alive, for Belinda was not above lying when she felt the truth invaded her privacy. In later years, she would say Charles was killed by enemy fire during the First World War, although his demise in 1919 was considerably less heroic.

When the *Yukon World* in Dawson announced Belinda's divorce, it confidently stated that she would again be known as Miss Mulrooney,[39] but in fact she did not reassume her maiden name. It is perhaps a measure of how strong public feeling was against divorce that Belinda preferred to be called by the name of the man who had betrayed her rather than face the stigma of being known as a divorced woman. Or perhaps more trying would have been the necessity of repeatedly explaining how big a mistake she had made in marrying him in the first place. It was far easier to be a "widow."

Belinda's troubles with Charles did not put a damper on romance for the other Mulrooney sisters. Handsome, clever Margaret was the sweetheart of many admiring miners and businessmen, but it was Nellie who made the first jump. The Dome City Bank became even more of a family affair on 9 January 1907, when Nellie married Jesse Noble.[40] After a dinner with a few intimate friends and a reception at the home of Mr. and Mrs. John McGinn, the newly-weds left at once on an extended honeymoon, going Out over the trail, headed ultimately for southern France. But the marriage may not have survived the honeymoon. They returned separately to Fairbanks in early summer. Jesse arrived first in June. Nellie followed nearly three weeks later, accompanied by her sister Agnes and her brother James.[41]

Belinda and Margaret had continued to operate the bank during the winter with good results. A statement sworn to by Belinda and Margaret on 30 July 1907 showed assets of $125,042.50, including secured loans of $76,000; cash, $24,185; due from other banks, $9,532.50; real estate, $10,000 and furniture and fixtures, $5,325. Surplus was $31,676.32, capital stock, $50,000, and due depositors, $43,366.18.[42]

A photograph taken in front of the Dome City Bank probably about 12 June 1907 shows Jack L. Tobin, pioneer of Fairbanks and layman on No. 1 A/D Dome, Margaret, Belinda, and Miller Thostesen, owner of No. 1 A/D Dome. In the gold pan on Margaret's lap is a 77.55 ounce "nugget" taken from Thostesen's claim.[43] This is the kind of publicity photo that not only helped the bank but also promoted mining in the entire Fairbanks region.

The Dome City Bank did so well that it weathered a nationwide financial panic later in 1907. Other banks in Fairbanks were forced to close temporarily, but throughout the crisis the Dome City Bank carried on business as usual.[44] There was of course good reason to have a bank at Dome City to handle the business and gold generated by the Dome Creek claims, but the bank's profitability also may have been due in part to the aggressive collection policy of its president. In July 1907, Jesse Noble and three other men were charged with gold dust robbery. They had appeared at No. 3 above Dome just as the owners of the claim were completing a cleanup and forcibly took 402 ounces of gold. Noble asserted the confiscation was justified, for the mortgage on the claim had not been satisfied.[45] The criminal charge was finally dropped and the matter settled in a civil case.

22.5. Left to right: Jack Tobin (1), Margaret Mulrooney (4), Belinda Mulrooney Carbonneau (3), and Miller Thostesen (2) examine a large nugget in a gold pan in front of the Dome City Bank, June 1907. *(Waugaman Collection)*

In another instance, the bank confiscated a gold deposit, the nugget in figure 22.5, to satisfy an overdraft. And on another occasion, Jesse Noble was indicted for pistol whipping a man he said was attempting to relocate No. 13 below on Goldstream. In this case Jesse was finally acquitted, but possibly not on the merits of the case. After long deliberation the jury was hung, but none of the members could stand the prospect of being confined longer in the inadequately heated jury room. The temperature outside had dropped to 60 degrees below zero. The jury decided they would rather be at home.[46]

If the rift between Jesse and Nellie had not occurred before they returned to Fairbanks, it did come later that fall, and Belinda, as lawyer John Clark put it, "disposed of a brother-in-law by heaving his trunk out of a window."[47] Late in October, Jesse Noble went to the District Court and initiated two actions. One was a criminal complaint against Belinda and Margaret, charging them with holding and concealing certain of his assets.[48] The other was a civil suit against his wife, Nellie, and her sister Margaret. He charged them with defrauding him of three mortgages and certain promissory notes, amounting in all to $15,915, plus his interest in two placer claims.[49] Judge James Wickersham issued a search warrant and ordered Deputy Marshal Charles Drebilbis to search the bank building, with particular attention to safe deposit box 13, and if necessary to search the persons of B. A. Carbonneau and Margaret Mulrooney. Whether the latter drastic action was required is not revealed, but the missing documents and some other property belonging to Noble were found. The judge ordered all of it turned over to Noble, who eventually moved to dismiss the actions against his wife and her sisters.

The motion to dismiss may have been connected with Jesse's buying out the Carbonneau/Mulrooney interests in the bank. Margaret reported that she sold her 296 shares of stock (which had been transferred to her from Belinda) to Jesse on 15 November 1907 at $100 each. He paid her $3,000 cash, and the rest was covered by a note, which Margaret had her brother Jim hold.[50] Thus ended the ownership interests of Belinda and her sister in the Dome City Bank, though both continued to be officers.

While all of this legal maneuvering was going on, Nellie Noble on 29 November 1907 gave birth to a boy who was named Robert.[51] Since Nell was no longer living with Jesse Noble, she and the baby were surrounded and supported by the Mulrooney sorority—Belinda, Margaret, and Agnes.

Judge Wickersham, in connection with the action of Scouse and Byrnes against Belinda, wanted another look at the affairs of the Dome City Bank.

He ordered Jesse Noble and Margaret Mulrooney to appear in his court on 26 December 1907 and to bring with them the books of the bank, showing names of officers, stockholders, the source of bank capital, and the royalty accounts for the contested claim on Dome Creek.[52] What transpired is not revealed by court records. Only five days later, Judge Wickersham resigned and stepped down from the bench after he had failed for the third time to gain Senate confirmation.

Two months later (17 February 1908) the former judge would write in his diary with double underlining: "Jesse Noble of the Dome City Bank employed me today as attorney for that bank—$1000 per annum retainer—fees for paper and attorney's fees allowed in notes and mortgages and reasonable fees in other cases." He did not, however, hold the position very long but resigned to run successfully for the office of Delegate in Congress from Alaska.

Belinda continued to need good lawyers and was on the losing end of several lawsuits. Back in Dawson she was sued by her former attorney, J. B. Pattullo. He had represented Charles and Belinda in several cases, beginning with the dispute over the terms of the Letourneau and Bernier mortgage in 1903. Now he claimed that his bill of $2,400 was unpaid. Belinda pleaded from afar of inability to pay; therefore, Pattullo petitioned for satisfaction through her only remaining asset in Dawson, the Fairview Hotel.[53] But first he had to show that the hotel actually was still Belinda's. Its title had been transferred in 1904 to the Klondike Gold Venture Company, Ltd.[54] According to Pattullo, this company was a trust set up for the sole benefit of Belinda, to hold the property until it could be transferred without fee to another company, The Canadian Gold Mining Concession Company, Ltd. Pattullo said this company also was owned solely by Belinda and that both companies had been set up to protect the Fairview from her creditors. Since Pattullo had been Belinda's attorney in a number of the cases where claims were made against her, he presumably was in a position to know.

Belinda testified that she had entered into an agreement with a person by the name of Schneider in New York City in June of 1904 to sell the Fairview to him for $25,000. The hotel was to be part of the holding of a company that Schneider and Charles Carbonneau were forming. Belinda said she received $4,000 down payment on the option, and that Charles and Schneider subsequently left for London to set up the company. She completed the transfer in July to the Klondike Gold Venture Company, having received a cablegram from Charles to do so. He acted under her power-of-attorney to complete the deal in London.

But papers produced as evidence showed the purchase price was $50,000 and that the company had been established on 16 April. This seemed suspicious because not only did it contradict Belinda's testimony, but it would mean that the company existed before a judgment was handed down on 8 June in the Letourneau and Bernier suit finding against the Carbonneaus. This suggested that the papers may have been back-dated. Belinda's and Charles's relationship was already shaky by that time, so perhaps Charles had collected a higher price and changed the date without Belinda's knowledge. In any case, Judge Macaulay felt that the question as to the legitimacy of the partnership should be tried separately.[55] Consistent with the contention that the companies were bogus, we have found no record of either the Klondike Gold Venture Company, Ltd. nor the Canadian Gold Mining Concession Company, Ltd. in the Public Records Office of England,[56] where the companies were supposed to have been registered.

In the case brought by Pattullo, the absent Belinda apparently was not represented by counsel. In fact, eight years later she stoutly denied that she ever owed Pattullo anything and that she knew nothing of any suit by him against her.[57] In any case, Pattullo won, and the Fairview was sold to satisfy Pattullo's bill.[58] Belinda had now lost what was the last vestige of her proud days in the Yukon.

Belinda's legal battles continued in Fairbanks as well. The Alaska Commercial Co. got a judgment of $845.25 for unpaid bills.[59] And by early 1908, the tide of the Scouse and Byrnes actions was definitely turning against her. After sorting through the conflicting accounts offered by both parties, the failing memory of both sides for critical details, and the attorneys' blocking of testimony that might reveal their own conflicts of interest, the court rendered its decision. Scouse and Byrnes won a judgment of $7,095.06 for undistributed profits, plus interest at 8 percent from 18 January 1908 and $905 in court costs.[60]

On 8 July 1908, Judge Silas Reid ordered the marshal to seize enough of Belinda's real and personal property to satisfy the writ of execution.[61] But Deputy U.S. Marshal Charles Drebilbis reported back ten days later that he had found only one lot, with a small cabin, in Belinda's name. It was seized and "sold" for $300 to Mabel Scouse.[62] All other property was in someone else's name.

In her testimony in court and before a referee, Belinda had proved a dissembling and obstructive witness, but that chicanery seems not to have diminished the esteem in which she was held by most of the residents of Dome and the vicinity. When it was announced in November 1908 that she and Margaret would be leaving on vacation, an impromptu farewell party was held in the Union Hall

22.6. Belinda Mulrooney Carbonneau and Margaret Mulrooney upon their arrival in Seattle, 7 December 1908. *(UW, Seattle Post-Intelligencer, 17192)*

in Dome. According to the *Fairbanks News* of 12 November, "Everybody in Dome and Vault was there to pay tribute to the popularity of the two ladies who have been the center of all social doings in that vicinity in addition to their close relations with the community as head and cashier of the Dome City Bank." Belinda was given an old ivory bucket and a crescent pin, and Margaret received a gold heart belt buckle "from the boys on the creeks." It was said they would visit in Seattle and Philadelphia and expected to return to Dome in March.

It must have been something of a shock to their friends and customers in Dome City when, on 27 December, they read in the *News* that Belinda had purchased a $25,000 tract of farming land in Yakima, Washington, and that "she will concentrate all her interests in the Yakima district and intends to dispose of her interests in the Dome City Banking and Investment Company immediately." Of course, the Carbonneau/Mulrooney interests in the Bank actually had been disposed of a year earlier.

IT SEEMS THAT Belinda may have tried once again to cut her losses by retreat. But on another front, it also seems she timed her exit well with regard to the prospects for further development in the Tanana District. She perhaps appreciated before many others did that the area was nearing its peak. In fact, Tanana gold production would begin decreasing in 1909–10; banks in Fairbanks began consolidating in 1909 (Cole, 121); and Dome City reached its maximum population of one thousand in 1909–10.[63] The following year, there were only four hundred people at Dome;[64] the Dome City Bank was out of business;[65] and Fairbanks's one remaining bank collapsed (Cole, 124). By 1915, Dome City no longer existed.[66]

23

Retrenching in Yakima, Washington

WHEN BELINDA LEFT Fairbanks and Dome City, she was once again in retreat—abandoning a boomed-out environment; pulling back from the frays with Jesse Noble, Mabel Scouse, and Bessie Byrnes; preserving the resources she had managed to protect in her family's care. But she was still in her warrior mode, planning her next campaign.

Belinda wasted no time. Upon landing in Seattle, she went almost immediately to Yakima, a small agricultural town about 110 miles to the southeast on the eastern side of the Cascade Mountains. In the wide, fertile valley where the Naches River joins the Yakima River, fine apples and other fruits could be grown. Furthermore, good connections to the Union Pacific and Northern Pacific Railways allowed efficient distribution of the produce.

Exactly how Belinda learned of Yakima is unknown. Developers of the Tieton project in Yakima promoted it to wealthy pioneers in Alaska, whose practice was to establish a second, winter home in a more temperate climate. According to one report, Belinda heard about Yakima while still in Fairbanks,[1] and she was among a vanguard of Alaskans who began settling in the area in 1909 and 1910.

By 9 January 1909, Belinda had taken up residence in the Yakima Hotel and was laying plans to make the town her home. She also was creating something of a sensation. Here was an apparently wealthy, thirty-seven-year old woman from the mining camps of the Klondike and Alaska, ready to invest in Yakima. Although she was married, and sometimes addressed as "Countess," no husband was in evidence. "How do you suppose she made her money?"[2] "You know how that kind of woman does it, don't you?" "Well I don't think she could be all that bad. Look at all the distinguished guests from the North she entertains." "How much money do you think she has?" "I don't know, but did you see all those diamond rings she wears?"[3] "Yes, and have you seen her furs on display in the window of the real estate office? There's a decorated moose hide and a rare silver-gray fox pelt. They say she has a lot more of them, worth $15,000!"[4] "I wonder what she is going to try to do here?"[5]

The land Belinda had bought was about four miles west of town and was planted in four-year-old peach and apple trees.[6] What Belinda planned to do was to grow fruit and develop land. Given her previous entrepreneurial occupations, that she arrived at the notion of becoming a gentlewoman farmer may be somewhat of a marvel. But in a way, Belinda was returning to her agricultural roots, shifting priorities in the face of recent defeats and disappointments. Perhaps she felt she had had enough of big-money promotions and devastated countryside. The shift had been gradual, starting just prior her marriage to Carbonneau. She began then to bridge the gulf between herself and her family, helping to support them, educating her siblings, spending more time with them, including them in her enterprises. They in turn had reassured her with their solidarity in times of trouble. By 1909 she had decided that the welfare of the family was paramount.

After Belinda's financial wipeout in the Yukon, she had drawn on the trust funds she had originally set up for her family's use. These funds had provided start-up capital for the Dome City Bank, which in turn helped generate new income. Though the money had been hers originally, and though Belinda undoubtedly was the force behind the financial recovery, nevertheless the new assets were in a real sense family money. They could be used to build a secure base for Belinda, her parents, her siblings, and their children. Perhaps Belinda also hoped to recreate the happy idyll of her childhood. A small farm in a beautiful, fertile valley seemed an ideal setting for the family to form a community where they could all be happy and prosper. But Belinda's by now well-developed toughness did not easily encompass the warmer, gentler approach to life that her new priorities might suggest, and her visions of the ideal were not always in harmony with those of her family.

The land Belinda was reported to have bought actually was not recorded in her name,[7] perhaps to isolate it from any further liens by Scouse and Byrnes. Margaret Mulrooney was listed as the owner, along with Henry Cook. Henry had staked the discovery claim on Dome Creek. He also owned Numbers 1 through 5 B/D, along with others;[8] therefore, Belinda and her sisters were well acquainted with him from Dome City. Throughout the development of this land in Yakima, it is difficult to sort out how much was due to Margaret and how much to Belinda. But it is safe to say that newspaper coverage of the project attributed most if not all to Belinda, and that Belinda took the leadership in most of the decisions. She was used to being in control, and apparently that suited Margaret.

Like Belinda's childhood home in Ireland, the farm property was about twenty acres. At a high point on the northeast corner of the gently rolling land, Belinda constructed a home, a center for her new life.[9] A. K. Thompson, architect, designed the house to her specifications,[10] using a blend of styles from the European continent and from Irish fortresses. Her contractor, Krause,[11] was ready to start construction by late February.

> Mrs. Carbonneau, the Alaskan banker who has recently invested in Yakima land, will begin immediately the construction of a $6000 dwelling to be erected on her land in the Wide Hollow valley. . . . The stately domicile will be built of concrete blocks.
>
> . . . The plan of the superstructure is much after the old castles of the Rhine. It will be two stories high. Two towers—one round and the other octagonal, will give the building a magnificent appearance. One of the towers is so arranged that its uppermost floor may be used for a balcony from which a very fine view of the country can be obtained.
>
> The house is to have all modern improvements. Mrs. Carbonneau has planned an ideal country home for herself and relatives.[12]

The concrete blocks were cast to have the appearance of dressed stone, but eventually nearly all became covered by a thick growth of ivy. The gables and roof were shingled with cedar shakes, and many large windows admitted ample natural light into the interior. Although there were no public utilities so far from town at the time of construction, nevertheless Belinda had the house wired for electricity as well as plumbed for carbide gas fixtures. A coal-fired steam boiler provided central heating originally.

The Mulrooney-Carbonneau house is not particularly large. Its original footprint was roughly 52 by 47 feet. But it is unusual. Its facade suggests solidity and strength, a Northern European fortress. And the interior feels spacious and ele-

23.1. An early view of Carbonneau Castle soon after it was completed in the summer of 1909. The toddler in the front yard is Belinda's nephew, Robert Noble. The woman on the steps at the east-facing main entrance is unidentified. Behind the house is the young fruit orchard. *(Waugaman Collection)*

gant. Yakima residents called the house Carbonneau Castle, and it is still known by that name.

The interior of the castle is arranged to facilitate a flexible style of living that could be very private, or shared with family members, or geared toward formal entertaining. It was furnished with Belinda's collections from Europe and the North; with carpets imported from England;[13] as well as with appointments from Frederick and Nelson,[14] a department store in Seattle that specialized in fine home furnishing and decorating.

The main entrance on the east side of the castle opens into a large room serving both as an entrance hall and a gathering place. Just opposite the doorway is a fireplace flanked by bookcases. In Belinda's day, comfortable, oversized leather chairs could be drawn up in front of the fire for evening conversations or for listening to the grand piano or the wind-up music box. A teakwood screen, heavily encrusted with ivory and jade figures, could be moved to block any drafts. In one corner of the room was a Verni Martin cabinet from Belinda's villa in Nice, displaying walrus ivory carvings done by her workmen in Alaska, a soapstone tree, and bijoux from Europe.[15]

The dining room in the north turret was furnished with an impressive chandelier, a large table of highly polished cherry, and a sideboard filled with fine china and silverware.[16] To the left from the main entrance in the south turret is a parlor, used as a billiard room for most of the years Belinda lived there. The entrance area can be isolated from the parlor and the dining room by finely carpentered, sliding, single-paneled doors. To the rear of the dining room is a kitchen, with perhaps a pantry originally in between. To the rear of the parlor is the side entrance hall from the south. A narrow, steep staircase leads from there to the upstairs.

The central room on the second floor, directly above the living room, is the "ballroom," with light-colored maple flooring. One neighbor of Belinda's, when asked whether the ballroom was ever actually used for dancing recalled, "Oh my goodness yes! [Belinda's] sister Margaret was quite a rounder, and they really had some good parties in the ballroom."[17] The ballroom also has a large fireplace and was used as a family gathering area, for it was flanked by the two main bedroom suites in the turrets, the one in the south turret being Belinda's. Carbide light fixtures in the ballroom are the only remaining visible evidence of the house's original lighting system.

Another steep, narrow staircase leads to the third-floor turret rooms, both of which have skylights and are sheathed on wall and ceiling with narrow tongue-in-groove woodwork. In addition, the north turret has several windows opening to the east. Connecting the two rooms is a low-ceilinged passageway. Belinda, never keen on domestic chores, used these turret rooms as accommodations for a cook and a maid.[18]

While the castle was under construction, Belinda lived in town at 315 South Fourth Street. With her were sisters Margaret and Nellie Noble with her young son Bob. Sister Agnes, by then Mrs. Jay Johnston, joined them while awaiting the birth of her first child.[19] Late in February, as construction on the castle was just beginning, their town home became the focus of local society when former Judge James Wickersham, the Alaskan delegate in Congress, visited Yakima on his way to see his political benefactor, President Theodore Roosevelt, before he left Washington.[20] Margaret was selected by the Commercial Club of North Yakima to travel to Seattle "and invite Judge Wickersham to stop and accept the hospitality of the men of the north who have made their home in the Yakima district," and she succeeded in her mission.[21]

When Delegate Wickersham's train arrived in Yakima on 24 February, he went first to Belinda's house, where he dined and was entertained until his 8 P.M. reception at the Commercial Club. There Wickersham spoke of the strong connections between Alaska and Yakima. Because Washington state benefited so much from Alaska's commerce as well as from its resources, Wickersham stressed how important it was for the Washington state congressmen to represent their mutual interests, because Alaska's delegate had no vote.

> "The state of Washington and the northwest get the greater part of the benefit of our treasure because it all comes to Seattle. We are your best customers for much that you produce. We give you yellow gold . . . , and pay 25 to 50 cents each, for your red apples, and send our people down here to purchase your land and help build up this great valley with their gold."[22]

Of course, this was great press in Yakima. After the reception, Yakima's former Alaskans hosted a banquet in the Yakima Hotel dining room, where the walls were decorated with several fox skins from Belinda's collection.[23]

BELINDA AND HER SISTERS were able to move into their castle in early August 1909. We know this from a social column of the local paper announcing that Joe Barrette, Belinda's old friend with whom she had first crossed Chilkoot Pass, was visiting her on "Nob Hill."[24] But Joe's visit was more than a social call. He, Belinda, and Margaret would carry out some business in the complicated style that had become Belinda's trademark since leaving the Yukon. Joe's mission in Yakima was the penultimate step in a set of twisting, confusing transactions dating back to 1904 in which business, friendship, bitterness, and the Yukon courts all played a part. To understand them, we need to return to the summer of 1904.

At that time, Belinda had returned to Dawson from Europe having separated from Charles Carbonneau on unfriendly terms. She needed cash, for most of her funds were tied up in various failing speculations; therefore, she arranged for a loan of $9,000 from her old friend Captain Norwood using a mortgage to the upper half of 40 A/D Bonanza,[25] among other properties, for security. The upper half of 40 A/D Bonanza was part of the payment she had received from the sale of her Grand Forks Hotel. Through his partnership with Belinda in the hotel, Charles had acquired half interest in the claim as well. Belinda had to use her power of attorney from Charles to execute the 1904 mortgage because the upper half of the claim was in both their names.

Later, when her former Dawson attorney James Pattullo sued Belinda for unpaid fees of $2471.38, he moved to recover the money through appropriation of Belinda's half of the upper half of 40 A/D Bonanza. Pattullo argued for only half of the half-claim because, prior to his filing suit, a change in ownership of Charles's portion had made action against it more problematic. Mining records showed that on 26 June 1907, Charles transferred his one-half interest in the partial claim to Margaret Mulrooney.[26] Since Charles and Belinda were divorced by this time, we might surmise that Margaret had continued to have some contact with Charles despite the bitter struggle between him and her sister. However, it was in fact Belinda in Dome City, Alaska, who used her power of attorney to execute the transfer in Charles's name.[27] Perhaps Belinda felt she had won full control of the property through the divorce proceedings. In any case, she also probably knew that Charles would never return to the Klondike to dispute the transaction.

Even though Pattullo was awarded Belinda's interest in the upper half of 40 A/D (along with the Fairview Hotel) to satisfy his bill, his title was secondary to the mortgage still held by H. H. Norwood. Then, according to claim records, Skipper Norwood assigned the mortgage to Margaret in October 1907.[28] However, Pattullo could not have known of the assignment for it was not recorded until two years later, on 1 September 1909. In the meantime in Dawson between 1907 and 1909, the Deputy Sheriff seized Belinda's interest in the claim, then sold it to an attorney, George Black for $550, with the proceeds apparently going to Pattullo via the courts. Black then immediately sold Belinda's interest to Pattullo for a dollar. By July of 1909, Belinda's friend Joe Barrette was interested in acquiring the 40 A/D Bonanza partial claim. He was able to buy Pattullo's (formerly Belinda's) half interest in the upper half of the claim for a dollar.[29] Although the actual price may have been greater, whatever it was, it was likely to have been discounted, because the property was still tied up by the mortgage to Skipper Norwood. But that was no problem for Joe.

Joe went to Yakima to get the one-quarter interest in the claim formerly in Charles's name and to clear the title to the other quarter with a little help from his old friends. This then is the trip when he visited the newly-constructed Carbonneau castle in Yakima in early August, 1909. On 10 August Margaret certified as paid the debt made in Charles's and Belinda's names and originally secured by the mortgage to Skipper Norwood, for the record would show that Norwood had already assigned the mortgage to her nearly two years earlier. This then would free the title so that the subsequent seizures and purchases that put Belinda's interest in Pattullo's hands now would be of unencumbered property; furthermore, Joe's purchase of that interest the previous month also would be good. Then Joe bought Charles's former quarter interest from Margaret for a dollar, for it had been in her name since June of 1907. Joe apparently then went back to Dawson to record the transactions that would give him clear title to all of the upper half of 40 A/D Bonanza—Norwood's assignment of the mortgage to Margaret, the discharge of the mortgage by Margaret, and the sale by Margaret of Charles's former interest to Joe.[30]

Another set of complicated transactions begun shortly after Joe's visit would put Carbonneau Castle and the surrounding ten acres safely into family hands only. About the time the castle was completed, trouble surfaced in the partnership between Henry Cook and Margaret, possibly over notes of Cook's that Margaret had bought from the Dome City Bank.[31] Margaret sued Henry for $8,200 plus interest and received a Writ of Attachment on his half of the Yakima property. It took four months before the dispute was settled by Henry's paying Margaret, and Margaret's moving for the case to be dismissed.[32] Shortly thereafter, Margaret and Henry paid off the mortgage they had on the Yakima property.[33]

In the meantime, Margaret had transferred her interest in the property to her mother Mary Mulrooney. Then by mutual transfer of interests, the original twenty acres was divided in half, with the northern ten acres plus improvements going to Mary and John Mulrooney, and the southern ten acres to Henry Cook.[34] John Mulrooney had to appear on these latter transactions because in Pennsylvania at that time, a married woman could not convey her own real property without the consent of her husband.[35]

In late August 1909 an announcement appeared in a Fairbanks paper letting friends of Belinda's know of her new home: "Mr. and Mrs. Carbonneau and Miss Margaret Mulrooney are now at their Yakima, Washington, chicken ranch."[36] The inclusion of Charles in the domestic scene on Nob Hill is almost surely an error, for it is improbable that Charles and Belinda even saw each other, let alone lived together, after their divorce.

Belinda and her family entertained many well-known guests at the castle over the years. Perhaps the most prestigious was a sitting president of the United States. Newspaper accounts of President William Howard Taft's visit to Yakima mention that he toured Nob Hill,[37] and according to neighbors, while in the Nob Hill area the president visited Belinda. The legend goes that Belinda did not have a chair wide enough to fit Taft. So she sent for a large, hand-carved Chinese chair at sister Agnes Johnston's, who was staying in town and returned with it in a wagon.[38] Another recollection of the visit was the enjoyment Taft got from watching a mother duck and her brood in the fountain on the front lawn of the castle.

While Belinda welcomed many illustrious guests to Yakima over the years, she generally was not a part of the local social life. Apparently Yakima society didn't know quite what to make of Belinda. She was straightlaced in some ways, yet unconventional in others. Her own sense of propriety often coincided with the customs of the day—she wore tailored skirts even under primitive conditions, enjoyed stylish hats, was fiercely loyal to her family, liked jokes but nothing off-color, and knew the art of substantive conversation. On the other hand, she was often blunt and impatient with small talk, was fiercely independent, and did not hesitate to wield power or take control. In her home she smoked cigarettes, drank whiskey[39] despite strong prohibition sentiment, and would just as soon sit with her feet on the table as on the floor. So Yakima's mothers warned their children, "Never go up there where that awful woman lives."[40] The only sense some could make of Belinda was that she must have been or perhaps still was a madam, an accusation she would have found highly offensive. But for the most part, Belinda did not bother herself with such rumors. As with her previous undertakings, she did what she thought was best and didn't worry about approval from others. She had too many important matters to look after. Her priorities now were to maintain the capital she had so she could support her extended family.

Amidst all the exciting new developments and visits with old friends from the north in 1909, also came sad news from the wilderness. Belinda's comrade, rival, and business partner, Alex McDonald, was dead.[41] Once the "King of the Klondike," with mines valued in the millions of dollars, by this time, at the age of about sixty,[42] Alex was nearly broke. He died of an apparent heart attack while sawing wood at the cabin where he had been prospecting on Slough Creek, near Clear Creek in the Stewart River district. Belinda had persuaded Alex to take out an insurance policy[43] so that his wife and child might have some financial support in the event of his death. It must have been a blow to Belinda to lose Alex so suddenly. He had seemed so big, so vital, such a challenge to her. She had shared so much of the best time in the Klondike with him, and her affection for him was genuine, if sometimes gruff.

Another surprising loss was the early death in 1910 of Belinda's friend Michael J. Heney, the builder of the White Pass Railroad. He was just forty-six years old and only a few weeks from completing another engineering feat, the Copper River Railroad in Alaska.[44]

In the spring of 1910 the census taker who called at Carbonneau Castle found a very full house. Besides Belinda, the head of the household, who is listed as a fruit farmer, there was sister Margaret, brother Jim, and sister Nellie Noble with her son Robert. It is a surprise to see Jesse Noble also listed.[45] The Nob Hill census was taken on 31 May, yet on 9 May and 18 June Jesse is reported to have been in Dome, Alaska.[46] However, it is possible that he made a quick round trip in connection with Nell's divorcing him. In Seattle on 5 July, Nell was granted a divorce on grounds of non-support and desertion, and Jesse, described as one of the wealthy mining men of the Fairbanks district, was ordered to pay $10,000 plus $100 a month permanent alimony, plus $500 attorneys' fees.[47]

Also at the castle for the 1910 census were Agnes and her husband Jay with their one-and-one-half-year-old son Charles. They were probably just winter visitors, waiting for the weather to warm before returning to Alaska. The final occupant was thirty-year-old Maude Stone, described as a boarder, who also may have been a domestic servant.

Back east in Pennsylvania, Belinda's parents, John and Mary, still lived in Archbald with Belinda's older brother Patrick.[48] Perhaps the grand house Belinda had bought for them in Glenside, Pennsylvania, had proved to be too much for them now that nearly all the children were grown. Within a short time,[49] John and Mary would move to Yakima, where Belinda built them an apartment adjacent to and just south of the castle.

For the next several years nearly all of her immediate family would either live or have extended visits at the castle or in Yakima. Belinda worked in her own orchard and managed Henry Cook's land as well,[50] pruning trees, thinning the apple sets, and irrigating. She had installed the irrigation and drainage system for the fields in cooperation with her neighbors.[51] When the fruit trees were mature enough to begin producing well, she sold her fruit by the train car load in Los Angeles and New York,[52] and she built a large warehouse/barn south of the castle to store equipment and to pack the crops for shipment. Brother Jim, now in his late teens, became her right-hand man in running the orchard, and sister Margaret helped with bookkeeping. Sister Nell remarried on 2 November 1911.[53] Her new husband, William F. "Wrong Font" Thompson, was editor and publisher of the *Fairbanks News-Miner*. After the wedding Nell moved to Fairbanks while Belinda and Margaret took responsibility for raising

Nell's son, Bob Noble, then four years old, with Nell occasionally visiting from Alaska.

The Alaska and Yakima Investment Company

In the fall of 1910, newspapers announced that Margaret Mulrooney, along with H. J. Snively, an attorney, were organizing the Alaska and Yakima Investment Company.[54] Official records show that Belinda and Nell Mulrooney Noble also were full partners and directors.[55] Margaret had had a business school education and some business experience through her work as the head cashier at the Dome City Bank. It made sense for her now to extend her activities with the investment company, for which she was appointed secretary. Her warm, good-humored disposition was more suited than Belinda's to making the necessary connections with a civilized public. Belinda's hardy, sober, freewheeling, no-nonsense approach suited the sometimes harsh, usually challenging, somewhat disorganized conditions of the mining camps in the North. But in more staid and settled society, she was often seen as cold, aggressive, bossy, and intimidating. As the years went on, Belinda and Margaret, working as a team, operated as an effective business unit, their talents complementing each other. However, there is little doubt that in most of the hard-nosed business dealings, Belinda remained the dominant force.

According to newspapers, the company consisted of investors from Alaska and Philadelphia and was incorporated at Olympia, Washington for $100,000. The purpose of the corporation was to develop city and country property in the Yakima Valley. Belinda and Margaret, through their hosting of Alaskan visitors interested in purchasing valley real estate, actually already had been acting as promoters. Their enthusiasm was genuine, based on their own satisfaction with the environment they were helping to shape. A recently purchased commercial property at the corner of First and A Streets in downtown Yakima was transferred to the company's holdings, as were the castle and the surrounding ten acres of orchard.[56] The investment company gave the appearance of a more structured framework for the Mulrooney sisters' financial activities.

But not everyone thought Margaret was such a good businesswoman. Back in Dome, Alaska, after the Mulrooney clan left, Jesse Noble had taken August F. Ruser as a partner to run the bank as its cashier while he himself worked two placer claims owned by the bank. Ruser not only ran the bank but reached some conclusions regarding its past operations. As a result, on 27 January 1911, he filed a suit in Yakima, Washington, in the name of the bank and against Margaret Mulrooney. In it he alleged that she, while cashier in 1907, had embezzled $10,500.[57] But Belinda contended that the suit was just a smokescreen for a plot by Jesse Noble aimed at getting back at Margaret, Nell, and herself. Here is how Belinda explained matters:

"... [I]n an action brought in the superior court of this state, Mrs. Noble was granted by Judge Wilson R. Gay [in Seattle] a divorce and a judgment for $10,000 damages and a half of Noble's estate.[58] That was a year ago, but Noble has never paid the alimony or the judgment.

"Some time ago Miss Margaret Mulrooney wrote her attorneys at Fairbanks to attach Noble's property. Noble, however, in the meantime had disposed of his holdings. He then threatened suit against Miss Margaret Mulrooney for $500 on a note which had been assigned to her and which she left with the bank. . . . Ruser and Noble made affidavits that Miss Mulrooney had assigned the note [to the bank]; but H. H. Scales, a bank examiner who afterwards became cashier of the institution made a counter affidavit that it had been left with the bank for collection, and the books proved that he was correct.

"Noble then sent a man named Cook [probably Henry] to see me [Belinda] at Yakima and through him made an offer to settle the Seattle judgment. Cook told me that Ruser and Noble had put up a job to sting my sister for $10,000, but that he could buy Ruser off, if she would pay him a certain sum. She refused the proposition absolutely, and the filing of the suit against my sister followed. The complaint was signed by Ruser and filed a year after the dissolution of the institution and the distribution of its securities. For the purpose of bringing the suit, Noble paid the bank license fees for another year so that he could sue in the name of the bank, but would be protected from resultant damage suits because the bank has no tangible assets.

"The filing of the suit created the greatest indignation amongst Alaskans now in Seattle who knew Noble and the Misses Mulrooney in Fairbanks, and it was agreed amongst them that the only way to get even was to drive Ruser out of town."[59]

What happened next was like a scene from the mining camps of the wild, wild west. Ruser became a lightning rod for Belinda's anger and frustration. She no longer had her great fortune, and her own reputation had been greatly tarnished during her time with Carbonneau and by her own subsequent efforts to recover. She knew how important a good reputation was in business, and she was determined that Margaret's would not be sullied. She also probably was agitated by the unrelenting legal maneuverings that continued from her

Fairbanks days. Ruser was walking head-on into a storm that had been brewing for years.

According to Ruser, he was lured to a Seattle hotel room where he was met by two burly fellows who pulled him into the room and locked the door. He said that as they held him, Belinda lashed him with a horsewhip for besmirching the name of her sister. When he cried out in pain, his mouth was stuffed with a towel. Finally, his assailants left and Ruser went to a police station to file a complaint against Belinda for assault. There was no doubt that he had been severely lashed and beaten.[60]

Belinda had no hesitation in acknowledging what she had done, but her version of what happened, as reported by the *Fairbanks Times* (28 January 1911), was a bit different than Ruser's.

> "It would be unbelievable among my friends in the North and here that I would let him attack my sister's reputation unfairly, and there was nothing left for me to do but whip him, which I did, thoroughly.
>
> "When Ruser states that I had two men helping me to chastise him, he states what is untrue. I needed no help. Twenty friends of ours here, all old Sourdoughs of Alaska, begged to be allowed to take the work off my hands, but it was a family affair and I attended to it to the best of my ability. A blackmailer simply received a little Alaska justice."

The *Seattle Times* noted, "Mrs. Carbonneau is not a female athlete of masculine proportions, but a quiet looking, neatly dressed little woman who weighs about 135 pounds. Ruser, the man she whipped, is more than six feet tall."[61]

About this time, fortunately, a cooler head intervened. Former Judge, now Delegate, James Wickersham arrived in Yakima, en route from Washington, D.C., to Seattle. He recorded the following in his diary:

MARCH 8 (1911)

Spokane in the morning, Yakima at 2 p.m. I stopped off here to see Mrs. Carbonneau and Margaret about Mrs. C's trouble with Jesse Noble and her recent horsewhipping of Ruser, the cashier of Noble's bank, for whom I was attorney. While I have no intention of appearing in these matters, I feel that I must see that these women are not mistreated for they have both been my friends and political and business supporters.

MARCH 9

Spent the day in North Yakima. Visited Mrs. C. and her sister in their suburban home, consulted with Snively, their attorney.

When Wickersham got to Seattle a few days later, he found Belinda and Margaret there, for a warrant had been issued for Belinda's arrest. He advised her to appear in court and to plead guilty—to take a fine and quit. Belinda accepted his advice and the sensational case was settled with a fine of $150[62] and apparently without further repercussions. In fact, it seems that the original complaint against Margaret was also dropped. But that would not be the end of inquiries into Margaret's business methods.

As Belinda and Margaret prospered in Yakima, Mabel Scouse and Bessy Byrnes festered in the far North. Though they had won their case in Fairbanks, they still had not recovered the money they had invested because Belinda had divested herself of all her assets there. Now she seemed to be accumulating wealth again in Yakima. Therefore, in 1911, at about the same time the trouble with Jesse Noble and August Ruser came to a head, Scouse and Byrnes again filed suit for what they considered to be their share of Belinda's current assets. This included the $8,000.06 plus interest awarded them in the Fairbanks case, and now an additional $10,000 plus interest they said Belinda had derived from the No. 3 A/D AL, first tier claim on Dome Creek.[63] Whether Belinda did not receive the summons to appear or simply ignored it is not known.[64] In any case, she did not appear, and Scouse and Byrnes now had an award of $18,000 plus interest against her.[65] However, when they tried to collect this amount in Yakima, they discovered that the property everyone had described as Belinda's was not held in her name and never had been. Belinda had won another skirmish, but Scouse and Byrnes continued the war.

In 1914 they once more filed suit against Belinda. And to make sure "their" money did not slip away by transfers to her relatives or associates, Scouse and Byrnes also named the Alaska and Yakima Investment Company, and most of Belinda's family—brother James, sisters Margaret and Nell, and parents Mary and John—as well as G. E. Waite and Henry Cook as co-defendants.[66] Belinda stood to lose even her castle and orchard if the court decision went against her. Now she would wage an all-out, head-on defensive battle that would last the next three years.

The evidence presented in the opening court hearings provided interesting reading for Yakima valley residents who had been curious about Belinda's past. The local newspaper gave an account of many of her accomplishments, estimating her accumulated wealth at one time as $1 million.[67] The judge hearing the case was said to exclaim as he left the courthouse after the first day of testimony, "That woman has Jack London and Rex Beach beaten by a mile!"[68]

The following day brought additional interesting testimony from Margaret concerning her management of the Alaska and Yakima Investment Company. Here is how the *Yakima Daily Republic* (16 September 1914) reported it.

> They found a condition of affairs which would have sent cold chills zigzag up the spinal column of an expert accountant, for the fair witness, with an indifference which gave even the examining attorney a shock, testified jauntily that she drew on the company's account at the bank, when it had one, to pay grocery, millinery and other personal bills for herself and Mrs. Carbonneau, that she did not expect to give any accounting of the affairs of the company, and that the stockholders of the company would have to take her own and Mrs. Carbonneau's word for it that everything was alright. In fact, she said, the purchase of the property on Nob Hill was purely a family affair, one which they expected to pay out sometime, and when it did they would settle things up, she thought, without difficulty. So far, she said the income from the property had been practically nil.

All of this was very revealing about Margaret's way of keeping accounts, and about the lack of success of Belinda's orchard. It also reflected the fact that the corporation was treated simply as a family holding company. But at issue in the Scouse and Byrnes suit was whether any of the plaintiff's original investments had survived to be the basis for any of Belinda's present assets. The old evidence was trotted out once again. Of special interest now was where the money for the Dome City Bank had come from and gone, and where all the gold was from the No. 3 A/D, first tier, RL Dome Creek claim.

Belinda and her codefendants contended that what money went into starting the bank had come from a trust account and gifts Belinda had given to her family long before the partnership with Scouse and Byrnes was formed. To support this claim, copious testimony and documents were produced describing the Carbonneau's wealth and life-style between 1900 and 1904 and the various gifts Belinda had bestowed. They argued that since the bank had been started with the money given to the family, the earning from the bank business belonged to the various family members. Of this, what Belinda had held in her own name was actually in trust for them. The funds from liquidation of the bank were combined with money from the sale of the family home in Glenside, Pennsylvania, to provide the funds for the property now held by the Alaska and Yakima Investment Company, Belinda and her sisters explained.

Regarding the gold from the Dome Creek claim—there wasn't any. James Kelly, who originally was a partner with Belinda and eventually bought what had been her interest, offered testimony for the defendants. He said this claim, which Scouse and Byrnes had thought was so successful, was instead a bust. According to Kelly, it had never paid beyond its operating expenses, and Belinda had never received any income from it.[69]

After thousands of pages of testimony; hundreds of exhibits; charges; and counter-charges, including forgery on the part of the plaintiffs, the suit for $18,000 was finally decided in favor of Belinda.[70] Scouse and Byrnes had to pay the costs of the longest,[71] hardest-fought legal battle in Yakima County history, in which the stenography fees alone totaled almost $4,000.[72] There was one final skirmish when Scouse and Byrnes appealed to the Washington State Supreme Court, but the decision of the Yakima Court was upheld.[73]

The financial shenanigans revealed by the Scouse and Byrnes trial may have raised eyebrows among Outsiders, but among Klondikers and Alaskans, Belinda was still okay. A few months after the beginning of the sensational trial, at the second annual sourdough banquet in Yakima valley, only two toasts were offered. The first was to Alaska. The second was a backhanded tribute, typical of pioneer "roasts," to Mrs. B. A. Carbonneau, "the sourest of the sourdoughs."[74]

There also were other indirect tributes to Belinda about this time. In 1915 a novel appeared that became very popular and must have given Belinda some hearty laughs. It was Harry Leon Wilson's comedy of manners, *Ruggles of Red Gap*. The novel's cast of characters includes former Alaskans and would-be gentry who are living in an agricultural valley much like Yakima, in a "fastest growing town" in Washington state. Belinda had met Wilson when she lived in Paris, and according to her, he took mannerisms of her speech and pieces of her life to concoct a central character in the novel, Mrs. Lysander John Pettengill, Ma Pettengill, "The Mixer." In the novel Ma Pettengill is depicted as confident, wealthy, down-to-earth, and intelligent. She is an inveterate practical joker; a nonconformist; a lover of gambling, whether at the table or at life; an enthusiastic fan of a justifiable fight; a shrewd planner; a defender of independent women; and not one to suffer fools gladly—all notable characteristics of Belinda.[75] Ma Pettengill proved so popular with both Wilson and his readers that he wrote another novel as well as short stories featuring her as the main character.[76]

Wilson's humorous stories were a welcome diversion in America from the grim realities of the war which had broken out in Europe. It must have worried Belinda that many of her friends and extended family were in danger there. Even before the United States finally declared war on Germany in April of 1917, the Mulrooneys had shifted into action. Brother Jim had joined Company E of the Second Washington Infantry and had been mustered out to guard a portion of the border with Mexico. With the declaration of war, he put his early schooling to good use and went to France to teach French to American soldiers. According to a newspaper report at the time, Margaret also was planning to go to France to do the same.[77]

Belinda apparently stayed in Yakima to grow food and look after her parents and nephew Bob, so she was at her castle in 1917 when she got more dispiriting news from an unexpected direction. The Fairview Hotel in Dawson, once Belinda's pride and joy, and a monument to her daring and tenacity, had burned to the ground.[78]

ONCE WORLD WAR I WAS OVER, it was time for Belinda to take stock of her life and face some difficult decisions. The Alaska and Yakima Investment Company had not flourished. The land boom in the Yakima Valley was over and real estate values decreased accordingly.[79] Although Belinda had tried to sell the ranch property and Carbonneau Castle with most of its furnishings along with Henry Cook's ten acres for $50,000,[80] she had not found a buyer. Neither was her orchard business a success. Her operations were reduced to ten acres of farming when Henry Cook liquidated his parcel in 1914.[81] "It was too small to make me rich and too large to leave," she used to joke. But the reality was that the Mulrooney magic had not worked because she had deviated from her tried-and-true ritual for success—anticipate the boom, diversify widely, move on when the boom is done. And now, having supported all of her family as well as herself for over a decade, her second fortune was gone. She was going to have to make changes once again.

Belinda's financial worries were not eased by the fact that she was now nearing her fiftieth birthday. Although she felt fine and was still energetic, she was reminded of the tenuousness of life by the loss of three of her closest male friends from Dawson. Two had died before the war—Alex McDonald in 1909 and dear, kind Joe Barrette in 1912—both in middle age while still mining in the North. The third was H. H. "Skipper" Norwood, who passed away in San Francisco in 1917.[82] Another blow came with the wreck of the steamer *Princess Sophia* in October 1918, en route from Skagway to Vancouver. Among the 379 persons lost were many Old Timers from the Yukon basin on their way Out for the winter, including William Scouse, Z. A. (Mabel) Scouse's husband.[83]

And then in 1919, word reached Belinda[84] that at age sixty-four, Charles Carbonneau also was now truly dead.

24

The Notorious Charles E. Carbonneau

T HE PATTERN OF Charles Eugene Carbonneau's life seemed to change little after Belinda divorced him in 1906. His style of business activity continued to be expansive and imaginative as he promoted various ventures around the globe. There were modifications to his locales of operation, however.

The Yukon and Alaska were close-knit enough that his reputation there as a promoter was ruined. With the Anglo-French Klondyke Syndicate going bankrupt in 1901,[1] and the Gold Run (Klondike) Mining Company in a shambles and headed in the same direction,[2] Charles no longer inspired confidence in his business acumen in northwest North America. His reputation was further tarnished there by accusations of criminal action in the salting of the No. 12 Gold Run claim and in the fraudulent management of the Gold Run company.[3]

His standing seemed even more shaky in eastern Canada and western Europe. The Anglo-French Klondyke Syndicate and the Gold Run (Klondike) Mining Company were, after all, English companies with stockholders primarily in Great Britain and France. In Europe Charles had been judged not just incompetent but a crook. He was convicted in 1905 in Paris of embezzling and swindling, for which he was sentenced to two years in prison plus a fine. He also was accused of other instances of embezzlement, but he managed to persuade court officials that he was ill and would be able to stand trial only after he recovered. Charles was temporarily excused by the court, after which he was spotted in England, Belgium, Italy, Montreal, and the eastern United States. However, as far as we have been able to determine, he never served his prison term nor paid the fine, and never was tried on the other charges. These circumstances led a Montreal paper to predict, "That's enough, we believe, to put an end to a career."[4] But Charles Carbonneau was more resilient than that.

Charles continued doing business by identifying other places for his schemes where he was out of the jurisdiction of French courts. The world was big enough and he was insignificant enough that there were plenty of people who had never heard of Charles E. Carbonneau or had since forgotten him. His mode of operation was as it had been in the Klondike—find American, French, or English investors for ventures in regions that were expanding and developing rapidly. These were usually in locales where the investors were unlikely to have direct communications.

In October of 1907 Carbonneau formed the Mexican and Cuban Estates Company.[5] He issued $300,000 in 6 percent bonds to raise capital to buy tobacco and other plantations in Cuba. Besides describing the very promising properties, the company's prospectus reassured investors by listing as a trustee and director Manuel Sobrado, then Minister of the Interior for Cuba. With this kind of official backing, the speculation seemed a good bet to succeed. Furthermore, advertisements were placed in London newspapers recruiting workers for the company's exotic plantations in the Caribbean, and many people applied for the positions.

Also in 1907, in partnership with Henri Rochette, Charles promoted another foreign venture. The Central Mexican Railway was to be extended by way of the Hugra-Cuenca Railway Company of Ecuador, the expansion to be financed with an offering of $1 million in shares. Publicity for this company included the information that among its wealthy Mexican supporters was Gustav Madero, brother to the politician, Francisco Madero, who would become president of Mexico in 1911.

It was not until 1913 that trouble connected with these Cuban, Mexican, and South American speculations came to public light. And then the revelations were spectacular.

Paris, Monday, April 14—The French police arrested Charles Eugene Carbonneau at Boulogne[-sur-Mer] after he had left a Channel boat and was getting into an elegant automobile, accompanied by a fifteen-year-old English girl, whom they sent back to England.

Carbonneau is wanted by the French police in connection with an alleged swindle in the construction of a railway line in Ecuador. Among the papers seized by the police were many referring to the Central Mexican Railway scheme launched by Rochette and Carbonneau five years ago. Shares of this company amounting to $1,000,000 were disposed of in France.

The Belgian and American police are also said to have charges against Carbonneau.[6]

When arrested, Carbonneau described the young woman in his company as his daughter. While it is possible that Carbonneau had a daughter born in 1898 while he was shuttling back and forth between the Klondike and Europe, we have found no independent verification of her existence. It seems more probable that Carbonneau had a sexual relationship with the girl accompanying him across the English Channel, speculation supported by the *Dawson Daily News* in 1906, where it is obvious that some who knew him in Dawson thought he had a penchant for young girls.[7]

Henri Rochette, Carbonneau's partner in the railway venture, was not one to increase confidence in the soundness or legitimacy of the investment. Like Carbonneau, Rochette had humble beginnings, but by promoting investments he earned $40 million in less than four years.[8]

The bubble elevating Rochette burst in 1908. When shareholders began to ask what was supporting all the speculation, they found nothing, and Rochette was placed under arrest for swindling. However, like any really good con artist, Rochette's genius was as much in manipulating people as in diddling securities. Rochette had many loyal investors and supporters, some of whom were in very high places. When he was released on bail a short time later, many of his creditors cheered him as he left the prison. Some detractors charged that government officials protected him even during the two years of investigation into his activities. Meanwhile he launched the Central American Railway scheme with Carbonneau. Following a long trial on the original charges of swindling, Rochette was convicted in 1912 and sentenced to two years in jail. However, still out on bail, he skipped the country. Located subsequently in Mexico City, where he held a position close to President Francisco Madero, he disappeared when the French government demanded his extradition, and took refuge in Switzerland.[9]

When Carbonneau was arrested and jailed in France in 1913 for the Central Mexican Railroad promotion,[10] these latest exploits of his partner Rochette had not yet come to light, for they were only then unfolding. In the meantime, two unhappy investors filed fraud charges against Charles in London concerning the Mexican and Cuban Estates Company.

The first, James Waddell, complained that Charles only pretended to own tobacco and other plantations in Cuba, under the name Cuban Land and Plantation Company. Waddell, impressed with the endorsement of the company by the Cuban Minister of the Interior, had applied for one of the plantation jobs advertised in the London newspapers. He found that in order to get the post, he had to purchase several hundred dollars of bonds in the company through Carbonneau. This he did, secured passage on a ship, and proceeded to Cuba.

> Waddell says that on his arrival in Cuba he, with dozens of others similarly engaged, ascertained that the company really had no business and possessed no property. Waddell and others were stranded, penniless and unprotected, in Cuba.
>
> . . . [It was charged that Carbonneau] kept secret from the plaintiff and other investors the public repudiation by Sobrado of any responsibilities and of the statement that he was a Director. The company never had any legal existence whatever, was never registered in Cuba, or incorporated in South Dakota (where the company was supposed to have been registered in September, 1907).[11]

A similar complaint was filed in London by Francis Henry Kinnear of New York, who had lost $2,500 and had also been left stranded in Cuba.[12]

On 5 April Charles applied for a postponement of the trial in London concerning the Cuban plantations charges, for it was at this same time that problems with the Central American railway company also began to surface. In requesting the postponement, Charles explained that he urgently needed to go to Mexico, because £60,000[13] of company funds had been used by the Maderos, who then were overthrown and assassinated. If Charles were to recover any of the money, he had to make his claims immediately.[14] The judge in London refused to allow a postponement,[15] but all parties agreed that Charles's evidence could be taken on commission before he left England for Mexico.[16] Having given his deposition, Charles did indeed leave England, but it was then that he was arrested by the French authorities on 12 April as he entered France.

Meanwhile, back in the high court in London, following several days of testimony on behalf of the plaintiffs, the situation looked bleak for Charles. The plaintiff's exhibits were compelling, and Waddell's and Kinnear's stories were corroborated by others. Then Charles's deposition was read on his own behalf.

If it was hard to discern the truth then, in 1913, it is even harder now to know Charles Carbonneau's true motives. If you are skeptical of his honesty, you could note that once again he proved that he could talk his way out of just about anything. And in doing so, he used tried and true methods of a skillful confidence artist—speak courteously and knowledgeably; cite support of those with power and authority; apologize for regrettable circumstances, but never admit any wrongdoing, never accept responsibility; find some way to be seen as a victim; if all else fails, claim that there is a conspiracy among those who are trying to ruin you. On the other hand, perhaps he, like the plaintiffs in the case, truly was just a victim of unfortunate circumstances, as he argued. Belinda had this to say about Charles's repeated business troubles.

> In building up a property, Mr. Carbonneau, as a promoter, thought in millions and created millions. Up to the time where he was about to put things over, reach the place where he could realize on it, he was splendid. But then . . . his associates would find some excuse to lose him—he was too extravagant in the management or something. When it came time to gather profits, he'd lose out. For some excuse or other, something would go wrong at that point. While he was building up, they would hang around, boost, and compliment his efforts. He would make up his mind that quick, to go to South Africa in a minute. But he would go as a gentleman, in the royal suite with body servants and everything. He really scared investors. What he was, what he stood for—a man handling so many problems. He was classed as second to none among promoters. (NW 56:2[292])

Charles's deposition in the suits against him in London had a similar ring.

> . . . Carbonneau said that he first floated the Mexican and Cuban Estates Company in New York. He registered it under the laws of South Dakota. The company had a nominal capital of $5,000,000. Many New York businessmen had big interests in it. The deeds of the property were drawn up by Vidal, a New York attorney. After the registration some difficulties arose, and ultimately he incorporated a new company called the Cuban Land and Plantation Company. Trust deeds were prepared for the Mexican company identical with those for the Cuban company. All debenture bonds were issued from the registered office in New York.
>
> Carbonneau's evidence proceeded to outline a big scheme which he said had been organized by financiers who had tried to get control of the company, to wreck the Cuban land concern. Notices, he said, were published in the principal New York daily papers, and Ministers of the Cuban Government received

anonymous letters alleging irregularities on the part of Carbonneau. His evidence was to the effect that the present proceedings had really been initiated by this opposition group of financiers, who were trying to ruin him, and that Kinnear was only a pawn in the game.[17]

Charles won the jury and was acquitted of all charges. But he was still under arrest in Paris concerning the Mexican railroad company and other charges of fraud.[18]

Apparently he was eventually released, though we do not know under what circumstances, for when we next hear of Charles the following year, he is a free man. Five months after the outbreak of the First World War in Europe, he steamed into New York harbor on the *Baltic* and registered at the Hotel Breslin. There his strange behavior and continual mutterings attracted the attention of the hotel personnel, who called in a doctor to examine their new guest. Charles related a story of heroic tragedy.

> Mr. Carboneau [*sic*] told the hotel clerks and Dr. Gibbons that he had been a Lieutenant in the French Army and had fought side by side with his five sons, that in one battle all six of them had been captured by the Germans, that in a fog they had fled from their German prison, that his five sons had been shot down in the attempt to escape, and that he, escaping unscathed, had made his way to England and sailed to America.[19]

Following this recital, Dr. Gibbons, knowing nothing of Charles's background, concluded that he was suffering from the strain of a terrific nervous shock and ordered him removed to the psychiatric ward of Bellevue Hospital for observation. Before going, Charles sent a cablegram "to his daughter in Paris, assuring her of his safety."[20] We have found no evidence that Charles ever had any children.

The sensational story of Charles's breakdown in New York City appeared not only in New York newspapers, but also was featured in both Fairbanks and Seattle.[21] Since Belinda's sister Nell was married to a newspaper owner in Fairbanks, there is little doubt that Belinda heard the news. Furthermore, all of the papers included background information linking Charles with Belinda. We can only guess what Belinda's reaction might have been to the revelation of Charles's breakdown. Perhaps she had already realized long ago that his connection with reality sometimes could be tenuous.

The final episode in Charles Eugene Carbonneau's notorious career came in February of 1919 when he and Rochette finally were to be put on trial for the

Central Mexican Railroad swindle. The two were charged as codefendants, but apparently it was all too much for Charles, for he had another mental breakdown while in prison. He became agitated and consequently was put in solitary confinement and constrained by a straitjacket. During the night, he apparently suffered another manic episode in the course of which he died of suffocation.[22]

In his own trial later that year, Rochette would claim that all of the problems with the Central Mexican Railroad had been due to Carbonneau. Rochette said that it was Carbonneau who sent part of the funds realized from the sale of the bonds to "a Mexican named Madero, who used them for revolutionary propaganda in that country."[23] The court was not convinced. Henri Rochette was sentenced to two years in prison and fined three thousand francs and costs.[24]

SO WAS THE SAD ENDING to the life of Charles Carbonneau. In many ways he and Belinda were very similar, so their affinity is understandable. Both began life in humble circumstances in Catholic families in Europe. They had arrived as immigrants in North America while children; and as young, bright immigrants often do, they had learned to bridge the gaps between the old and new worlds with great facility. They each were determined to make their own way and stylishly. They were imaginative thinkers, interested in the wider world around them, and yet comfortable with going their own way, operating independently. As adults they found entrepreneurism a profitable channel for their ambition, talents, gamesmanship, and energy. These similarities would lead Belinda in later life to say, despite all the problems they had, "In some ways there wasn't any pair better mated than we were" (NW 56:3[293]).

But Charles and Belinda were quite different in other ways. Until she met Charles, Belinda used and risked her own resources to build up businesses,[25] and in quite a few of these she was highly successful. Belinda was more accountable at all stages of her ventures, whether assuming risks, reaping benefits, admitting error, or accepting praise. Also underlying Belinda's success was a more realistic grasp of what was within her abilities to accomplish. Charles's ventures were usually more grandiose and involved risking the investments of others. None of the companies he started from his Yukon days on turned a profit for anyone but himself. Charles's and Belinda's partnership was no exception.

The contrasts between Charles and Belinda illustrate that a thin line separates speculative entrepreneurship from a confidence game. It is hard for an investor to judge whether a new company, based on unproved products and untried management, is an imaginative and legitimate venture or is simply capitalizing on a craze for the benefit of the promoters. At the beginning stages of an enterprise, Charles engendered confidence in his ability to reap profits from gold mining and other risky undertakings. But he consistently failed to sustain that confidence. Whether Charles's malfeasance justified the loss of trust is open to interpretation. In any case, Charles repeatedly managed to get so out of touch with his colleagues that, according to him, they would oppose his legitimate efforts to the point of bringing down the company.

Furthermore, Charles illustrates that the personality traits of entrepreneurs in more extreme form are often associated with mental instability.[26] The imagination required to think of things differently and creatively, when not balanced by reality checks is delusion. The self-confidence necessary to act on new ideas in its extreme is megalomania. And risk-taking, if untempered by realistic evaluation of the alternatives, resources, and potential costs and benefits, is impulsive folly.

Charles Carbonneau had a profound effect on the life of Belinda Mulrooney. The beginnings of her association with him launched her into an expansive stage of her life—a time of prosperity when she hoped both to establish her own happy, loving family and to explore ever-wider geographical and cultural circles. While her horizons did widen after their marriage, Belinda's other dreams were soon quashed. The couple had no children, though we do not know why. And Belinda eventually realized that Charles had married her primarily for her money, which was soon used up in speculative ventures and very high living.

Belinda's divorce was another turning point in her life, the beginning of a more bitter stage. Her humiliation over being duped and financially ruined was very deep, as was her disappointment in never being able to have children of her own. She set out with dogged determination to get back on her feet financially. With the help of her family, she managed to do so, though not without some wily business maneuvers of her own. And just below her usually serious composure roiled a rage that surfaced as righteous indignation toward anyone she thought was trying to take advantage of her or her sisters.

Only after fifteen years[27] did Belinda seem ready for another change. Perhaps overwhelmed by the devastation of World War I and the mortality of the influenza pandemic of 1918–19,[28] as well as by the regrettable circumstances of Charles's death, Belinda's rage finally did subside, releasing her into a more reflective sixth decade of life.

Belinda Matures

T THE START of the 1920s, with her orchard business limping along, Belinda soberly evaluated her position. It was not good. Her nest-egg was dwindling, and she was having a hard time meeting day-to-day expenses. To increase her income, Belinda decided to rent her castle. She would continue to run her orchard from the apartments she had built to the south of the castle. This arrangement meant that brother Jim, sister Margaret, and nephew Bob, as well as Belinda, would be living with her parents.[1]

The first summer of renting, 1920,[2] she left the castle intact, fully furnished. In fact, the renters, the Gue family, were more like boarders, for Belinda managed the house and meals, kept her cook, Ben, and ate her evening meals with them.

The Gue offspring, Gladys and Marjorie, were sixteen and seventeen years old, respectively. They were excited about staying at the famous castle. With its spacious grounds, tennis court, and billiard room, it seemed almost a resort. Gladys and Marjorie also were intrigued by what they had heard of Mrs. Carbonneau. Some of their contemporaries were even deliciously scandalized, for they thought Mrs. Carbonneau to be quite risqué, with her cigarette smoking and liquor drinking. While women's smoking was becoming more accepted in

25.1. The front of Carbonneau Castle. *(Mayer Collection, date undetermined)*

some parts of America at this time, in small-town, rural Yakima, it simply was not done by the "right kind" of women. Belinda's drinking of liquor was even more scandalous. She, like many Klondikers, viewed whiskey as a kind of tonic, to be taken regularly, but in moderation. However, nationwide prohibition was enacted 16 January 1920; while Washington, like many other states, already had passed its own version several years earlier, in 1914. So to some, Belinda's shot a day was viewed as a federal offense. As if her current behaviors weren't enough to raise eyebrows, Belinda's having run hotels in the Klondike and having made a lot of money—somehow—fueled speculation that she actually had been a bordello madam. Maybe she still was? Their friends couldn't understand how the Gues would dare to take their teenage girls to the castle for the summer. But Gladys's and Marjorie's parents were more open-minded.

> Before we [moved] out, Mrs. Carbonneau had invited us out for dinner. . . . And Dad told us, "Now then, you will probably see Mrs. Carbonneau smoke a cigarette." Well, we had never seen a woman smoke a cigarette in our lives! In those days, you know. Well, of course, we sat there at the table, and we couldn't wait, my sister and I. We were rolling our eyes around and wondering when this was going to happen.
>
> And he also said, "And she probably will have a drink." Well, this was something else that we were all excited about. So after dinner . . . we went out and sat by the fireplace [in the ballroom]. We were absolutely goggle-eyed over it

all, you know. It was so exciting. And she smoked her cigarette, and we waited for her to take this drink. And she drank it out of a little shot glass.[3]

Having acquired the habit of smoking while in Europe in 1901, Belinda by this time was thoroughly addicted to nicotine. The Gue sisters probably would have been more shocked had they known that Belinda also chewed tobacco at times. According to brother Jim, when she chewed in the house, she would go out to the kitchen and spit the tobacco juice out the back door. "To fertilize the roses," she said.[4]

Once Marjorie and Gladys got to know Belinda, they were very favorably impressed by her.

> It wouldn't bother [Mrs. Carbonneau] in the least to [know she was thought to be risqué]. She was completely herself. But she had this reserve about her that she didn't go out to shock anyone. That would be the last thing in the whole wide world . . . she would ever think of doing.
>
> She was a delightful person. And [she] always just intrigued us, because she was so different . . . from the other people we knew.[5]
>
> She wore these *pince nez* glasses, and they were always just a little bit cock-eyed, you know. Just a little bit. She had beautiful, raven black hair,[6] as I remember, and . . . the way she held her mouth, you could sort of see that when she was up in the Klondike, if somebody did something that she didn't like, I'll bet you . . . the words could crack out of that little mouth of hers! But she was an absolute delight. . . . There was quite a bit of reserve, dignity. But [she was] very warm, delightful.
>
> She was herself completely under all circumstances. And she didn't want any nonsense around. Fun, yes, she loved that. But there was a line.
>
> She wore tailored things. . . . Usually even around the house there, she always wore tailored suits. She'd reach into this [left] breast pocket to take out her cigarettes. And no wasted, fluffy motions or anything else.
>
> She's a person, once you have known her, you never completely get her out of your mind.[7]

The Gue sisters remember being captivated by Belinda's stories of the Klondike and Alaska, told as they gathered after dinner for conversation in the ballroom.[8] They also recalled that in 1920 Belinda's brother Jim, then twenty-seven years old, was doing most of the labor to run the orchard.[9] Though they never saw Belinda work outside that summer, her weather-beaten complexion testified to her active outdoor life, as well as to the fact that she didn't care to try to hide the signs of her age and essence with creams or makeup.

25.2. The Gue sisters, Marjorie at left and Gladys at right, sit between (*l. to r.*) Louis Delaguerra, Belinda's nephew Bob Noble, and Guy Cooper on the front steps of Carbonneau Castle in about 1920. Delaguerra and Cooper played on the Yakima baseball team. *(Gue Collection)*

The Gue sisters had Belinda's bedroom on the second floor of the south tower for their own. They were thrilled by the soft richness of the sable fur blanket Belinda had left on her bed, and they played with it by draping it around their shoulders to form a royal robe. Apparently Belinda also took a liking to the girls. Although neither Gladys nor Marjorie knew exactly why, she generously gave them her Ford Model T sedan to proudly drive to high school.

The Gues stayed at Carbonneau Castle only about four months. Next Belinda rented to the Bunting family, presumably with arrangements similar to those she had had with the Gues. Later still, Belinda's home became The Castle Club, for men only, still furnished with Belinda's belongings and with the kitchen overseen by her cook.[10] Nevertheless, by 1921 it was obvious she would need more operating capital. The only way to get it was to sell part of her land. In preparation for this the family corporation, the Alaska-Yakima Investment Company, transferred title to Belinda personally.[11] Then, in 1922, she sold part of her ten acres to Melissa Bell. A year later the investment company was dissolved, apparently for failure to pay fees.[12]

By 1924 Belinda and her family had decided to scale back even further by moving to a new, more modest home in Seattle. Belinda bought two lots on a

25.3. Belinda relaxes on the lawn of her estate on a hot day in the summer of 1920. The men are unidentified members of the Yakima baseball team. The Model T Ford Belinda gave the Gue sisters to drive is in the background. *(Gue Collection)*

hilltop in southwest Seattle.[13] To the north was an unrestricted view of downtown Seattle and the Elliot Bay waterfront. In the distance to the west were the peaks of the Olympic Mountains. To the east, across unpaved 37th Avenue SW, were an orchard and the newly built Mount St. Vincent Home for the Aged, beyond which on a clear day could be glimpsed the peaks of the Cascade Mountains. Mount St. Vincent Home was a beneficiary of the estate of Belinda's Alaskan friend, Michael J. Heney, builder of the White Pass and the Copper River Railroads.[14] Perhaps because of her friendship with Michael, Belinda was able to arrange to stay at the facility for a couple of months in late 1924 while her own home across the street was being built.[15]

A mortgage on the castle property[16] helped to finance Belinda's new house at 4817 37th Avenue SW. The Seattle home's basic dimensions were thirty-one feet wide by twenty-four feet deep, but good-sized covered porches extended the space at both the front and back. The shingled, craftsman-bungalow style disguised the fact that the full basement, largely exposed on the sloped north and west sides, also was a four-room living unit, accessible only by the stairs at the back. From the front view the large, symmetrical windows on either side of the porch presented an attractive, balanced exterior. Much of the charm of the original structure has been obliterated by renovations, but it still stands (in 1998) at the same address.

According to the Seattle directory, Belinda as well as her parents, John and Mary, moved to the new house in Seattle in 1925.[17] Apparently her parents lived upstairs while Belinda lived downstairs. But it seems Belinda still was spending some of her time in Yakima running her orchard, for we hear of Belinda in Yakima in 1928 from Helen Hawkins, who carried out a series of interviews with her there.[18]

THERE WERE several important elements underlying Belinda's seemingly "magic" or "lucky" achievement prior to 1900. First, Belinda had a high degree of geographic mobility, which meant she got to a booming environment quickly and was ready to move on to the next once the peak of the boom was past. Second, these boom environments were often primitive and disorganized, so that operating in them required flexible problem solving, stamina, and high tolerance for ambiguity. Third, Belinda could act quickly and decisively. Finally, she diversified her investments so no one undertaking was critical, while the odds were increased for finding a winner.

By the 1920s, Belinda also had found where her weaknesses were. She was not so skilled at the long-term, steady-state management of a business, which required not only her strength of vision but also a more systematic attention to detail than was her natural bent. This lack of attention to detail was what got her into trouble with the Scouse and Byrnes partnership. Belinda seems to have learned from this experience, for in setting up the Dome City Bank, sister Margaret was put in charge of all aspects of the bookkeeping and accounting. Nevertheless, Belinda's newfound wisdom did not save her from the longer-term repercussions of the failed partnership with Scouse and Byrnes.

Another drawback for Belinda was that she was very earnest, outspoken, and disinclined to hold her socially unsanctioned behaviors in check for long; therefore, dealing with a more conventional public on a regular basis was a strain. Furthermore, away from the rough-shod expansion of a booming frontier, she was likely to be seen as an oddity. Her self-confident, problem-solving skills were more likely to be considered an aberration than an asset to a woman's mental domains. This, of course, was more society's weakness and loss, though Belinda paid the personal costs of censure.

In light of these considerations, the general decline of Belinda's fortunes in the second decade of the twentieth century perhaps is more understandable.

She made a decided shift in her goals following her divorce from Charles. Financial gain was no longer her main objective. Money, she began to feel, was meaningless unless it was used for what was most important. Now her family became her highest priority, and if there were compromises to be made, now her duty to her family would prevail over taking risks in the hope of amassing wealth. Therefore, many of the elements of the Mulrooney "magic" were no longer operating.

Although it boomed for a while, Yakima was decidedly "settled," and there was less room and less support for her eccentricities to operate creatively. Nearly all of Belinda's resources were tied up with the Yakima property; therefore, she did not have money available for the more diversified speculations that had so often paid off in her early life. And because she chose to look after her elderly parents and young nephew while living a planted, agrarian life-style, she was no longer free to move on when Yakima's boom did not last. There may have been one exception to this lack of mobility, however. We have one reference to Belinda's having applied her winning formula once again, trying her luck around Goldfield, Nevada.

> . . . Years [after 1898] she was again my hostess in a hotel in the camp that rose on the Nevada desert after the Goldfield strike.
>
> "Just couldn't keep away," she said. "It's in the blood, I guess. I lost most of the fortune I made in the Klondike, but am making another."[19]

However, we have no specific indication of when this incident might have occurred, nor have we located any records verifying that Belinda was in the Goldfield area.

Probably the most painful lesson Belinda learned from looking back on her earlier life was that she could be such a poor judge of the character of men when it came to romantic relationships. She was not likely to find a steady, trustworthy partner among the smooth-talking, expansive, imaginative "gamblers" she found so attractive. Because of Belinda's persistent public cover-up of what happened between her and Charles Carbonneau, it is hard to know how successful she was at integrating this knowledge. According to family members, Belinda was very embarrassed about having been taken in and defrauded by him.[20] Only on rare occasions did she admit in public that she had dumped him. Usually she claimed that Charles had died while they were still married. Though Belinda was somewhat more open with her family, where she jokingly called him the "no-account Frenchman,"[21] even with them she never talked about details of their relationship. The incident with Agnes's kidnapping and Charles's probable philandering, about which Belinda's sisters and brother could have had some direct knowledge, also were not discussed. Or it may be that if they were discussed, the conversation was in French so that the younger generation could not understand.[22] And no one in the family, at least among the generations surviving in the 1990s, knew exactly what did happen to Charles Carbonneau after their divorce. Furthermore, from all we have been able to gather, Belinda did not have any romantic relationships following her divorce. Apparently, after the disaster with Charles, Belinda simply gave up on that kind of association with men.

As Belinda neared the age of fifty, she seems to have become more reflective about her life. What, after all, did her early accomplishments mean? Starting with nothing and despite several reversals, she had by her own efforts made fortunes from a variety of businesses. She had helped to build towns and to develop a whole new area of North America. For the most part she had tried to carry out her business affairs honestly, though from some people's perspectives she had been less than trustworthy. She had materially improved the situation of her whole family, and while she had birthed no children of her own, she could derive satisfaction from knowing her support and care of her siblings and some of their children had made a significant contribution to nurturing later generations.

There are indications that near the half-century mark of her life, though modest about her achievements, Belinda did wish to be remembered for her early contributions to the development of the North. One is that she became a charter member of the Pioneer Women of Alaska, organized 19 February 1916 in Fairbanks to preserve the names and histories of women who settled early in Interior Alaska.[23] Another is that in the 1920s Belinda consented to an extended interview about her maiden years. Perhaps she felt the story of her early life would also be a kind of legacy, and if she told her own version, it would be more accurate than the romanticized legends that so far had appeared. Besides, she needed money. Here might be another way to make some. In any case, when the opportunity presented itself to tell about her life as she wished for it to be remembered, Belinda seized it.

Helen Hawkins,[24] a Spokane newspaper woman, wanted to write the true story of the woman about whom she had heard so many rumors. And Belinda found Helen to be a sympathetic and perceptive listener. If Belinda was at first hesitant about the interview, that reserve soon disappeared. She became an enthusiastic participant in the project. Apparently she became invested enough in the telling of her story that when it seemed that Helen's efforts were not going to result in a publication, Belinda put the material in the hands of another person to try to get it out.[25]

At first Belinda was self-conscious about Helen's constant scribbling of notes. Unlike modern interviewers, Helen did not have the benefit of a tape recorder. Instead she depended upon her fast-as-lightning scrawl and her prodigious memory to catch most of the words as well as the tone of her subject.

Belinda did not pour out her entire life story to Helen Hawkins. Rather, she presented the aspects of her life of which she was most proud. Her recollections would cover the period from her birth through the day of her wedding Charles Carbonneau. It was not the whole story, but it was a substantial and impressive undertaking. When it was done, Helen Hawkins's notes and various typed drafts of manuscripts would fill enough file folders to stuff a large cardboard carton.

Like any memoir, Belinda's recounts events from only her own perspective and includes many errors of fact and interpretation. At times the story is distorted, whether intentionally or unconsciously, to preserve Belinda's sense of propriety, or to hide the true identity of certain characters, or to protect her own ego. Fortunately, Belinda's ego was quite strong. Consequently, for the most part we have found the information in the memoirs to be verified by independent sources. For example, rather than omitting many of her missteps, or "spasms" as she called them, Belinda includes them as examples of how she learned the hard way or as humorous anecdotes with herself as the butt of the joke. Since the memoirs end with her marriage to Charles Carbonneau, they of course do not include the most problematic part of her life. This is unfortunate, for it would have been interesting to hear what sense Belinda then made of those difficult years.

Much of the material collected by Helen Hawkins tells of events and circumstances we would have no other way of knowing about except from Belinda. From this basis, once given the leads of where to look, we have in many cases been able to piece together an even more factually accurate version of Belinda's life. The fruits of Helen Hawkins's work are most evident in our telling of Belinda's story up through 1900. But the interviews are also valuable for their glimpses of Belinda in her mid fifties, as Helen Hawkins gives us her own perspective on Belinda in 1927 or 1928.[26] These images from a sympathetic and observant contemporary of Belinda's are especially valuable.

We learn, for example, that when Helen Hawkins first met Belinda, who was then about fifty-five years old, she was surprised that she looked like an old lady—small, unassuming, weathered, and rather unkempt. Helen had imagined a more imposing, attractive, socially extroverted person from all the stories she had heard about the famous Mrs. Carbonneau. It was only when Belinda began speaking that the strength of her character, her charm and her vitality became apparent. Soon, Helen was completely won over. "To this day she can dim the most beautiful woman by the potency of her charm, a charm that depends on nothing that draws the eye. Tired, slumping, careless as she looks now, she can galvanize a roomful by her speech."

At the time Helen began the interviews, Belinda was in the process of selling her castle.[27] She had moved herself and many of her antiques and mementos from the castle into an apartment in what had been originally the warehouse for the orchard business.[28] Amidst the cluttered reminders of her more prosperous years, Belinda at this time lived very simply. By 1928 her brother Jim had moved to Fairbanks, so now Belinda was the one who tended the orchard. She no longer wore her trademark tailored suits, but would often do the interviews in an old black sateen dress and muddied slippers.

> She smokes while she talks. . . . She wears dresses with the effect of having put them on in a great hurry, considering time at the mirror lost. Her hair, thick and glossy . . . , glistens with many auburn lights.
> . . . Her way of sitting is as widespread as a man might lounge. She taps a fresh cigarette on the palm of one hand, lights it and disappears behind a smoke screen of blue. She outspreads her long, strong hands and makes a comb of her fingers, pushing her hair back from her furrowed forehead, not trying to hide its lines or weather-beaten texture. She looks sometimes like a gnome from behind her horn rimmed spectacles.

Most of the interviews took place at Belinda's warehouse apartment, but there are also glimpses of Belinda in a few other settings as well. Once she and Helen were talking in a restaurant in Yakima when suddenly Belinda hunched slightly into her seat, looking uncharacteristically guilty. She quickly stubbed out her cigarette as a man who had entered the restaurant bowed to her in greeting. Belinda explained that the man was an old Alaskan, whom she believed had never seen her smoke. So even though she was usually sure of herself and did as she pleased in her own home, Belinda observed propriety and did not want to intentionally shock anyone, as the Gue sisters had noted.[29]

At another time, the interview was conducted at a cabin in the Rainier forest. Here we see that Belinda was still very much at home in the wilderness. And like any true nature lover, she was restored by being there.

The Countess came in from a walk by the river. She always washes in every stream she finds, whether it is a rill in a hill pasture, an irrigation ditch, or a white frilled river. This morning she had been performing her ablutions in the Upper Nachez. She stalked into the cabin, her heavy shod feet almost trotting with the joy of being in the mountains again. In gray tweed knickers and a brown sweater buttoned up under her chin, she was grinning.[30]

The Seattle Years

When Belinda finally decided she needed the equity she had in the castle to live on, she sold it to the Dr. George[31] Riemcke family. After the Riemckes moved in, Belinda did return for a visit, for she still owned part of the adjoining orchard. She found Mrs. Riemcke in the parlor, sewing drapes for all of the windows of the castle. Belinda's comment to her—"My God, woman! There's no man on earth worth all the effort you're putting in!"[32]—clearly reflects Belinda's attitudes on housework and domestic relations, as well as her lack of diplomacy.

In 1928 Belinda added to the development on her Seattle property by building a shingled, gambrel-roofed structure on the alley behind her home.[33] This originally may have been intended as a small barn, but the 25-foot by 20-foot annex was soon converted to a four-room single-family dwelling.

Belinda's permanent move to Seattle in 1929 or 1930[34] may have been triggered by the death of her father, John, on 31 December 1929.[35] Now her eighty-year-old mother would need companionship and caretaking. Through the depression years of the thirties, Belinda and brother Patrick and sometimes sister Margaret would live with the elderly Mary Mulrooney in southwest Seattle.[36] Margaret was no less devoted than Belinda and Patrick; but she by this time had married Alonzo Gauslin, and they moved to Olympia, Washington, for a time.[37]

By 1933 Belinda had sold the remainder of her Yakima orchard[38] and had enough money to invest in another house.[39] First an adjoining lot on 37th Avenue NW was bought in mother Mary's name. Then it was transferred to brother Jim the next year,[40] and he built a duplex[41] on it at 4811 37th SW.[42] Although this new property was in Jim's name, family informants[43] referred to this second house as Belinda's as well. Therefore, we speculate that financing was derived from Belinda's earlier fortune and was put into Jim's name as an estate management device. The new house was twenty feet wide and thirty feet deep, with a six-foot-wide covered porch running across the back. The building was split symmetrically left and right into two, two-room apartments. The exterior was

25.4a. Belinda's house in Seattle at 4817 37th Avenue SW. *(Waugaman Collection)*

b. The gambrel-roof house built in 1928 behind Belinda's first Seattle home. This photograph was taken in 1937 as part of a Works Project Administration project to document Seattle development. *(DAPR, PS)*

c. The duplex built in 1933 at 4811 37th Avenue SW, next door to Belinda's house. It was renovated in the late 1940s and demolished in 1990. *(DAPR, PS)*

covered with three-inch cedar boards and when viewed from the front was very plain. But the west side at the rear of the apartments was pleasing with its ample porch facing toward the Olympic mountains.[44]

Now there was enough space to house family members as well as to rent for income. Belinda lived on one of the floors of her own home, but rented the other floor as well as the little house out back.[45] In the duplex next door brother Patrick was in one side and mother Mary lived on the other side. This arrangement apparently gave all of them the privacy they needed while ensuring that Mary Mulrooney was looked after. At the same time, Mary was able to continue in the domestic activities that she so enjoyed.[46]

The Great Depression was a difficult time for just about everyone in the United States. Belinda and her family were no worse off than most, and thanks to Belinda's frugality and the family solidarity, Belinda, Mary, and Patrick in Seattle managed to live satisfactorily. Margaret, Agnes, Nell, and Jim got along with their own families in Olympia and Alaska. Back in Yakima, when nephew Bob Noble left his wife and children to go into the merchant marine, his estranged wife decided to try her fortune in Hollywood. The two Noble children, Janet and Patrick, were left in the care of their maternal grandmother, Mabel Crum, who also was Belinda's good friend. Belinda, like Mabel, was very concerned for the children, and when she could, she sent them financial assistance.[47] So even when she was not so well off herself, Belinda was looking after the welfare of the children of her extended family.

The winter of 1935–36 was a particularly gloomy time for the Mulrooneys, for two of Belinda's sisters, both considerably younger than she, died within a four-month span—Helen "Nell" Noble Thompson, on 7 November 1935,[48] and Agnes Johnston, on 3 March 1936.[49]

As the Great Depression ground on, Belinda managed to earn some income as a seamstress for the Works Project Administration.[50] She kept alert to business opportunities, but she no longer had the wherewithal to act on her hunches. So, for example, she had wanted to invest in some unlikely-looking land south of Seattle and urged her brother Jim and his wife Betty to buy some even though she couldn't. They decided not to, but regretted it later when Boeing Aviation purchased all the area, including the parcels Belinda had had her eye on, for its facilities next to what became Boeing Field/King County International Airport.[51]

At age sixty-seven, Belinda became the eldest member of her family when her mother died on 16 April 1940.[52] From then on the duplex on 37th Avenue SW was either shared with siblings or rented out. During the years of the Second World War and until his death in 1946,[53] Patrick shared the duplex with his sister Margaret and her husband, Alonzo Gauslin.[54] Brother Jim Mulrooney transferred the property to the Gauslins in 1947.[55]

Even before the United States entered the Second World War in 1941, Seattle was starting to grow from increased production in the shipyards. Once war actually was declared, there was really a boom and housing was in very short supply. Belinda's real estate then became even more valuable. She could accommodate up to five families, including herself, in separate units on the 37th Avenue SW properties.

Belinda also found other ways to earn some money and to contribute to the war effort. As in her younger days, she was willing to work at whatever job seemed interesting and profitable. She found employment at Associated Ship Builders in Seattle, whose yards were on Harbor Island at 2727 16th SW,[56] located at the base of the hill where Belinda lived. She helped to make steel minesweepers by working as a scaler—cleaning rust and corrosion from the steel before the welders did their job and removing the crusty slag following the weld. She also may have been responsible for keeping the pier and offices at the ship yard clean.

Belinda was fiercely patriotic, and when an interviewer for the shipyard newsletter asked her about her reasons for working, she replied, "Well, why not? I've really worked all my life, and this is certainly no time to be idle. We've got a war to win."[57]

The shipyard newsletter article has a lot of misinformation in it, but it does accurately reflect one significant shift in Belinda's life. During her early years, she supported church work but was against organized religion, and her ideas about religion were very pragmatic: "Work as hard as you can, but don't trust to luck. Have faith and God will help you. But I don't believe in bothering Him about little things all day long."

Consistent with this philosophy, in the Klondike Belinda had supported the efforts of the clergy to care for the sick and to promote charity among the miners, but she resisted their attempts to recruit her. Later, in Yakima, because the pioneer preacher S. Hall Young mentioned her in his books,[58] the Presbyterians invited her to come to their church. She told them she was Catholic. On the other hand, when the Catholics tried to get her to join, she told them she was Presbyterian.

But now in her later years, Belinda became more reflective and more open to religious concerns.[59] She used the occasion of the shipyard interview to tell of a more spiritual side of Alaskan and Klondike history, a side she felt was often neglected.

25.5. Belinda at work in the Associated Ship Builders' yard, about 1943. *(Flood-tide, Associate Ship Builders. Gilge Collection)*

Someday a story should be written about the work of Bishop Rowe,[60] [Father Judge],[61] and Dr. [*sic*] Young,[62] who established the first churches there. The spiritual side of the development of Dawson, amidst the confusion and excitement of the gold rush has never been touched upon in fiction, and should be, for there was a very great strength of religious feeling and a practical demonstration of the brotherhood of man.[63]

Belinda liked her shipyard employment so much that even after World War II ended she continued working on Harbor Island for a time, switching to the Todd Ship Yard[64] to build commercial vessels. Following the war, Seattle continued to grow. In the late 1940s the land around Belinda's 37th Avenue NE real estate underwent extensive development, so that by the early 1950s nearly every lot had a new, trim, single-family home on it.[65] On her own property, Belinda was no longer surrounded by her immediate family. Sister Margaret and her husband Lonnie Gauslin now owned the duplex and lived in one side of it, but non-related families rented the other residences. Of these new neighbors, Belinda became particularly close to Irene Gilge, who with her husband and

25.6. Belinda in 1946 at age 74.
(Vitzthum Collection)

children rented the gambrel house behind Belinda's house from about March 1943 through 1957.[66] Belinda and Irene talked frequently, and Belinda often celebrated holidays with the Gilges. As Belinda grew older, Irene would stop by with a plate of food because she knew Belinda didn't like to cook. And it was because of Irene's friendship and admiration for Belinda that some of her photographs and papers were saved after Belinda's death.[67]

As independent as Belinda was, at age eighty-five, even with the help of her neighbors, she knew she could no longer count on living out the rest of her life on her own. Margaret was gradually deteriorating mentally, and rather than helping Belinda, needed to be looked after herself.[68] On 15 September 1957 Belinda moved across the street and into a room on the fifth floor of Mount St. Vincent Nursing Home. Her sister Margaret followed three months later,[69] her husband having died. According to a family member, when moving to the home both sisters signed over what remaining property they had to the nursing home in exchange for their lifetime care.[70]

Belinda's world was shrinking, along with her body. But she was still alert, her mind still sharp. Although she was not gregarious, she enjoyed good conversation. She got to know most of the residents of the home, would greet them by name, and knew something about their lives. She also loved to read good books, with history, westerns, and mysteries being among her favorites.[71] She delighted in the sweeping view she had from her fifth-floor window of Seattle's busy waterfront. Her wanderlust had abated long ago, but it was not entirely extinguished. For example, friends chuckled when Belinda seized the opportunity to "break out" without telling anyone in order to accompany a friend to Reno on a gambling jaunt.[72] She spent a good deal of time with sister Margaret. And she enjoyed visits from younger members of her family. Her grandniece remembered that a shot of whiskey was always part of the visiting ritual.

> She always had her glass of whiskey, at least once a day, even at St. Vincent. She thought she was smuggling the bottles in,[73] but all the nuns knew. And they didn't care, because what's one little shot of whiskey?
>
> She always wanted to see the children and would buy ice cream for them. And she always gave [the adults] a glass of whiskey. She had all her little whiskey glasses lined up on a shelf in her room, not covert at all. You couldn't go in there and talk to her without having one, that was just the way it was. She would not accept "No" for an answer.
>
> [She would have an occasional cigarette, perhaps two or so a day], and she used ivory cigarette holders.[74]

As she got older, Belinda confirmed her religious feelings by returning to the Catholic Church,[75] from which she had been alienated by her divorce from Charles Carbonneau in 1905. She also became even more reticent about her early life. She would declare, "I'm not important," or "It's all just water under the bridge."[76] However, she did give at least two interviews while she lived at Mount St. Vincent Home. Both of them appeared in 1962, the year Belinda celebrated her ninetieth birthday, and both primarily covered her adventurous years prior to 1910. However, they do also offer glimpses of the still lively, though elderly, Belinda.

For example, we learn that tears still came to Belinda's eyes when she spoke of her beloved, faithful St. Bernard Nero (Mackay, 4–6). While she still enjoyed

25.7. Belinda in 1962 at age 90.
(DeArmond Collection)

games of chance such as the bingo at Mount St. Vincent Home, she discounted her high life in Europe and her gambling there as "an empty thing" (Franklin, 22–23, 28–29). She talked disparagingly of all the greed and gold-crazy lust that propelled the gold rushes. And she credited her old friend Michael J. Heney with being the best example of what good gold might do. "Mike distributed the bulk of his wealth among relatives and charities" (Mackay, 6). By this criterion Belinda had done well also.

When asked about Dawson, she declared she had no wish to see it again.

> It'll never be the same again. And I remember it best as it was, a place where there was confidence, trust and fellowship. Oh! It was tough, but I tell you, I loved it for a fact! (Franklin, 29)

Belinda Mulrooney Carbonneau died on 3 September 1967 at the age of ninety-five years. Though still mentally alert, she had become more and more frail with advancing years, until on 14 March 1967, she was transferred to the Cascade Vista Nursing Home in Redmond, Washington.[77] There in late August while getting out of bed, Belinda fell and fractured a hip.[78] She was transferred then to the Swedish Hospital, where she died of pneumonia as a complication of the hip fracture.[79]

It is ironic that despite her unusual and extensive accomplishments on the Northwest frontier, Belinda's death received little notice beyond her immediate family. She had outlived nearly all of her contemporaries, so no one was alive who knew first-hand what she had accomplished. And the feminist revival that would acknowledge and seek to understand women's roles in United States and Canadian history had not yet gotten well underway.

There is also great irony in the official account offered of Belinda's life on the certificate of her death. Belinda Agnes Mulrooney Carbonneau had been a pioneer of the Yukon and Alaska. She was probably the first stewardess on board a ship in Alaskan waters at a time when most Americans were unaware of the wonders of the new territory, and she served as purchasing agent for both the Native American and Caucasian families already living in Southeast Alaska. She was an imaginative speculator, a builder of restaurants, cabins, hotels, and castles. She founded one town and helped to build other new towns in the Yukon and Alaska. She also helped to develop telephone and water services in these towns. She founded investment companies. She was a gold prospector and miner, and she managed one of the largest mining companies in the Klondike. She founded and managed a bank. She became a fruit grower and a promoter of central Washington state agriculture. During the Second World War, she contributed to the war effort by helping to build ships. She supported and educated her family and became a loyal daughter, sister, and aunt. Despite all of these accomplishments and vocations, on her death certificate Belinda is described as a housewife,[80] the one occupation she assiduously avoided.

Notes

Preface

1. Goldin, *Understanding the Gender Gap.*

Chapter 1. Ireland: Fostering Self-Reliance

1. Carns is also spelled Kearns (NW 2:1), Carnes, or Carins (B. Mulrooney, County Sligo, *Birth Certificate*). The village is in the valley of the Carns River, less than two miles north of the County Mayo border and northeast from Ballina about eleven miles by road.

2. This is the date Belinda usually celebrated as her birthday, according to her sister Margaret (Carbonneau and Gauslin to Dougher, 5 January 1959). However, parish records give the date as 18 May, and her county birth certificate has 10 June 1872. In 1928 Belinda gave her birth year as 1873 (NW 2:1), as does the 1920 census for Yakima, Washington. The 1910 census for Yakima suggests she was born in 1875. Records at Mount St. Vincent Home, Seattle, list Belinda's birth date as 16 May 1872.

3. *Parish of Castleconnor Records*, Register B2, p. 097, Entry 1465, 18 May 1872; County Sligo, *Birth Certificate*, 10 June 1872.

4. Mary's last name is reported as O'Connor by her grandson, Robert Noble, on Belinda's death certificate, 3 September 1967 (*Seattle Death Records*, Registration District 6577, State file no. 19864). O'Connor also appears in the Hawkins Collection. However, Connor is the name given on Belinda's birth certificates (Parish and County) and on Mary's parish records. On the other hand, Belinda's grandfather is listed as James Connors on tenement records.

5. Mulrooney is the standard spelling. Belinda's birth certificate, however, spells it Mulroony, and as late as 1 May 1899 (*Yukon Territorial Records*, Liquor License, Grand Forks Hotel) Belinda was signing her last name variously as Mulroney or Mulrooney; Mullrooney is also a variant. Belinda stated her father had come from County Mayo (Hawkins).

6. Information about the farm is from County Sligo, *Valuation of Tenements,* 45; courtesy of Larry and Rose Dougher Vitzthum. *Parish of Castleconnor, Birth Records,* show children who were siblings of Mary Connor born to James and Alice Howley Connor. However, a record of Mary's own birth in about 1850 or 1851 (U.S. Census, 1880, 1900, 1910, and 1920) has not been found. Courtesy of Rose Dougher Vitzthum.

7. See for example Chambers, *Granuaile.*

8. *Parish Castleconnor Marriage Records,* Register M2, p. 20, entry 290.

9. *Lippincott's Gazetteer,* 392.

10. U.S. Census 1880, 1910, 1920; however, the census for 1900 (Archbald, Pennsylvania), unlike the others, gives the year of John Mulrooney's birth as 1850.

11. O Gráda, *Ireland Famine,* 83–84; on the potato famine see also Solar, "The Great Famine" and Mokyr, "The Deadly Fungus."

12. Maria's parents had two other children, born in 1852 and 1854, who did not live long enough to be named (*Parish of Castleconnor Birth Records,* 15 August 1852 and 5 June 1854; courtesy of Rose Dougher Vitzthum).

13. But see O Gráda, *Ireland Famine,* for complexities in the interpretation of post-famine inheritance patterns.

14. Clarkson, "Conclusion," 220–36.

15. The Irish were second only to Germans between 1820 and 1910 (*Information Please Almanac,* 254).

16. *Parish Castleconnor Marriage Records,* Register M2, p. 20, entry 290.

17. John's date of immigration is variously reported as 1872 to 1874 in U.S. census data. A John A. Mulroney, from Great Britain and Ireland, arrived in Philadelphia in 1872 and declared his intention to naturalize 6 August (Filby and Meyer, eds., *Passenger and Immigration Index.* Filby, ed., *Philadelphia Naturalization Records,* 488). This person is the right age, twenty-seven years (Pennsylvania, *Quarter Sessions Record,* 6 August 1872); he arrived in Philadelphia, where Belinda's family had connections; and Mulrooney (and its variants) was an uncommon name (Matheson, *Surnames in Ireland,* 66); therefore, we assume this is Belinda's father.

18. Maria's arrival date is reported as 1874 to 1877 in various U.S. census data. Because married women derived citizenship from their husbands, and before 1906 often no immigration information about them was recorded (Newman, *Naturalization Processes*), it is not surprising, though unfortunate, that we could find no record of Maria in immigration and naturalization records.

19. Ainsworth and Bowlby, "Ethological Personality Development," 331–41.

20. William Connor via Rose Vitzthum, Vitzthum to Mayer, 6 October 1988.

21. Ibid., 12 August 1992. The date is given as 1886 in the 1910 U.S. Census and as 1884 in the 1920 U.S. Census (Yakima, Washington). Once again, probably because data on immigration of children was not recorded systematically until 1906 (Newman, *Naturalization Processes*), we did not find the exact date of Belinda's arrival in the United States in the appropriate records.

22. January 1879 according to 1900 U.S. Census; 1879 according to 1880 U.S. Census and *1946 Seattle Death Record;* 1877 according to 1910 U.S. Census.

23. March 1884 according to 1900 U.S. Census; 1884 according to *1935 Seattle Death Record* and Vitzthum to Mayer, 27 January 1993.

24. Vitzthum to Mayer, 27 January 1993. The 1900 U.S. Census reports the deaths of three children, however.

Chapter 2. Pennsylvania: Unhappiness, Deceptions, and New Opportunities

1. Hawkins. Assembly of the statue did not start until the summer of 1886, and it was completed in October of that year. This suggests that either Belinda arrived in the United States in 1886 or later, or that her comments about the statue were based upon experiences after she first arrived. From other information we concluded that Belinda arrived in the United States in the spring of 1885, but 1886 is also a viable alternative.

2. NW (chap. 2:1) says Scranton was the site of the Mulrooney home, but it was actually in Archbald (1880 U.S. Census, Archbald, Pennsylvania; also William Connor via Florence Nelson Long, Long to Mayer, 20 June 1982).

3. Murray to Mayer, 16 December 1997.

4. Betty Mulrooney, interview by Mayer.

5. Carbonneau and Gauslin to Dougher, December 1965; 1920 U.S. Census, Yakima, Washington; *1973 Seattle Death Records.*

6. 1900 U.S. Census, Archbald, Pennsylvania; *1936 Seattle Death Records.*

7. The timber rattlesnake, *Crotalus horridus,* used to be widespread in the mountains and forests of Pennsylvania. Now the shy, usually placid reptiles have been displaced by humans and have been hunted so intensively that they have nearly disappeared from many places where they were once common.

8. *Pennsylvania Statute Law 1920,* §13580 (30 June 1885; P.L. 2020, §1).

9. This amount may represent the combined earning of all her jobs. The $25 in the late 1880s would have purchased commodities worth about $427 in 1998. Belinda reported the $25 amount in a 1928 interview; therefore she may have converted it already to 1928 dollars, in which case it would be equivalent to about $208 in goods in 1998, still a considerable sum (McCusker, "How Much Is That?" Table A2, pp. 329–32; extended by *Consumer Price Index [1982–84]*). Derks, *Value of a Dollar,* 14–15.

10. Typical fares to Queenstown, County Cork, were about $20 steerage, $30 second class, and $50 and up for cabin (*New York Times,* 1 July 1899, p. 7, col. e). She would need additional funds to get from Queenstown to Ballina, County Mayo, and for land transportation in both the U.S. and Ireland.

11. Vitzthum to Mayer, 12 November 1992, 27 January 1993.

12. *Philadelphia City Directory, 1890,* 745.

13. Goldin, *Understanding the Gender Gap,* 11, 223, 47, 17.

14. Ibid., chap. 3.

15. Franklin, "She Was the Richest," 23.

16. The George K. Cummings family residence was located on Cresheim Avenue, near Springfield Avenue *(Philadelphia City Directory, 1890).*

17. Isabelle was born to J. G. and Mary Owen Brown in about 1864 (Hoppin, *Art of J. G. Brown,* 33).

18. According to Martha J. Hoppin, Curator of American Art, Museum of Fine Arts, Springfield, Massachusetts, and author of *Country Paths and City Sidewalks: The Art of J. G. Brown,* J. G. Brown did only two paintings from 1890 to 1895 with a young woman and small boy in them. One is "The Sidewalk Dance," the other is "The Gang." Since the setting for "The Sidewalk Dance" was identified in the estate sale catalog as outside the Browns' residence at 250 West 42nd Street (Hoppin to Mayer, 14 July 1992), it seems more likely to be depicting Belinda and Jack.

19. The *Philadelphia City Directory* shows the Cummings family at the Chestnut Hill address as late as 1890, but not in 1891–93. They appear in the *Chicago City Directory* in 1892 and 1893. It is not clear where they lived in 1891.

20. Franklin, "She Was the Richest," 23.

21. Hawkins. However, six hundred dollars is considerably more than what she would have earned at three dollars per week over a two-year period with the Cummings family. It would be equivalent to about $10,700 in commodity purchasing power in 1998 (McCusker, "How Much Is That?"; *Consumer Price Index [1982–84]*).

22. It is not clear exactly when Belinda left for Chicago. According to Hawkins Collection materials, she was still working for the Cummings family when she left. That would mean no later than early 1892, because G. K. Cummings appears in the Chicago directory at that date. In another interview given later in her life (Franklin, "She Was the Richest," 23), she says she went to Chicago in 1892. Construction of the Columbia Exposition began in early 1891, and the grounds were dedicated on the anniversary of Columbus's landing in the Americas, 12 October 1892. But the fair did not open officially until 1 May 1893.

23. Goldin, *Understanding the Gender Gap*, 17.

24. Winslow and Solomon, "Entrepreneurs Are More Than Non-Conformists," 202–13.

25. Wortman, *Women in American Law*, chap. 2.

26. Lerner, "Lady and Mill Girl."

27. Sachs and Wilson, *Sexism and the Law*, 70. See also Goldin, *Understanding the Gender Gap*, 47–49, and Goldin, "Economic Status of Women," for similar occupations of females in Philadelphia as late as the 1790s.

28. Blackstone, *Commentaries*, bk. 1, chap. 15, 442.

29. However, a distinction was made for the real property (land and buildings) a wife brought into the marriage. Although the husband controlled it, he could not sell it without his wife's consent, because it descended to his wife's legal heirs. See, e.g., Wortman, *Women in American Law*, 1:13–19.

This account leaves out the possibility for modification of property rights by equity jurisprudence; however, there is debate about the extent to which equity had an impact on women's lives. See, e.g., Sachs and Wilson, *Sexism and the Law*, 77–80, and Basch, *Eyes of the Law* for a fuller treatment of this issue. This account also leaves out the widow's dower right, which provided her with a life tenancy in one-third of the real property if there were children, or in one-half if there were no children. See Wortman, *Women in American Law*, 1:17–19.

30. Consistent with this interpretation, a quantitative analysis suggests that the decline in labor force participation rates for female heads of households in Philadelphia from 1790 to 1860 was gradual and that there was a similar shift in male occupations away from proprietorships and into industrial jobs (Goldin, *Understanding the Gender Gap*, 47–49).

31. The right to vote on certain issues had been extended to women in some colonies, but it was rescinded after 1776 (Sachs and Wilson, *Sexism and the Law*, 74).

32. See for example Basch, *Eyes of the Law*; Chused, "Oregon Donation Act," 44–78; Siegel, "Modernization of Marital Status Law," 2127–211.

33. Sachs and Wilson, *Sexism and the Law*, 78.

34. A woman was not admitted to the bar until 1869—Arabella A. Mansfield in Iowa. Even after that the right to practice law was only sporadically and capriciously granted to a few women, then reversed, until passage of the Nineteenth Amendment in 1920 (Weisberg, "Barred from the Bar").

35. Sachs and Wilson, *Sexism and the Law*, 78. For a provocative discussion of sources influencing discontinuity between judgments and implementations, see Judge Judith Resnik's comments in Heilbrun and Resnik, "Convergences," 28–30.

36. Justice Joseph P. Bradley, concurring opinion in *Bradwell v. The State of Illinois*, 83 U.S. 130 (1873).

Chapter 3. A Young Entrepreneur Exploits Chicago and the World's Fair of 1893

1. Bancroft, *Book of the Fair*, vol. 1, title page.

2. See Hales, *Constructing the Fair*, 15.

3. Higinbotham, *Report of the President*, 86. For other perspectives on the Midway Plaisance, see Bloom, *Autobiography*, 107, 137; Muccigrosso, *New World*, 155.

4. *Souvenir of a Ride; Chicago Record*, 12 July 1893; Muccigrosso, *New World*.

5. *Chicago Record*, 28 July 1893, p. 3, cols. a–c. By September and October, daily attendance was nearly 150,000.

6. Muccigrosso, *New World*, 153, 83.

7. Hales, *Constructing the Fair*, 3; Gilbert, *Perfect Cities*, 1.

8. Mackay, "Saga of Belinda," 4, says 1892. A date prior to 16 May 1893, Belinda's twenty-first birthday, agrees with NW 3:1, where Belinda reports she carried out some of her early business transactions while she was still underage.

9. These may be the two women from Philadelphia with whom she had planned to go to Chicago.

10. U.S. Census Bureau, *Special Reports*, pp. cxxv–cxxvi.

11. NW 3:1; *Klondike News*, 1 April 1898, p. 4.

12. Kanowitz, *Women and the Law*, 8.

13. U.S. Census Bureau, *Special Reports*, pp. cxxv–cxxvi.

14. Franklin, "She Was the Richest," 23; Hawkins.

15. Anderson to Mayer, 9 April 1997; *Garden City Observation Wheel Company v. Ferris Wheel Company*, stipulation of Somers.

16. *Garden City Observation Wheel Company vs. Ferris Wheel Company*, testimony of R. Bateman, 6 July 1893.

17. Anderson to Mayer, 9 April 1997.

18. *Chicago City Directory, 1893*, 1180, 2139; Business Directory, 2139. However, this address is thirty blocks, a considerable distance, north of the Midway Plaisance.

19. Bloom, *Autobiography*, 139.

20. Hawkins. His name is also given as Ginnis and McGinnis. A John Guinness is listed under "Officers Retired during 1893" in *Chicago Police Reports, 1891–1894*, 137.

21. In parish records of tenements for Carns, a Patrick McGuinness leased land adjacent to Belinda's grandparents, James and Alice Connors (*Valuation of Tenements, Parish of Castleconnor*, 45; Courtesy of Rose Dougher Vitzthum).

22. Mackay, "Saga of Belinda." If this is true, then purchase of her first property occurred after the Midway Plaisance was in operation. Alternatively, Belinda may have first met Officer McGuinness earlier than the raid on the Streets of Cairo. Most evidence, though inconclusive, points to the latter possibility.

23. U.S. Census, 1900, 1910. However, U.S. Census for 1920 puts the year as 1893, and Jim's wife reported the date as 29 September 1894 (Betty Mulrooney to Johnston).

24. Muccigrosso, *New World,* 84, 158, 181.

25. NW 3:3. However, we have not been able to locate such a newspaper story.

26. *Chicago Tribune,* 2 August 1893, p. 6, col. e; *Chicago Record,* 2 August 1893, p. 1, col. e.

27. In fact, a hundred years later, of all the magnificent structures of the Exposition, the Palace of Fine Arts is the only major building remaining at the fairgrounds. It now houses the Museum of Science and Industry. It was the only building on the exposition grounds to be constructed of more permanent materials—masonry, with concrete foundations. Its exterior was reconstructed in marble and limestone in 1940. The fires that destroyed the rest of the buildings were probably deliberately set. See Hales, *Constructing the Fair,* 29, 48; also Sinkevitch, *AIA Guide to Chicago,* 422.

28. *Chicago City Directory, 1893,* shows George K. Cummings as a partner with Duncan G. McDougall in an electrical specialties business, with a residence at 4228 Oakenwald Avenue (pp. 421, 1051, 1930).

29. Belinda gives the figure of $8,000 in NW 3:3; it would be equivalent to about $144,000 in 1998 composite consumer prices (McCusker, "How Much Is That?" Table A-2, 329–32; extended by *Consumer Price Index [1982–84]*). For contemporary wages, see for example Muccigrosso, *New World,* 38, (43): carpenters earned $2.50 to $3.00 per day. A six-day work week for fifty-two weeks would thus yield $936. Policemen's salaries were $720 to $1000 a year.

Chapter 4. Launching into the Pacific Northwest

1. *Chicago Tribune,* 14 August 1899, p. 12, cols. c–d.

2. Betty Mulrooney, interview by Mayer.

3. Sutro Heights is a park overlooking the Pacific Ocean at the western end of the street now named Geary Boulevard, but which was Point Lobos Avenue in Belinda's time. We have been unable to find evidence for a racetrack near that location in 1894–95. The Bay District Race Track was perhaps the nearest. It was bounded by First Avenue (now Arguello Blvd.), Fulton Street, Fifth Avenue, and A (now Anza) Street, on the northeast boundary of Golden Gate Park. It operated until 27 May 1896 (Hansen, *San Francisco Almanac*). Belinda says she went to the racetrack with a well-to-do family named Nolan (Hawkins).

4. In one interview she describes this as a dairy and ice cream parlor (Franklin, "She Was the Richest," 23).

5. The Fairmount Hotel was located at 1714 Market Street (*San Francisco Directory, 1894, 1895*). It is not to be confused with the famous Fairmont Hotel on Nob Hill, which was not completed until 1907 (Hart, *Companion to California,* 133–34).

6. In 1894 Mrs. C. Goodell was the proprietor of the Fairmount Hotel. In 1895 new owners are listed, Knights and Jones (*San Francisco Directory, 1894, 1895*).

7. William Cramp (1807–1879) founded the company in Philadelphia in the 1830s. It was held as a close corporation by the Cramp family until 1915, though the yards maintained the Cramp name until their closure in 1927. The Philadelphia yard was reopened in 1940. After the Second World War, it was sold to the U.S. Navy (Farr and Bostwick, *Shipbuilding at Cramp and Sons*).

This Mrs. Cramp may have been the wife of Charles H. Cramp, who headed the shipbuilding company after his father and during the 1880s and 1890s. However, other sons of William Cramp also filled leading positions in the business and acted as directors. These were Theodore, William M., Jacob, and Samuel H. Cramp (Dun Collection, *Philadelphia*, vol. 141, 124).

8. The *State of California* in 1878; the *City of Puebla* in 1881, bought by the steamship company in 1887; and *Queen of the Pacific*, 1882, renamed simply *Queen* in 1888 (Farr and Bostwick, *Shipbuilding at Cramp and Sons*, 21, 25).

9. The steamers *Santa Rosa* and *Pomona* sailed for San Diego every four days *(Northern California State Directory, 1893–94)*.

10. Hawkins; *Klondike News*, 1 April 1898, p. 4, col. b.

11. The *Topeka* also made occasional trips between Puget Sound and San Francisco, with a stop in Portland. Therefore, Belinda may have taken the *Topeka* or the company's regular ship from San Francisco, the *Umatilla (Northern California State Directory, 1893–94)*.

12. Franklin, "She Was the Richest," 23. Wallace was born 22 January 1853, in Newbergh, Scotland (Wright, *Marine History*, 368).

13. Palmer, *In the Klondyke*, 150–51. Sixty-five years later, Belinda would tell a less subtle, more belligerent variation of this story:

> A burly leader of a group of would-be miners knocked on the stewardess' door one day and presented a fancy pair of dirty high-top boots.
>
> "I want to get these boots polished," he said. "When you're finished, just leave them on the deck outside your door."
>
> "Listen, and this goes for every man on board who needs a little valuable lesson-learning quick. Go clean them and polish them yourself. Anybody who leaves boots at my office will find them filled with sea water."
>
> The story spread . . . in high good humor, and never again did any passengers risk getting out of line. (Mackay, "The Saga of Belinda," 4)

14. U.S. Census Bureau, *Special Reports*, cxxv. In the 1890 census 3.8 percent, and in 1900 4.3 percent of retailers were women. Only 44 females are listed in the Trade and Transportation category of occupations in Alaska in 1900. The table for Alaska does not break this number down further, but in the overall census, 6.8 percent of females in Trade and Transportation were retail merchants. If the same proportion holds for Alaska, it suggests there were only about three such female retail dealers.

15. Clark, *History of Alaska*, 196–97.

16. Told to R. N. DeArmond by an early Juneau resident; DeArmond to Mayer, 21 May 1988 and 9 May 1995.

17. See for example Emmons, *The Tlingit Indians*, 6.

18. *Juneau Alaska Searchlight*, 30 September 1896.

19. NW 5:1. In February 1897, the mail carrier from Circle City arrived in Juneau with news of the Klondike strike (DeArmond to Mayer, 21 May 1988). According to William Ogilvie, surveyor for the Canadian Government, it was seventy-three-year-old Captain William Moore, founder of Skaguay, who carried the mail from Circle City in late November 1896, over the trail and passes, to Juneau (*Early Days*, 212–13). Belinda identified her source of information about the strike as a man called Two-Finger McKay.

Chapter 5. Chilkoot: Going In in 1897

1. A sweeper is a tree on the riverbank whose roots have been partially undercut so the top of the tree falls over the water, held by the remaining embedded roots. The projecting treetop, just above the water's surface or partially submerged, can knock a person out of a boat, pin her with the tremendous force of the water against its branches, or capsize and damage the boat.

2. *Klondike News,* 1 April 1898, p. 4, col. a.

3. *Klondike Semi-Weekly Nugget,* 28 March 1901, p. 2, col. b.

4. *Juneau Alaska Searchlight,* 3 April 1897, p. 8; *Klondike News,* 1 April 1898, p. 4, col. a. The date is reported as 2 April in Hawkins Collection notes.

5. Nathan Kresge in *Seattle Sunday Times* (22 February 1931, pp. 3, 5) gives the names of people in the party. The Minnicks are listed as Minch on the *Mexico* passenger list (*Juneau Alaska Searchlight,* 3 April 1897, p. 8).

Joe's name also appears as Jo or J.O., and Barrett. We have taken the preferred spelling from his signature on his will, dated 17 July 1912 (Yukon Territorial Court, *Records 1897–1950, Estates*), where his first name is given as Lazare.

6. *Dawson Daily News,* 22 July 1912, p. 4, col. d.

7. NW 6:3; Hawkins.

8. Joe Barrette is apparently the model for "Poleon" in Rex Beach's *The Winds of Chance,* which has a Belinda-like character as heroine (NW 6:3).

9. The distance is closer to thirteen miles (U.S. Park Service, *Map of Chilkoot Trail*). Because Belinda probably had no map, it is not surprising that her estimates of distances are inaccurate. And as any packer knows, difficult trails usually seem longer than their physical measure.

10. The first fuel was at Happy Camp, which is about seven to eight miles from Sheep Camp and about four miles beyond Chilkoot Pass (U.S. Park Service, *Map of Chilkoot Trail*).

11. Packing for prospectors and eventually for stampeders became a major source of income for Native Americans of the region—male and female, adults and children. They were primarily of the Tlingit tribe, who traditionally controlled Chilkoot Pass. But Haidas, their neighbors to the south, and interior groups also profited.

12. Belinda says "cross-cut saw," but the cross-cut saw is used only for cutting across the grain. A whipsaw, a long rip saw with an especially broad blade and with handles at each end, was needed to saw boards. The log to be sawn was put up on a rack, about six feet off the ground. One person stood on top and pulled the saw up, and a second person underneath powered the downstroke, while both tried to keep a straight line.

13. At the outlet of Lake Bennett is Carcross. It is not clear whether Belinda's party was able to float from there or whether they had to continue by sled another forty miles across Nares, Tagish, and Marsh Lakes to the mouth of Marsh Lake, where at least one part of the Hawkins material suggests they put into the water.

14. The date of Belinda's arrival was reported as 10 June in the *Klondike News* (1 April 1898, p. 4). But mining records (Yukon, Mining Recorder, *Henderson Creek,* vol. 133, 295) show she located a claim on 14 June 1897, at 22 below discovery on Henderson Creek, which is near the mouth of the Stewart River, about seventy miles upstream from Dawson. It is unlikely that Belinda retraced her journey upstream to make the claim after arriving at Dawson. Indeed, the *Klondike News* story confirms the staking was done before arriving at Dawson.

15. Esther and Belinda would become good friends. Esther's names are sometimes spelled Ester and Duffy. We have taken her signature on an application for a mine grant (Dawson, *Mining Records, No. 5 Ora Grande,* 25 November 1897) as the definitive spelling.

Chapter 6. Building Dawson

1. Gates, *Gold at Fortymile Creek,* 19, 6–8.

2. On 1 September 1896 (Kitchener, *Flag over the North,* 208).

3. Adney, *Klondike Stampede,* 179.

4. *Klondike News,* 1 April 1898, p. 18, col. a.

5. Kitchener, *Flag over the North,* 214

6. Ogilvie, *Early Days,* 216.

7. Kitchener, *Flag over the North,* 208; Adney, *Klondike Stampede,* 180.

8. Kitchener, *Flag over the North,* 214. These boats had over-wintered at camps downriver from Dawson and so got to the new town sooner than could the steamers from Outside.

9. Hawkins; NW 12:1–2.

10. Johns, "Early Yukon," 135 f., 147; Gates, *Gold at Fortymile Creek,* 118.

11. For example, she located No. 5 Ora Grande, a tributary of Eldorado Creek, on 25 November 1897 (Dawson, *Mining Records.*)

12. London, *Daughter of the Snows,* 39, 85.

13. *Klondike News,* 1 April 1898, p. 4, col. c.

14. NW 7:2. However, the *Klondike News* (1 April 1898, p. 4, col. c) reported charges of $1.50 to $4.50 per meal.

15. Gates, *Gold at Fortymile,* 162; Johns, "Early Days," 170, 196.

16. Bill McPhee was a well-known pioneer. In Juneau in 1887 he opened a saloon and theater, the Opera House, with a partner, Herman Hart. He crossed Chilkoot Pass to the interior to prospect in 1888 (*Dawson Daily News, Mining Edition,* September 1899, p. 27, col. d), and eventually established a saloon at Forty Mile, where he was known for his good-natured generosity (e.g., Young, *Hall Young of Alaska,* 343). When the Klondike strike was made, he quickly moved to Dawson and started yet another saloon, The Pioneer, in partnership with Catherine's husband Harry Spencer and with Frank Dinsmore.

17. Since Joseph Ladue had left in early June for the Outside (he was among the *Excelsior*'s passengers landing at San Francisco on 15 July 1897) and Arthur Harper had left soon after (he was a passenger into San Francisco with William Ogilvie [*Early Days,* 223], who left Dawson about 14 July 1897), Belinda probably dealt with Thomas Kirkpatrick.

18. If Harry Cribb was indeed involved from the beginning, it would suggest either that the cabins were built in the fall of 1897, or that the information that he arrived in Dawson in October of that year (*Alaska-Yukon Magazine* 7 [January 1909]: 306) is inaccurate.

19. Second Street and Second Avenue, like the other numbered streets and avenues, often were confused in the early days. Belinda's cabins were on Second Avenue in the block between Third and Second Streets. To reduce confusion, Second Street was renamed Queen and Third Street became King.

20. *Klondike News,* 1 April 1898, p. 11.

21. The Presbyterian minister, who did not in fact hold a doctorate.

22. *Klondike News,* 1 April 1898, p. 18.

23. Gussie LaMore interview by Alice Rex, *San Francisco Examiner,* 3 October 1897.

24. In 1900, 14.3 percent and in 1890, 12.5 percent of restaurateurs were female (Census Bureau, *Special Reports,* cxxv). We did not find similar detailed data for women in Canada.

There is no listing for "contractor" in the 1900 census occupations analysis. But nearly all categories under "Building Trades" are at 0.1 percent for females except for painters (0.6 percent), paper hangers (1.1 percent), and mechanics (0.3 percent).

Chapter 7. Grand Forks, the Heart of Gold Country

1. *Dawson Daily News Mining Edition,* September 1899, p. 27, col. b.

2. To stake a claim according to regulations, the locator planted a post at each corner and cut lines through the woods between them so each post could be seen from the preceding one. On a roughly north-flowing stream, such as Bonanza Creek, the locator numbered the posts by standing facing south. The first post would be over the left shoulder toward the east, while the second post would be southerly from that following the valley and five hundred feet from No. 1. No. 3 would be across the valley from No. 2; and No. 4 would be five hundred feet from No. 3 following the valley to a point across the valley from No. 1. Each post had to be not less than three feet high, not less than three inches square at the top, and squared for at least a foot. On the first post, written in durable pencil or inscribed, was the number of the claim, the full name of the locator, the date of location, the letters "M.L.P." (Mining Location Post), and the number of the post. The other posts contained "M.L.P." and the number of the post (Ogilvie, *Early Days,* p. 165). Ogilvie estimated it would take a good axman about half a day to stake a claim according to regulations. In the early days of the Klondike, few took the time to do it completely. Once the claim was staked, the locator hurried to the nearest recorder with a sample of gold, made an affidavit of discovery, and paid fifteen dollars for recording and a lease of one year.

3. Surveyors stretched a chain of one hundred links, sixty-six feet long, to measure distances. Each end of the chain was carried by a chainman.

4. Ogilvie, *Early Days,* 209; Berton, *Klondike Fever,* 78–79. Dick Lowe was the wealthy miner who bought the first and then third of Belinda's cabins in Dawson (Hawkins).

5. We rely here on Tappan Adney's description from the fall of 1897 (*Klondike Stampede,* 257).

6. U.S. Census Bureau, *Special Reports,* cxxv. About 15 percent of hotelkeepers in the United States were women at this time. About 3 percent of saloonkeepers were women. See Leo Kanowitz, *Women and the Law,* 129, for examples of legal restrictions to women's bar-keeping.

7. She was at Grand Forks Hotel with Sadie when the Dominion Creek stampede took place (NW 10:6); she staked her claim on 23 August (Yukon Mining Recorder, *Dominion Creek,* 351). Therefore, the hotel had to have been occupied prior to this.

8. *Yukon World,* 8 February 1907, p. 4, col. a.

9. Estimated from a photo/illustration in the *Klondike News* (1 April 1898, p. 2), using Belinda's height as about five feet, two inches. This image is of poor quality, but it is the earliest we have found of the hotel and does not include the later additions.

10. The *Dawson Daily News Mining Edition* (September 1899, p. 13, col. b) reported a glass window and frame cost $100 in late 1897. This would be equivalent to about $1,950 in 1998 (McCusker, "How Much Is That?" Table A2, 329–32; extended by *Consumer Price Index* [1982–84]).

11. Later it also was referred to as Eldorado and Bonanza.

12. It actually may be Walker Gilmer whom Frederick Palmer identified as "Andrew" in the passage quoted above.

13. NW 10:3. It may be this cabin that the 31 May 1899 survey of Grand Forks showed as located on lot 5, block B, and that Belinda co-owned with Old Timer Bill McPhee, co-owner of Dawson's Pioneer Saloon.

14. NW 11a:3. Belinda had promised Sadie wages, provisions, and an outfit for the winter.

15. *Dawson Daily News Mining Edition*, September 1899, p. 27, col. b.

16. *Dawson Daily News*, 9 January 1909, p. 4, col. f.

17. See for example *Klondike News*, 1 April 1898, p. 14; Haskell, *Two Years*, 359; *Dawson Daily News Mining Edition*, September 1899, p. 21.

18. Tom Chisholm had known Alex McDonald for a long time; they had come from the same county in Nova Scotia. Although Alex was related to other Chisholms there, he and Tom were not related (*Dawson Daily News*, 9 January 1909, p. 4, col. f). Tom became owner of the Aurora saloon in Dawson.

19. Belinda mentions services conducted by the Presbyterian minister S. Hall Young, who arrived in Dawson 9 October 1897; Father William H. Judge, S.J., the Catholic priest from Forty Mile who reached Dawson 6 March 1897; and Bishop Peter Trimble Rowe, who was in charge of the American Episcopal Church in Alaska. While Dawson was not his territory, he may have visited there as early as Belinda suggests. The Reverend R. J. Bowen represented the Anglican church in Dawson in the early days. Reverend Young wrote to his church sponsors on 1 December 1897 about preaching at the Grand Forks Hotel on 21 November (*Church at Home and Abroad*; see also Young, *Hall Young of Alaska*, 352–53).

20. Walker Gilmer interviewed by Joan Arnold, in an unidentified Seattle newspaper (Hawkins).

21. Dawson, *Registered Documents, Power of Attorney*, Yola Grignon to Belinda Mulroney, 29 July 1898.

22. *New York Times*, 21 February 1898, p. 5, col. b.

23. Clarence J. and wife Ethel Berry, along with Fred (F. C.) Berry, were among the original locators on Eldorado Creek, having rushed from Forty Mile in August of 1896. They owned interests in claims 3, 4, 5, and 6, some of the richest ground on the creek.

24. Tom O'Brien had been in the Yukon prospecting as early as 1888 (Gates, *Gold at Fortymile*, 52), and he later kept a saloon at Forty Mile (Johns, "Early Yukon," 104). He undertook many business ventures in the Dawson area, including the telephone company, a saloon/theater, a railroad between Dawson and Grand Forks, and a beer brewery.

25. NW 16:1–2(113). The *Dawson Daily News Mining Edition* (September 1899, 27 b) also credits Belinda with being "the main promoter of the telephone line."

Chapter 8. Mining in the Winter of 1897–98

1. We find no registered Eldorado creek claims for her from this period; however, Belinda did purchase portions of three Eldorado bench claims (*Dawson Daily News Mining Edition*, September 1899, p. 27). She may also have been referring here to unregistered interests in claims held by others.

2. Belinda claimed 47 B/L/D on Dominion on 23 August 1897 (Yukon, Mining Recorder, *Dominion*, 351, 352). This claim was later renumbered to 73D B/L/D.

3. *Kansas City Star*, 7 April 1898, p. 4.

4. On 10 December 1897, Belinda located LL of 5 Skookum Bench (Yukon, Mining Recorder, *Bonanza*, vol. 13, 42). She bought the bench on 4th tier opposite upper half LL of 1 B/D Bonanza, from its locator Christopher Ellis, for $250, 21 July 1898 (Dawson, *Registered Documents*, Bill of Sale, #10309; also *Mining Records*, sec. 3, 32).

5. See for example Yukon, Mining Recorder, *Reindeer*; Dawson, *Registered Documents*.

6. *Klondike News*, 1 April 1898, p. 36.

7. *Kansas City Star*, 7 April 1898, p. 4.

8. *Klondike News*, 1 April 1898, p. 36; *Kansas City Star*, 7 April 1898, p. 4. Among the Yukon members, it was apparently Dr. C. C. Savage who was the primary Kansas City connection.

9. Ibid.

10. *Klondike News*, 1 April 1898, p. 36. But there seems to be an error in this article about the numbers on Reindeer, for Number 4 *Below* was the claim Belinda put into the company. Records show Belinda located this claim on 6 December 1897 (Dawson, *Mining Record*, Application for Placer Grant, #3348, *Mining Records*, microfilm roll 2, Dawson City Museum, Yukon) and transferred it to McNeil on 21 December 1897 (Yukon, Mining Recorder, *Original Locators, Reindeer*, Instr. 3349).

11. The *Klondike News* (1 April 1898, p. 36), however, reported that the company was capitalized for $3 million, with shares selling at $50 each. There are numerous errors throughout this source, so we have relied more heavily on the information printed in the *Kansas City Star* (7 April 1898, p. 4). It is not clear whether the Eldorado-Bonanza Quartz and Placer Mining Company is the same as the Bonanza-Eldorado Company reported in the 21 February 1898 *New York Times* to be capitalized for the extraordinary sum of $200 million. (Estimates vary as to the *entire* yearly value of Klondike gold production, but all are at most one-tenth of the *New York Times* figure [*Klondike Nugget*, 22 March 1899, p. 1, col. b; Johnson, "Yukon's Gold Yield;" Canadian Department of the Interior, cited in Ross, *Canadian Bank of Commerce*, 478].) On the other hand, the *New York Times* information about the Bonanza-Eldorado Company was attributed to a James E. Scovel, who apparently was the person acquiring equipment for Belinda's Yukon Telegraph and Telephone Syndicate, and who presumably also would have heard of the mining company. If they are the same company, the information is greatly muddled, and the exaggerations are perhaps symptomatic of the growing "Klondike Fever" on the Outside.

12. Note that while the advertisement appeared in the 7 April 1898 edition, the copy was probably prepared before 26 December 1897, when McNeil and Savage left Dawson.

13. *Klondike News*, 1 April 1898, p. 36.

14. See, however, Wilson Foster's later assessment of quartz mines summarized in the *Daily Klondike Nugget*, 3 March 1903, p. 3, col. a.

15. Cook to Mayer, 8 August 1995.

16. Berry to Mayer, 31 January 1997.

17. Green to Mayer, 28 April 1998.

18. Clarence and Ethel Berry had spent the winter of 1897–98 in California, but returned to the Klondike in time for the spring cleanup.

19. Morrison, *Politics of the Yukon*, 11.

20. Armstrong, *Yukon Yesterdays*, 83. Royalty rates were changed in the spring of 1898, March 1899, and the spring of 1901. See Morrison, *Politics of the Yukon*, for specifics.

21. See Sachs and Wilson, *Sexism and the Law*, chaps. 1 and 2, for a synopsis of key cases. As late as 1929, this point was still being litigated in Canada (38–40).

22. Ogilvie to Surveyor General Deville, 6 November 1896. Reprinted in *Yukon World*, 1 March 1904, p. 2 and 2 March 1904, p. 2.

23. See for example *Kansas City Star*, 28 January 1898, p. 12, col. c.

24. Ogilvie, *Early Days*, 162–63.

25. Ogilvie to Surveyor General Deville, 6 November 1896. Reprinted in *Yukon World*, 1 March 1904, p. 2, cols. e–f.

Chapter 9. Winds of Change

1. Gates, *Gold at Fortymile*, 61; Johns, "Early Yukon," 159; NW 10:1; Young, *Hall Young of Alaska*, 345.

2. While Belinda explicitly denies Alex McDonald's financial involvement with the hotel, still others thought that Alex was a partner in the business. For example, Tappan Adney, (*Klondike Stampede,* 392) reported that the hotel was "opened by Alex McDonald and Miss Mulrooney." We have been unable to determine whether this is simply a prejudice that such a project was unlikely to be accomplished by a woman on her own, or whether it is based on now inaccessible information about McDonald's actual involvement.

3. NW 42:1(226). There is ambiguity about when this fair was actually held. Belinda says March of 1898 or 1899. In favor of 1899, she says she donated in the name of her Fairview and the Grand Forks Hotels, and the Fairview was not even started in March of 1898. On the other hand, she says Father Judge and Reverend Hall Young attended. Father Judge died 16 January 1899, and Reverend Young left Dawson about 6 August 1898. Since this event is not reported in the local papers, which were established in 1899 but not 1898, and the tone of the proceedings fits more with the earlier date, we have concluded 1898 is the more likely.

4. Gates, *Gold at Fortymile*, 118; Johns, "Early Yukon," 135–36.

5. *Klondike Nugget*, 7 September 1898, 1 c.

6. In fact, in her 1928 interview, Belinda emphatically denies that Esther was doing anything other than mining (NW 31:4[179]).

7. The $5,000 would purchase consumer goods in the United States worth about $97,500 in 1998. If Belinda was already converting it to 1928 prices, the value in 1998 would be $47,500. (McCusker, "How Much Is That?"; *Consumer Price Index [1982–1984]*). In this and subsequent calculations of monetary values from Dawson, we assume parity between United States and Canadian dollars.

8. George Burns (or Byrnes) was an early prospector on the Yukon (Judge, *An American Missionary,* 257, 282) and a well-liked mine owner on Eldorado Creek.

9. George Noble was a civic-minded barkeeper at the Worden Hotel in Dawson (*Klondike Nugget*, 22 October 1898, p. 3, col. a), who later was involved in the Tivoli Theater (*Klondike Nugget*, 29 April 1899, p. 4, col. a), and managed the Criterion Theater, saloon, and dance hall (*Klondike Nugget*, 10 May 1899, p. 1, col. b).

10. Edgar A. Mizner was an engineer hired by the Alaska Commercial Company to supervise the company's affairs in the Klondike. According to Alva Johnston *(Legendary Mizners)*, he was responsible for inducing his three brothers—William, Addison, and Wilson—to seek their fortunes in the Yukon. Wilson, the black sheep and youngest, cut a swath in the North as a gambler, cardsharp, con artist, prize fighter, ballad singer, and early associate of Soapy Smith. While more steady than his younger brother, Edgar in Dawson also was

known as a formidable bare-fist fighter (Johnston, *Legendary Mizners,* 122–23). All the brothers were good singers.

11. Gordon C. Bettles had been prospecting and mining in the Yukon basin as early as 1888 (Bettles, "Early Yukon River History," 109–14).

12. Belinda says she danced with Joseph Ladue, one of the founders of Dawson townsite, on 17 March 1898. But this is probably not the case. Ladue left Dawson in June of 1897. On 31 August 1898, the *Klondike Nugget* (p. 4, col. a) reported that Ladue had just arrived from New York. Though it does not say exactly when he had left, comments in the article make it sound as though he had not seen the town for at least a year.

13. Adney, *Klondike Stampede,* 439; F. C. Wade gives the date as 26 February 1898 (Canada, *Sessional Papers, vol. 33,* 15).

14. Adney, *Klondike Stampede,* 432. E. LeRoy Pelletier also estimated that Dawson was 90 percent Americans (*New York Times,* 8 May 1898, p. 6, col. d).

Chapter 10. A Fair View in Dawson

1. NW 14:2–3(104–5); 15:5(110). Belinda also described the heating plant as based on a boiler from a steamboat that had wrecked downriver.

2. *Klondike Nugget,* 27 July 1898, p.1, col. b. In testimony given about ten months later, Belinda mistakenly says her "house" started running on 27 August (Canada, *Sessional Papers,* 33:33).

3. Princess Street was originally called First Street. See plat map, fig. 6.1.

4. One description of the hotel says the walls of these rooms were made of canvas, pasted over with wallpaper (Berton, *Klondike Fever,* 313). However, Belinda says (Johnston Collection), "[T]he bedroom partitions were uprights, 4" x 6", boarded on both sides. We used canvas over the boards which was painted by a German artist . . . from San Francisco."

5. Colonel James Domville, Member of Parliament from the county of King, New Brunswick, was visiting Dawson at the time.

6. Estimated by the Northwest Mounted Police, census taken about 23 July 1898 (*Klondike Nugget,* 30 July 1898, p. 4, col. c).

7. Samuel Benfield Steele arrived in Dawson in the late summer of 1898 to head the Northwest Mounted Police, replacing Inspector Charles Constantine, who also had won the respect and admiration of the pioneers.

8. LeRoy Tozier arrived in Dawson from Olympia, Washington, in the fall of 1897. He practiced law in Dawson a short time, and also became a real estate broker. (*Alaska-Yukon Magazine* 7, no. 4 [January 1909]: 315.)

Chapter 11. The Skagway Caper

1. The events in this chapter have been told in various versions by Belinda herself as well as by others who used them as a basis for fictional writing. We believe the description appearing in the 1928 interviews to be the most accurate. However, we have eliminated obvious inaccuracies, and we comment on questionable details in the accompanying notes. The 1928 interviews have Belinda leaving just after 4 July 1898 (NW 18:1[122a]). But the Fairview

did not open until 27 July, and all other indications point to the trip starting in late August or early September.

2. NW 18:3(123), 18:5(125). Colonel Steele arrived in Dawson 5 September 1898 (*Klondike Nugget,* 7 September 1898, p. 1, col. d). There was as yet no regularly scheduled postal system to or from Dawson, a source of great irritation to the isolated Yukon residents (e.g., *Klondike Nugget,* 2 July 1898, p. 3, col. b; 12 January 1899, p. 1, col. c; 28 January 1899, p. 2, col. b; *Klondike Miner,* 26 May 1899, p. 1, col. d; Pelletier, *New York Times,* 8 May 1898, p. 6).

3. This steamboat was run by Lafe Hamilton (NW 18:2[122b]).

4. Skagway is the modern spelling of the coastal Alaskan town referred to as Skagua or Skaguay in its early days.

5. This person was identified as Black Sullivan, a pioneer from Dawson, who was building boats with a partner at Bennett (NW 18:4[124]).

6. In the sometimes gossipy *Daily Klondike Nugget,* Heney is also described as fond of telegrams, pretty women, and whiskey (10 April 1903, p. 1, col. a).

7. This is apparently Miss Burkhard. See for example *Skaguay News,* 16 September 1898, p. 2, cols. a–b. The Burkhard Hotel was built on McKinney Street in 1897 (*Skaguay News,* 5 November 1897, p. 3, col. d), and so was among the oldest of the fifteen large hotels and boardinghouses in Skagway as of 14 October 1898 (*Skaguay News,* 14 October 1898, p. 1, col. c). Perhaps at this time it was expanding its facilities.

8. E. R. Peoples advertised "upholstered goods and furniture, shades and carpets" and was located at Broadway and Johnson, Skagway (*Skaguay News,* 16 September 1898, p. 4, cols. d–e). He was also Skagway's undertaker.

9. Captain William Moore was an early pioneer in Alaska. He piloted steamboats along the northwest coast and its rivers. He is credited with founding Skagway and promoting the White Pass trail as the best route to the interior.

10. NW 48:3(256). A newspaper clipping, unidentified but probably from Pennsylvania and datable to about April 1899, confirms that Belinda's parents "hear from her frequently and she does not fail to send them substantial evidence of her success." Courtesy of Janet Noble Bouillon.

11. Other sources identify the load as belonging to Dawson saloonkeeper and Belinda's friend Bill McPhee (e.g., Berton, *Klondike Fever,* 312).

12. In the 1928 interviews and in later tellings, Belinda says she met the boss gambler Jefferson "Soapy" Smith while in Skagway, and that it was Smith and his men who helped her get her outfit to Bennett. However, Soapy Smith had been killed in Skagway on 7 July 1898. Since the Fairview did not open until late July and the *Skaguay News* reported that Belinda did not arrive there until a few days before 16 September, it is unlikely that Belinda had any contact with Soapy Smith. The shell game man whom Belinda calls "Broad" and whom she hired, may have been associated with Smith previously. We have been unable to determine whether Broad was his real name or an pseudonym.

Chapter 12. *Racing with Winter*

1. As it turned out, travelers as late as December were finding the lakes and rivers of the upper Yukon unfrozen (*Klondike Nugget,* 9 January 1899, p. 1, col. d).

2. NW 28:2(168). However, other reports of the death of Ella Card's seven-month-old daughter identified the site as at the end of Chilkoot trail, near the rapids between Lakes

Lindeman and Bennett (*Juneau Alaska Searchlight*, 5 June 1897, p. 8; Hartshorn, ms., 6). The Hartshorn material may be a transcription of a section of Haskell's *Two Years*, 341.

3. *Klondike Nugget*, 1 October 1898, p. 4, col. a. The *Nugget* reported that Belinda arrived on the steamer *Ora;* however, in the 1928 interviews Belinda implies that she took her scows all the way to Dawson. She also says the remainder of the trip from Whitehorse was easier (NW 29:1[169]), so perhaps she felt it was safe to have the scows come down without her.

4. *Klondike Nugget*, 20 August 1898, p. 3, col. b.

5. Ibid., 13 August 1898, p. 1, col. c.

6. Ibid., 19 October 1898, p. 1, col. b.

7. *Yukon Midnight Sun*, 22 October 1898, p. 4, col. e.

8. NW 29:1–2(169–70). In the original of this passage, Belinda describes the scene as though she arrived with the scow. Newspaper reports suggest the account we give here is more accurate.

9. *Klondike Nugget*, 1 October 1898, p. 3, col. a; Greenhous, *Guarding the Goldfields*, 151. Faith Fenton was the pen name of Alice Freeman. She traveled to the Yukon with four nurses, recruited for the Klondike by the Victorian Order of Nurses, and with the Yukon Field Force.

10. Customs Collector D. W. Davis is reported as early as 28 May 1898 in Dawson (*Klondike Nugget*, 29 May 1898; reprinted in *Klondike Nugget*, 22 October 1898, p. 1, col. b).

11. *Klondike Nugget*, 19 October 1898, p. 4, col. a.

12. Ibid., 15 October 1898, p. 1.

13. Ibid., 5 November 1898, p. 1, col. d.

Chapter 13. Charles Eugene Carbonneau

1. *New York Times*, 22 December 1914, p. 8, col. b.

2. *Klondike Nugget*, 20 August 1898, p. 4, col. c. According to one account, Charles first registered at the Regina hotel (Dill, *Long Day*, 83), but we have not found independent verification of this.

3. Dill, *Long Day*, 81; Mackay, "Saga of Belinda," p. 6.

4. *B.C. Review* (London), 11 October 1902, p. 184.

5. Yukon, Mining Recorder, *Creek Claims, Bonanza*, vol. 3. Pelkey staked the Bonanza claim September 10, 1896. In early 1898 he was reported as being Outside for rest and recreation, and scheduled to return in August. Thomas Pelkey was Canadian-born, but he had lived in Williamsport, Pennsylvania for many years. He came to Fortymile in about 1894. (*Klondike News*, 1 April 1898, p. 3, col. a.)

6. *Klondike Nugget*, 20 August 1898, p. 3, col. b. The party was held on 17 August.

7. Yukon, Mining Recorder, *Creek Claims, Bonanza*, vol. 3, and *Eldorado*, vol. 22. No. 2 left fork Lucky Gulch at No. 26, ascending Lucky Creek, and No. 7 left fork Lucky Creek (England, *AFKS, Agreement for Sale*, 11 November 1898 rec. 4).

8. Dawson, *Mining Records*, Placer Mining Roll 8, p. 11, New Records, Eldorado 3A, inst. 121. Pelkey, with partners, had bought the fractional claim 3A on Eldorado on 6 May 1897.

9. See for example *Klondike News*, 1 April 1898, p. 3, col. a; *B.C. Review* (London), p. 184.

10. Belinda says Charles was in the company of Pelkey when they first met, and he had at that time an option on Pelkey's mine (NW 45:2–3[234–35]). Pelkey and Carbonneau arrived in Dawson some time before the evening dinner party on 17 August. The mines were pur-

chased on 26 August. Belinda left Dawson for the Outside before the end of the month (*Klondike Nugget*, 31 August 1898, p. 4, col. c). Therefore, Charles and Belinda probably first met between 16 and 26 August 1898.

11. This is probably J. K. Leaming.

12. *Skaguay News*, 23 December 1898, p. 2, col. b; *Klondike Nugget*, 11 January 1899, p. 4, col. a

13. At £1 to $4.831 (Mitchell, *British Historical Statistics*, Table 22, 702), the capitalization would be equivalent to about $4,700,000 in consumer goods purchasing power in 1998 in the United States (McCusker, "How Much Is That?" Table A-2, 329–32; *Consumer Price Index* [1982–84]).

14. England, *AFKS Memorandum of Association*, 10 November 1898, rec. 2.

15. Ibid. *Articles of Association*, 10 November 1898, rec. 3.

16. Ibid. *Agreement for Sale*, 11 November 1898, rec. 4.

17. Ibid. *Agreement for Appointment of Manager*, 11 November 1898, rec. 5.

18. Ibid. *Agreement for Sale*, 11 November 1898, rec. 4.

19. Yukon, *Free Miner's Certificates*, vol. 188, 7 December 1898, cert. 20574, pp. 1, 2.

20. *Skaguay News*, 23 December 1898, p. 2, col. b.

21. Ibid.; *Klondike Nugget*, 11 January 1899, p. 4, col. a. These two sources vary in the numbers of men and dogs in Carbonneau's party. We have chosen to use the information from the *Klondike Nugget* because it is more elaborated, though it may not be more accurate.

22. Yukon, RCMP, *Persons Inwards and Outward; Persons Inwards from Dec. 18, 1898*.

23. *Klondike Nugget*, 7 January 1899, p. 4, col. c; 11 January 1899, p. 4, col. a. However, a subsequent article in the rival *Klondike Miner and Yukon Advertiser* (27 January 1899, p. 2, col. e) pointed out the errors of Carbonneau's version of the strife between Norway and Sweden.

24. He left 17 December 1898 from Skagway (*Skaguay News*, 23 December 1898, p. 2, col. b) and arrived 9 January 1899 in Dawson (*Klondike Nugget*, 11 January 1899, p. 4, col. a). Therefore, the eighteen days the *Klondike Nugget* article reported him as on the trail is not accurate.

25. *Klondike Nugget*, 11 January 1899, p. 4, col. a.

26. Yukon, Mining Recorder, *Creek Claims, Bonanza*, vol. 3 for Bonanza 41 A/D, inst. 692; and *Eldorado*, vol. 22 for Eldorado 3A, inst. 690; 11 January 1899.

27. *Klondike Nugget*, 4 January 1899, p. 4, col. b.

28. In early 1899 Walter C. Watrous, with the *Klondike Nugget* newspaper, organized an express service to carry mail and occasional passengers between Dawson and Skagway. See, e.g., *Klondike Nugget*, 4 January 1899, p. 3, col. b; 25 January 1899, p. 4, col. c; 1 February 1899, p. 1, col. c; 15 February 1899, p. 4, col. b.

29. *Seattle Post-Intelligencer*, 2 February 1899, p. 5, cols. c–d.

30. *Dawson Daily News Mining Edition*, September 1899, p. 28, cols. c–d.

31. London, *AFKS Summary of Capital and Shares*, 16 March 1899, rec. 8; shares were approximately equal to $4.83 each and equivalent to about $94 in 1998 consumer goods purchasing power in the United States (McCusker, "How Much Is That?" Table A-2, 329–32; *Consumer Price Index* [1982–84]).

32. Charles's father and mother are identified as F. L. and Emma Beaudry Carbonneau on the Dawson Catholic Church's marriage register, 1 October 1900. They are listed as François and Aurelie Beaudry Carbonneau in the Loiselle File record of his marriage to Alice Boilard in 1885.

33. J. E. Girouard was an attorney who served as the Registrar of the Yukon and as a member of the Yukon Council. His law office ad first appears in the *Klondike Nugget* on 3 December 1898, p. 4, col. c. F. X. Gosselyn arrived in Dawson 11 January 1899, as Crown Tim-

ber and Land Agent (*Klondike Nugget,* 12 January 1899, p. 4, col. c). Calixte Aime Dugas was appointed Superior Court Judge 12 September 1898 and arrived in Dawson about 19 October 1898 (*Yukon Midnight Sun,* 22 October 1898, p. 1, col. f; *Klondike Nugget,* 19 October 1898, p. 4, col. a and 22 October 1898, p. 4, col. a.

34. W. S. Dill (*Long Day,* 97) says Charles sent a rose to Belinda every day after they met. There are obvious errors in this memoir, and it seems doubtful that Dill got this information from first-hand observation, but this story does capture Charles's style and appreciation for the grand gesture.

Chapter 14. Belinda at Her Peak

1. NW 58:4(302); Gould to Mayer, 2 July 1998.

2. *Yukon Midnight Sun,* 22 October 1898, p. 4, col. b. The performance was on 18 October.

3. *Klondike Nugget,* 4 January 1899, p. 4, col. c; 11 January 1899, p. 4, col. b; 14 January 1899, p. 1, col. c; 31 December 1898, p. 4, col. a.

4. *Yukon Midnight Sun,* 22 October 1898, p. 4, col. a. The Tivoli was the new incarnation of the Combination Theater (*Klondike Nugget,* 8 October 1898, p. 4, col. b).

5. *Klondike Nugget,* 26 October 1898, p. 1, cols. a–b.

6. *Yukon Midnight Sun,* 22 October 1898, p. 1, col. a.

7. *Klondike Nugget,* 31 December 1898, p. 4, cols. b–c.

8. Ibid., 28 December 1898, p. 3, cols. a–b; 31 December 1898, p. 4, cols. b–c. At this event, there were reprises of the debate over the criteria for respectability of women.

9. Morrison, *Politics of the Yukon,* 18, 132; Guest, *History of Dawson,* 196.

10. *Klondike Nugget,* 24 December 1898, p. 4, col. c. Listed as J. H. C. Ogilvie in a later report (*Klondike Nugget,* 26 April 1899, p. 4, col. a), Captain J. H. C. Ogilvie was an officer in the Yukon Field Force, sent from Fort Selkirk to Dawson in early October 1898 (Canada, Walsh to Evans).

11. U.S. Census, 1900, Archbald, Lackawanna County, Pennsylvania, 4 June 1900, Enumeration District 2, Sheet 1B, Ln. 68. While the initials "J. J." might correspond to either Belinda's brother or her father, other evidence suggests neither of them was in the Klondike as early as 1898. Our first record of Belinda's brother, called Patrick or Joe, is as a guest at a dinner party in Dawson on 1 October 1900, about two years after the formation of the water company. Belinda's father John also was in Dawson, according to Betty Mulrooney (interview by Mayer). Though she did not know the exact date, she thought he had gone In and stayed for about two years. The *Klondike Nugget* announced his arrival on 23 June 1901. Other early Mulrooney/Mulroney visitors in Dawson include a J. F., who passed through Tagish on 29 May 1898 (Yukon, RCMP *Register of Boats through Tagish*); however, this person was from Portland, Oregon, not Pennsylvania. A J. A. Mulroney filed a claim on a tributary of Hunker Creek on 20 September 1898 (Yukon, Mining Recorder, *Index of Original Locators,* vol. 1, p. 296, No. 1 on tributary at 13 Above, Hunker, Inst. 11042). J. H. Mulrooney is listed as a miner in the Dawson directory for 1901 (Ferguson, *Dawson Directory*). J. S. Malooney mined No. 18, Gold Bottom in 1901 (Allen, *Dawson, Yukon Territory*).

12. *Klondike Nugget,* 4 January 1899, p. 2, col. c.

13. See *Klondike Nugget,* 7 January 1899, p. 1, col. a and subsequent issues for further details.

14. Ibid., 18 January 1899, p. 1, col. c.

15. Ibid., 12 April 1899, p. 3, col. a.

16. Ibid., 24 December 1898, p. 4, col. c.

17. Ibid.; 26 April 1899, p. 4, col. c; 29 April 1899, p. 4, col. b.

18. NW 16:3(115). The apparent discrepancy in price between what was stated in the original petition and this quote may be accounted for if the "pail" held two and a half gallons.

19. *Klondike Nugget,* 26 April 1899, p. 4, col. c; 29 April 1899, p. 4, col. b.

20. The *Daily Alaskan* (*Skaguay,* 21 February 1899) lists many of the guests. Coverage in the *Skaguay News* (24 February 1899) was more general.

21. Credit for the first strike on Adams/Cheechako Hill is given to O. B. Millett in the spring of 1898 (*Dawson Daily News Mining Edition,* September 1899, p. 15, col. b).

22. While Belinda says she is describing her Cheechako Hill claim, in what follows we may be getting instead a blend of her claims on Cheechako and Gold Hills.

23. This may be the Lawson who is mentioned as a partner with Norwood and who supervised their extensive operations on American Hill, opposite 17, 18, and 19 B/D Bonanza. See, e.g., *Dawson Daily News Golden Clean-Up Edition,* 1902, p. 12.

24. George (Skiff) Mitchell was a lumber man from Eureka, California (Berton, *Klondike Fever,* 58) who had been mining in the Yukon basin as early as 1887. (Judge, *An American Missionary,* 257; Gates, *Gold at Fortymile,* 39). He bought No. 1 Eldorado for a pittance soon after it was staked and owned interests in other valuable claims. He is credited with directing, on a lark, G. A. Lancaster to prospect the ground on Gold Hill in the summer of 1897 (*Dawson Daily News Mining Edition,* September 1899, p. 17, col. d). Lancaster's quick and amazing success triggered a local stampede to stake hillside claims and was probably what first drew Belinda out from Dawson to what was to become Grand Forks.

25. This is probably Andrew Jackson Maiden, a Yukon Pioneer (Gates, *Gold at Fortymile,* 161). We did not find records for his Cheechako Hill location. However, he is shown as locator of Bench LL 2 Eldorado on 14 January 1899 (Yukon, Mining Recorder, *Original Locators, Eldorado.*). This claim would be part of Gold Hill, and Belinda was reported to have interests in two claims in this area (*Dawson Daily News Mining Edition,* September 1899, p. 27, col. c).

26. This statement is not consistent with records for the Cheechako Hill claim, described as Bench on 4th Tier opposite upper half LL of 1 B/D Bonanza, bounded on west by O. B. Millett, south by F. W. Ward, and north by E. J. Irvin. Records show Belinda bought it for $250 from Christopher Ellis on 21 July 1898, after he alone staked it on 14 February (Dawson, *Mining Records,* 32, microfilm roll 3, sec. 3).

27. *New York Times,* 8 May 1898, p. 6, col. a.

28. Quoted by Young, *Hall Young of Alaska,* 321.

29. Adney (*Klondike Stampede,* 419) reports seeing steam thawing introduced in Dawson in the summer of 1898. This dating is consistent with an article in the *Klondike Nugget* (11 March 1899, p. 1, cols. b–c) in which steam thawing and tram cars are mentioned as "improved methods of working earth" on Gold Hill.

30. French Hill was on the left side of Eldorado Creek looking downstream, about a mile and a half from Grand Forks, between Irish Gulch and French Gulch.

31. NW 37:4–5(205–6). Belinda's claim on Cheechako Hill was bounded by those of the Yukon Gold Fields, Ltd., on the south and that of Senator Jeremiah Lynch (*Dawson Daily News Mining Edition,* September 1899, p. 27, col. a).

32. In 1898–99 this meant above the ankles, perhaps calf-length.

33. Gould to Mayer, 29 January 1998.

34. O'Connor, *High Jinks on the Klondike,* 82. It is hard to judge whether the one dollar per day wage is accurate. E. LeRoy Pelletier reported that in December of 1897 many men were

glad to work simply for grub (*New York Times,* 23 January 1898, p. 1, col. g). But after that winter, wages were higher. Work on Belinda's Cheechako Hill claim would have been a year or
more later.

35. *Dawson Daily News Mining Edition,* September 1899, p. 27.

Chapter 15. Spring 1899, and Carbonneau A-Courting

1. Morrison, *Politics of the Yukon,* 105 n. 43; Adney, *Klondike Stampede,* 438; Young, *Hall
Young of Alaska,* 369.

2. Morrison, *Politics of the Yukon,* chap. 3.

3. F. C. Wade to E. Wade, 20 April 1898.

4. Charles married Alice Boilard on 4 August 1885, in St-Paul-du-Buton, Montmagny
County, Quebec. (*Loiselle File.* Courtesy of Serge Barbe, City of Ottawa Archives.)

5. For a summary of legal changes during the late nineteenth century, see Constance B.
Backhouse, "Married Women's Property Law in Nineteenth-Century Canada," 211–57.

6. "An Ordinance to Facilitate the Conveyance of Real Estate by Married Women, No. 6.
Ordinances of the NWT, 1886, 178–79.

7. *Revised Ordinances of the NWT, 1888,* Sched. A: Ordinances Repealed, 12; "An Ordinance
Respecting the Personal Property of Married Women," *Ordinances of the NWT, 1898,* Chap.
47, p. 421 (No. 20 of 1890, s.2).

8. *Klondike Nugget,* 8 April 1899, p. 4, col. a.

9. *Kansas City Star,* 31 October 1898, p. 6, col. e, reprint of story about Alex McDonald
from the *San Francisco Examiner; Klondike Nugget,* 12 April 1899, p. 1, col. d.

10. *Klondike News,* 1 April 1898, p. 14.

11. *New York Times,* 22 December 1914, p. 8.

12. The entire output of the Yukon from 1885 through 1908 has been estimated at $150
million (*Dawson Daily News Special Edition,* 21 July 1909).

13. Denison, *Klondike Mike,* 227; Armstrong, *Yukon Yesterdays,* 50.

14. Later Belinda recalled (NW 37:3[204]) that cleanup began on 15 April, but stories in
May issues of the *Klondike Nugget* suggest it was actually somewhat later that year.

15. *Klondike Nugget,* 29 April 1899, p. 4, col. a.

16. Ibid., 27 April 1899, p. 1, col. d.

17. NW 41:2(222). The Pioneer Saloon was next to the Northern Restaurant on Front
Street (First Avenue). By this time both of Bill McPhee's partners, Harry Spencer and Frank
Dinsmore, had died.

18. *Dawson Daily News Mining Edition,* September 1899, p. 28.

19. Yukon, *Bonanza Townsite Record.* This may be the same cabin Belinda shared with
Sadie O'Hara.

20. *Yukon Midnight Sun,* 22 October 1898, p. 4; *Klondike Nugget,* 22 October 1898, p. 3, col. b.

21. *Klondike Nugget,* 19 October 1898, p. 4, col. b.

22. *Klondike Nugget,* 27 April 1899, p. 1, col. c; 29 April 1899, p. 1.

23. *Klondike Nugget,* 15 October 1898, p. 3, col. b; 4 January 1899, p. 3, col. a; 7 January 1899,
p. 1, col. b.

24. Ibid., 12 April 1899, p. 3, col. b.

25. Kelcey ("Lost in the Rush") estimates fewer than 100; Guest (*History of Dawson,* 220)
estimates fewer than 150.

26. *Klondike Nugget,* 6 May 1899, p. 1, col. d.

27. A Dr. Simpson is mentioned as a bystander during an altercation between Drs. J. W. Good and George E. Merryman at the Fairview bar (*Klondike Nugget, Supplement,* 2 August 1899, p. 2, col. b).

28. *Klondike Nugget,* 29 April 1899, p. 2, col. c.

29. N. A. Fuller was one of the four men most frequently named in connection with the original discovery of gold on Gastineau Channel in 1880 and the founding of Juneau, Alaska. He eventually became assistant manager of the Treadwell Mine on Douglas Island. About 1890 he went to Michigan, made a number of investments and went broke. He returned north during the Klondike Rush, where he was involved with the Dawson telephone and public utilities systems. Later he installed the telephone system at Fairbanks and owned it for a time. Fuller left the North about 1908, lived in California for a number of years, and died in Detroit, Michigan, on 21 November 1930. See R. N. DeArmond, *Founding of Juneau,* 159.

30. *Klondike Nugget,* 6 May 1899, p. 4, cols. b–c.

31. Ibid., 20 May 1899, p. 4, col. b; 10 May 1899, p. 4, col. b; *Klondike Miner and Yukon Advertiser,* 12 May 1899, p. 4, col. d; NW 48:2(255).

32. *Klondike Nugget,* 12 January 1899, p. 4, col. c.

33. Handwritten agreement on Fairview Hotel stationery for Private Partnership, dated 15 March 1899 (Carbonneau Collection, Yakima).

34. Stander was born 4 (or 16) June 1867 in Unterkrein (Dolenjska) Province, which has been part of Austria, Yugoslavia, and now Slovenia. He immigrated to the United States in about 1887. He died 2 April 1952 in Morningside Sanitarium in Portland, Oregon.

35. *Klondike News,* 1 April 1898, p. 1.

36. Dawson, *Mining Records,* microfilm roll 2, 40 A/D Bonanza, inst. 166M, 25 October 1897.

37. NW 48:1(254); Yukon, Mining Recorder, *Bonanza Creek, 40 A/D,* vol. 3, p. 420 f., Inst. 1277.

38. NW 48:1(254). However, an article in the *Dawson Daily News Mining Edition* (September 1899, 27 b) reports the sale price for the hotel was $24,000.

39. *Klondike Nugget,* 17 May 1899, p. 4, col. b. Max Endelman was in Alaska as early as 1887, for he had property at that time in Sitka. A story in the *Klondike Nugget* (1 November 1899, p. 20) reported he arrived in 1886. In July 1888 he moved to Juneau upon being appointed a deputy U.S. Marshal there. He became manager of the Opera House, which had been built by Bill McPhee, but who probably was no longer an owner when Endelman was manager. The Opera House was a combination theater/bar/dance hall and, probably, bordello. The *Yukon Midnight Sun* (22 October 1898, p. 1) reported that Max had leased both the Eldorado and Bonanza claims of Stander; there had obviously been an extensive relationship between the Standers and Endelman before the Grand Forks hotel transaction.

40. Dawson, *Mining Record Book,* 24, microfilm roll 21, Lower half, No. 12 Gold Run; *Registered Documents,* microfilm roll 2, Bill of Sale, Inst. 41H.

41. Yukon, Mining Recorder, *Bonanza Creek, 40 A/D,* vol. 3, p. 420 f., Inst. 2069; Inst. 3743, 11 July 1899 (since Charles was not in Dawson in July, someone else must have seen to this recording.); Inst. 6499, 5 September 1899.

42. *Klondike Nugget,* 7 June 1899, p. 1, col. d.

43. Yukon, Mining Recorder, *Bonanza Creek, 41 A/D,* vol. 3; *Creek Claims, Eldorado 3A,* vol. 22, p. 420 f.; Insts. 2121, 2119, and 2120, 8 June 1899.

44. Meadows to Pepin, 2 March 1898 (*Santa Cruz [Calif.] Sentinel,* 23 April 1898, p. 1).

45. *Skaguay News,* 24 February 1899, p. 2, col. c.

46. Mining records show at least $18,819 being extracted by 7 June (Yukon, Mining Recorder, *Royalties, Eldorado 3A,* vol. 200, p. 97, 7 June 1899).

47. Henderson, *How Con Games Work.*

48. *B.C. Review* (London), 11 October 1902, p. 184.

49. Yukon, Mining Recorder, *Creek Claims, Eldorado,* vol. 22; *Bonanza,* vol. 3.

50. London, *AFKS, Extraordinary Resolution,* 13 June 1901, rec. 11.

51. Yukon, Mining Recorder, *Royalties, Eldorado 3A,* vol. 200, p. 97, 7 June 1899.

52. *Klondike Nugget,* 10 June 1899, p. 1, col. b; NW 46:7(245).

53. H. T. Wills was head of the Canadian Bank of Commerce and the brother of Dr. A. E. Wills, Surgeon to the Northwest Mounted Police.

Chapter 16. The Klondike Rush Is Over

1. One account has Joe Barrette being the person who initially introduced Charles to Belinda (Dill, *Long Day,* 92). Numerous other factual errors in this source suggest it should not be taken literally, but it probably does accurately reflect that Barrette and Carbonneau, both French Canadians, were on friendly terms. Such positive regard for Charles from one of Belinda's Old-Timer mining friends was unusual.

2. *Klondike Nugget,* 15 November 1899, p. 3, col. a.

3. This occupation appears on the *Marriage Register* at the Dawson Catholic Church for Charles and Belinda, 1 October 1900. See also Mike Mahoney (Denison, *Klondike Mike,* 226); and Joe Putraw, foreman of No. 16 Eldorado (Dill, *Long Day,* 84–85).

4. *B.C. Review* (London), 11 October 1902, p. 184.

5. *Klondike Nugget,* 17 May 1899, p. 4, col. a.

6. F. C. Wade to E. Wade, 20 April 1898.

7. Young, *Hall Young of Alaska,* 369–71; Adney, *Klondike Stampede,* 438–39. See also Morrison, *Politics of the Yukon,* 16, 23.

8. For example, Wade was recommended to succeed William Ogilvie as Yukon Commissioner in 1901, but Prime Minister Wilfrid Laurier appointed James H. Ross instead (Morrison, *Politics of the Yukon,* 37).

9. Canada, *Sessional Papers,* vol. 33. Skeptics declared the investigation a whitewash.

10. *The Province (Vancouver),* 25 July 1899, p. 1, cols. f–g.

11. Ibid., 27 July 1899, p. 4, col. b.

12. Ibid., p. 8, col. a.

13. Adams or Cheechako Hill was on the west side of Bonanza Creek, opposite claims Discovery through about 6 B/D Bonanza. Norwood's main holding, however, as a partner with Lawsen and Fuller, was at American Hill, between Magnet Creek and American Creek, opposite claims 17 through 19 B/D Bonanza (*Dawson Daily News Golden Clean-Up Edition,* 1902, p. 12); NW 57:3(296). See also Dill (*Long Day,* 228–29) for a description of Norwood's "very substantial cabin" and his "prodigal hospitality."

14. See, e.g., Mayer, *Klondike Women,* 190–94.

15. An advertisement for Nellie's Can-Can Restaurant and Short Order House appears in the *Klondike Nugget* (28 June 1898, p. 1). She also opened the Cassiar Restaurant on 22 October 1898 (*Yukon Midnight Sun,* 22 October 1898, p. 4, col. d).

16. Canada, *Sessional Papers,* vol. 33, 33 (deposition by Belinda Mulrooney). Many unlikely details of Dawson life appear in the transcripts from Ogilvie's Commission of Inquiry.

17. *Klondike Miner,* 12 May 1899, p. 1, col. c; 26 May 1899, p. 4, col. e.

18. *Klondike Nugget,* 20 May 1899, p. 1, cols. b–c.

19. Ibid. See also Canada, *Sessional Papers,* vol. 33.

20. *Klondike Miner,* 26 May 1899, p. 4, col. e.

21. Canada, *Sessional Papers*, vol. 33, 28.

22. *Klondike Nugget*, 20 May 1899, p. 1, cols. b–c. See also Canada, *Sessional Papers*, vol. 33, 5–6, 32–34. The commission decided there was no evidence to support the charges against any of the officials. However, this Skookum Hill claim would continue to be at the center of conflict and government action for Nellie Cashman. See Mayer, *Klondike Women*, 221, 249n.

23. Canadian Department of the Interior data, quoted in Ross, *Canadian Bank of Commerce*, 478; Johnson, "Yukon's Gold Yield."

24. *Klondike Nugget*, 26 August 1899, p. 1, col. a; *Supplement*, 19 July 1899, p. 2, col. a.

25. *Klondike Nugget*, 24 June 1899, p. 1, col. a.

26. See Guest, *History of Dawson*, chap. 7, for a description of the increasing control exerted on these establishments beginning at the end of 1898. They did not finally close until 1919, however.

27. *Klondike Nugget*, 10 June 1899, Extra, p. 1, col. a.

28. Ibid., 24 May 1899, p. 1, col. a.

29. Ibid., *Supplement*, 10 June 1899, p. 4, col. b.

30. Ibid., 27 May 1899, p. 1, col. d.

31. Ibid., 8 July 1899, p. 1, cols. b–c; 12 July 1899, p. 1, cols. b–c.

32. Ibid., 14 June 1899, p. 1, col. d.

33. Ibid., 22 July 1899, p. 4, col. a.

34. Ibid., 30 September 1899, p. 1, col. c; 4 October 1899, p. 2, col. d.

35. Ibid., 12 July 1899, Supplement, p. 1, col. d.

36. *Dawson Daily News Mining Edition*, September 1899, p. 27. This story also credits her with owning 12B Gold Run; however, *Mining Records* (Dawson, Microfilm roll 21, Sect. 2, New Records) show 12B owned at this time by the original locator August Olson. Nevertheless, T. F. Lawson and R.(H?) H. Norwood would soon acquire the claim. If this is, in fact, Captain Norwood and his partner, perhaps Belinda had an unrecorded interest through them.

37. Yukon, Mining Recorder, *Bonanza Creek, 41 A/D*, vol. 3.

38. *Klondike Nugget*, 14 June 1899, p. 4, col. b. The *Dawson Daily News Mining Edition*, September 1899, reported that the Fairview was under lease to Gates and Cox (p. 27, col. b).

39. *Klondike Nugget*, 23 September 1899.

40. *Klondike Semi-Weekly Nugget*, 30 August 1899, p. 8, col. b.

41. *Klondike Nugget*, 7 October 1899, p. 6, col. b.

Chapter 17. Belinda's Triumphal Tour

1. NW 49:3–4(261–62). Belinda's and the crew's effort to conceal her having worked on the *Topeka* was probably futile, for many of the true Old Timers would have been familiar with both the boat and its crew.

2. U.S. Census 1900, June 4, Archbald, Lackawanna County, PA; Enum. Dist. 2, St. 1B, Ln. 68; Microfilm T-623, Roll 1418, vol. 101.

3. NW 51:4(271); Yakima, *Scouse and Byrnes v. AYIC*, no. 9439, Depositions of Margaret Mulrooney, 1 December 1915, and Helen Mulrooney (Mrs. William F.) Thompson, 18 March 1916; Johnston to DeArmond, 3 October 1988.

4. NW 51:6(273). In the 1928 interviews Belinda says she sailed for Queenstown; however, advertisements for this ship identify Southampton as its destination port (*New York Times*, 15

November 1899, p. 13, col. f). Queenstown was the former name of the port of Cobh, Ireland, in Cork Harbor.

5. See for example *New York Times*, 15 November 1899, p. 13, col. f.; 5 December 1899, p. 8, col. g. Belinda's trip on the *Kaiser Wilhelm der Grosse* probably started from Hoboken, New Jersey, on 28 November 1899 or 4 January 1900. Other scheduled crossings would have been out of the possible time frame.

6. Recall, however, that Belinda did say she had written to her grandmother frequently and had promised her a visit (NW 48:3–4[256–57]).

7. See for example *Dawson Daily News*, 28 July 1904, p. 1, col. a.

8. Marcel styling was done with a hot curling iron, leaving parallel sets of deep waves in the hair.

9. NW 53:2–3(280–281); Hawkins.

10. NW 53:1(279). It was apparently through this family in Bordeaux that Carbonneau claimed his title.

11. This latter destination presumably had to do with her siblings' schooling there.

12. *Klondike Nugget*, 20 May 1900, p. 6, col. e; NW 53:5(283).

13. NW 54:1–2(284–85). We have been unable to determine what happened to Nero after this date.

14. *Klondike Nugget*, 20 May 1900, p. 6, col. e.

Chapter 18. A Wedding

1. *Dawson Daily News*, 18 May 1900; *Klondike Semi-Weekly Nugget*, 20 May 1900, p. 6, col. e.

2. In the 1928 interviews, Belinda said she came in by sleigh and had an exciting race with Alex McDonald to be the first from Whitehorse to Dawson. This account does not agree with the newspaper reports at the time and may refer to another trip. However, the other trip would have had to be some time after the telegraph wires were in use (about September 1899), for they play a part in the story.

3. *Klondike Semi-Weekly Nugget*, 29 March 1900, p. 1, col. b; 1 April 1900, p. 4, col. b; and 15 April 1900, p. 6, col. a.

4. Yukon, *Free Miners Certificates*, vol. 188, 41.

5. *Klondike Semi-Weekly Nugget*, 10 June 1900, p. 6, col. c. Another possibility is that the seldom neutral *Klondike Nugget* was taking a dig at Carbonneau's business speculations, for (ignoring a missing "s") "des longs champs" means literally "of the long fields."

6. *Klondike Semi-Weekly Nugget*, 24 May 1900, p. 8, col. c.

7. *Dawson Daily News*, 29 January 1900, p. 1.

8. *Klondike Semi-Weekly Nugget*, 20 May 1900, p. 4, col. b; 24 May 1900, p. 4, col. d; 27 May 1900, p. 6, col. b; 14 June 1900, p. 8, col. b.

9. Ibid., 3 June 1900, p. 4, col. d.

10. Ibid., 17 May 1900, p. 3, col. c; 27 May 1900, p. 1, col. b.

11. *Klondike Nugget*, 12 July 1899, p. 3, cols. a–b; *Dawson Daily News Mining Edition*, September 1899, p. 28.

12. *Klondike Semi-Weekly Nugget*, 7 June 1900, p. 5, col. e. In the estimation of E. LeRoy Pelletier, *New York Times* correspondent, No. 26 A/D Bonanza was one of the richest claims in the whole region (*New York Times*, 5 November 1899, p. 4, col. a).

13. Yukon, Mining Recorder, *Creek Claims, Eldorado 3A*, vol. 22, 11 November 1899.

14. *Klondike Semi-Weekly Nugget*, 17 May 1900, p. 4, col. d; Yukon, Mining Recorder, *Creek Claims, Eldorado 3A*, vol. 22, 25 May 1900; *Bonanza Creek, 41 A/D*, vol. 3, Inst. 12502.

15. *Klondike Semi-Weekly Nugget,* 3 June 1900, p. 6, col. b.

16. Betty Mulrooney to Johnston.

17. Lower half, No. 12 Gold Run, 7 June 1900, for $9,500 (Dawson, *Mining Recorder Records,* 12, New Records, microfilm roll 21, Sect. 2).

18. Nels Peterson had been in the party with Belinda when she first entered the Yukon in the spring of 1897. (See chapter 5.) He and his partner Nathan Kresge were among the earliest to file rich claims on the hillsides above Grand Forks in 1897. Peterson later invested and lost much of his gold in a steamship company, the "Flyer Line," which provided service between Dawson and Whitehorse. See for example *Klondike Semi-Weekly Nugget,* 9 December 1900, p. 1, col. b.

19. NW 58:1(299). This calculation is based upon twelve troy ounces to the pound. Although this was an unusually large nugget, others as big had been found on nearby claims. See for example *Klondike Miner and Yukon Advertiser,* 17 February 1899, p. 4, col. c, on Henry Berry picking up a seven-pound nugget on No. 5 Eldorado; and *Klondike Semi-Weekly Nugget,* 20 May 1900, p. 8, col. a, on discovery of a seventy-seven-ounce nugget.

20. Yukon, Mining Recorder, *Bonanza Creek, 40 A/D,* vol. 3, p. 420, 29 June 1900.

21. See for example Commissioner Ogilvie's correspondence circa 6 May 1899 concerning surfeit of liquor (Yukon, *Records*).

22. Yukon, *Territorial Records,* File 576939. This statement of permits issued came from the Department of the Interior in Ottawa, and a letter dated 18 August 1900, from P. G. Keyes in Ottawa to J. T. Lithgow, Comptroller at Dawson, suggests the fees were actually paid in Ottawa. We found no other reference to Carbonneau's having made another trip Outside at this time, however.

23. The *Klondike Nugget* (16 August 1900, p. 4, col. e) says the Mintos stayed at the home of Major Z. T. Wood, who was commander of the Northwest Mounted Police at Dawson (e.g., *Klondike Semi-Weekly Nugget,* 6 January 1901, p. 2, col. d).

24. The poor condition of roads, especially those to the creeks, was a major complaint of the Klondikers. For example, Charles Carbonneau was one of several Eldorado Creek claim operators signing a petition in the fall of 1899 to Commissioner Ogilvie complaining of the "abominable condition" of the trail up the creek from Grand Forks. They requested a good wagon road, arguing they already had paid enough royalties and taxes to justify the reasonable expense needed for safe transportation of goods, gold, and machinery (*Dawson Daily News,* 15 September 1899, p. 1, col. g).

25. NW 59:1–4(303–6). A newspaper account of the Mintos' trip to and from the Bonanza area on August 15 says the carriage that Crown Prosecutor F. C. Wade, Commissioner William Ogilvie, and Registrar J. E. Girouard were riding in broke down on the way to Grand Forks, forcing them to hike. On the way back to Dawson, a horse pulling a wagon going the other way stepped into a mud hole and impaled itself on a pointed stick, whereupon it bled to death. The dead horse was just being removed from the road when the Minto party arrived. So there were mishaps, but there is no incident reported such as the one described by Belinda. Neither is Belinda listed as one of the party that day, though F. C. and Edith Wade and Alex and Margaret McDonald were. However, on August 16 another excursion up Bonanza Creek was taken over the ridge road. It may be this latter trip that Belinda describes. (*Klondike Semi-Weekly Nugget,* 20 August 1900, p. 4, col. e.)

26. This is apparently John P. Sale and Company, formerly Pond and Company, Jewelers (*Dawson Daily News Mining Edition,* September 1899, p. 11, col. c).

27. *Klondike Semi-Weekly Nugget,* 19 August 1900, p. 2, col. b.

28. *Klondike Semi-Weekly Nugget,* 30 August 1900, p. 8, col. a. The agreement to sell to

G. Sanberg, J. W. Granvas, J. W. Westerlund, and R. C. Davis was drawn up 18 August 1900. The final transfer was filed 5 July 1901 (Dawson, *Mining Recorder Records,* 32, Inst. 14154, 20425, microfilm roll 3, Sec. 3).

29. Yukon, Mining Recorder, *Bonanza Creek 53 B/D,* vol. 2, p. 124, Inst. 17595, 8 September 1900.

30. Vitzthum to Mayer, 28 December 1992; 2 January 1993. However, Belinda's sister Helen/Nell years later testified that a house was purchased for her (Yakima, Case 9439, *Scouse and Byrnes v. AYIC, No. 9439,* Deposition of Mrs. William F. Thompson, 18 March 1916). It is possible that more than one home was purchased in Glenside.

31. Belinda also said that Wilson Mizner was among those who boycotted the celebration (NW 60:3[311]), but she may have meant Edgar Mizner. According to brother Addison, Wilson had left Dawson for Nome with the first boat downriver in June 1899 (Mizner, *The Many Mizners,* 166). Only Edgar Mizner was still living in Dawson at the time of Belinda's and Charles's wedding.

32. *Klondike Semi-Weekly Nugget,* 30 August 1900, p. 8, col. a; 4 October 1900, p. 2, col. d.

33. These may have been part of the thousand-gallon shipment Carbonneau had brought in earlier that summer.

34. *Klondike Semi-Weekly Nugget,* 4 October 1900, p. 7, col. e; NW 61:2(314).

35. However, the *Nugget* reported Father Demerais as presiding (*Klondike Semi-Weekly Nugget,* 4 October 1900, p. 7, col. e), while marriage records for St. Mary's Church (Yukon Archives, microfilm CM#016-001) show the signature of Father Gendreau.

36. NW 60:3(311). This number was confirmed by Mrs. Blaker to Betty Mulrooney (interview by Mayer).

37. *Klondike Semi-Weekly Nugget,* 4 October 1900, p. 7, col. e.

38. Betty Mulrooney, interview by Mayer. This menu is now in the Johnston Collection.

39. Joe's brother Norbert had also been an early prospector in the Yukon, coming In with Alex McDonald in 1895 (*Dawson Daily News,* 9 January 1909, p. 4, col. f).

40. This is probably R. P. McLennan, who would become mayor of Dawson in 1903 (*Daily Klondike Nugget,* 12 January 1903, p. 4, col. f).

Chapter 19. Carbonneau and Carbonneau

1. Goldin, *Understanding the Gender Gap,* 17, Table 2.1; 12. The 4 percent is an extrapolation of the tabled data. The overall rate for white married women was 3.2 percent. For nonwhite married women it was 26 percent.

2. Dawson, *Registered Documents,* Inst. 15148, 8 October 1900, microfilm roll 19; Inst. 15154, 9 October 1900, $8,500, microfilm roll 20; Inst. 15179, 10 October 1900, $10,000, microfilm roll 20.

3. England, *AFKS Extraordinary Resolution,* 13 June 1901, rec. 11.

4. *B.C. Review* (London), 11 October 1902, p. 184.

5. Yukon, Mining Recorder, *Bonanza Creek 40 A/D,* vol. 3, p. 420 f. Inst. 15441, 24 October 1900.

6. *Klondike Semi-Weekly Nugget,* 10 January 1901, p. 3, col. a; p. 2, col. a.

7. *Yukon Sun and Klondike Pioneer,* 23 February 1901.

8. For example, ibid., 5 February 1901; 9 March 1901.

9. Ibid., 23 February 1901. See also *Dawson Daily News,* 28 January 1901, p. 4, col. f.

10. *Yukon Sun and Klondike Pioneer,* 30 March 1901.

11. *Weekly News (Dawson),* 10 May 1901.

12. *Klondike Semi-Weekly Nugget,* 4 April 1901, p. 7, col. e. These depths for the gold layers are at variance with those reported later in the *Dawson Daily News,* 25 November 1902.

13. *Dawson Daily News,* 30 March 1901.

14. *Klondike Semi-Weekly Nugget,* 1 June 1901, p. 5, col. f.

15. *Klondike Nugget,* 5 June 1901.

16. *Yukon Sun,* 9 March 1901.

17. A. E. C. McDonald, Coroner, with six jurors (*Klondike Semi-Weekly Nugget,* 14 March 1901, p. 4, col. b). Strangely enough, inspection of the underground tunnels and of the ubiquitous steam boilers was not one of the duties of the government-appointed mining inspectors. The *Nugget* editor urged the authorities to require routine examinations by the mining officials.

18. *Yukon Sun,* 16 March 1901; 6 April 1901.

19. Ibid., 6 April 1901; 13 April 1901.

20. Ibid., 11 May 1901.

21. Dawson, *Mining Recorder Records,* Lower half No. 12 Gold Run, Inst. 12492, 7 June 1900. New Records, p. 24, microfilm roll 21, Sect. 2. Ibid., Upper half No. 12 Gold Run, Inst. 17145, 11 March 1901; *Klondike Semi-Weekly Nugget,* 24 March 1901, p. 8, col. c.

22. See for example the description of work on Gold Run Creek in *Dawson Daily News Golden Cleanup Edition,* 1902, 56–57.

23. Johns, "Early Yukon," 141, 247–248. Here the last name is spelled Shute.

24. *Klondike Nugget,* 8 August 1898, p. 3, cols. a–c.

25. For example, ibid., 31 December 1898, p. 3, col. b.

26. *Klondike Nugget,* 29 November 1899.

27. *Klondike Semi-Weekly Nugget,* 26 June 1901, p. 1, col. d.

28. Betty Mulrooney to Johnston, 31 March 1977.

29. Dawson, *Registered Documents,* Bill of Sale, Inst. 21245, 31 July 1901, $1.00, microfilm roll 25; Declaration, Inst. 21245, 31 July 1901.

30. Yukon, *Dawson Building Catalogue,* vol. 3, Block HA, Lot 11, Area 3, 5 August 1901.

31. *Klondike Semi-Weekly Nugget,* 24 July 1901, p. 5, col. d.

32. Ibid., 26 October 1901, p. 1, col. a; p. 3, col. a; p. 5, col. a; p. 5, col. a.

33. Yukon, Mining Recorder, *Royalties, Eldorado 3A,* vol. 200, p. 97.

34. Dawson, *Registered Documents.* Bill of Sale, Inst. 21906, 23 August 1901, for $1.00; Bill of Sale, Inst. 21950, 24 August 1901; Agreement of Sale, Inst. 21954, 24 August 1901, microfilm roll 25; Yukon, *Dawson Building Catalogue,* vol. 3, Block HA, Lot 11, Area 3, 8 October 1901.

35. *Klondike Semi-Weekly Nugget,* 20 July 1901, p. 5, col. c.

36. Green, *The Gold Hustlers.*

37. NW 39:1–2(210–11). It is not clear which claim Belinda is referring to here. According to Mining Recorder records, she did not own 47 B/D Bonanza. She did have a part interest in 53 B/D, bought September 20, 1897 (Yukon, Mining Recorder, *Bonanza Creek,* vol. 1, pp. 17–18, Inst. 619). This claim had originally been numbered 57 B/D when it was located in August of 1896. However, Belinda sold her interest in 53 B/D to William White for $1.00 just before she married Carbonneau (Yukon, Mining Recorder, *Bonanza Creek,* vol. 2, p. 124, Inst. 17595–16174, 8 September 1900). We found no record of Treadgold ever owning this claim. Neither did Belinda ever have a recorded interest in some of the other claims on Bonanza

that Treadgold owned in 1901, namely 34 B/D, 36 B/D, 86 B/D, 3 A/D, or 5 A/D. However, by 1903 he owned key claims covering over two miles of Bonanza (Green, *Gold Hustlers,* 27, 68), and Belinda may have held unrecorded interests in many of these.

38. *Klondike Semi-Weekly Nugget,* 31 August 1901, p. 3, col. d.

39. *Daily Klondike Nugget,* 16 April 1902, p. 1, col. c.

40. *Klondike Semi-Weekly Nugget,* 28 August 1901, p. 7, col. c.

41. Ibid., 16 November 1901, p. 4, col. c. Letourneau's first name is erroneously given as Edward here.

42. Dawson, *Registered Documents,* Lay Agreement, Instr. 23392, 10 September 1901 (7 October 1901), microfilm roll 25; Mortgage, Instr. 23393, 28 September 1901, microfilm roll 26; *Daily Klondike Nugget,* 14 June 1902, p. 6, col. a.

43. *Klondike Semi-Weekly Nugget,* 7 December 1901, p. 4, col. d.

44. *Dawson Daily News,* 2 October 1901.

45. It may also be the same McLennan whom Charles faced in court in the spring.

46. *Klondike Semi-Weekly Nugget,* 30 November 1901, p. 1, col. a; 27 November 1901, p. 1, col. a.

47. *Daily Klondike Nugget,* 12 January 1903, p. 4, col. f.

48. The last date we have for them in town is Charles's signature on a document dated 7 October (Dawson, *Registered Documents,* Lay Agreement, Instr. 23392, 10 September 1901 [7 October 1901], microfilm roll 25).

49. *Daily Klondike Nugget,* 9 April 1902.

50. This address is given for Charles on a document dated 31 December 1902 (Dawson, *Registered Documents,* Bill of Sale, Inst. 33334, 33335, microfilm roll 35). Nearly all the information about the residence in Paris comes from Jim Mulrooney, Belinda's younger brother (Betty Mulrooney to Charles Johnston, 31 March 1977).

51. This is apparently Gabrielle-Charlotte Réjane, whose specialty was light comedy. She performed on stage and in movies and eventually owned her own theaters (Hartnoll, *Oxford Companion to the Theatre,* 793).

52. Some (e.g., Dill, *Long Day,* 101; Berton, *Klondike Fever,* 425) have reported the harness of the rig was profusely ornamented with gold, and that when the carriage stopped, an Egyptian footman leapt to the ground to unroll a red, velvet carpet. However, Belinda said (Johnston Collection), "The scene . . . is false and ridiculous. That stunt was pulled by the daughter of Leopold, the King of Belgium."

53. Johnston to DeArmond, 24 January 1989.

54. Betty Mulrooney, interview by Mayer.

55. *Daily Klondike Nugget,* 9 April 1902, p. 6, col. c.

Chapter 20. Mining Gold Run

1. For example, they already had one agreement with Louis Spitzel on December 12, 1901, concerning sale of the properties, but it was not exercised (Dawson, *Registered Documents,* Inst. 26605, 12 December 1901, microfilm reel 29).

2. Dawson, *Mining Recorder Records,* Gold Run 12A, 29–30, Inst. 13351, 18 June 1900, $100,000; refinanced with Inst. 16092, 23 February 1901; Inst. 26320, 1 April 1902, $536,692.47, microfilm Roll 21, Sect. 2, New Records.

3. *Daily Klondike Nugget,* 20 June 1902, p. 2, col. c; 30 January 1903.

4. *B.C. Review* (London), 11 October 1902, p. 184.

5. *Daily Klondike Nugget,* 14 June 1902, p. 6, col. b.

6. Dawson, *Registered Documents,* Inst. 23393, 28 September 1901, microfilm roll 26.

7. *Daily Klondike Nugget,* 14 June 1902, p. 6, col. a; 19 June 1902, p. 5, col. b.

8. Ibid., 23 June 1902; 14 June 1902, p. 6, col. a. On their behalf, Wilfred Thibault, book-keeper for the claim, testified that the laymen had been working steadily, and that the last two cleanups had netted 296 ounces. An additional 197 ounces had been extracted since the arrival of the receiver, Baptiste. At approximately $17.60 per ounce (*Dawson Record,* 29 February 1904), the total of 493 ounces would have yielded $8,677. By the lay agreement, royalty would be paid out of this amount and then half of the remaining gross output would automatically go to the Carbonneaus, the other half to the laymen from which they would pay expenses and the mortgage. Therefore, it is not obvious how the debt to the Carbonneaus was reduced to $13,700, as the defendants contended.

9. *Dawson Record,* 18 September 1903; Dawson, *Registered Documents,* Inst. 23392, 10 September 1901, microfilm roll 26.

10. *Daily Klondike Nugget,* 14 June 1902, p. 6, col. b.

11. *Dawson Daily News,* 18 June 1902.

12. This was apparently done under some sort of trust agreement, for Chute and Wills still had a say in how the property was to be further disposed. On the same day the Chute and Wills partnership's mortgages to the bank were marked paid; therefore, their Gold Run property was by then no longer encumbered.

13. Dawson, *Registered Documents,* Inst. #27123, 19 May 1902, microfilm roll 30. The bank is represented in this and related transactions by its officers, D. A. Cameron, P. C. Stevenson and/or H. T. Wills, the latter being the brother of Dr. A. E. Wills; Insts. 27120, 27121, 27122, 19 May 1902; Inst. 28173, 23 June 1902, microfilm roll 31. The upper half of No. 12 Gold Run was also cleared of a mortgage that had been executed by its former owners, before Belinda had bought it (ibid., Inst. 28187, 21 June 1902), thereby unencumbering it; Inst. 30591, 23 June 1902; *Dawson Daily News,* 10 July 1903.

14. *Daily Klondike Nugget,* 24 June 1902.

15. Dawson, *Registered Documents,* Inst. 33332, 24 June 1902, microfilm roll 35.

16. *Dawson Daily News Golden Cleanup Edition,* 1902, p. 54, indicates that the claim usually was regarded as Belinda's.

17. A regular feature of the *Dawson Daily News* was a list of guests at several of the hotels in the city.

18. Notarized transcripts of telegrams dated 5, 14, 21 August; 8, 22, 27 September; and 10 October 1902, sent to Dr. A. E. Wills by Canadian Bank of Commerce, Dawson (Carbonneau Collection, Yakima).

19. *Daily Klondike Nugget,* 17 June 1902, p. 1, col. h; 18 June 1902, p. 1, col. f; p. 2, col. a.

20. Technically, Gold Run Creek was a tributary of Indian River, not the Klondike.

21. *Dawson Daily News,* 26 September 1902; 22 October 1902. According to Canadian Bank of Commerce records, Chief Wills had been relieved of active duties as manager so he could be appointed as local director and supervisor of the business (Cate to Mayer, 25 November 1996).

22. Yukon, *Court Records,* vol. 1, File 277–02, 20 August 1902.

23. England, *GR(K)MC Application for Company Limited by Shares,* 1 October 1902, rec. 1.

24. Although the British pound sterling was valued at $4.876 U.S. on average in 1902 (Mitchell, *British Historical Statistics,* Table 22, 702), contemporary documents and newspa-

pers used a value of $5.00; therefore, to avoid further confusion in an already complex story, we adopted this convention. The $2 million would buy consumer goods worth about $37.8 million in 1998 in the United States (McCusker, "How Much Is That?" Table A-2, 329–332; *Consumer Price Index [1982–84]*).

25. England, *GR(K)MC Statement of Nominal Capital*, 1 October 1902, rec. 3.

26. Ibid., *Application for Company Limited by Shares*, 1 October 1902, rec. 1.

27. Ibid., *Return of Allotments*, 4 October 1902, rec. 9.

28. Ibid., *Register of Directors and Managers*, 4 October 1902, rec. 7.

29. *La Patrie* (Montreal), 10 February 1905, p. 1, col. f.

30. England, *GR(K)MC Articles of Association*, 1 October 1902, rec. 5.

31. Ibid., *Agreement for Sale and Purchase*, 4 October 1902, rec. 8. The exact number of shares going to the Canadian Bank of Commerce and used to raise cash may have varied somewhat from that stated. There are minor discrepancies in the various incorporation documents.

32. Ibid., *Summary of Capital and Shares*, 31 December 1903, rec. 14. One of these Bearer Warrants in the Waugaman Collection is dated 28 November 1902.

33. Ibid., *Report*, 12 December 1902, rec. 10; *Agreement*, 22 December 1902, rec. 13.

34. Ibid., *Articles of Association*, 1 October 1902, p. 25, rec. 5.

35. Dawson, *Registered Documents*, Mortgage, Inst. 33334, 31 December 1902, microfilm roll 35; *Dawson Daily News*, 10 July 1903, 7. It is interesting that no due date is specified in the mortgage instrument.

36. Dawson, *Registered Documents*, Mortgage Assignment, Inst. 42207, 1 May 1903, microfilm roll 43. We note that even as a ninety-year-old, Belinda remembered that the bank had loaned $700,000 for the company (Mackay, 5).

37. Ibid., Bill of Sale, Inst. 33333, 31 December 1902, microfilm roll 35; Mortgage, Inst. 33334, 31 December 1902; Bill of Sale, Inst. 33335, 31 December 1902; England, *GR(K)MC Return of Allotments*, 31 December 1902, rec. 11; *Form E, Summary of Capital and Shares*, December 31, 1903, rec. 14.

38. On 13 January 1903 (*Dawson Daily News*, 24 August 1905).

39. *Daily Klondike Nugget*, 30 January 1903, p. 1, cols. a–b; 4 March 1903, p. 1, cols. c–e.

40. This and other details of the case are from the *Dawson Daily News*, 10 July 1903, p. 7.

41. Friends would later report that he was offered $80,000 to withdraw his suit (*Yukon World*, 24 June 1904). It also seems that Chute may have been guaranteed isolation from liability for the mortgage, for the next day, 18 March 1903, the Chute and Wills partnership also officially was dissolved (*Daily Klondike Nugget*, 20 March 1903, p. 4, col. f), and when A. E. Wills assigned the mortgage to the Canadian Bank of Commerce, he was the only one assuring payment in case of default by Carbonneau (Dawson, *Registered Documents*, Mortgage Assignment, Inst. 42207, 1 May 1903, microfilm roll 43).

42. *Daily Klondike Nugget*, 4 March 1903, p. 1, cols. c–e.

43. *Dawson Daily News*, 3 July 1903; 10 July 1903.

44. Ibid., 24 August 1905; 9 July 1903; 13 July 1903.

45. Betty Mulrooney to Johnston, 31 March 1977.

46. The last record we find of Carbonneau in the Yukon is a Free Miner's Certificate issued to him on 19 May 1905 (Yukon, *Free Miner's Certificates*, vol. 191, p. 67, #103903). It is not clear whether this was at Dawson or at Gold Run. We do not think Charles filed personally, but rather had the paper work done by someone else.

47. Betty Mulrooney, interview by Mayer.

48. *Yukon Sun (Dawson)*, 22 April 1903, p. 3, col. a.

49. *Dawson Daily News*, 31 August 1912. The name is also spelled Kruger.

50. *Dawson Record*, 28 July 1903.

51. Betty Mulrooney to Johnston, 31 March 1977.

52. For example No. 12 Gold Run (*Dawson Daily News*, 29 July 1903).

53. Yukon, Mining Recorder, *Bonanza Creek, 41 A/D*, vol. 3, 12 September 1903, to Eugene Smith, Inst. 39766; *Original Locators, Dominion Creek*, vol. 33, 8 October 1903, to Henry Renkin, Inst. 35404, filed 15 July 1903.

54. *Daily Klondike Nugget*, 16 December 1902, p. 3, col. a; Yukon Territorial Court, *Records*, vol. 1, File 277–02; *Dawson Daily News*, 15 September 1903.

55. *Dawson Daily News*, 16 October 1903; 21 October 1903.

56. Betty Mulrooney, interview by Mayer.

57. *Seattle Post-Intelligencer*, 3 March 1920; 15 November 1903, p. 16, col. c.

58. Betty Mulrooney, interview by Mayer; Betty Mulrooney to Johnston, 31 March 1977. This account is verified by newspaper stories of the tragic death (*Seattle Post-Intelligencer*, 15 November 1903, p. 16, col. c; *Seattle Times*, 15 November 1903, p. 1, cols. a–c).

59. *Dawson Daily News*, 16 November 1906.

60. *Who Was Who 1897–1915*, 1:574.

61. Betty Mulrooney to Johnston, 31 March 1977.

62. *La Patrie* (Montreal), 10 February 1905, p. 1, col. f.

63. England, *GR(K)MC Form E, Summary of Capital and Shares*, 31 December 1903, rec. 14; *Agreement*, 22 December 1902, rec. 13; *Dawson Daily News*, 10 July 1903, p. 7.

64. *Dawson Daily News*, 12 March 1904.

65. *Yukon World*, 24 June 1904.

66. *Dawson Daily News*, 24 August 1905.

67. Ibid., 8 June 1904; 29 November 1905.

68. Ibid., 27 December 1911, p. 3, cols. a–c.

69. Ibid., 24 August 1905.

70. U.S.A., *Carbonneau v. Carbonneau*, Case 539.

71. Yukon, Mining Recorder, *Bonanza 40 A/D*, vol. 3, p. 420 f., 15 July 1904, Inst. 40239; *Yukon World*, 19 July 1904.

72. *Yukon World*, 24 August 1904. She did not present the papers firing Wills.

73. Pattullo and Ridley to Mrs. C. E. Carbonneau, 15 July 1904 (Carbonneau Collection, Yakima).

74. There is confusion in this article between H. T. "Chief" Wills of the Canadian Bank of Commerce and his brother Dr. A. E. Wills, so it is not clear who is supposed to be speaking here. Since it was A. E. Wills who was acknowledged co-owner and co-manager of Gold Run, we have assumed that it is Dr. Wills who Belinda is saying appointed her. However, given the ill-feeling between A. E. Wills and the Carbonneaus and the fact that Belinda was good friends with H. T. Wills, the quote sounds more like it might have come from H. T. Wills.

75. Mackay, "Saga of Belinda." This article is based not only on Mackay's interview with Belinda while they were both residents at Mount St. Vincent Home in Seattle (Mitchell to Mayer, 19 June 1997), but also on his own experience and personal knowledge of events in Dawson.

76. *Yukon World*, 19 July 1904; copy of lay agreement, courtesy of Jim Robb, Whitehorse.

77. Handwritten note, apparently by Belinda (Yukon Archives).

78. *Yukon World,* 20 July 1904.

79. *Seattle Post-Intelligencer,* 10 January 1909.

80. Pelletier, *New York Times,* 23 January 1898, p. 2, col. b.

81. *Klondike Semi-Weekly Nugget,* 7 June 1900, 5 c; 10 June 1900, p. 1, col. a.

82. *Yukon World,* 7 August 1904.

83. England, *GR(K)MC Register of Change of Directors or Managers,* 17 August 1904, rec. 18; *Return of Allotments,* 4 October 1902, rec. 9; *Form E, Return of Allotments,* 31 December 1903, rec. 14.

84. *Yukon World,* 24 August 1904, 3 b; England, *GR(K)MC Register of Directors or Managers,* 17 August 1904, rec. 18.

85. *Yukon World,* 24 August 1904, p. 3, col. a.

86. *Dawson Daily News,* 24 August 1905.

87. However, Wills also had let a few lays. For example, the *Yukon Sun* (10 May 1903) reported lays on Numbers 16, 17, 18, 22a, and 27.

88. *Yukon World,* 24 August 1904, p. 3, cols. a–d.

89. Ibid.

90. Ibid., p. 2, col. e.

91. Ibid., 8 October 1904.

92. *Dawson Daily News,* 22 September 1904, p. 3, col. e; 1 March 1905, p. 4, col. b; 22 September 1904, p. 3, col. e.

93. *Yukon World,* 15 July 1904. However, original court documents show the judgment came to $2,935.50 (Yukon Territorial Court, *Records,* vol. 1420, File 277–02).

94. *Dawson Daily News,* 29 November 1905; Yukon Territorial Court, *Records,* vol. 1472, File 2.

95. *Yukon World,* 13 October 1904.

96. However, we do find a Free Miner's Certificate issued to her on 11 May 1905 at Dawson. It is possible that someone else filed the paperwork for her. (Yukon, *Free Miner's Certificates,* vol. 191, p. 67, 103805).

97. U.S., *Scouse and Byrnes v. Carbonneau,* Case 409, depositions concerning activities involved in setting up partnership; Depositions of E. O. Finlaison and L. Byrnes.

98. *Dawson Daily News,* 12 October 1904; Dawson, *Mining Recorder Records, Creek Claims, Eldorado 3A,* p. 12, 24 August 1901, Inst. 21954, microfilm roll 8. It is not clear why the Carbonneaus were brought in on the action. It seems likely that when the Carbonneaus agreed to sell their Eldorado 3A claim to Thompson in 1901, they may have taken back a mortgage on the property, which obligation perhaps had been transferred to the bank. Or perhaps they had an unrecorded obligation to the bank associated with the claim. Something like these scenarios is supported by the fact that when the case was finally settled, Thompson got free and unencumbered title to the claim, while the Carbonneaus were foreclosed and debarred (Dawson, *Registered Documents,* Judgment, Inst. 46811, 30 June 1906).

99. *Dawson Daily News,* 15 February 1905, p. 4, col. d.

100. *La Patrie* (Montreal), 10 February 1905, p. 1, col. f, quoting *Le Journal* (Paris), 29 January 1905. Translation courtesy of Virginia Rusinak.

101. Ibid.

102. *Dawson Daily News,* 2 August 1905.

103. Ibid., 27 April 1911.

104. Green, *Gold Hustlers,* 130, 249, 294.

105. Klein, "History of Teck Corporation."

Chapter 21. Starting Over in Fairbanks

1. Sometimes spelled Scowse or Scouth. Mabel also is referred to as Mrs. Z. (Zidania) A. Scouse.

2. U.S.A., *Scouse and Byrnes v. Carbonneau,* Case 409, Complaint, 18 September 1905.

3. Ibid., Deposition L. Byrnes, 1 August 1907, 13. Mabel may have come In prior to 1899.

4. Dawson City Museum, *Pan for Gold* data base, 1997. Neville Armstrong (*Yukon Yesterday,* 87–91) got Thomas's name wrong, but says the brothers owned Eldorado 14, 15, and (for a time) 16, plus a claim on Adams Gulch. William Scouse was the original staker of Eldorado 14 in 1896 (William Douglas Johns in Adney, *Klondike Stampede,* 326). He also was involved in a partnership with C. E. Carbonneau on Eldorado 14 and 15 (*Dawson Daily News Mining Edition,* September 1899, p. 28, col. c). Scowth is listed as an owner on Bonanza 32 A/D in the *Dawson Daily News Golden Cleanup Edition* (1902, p. 29). The Scouse brothers and perhaps Mabel may have held interests in Klondike Consolidated, for in 1901 this company, besides Bonanza 32 A/D, also was identified as the owner of Eldorado 12, 13, 14, and 15 (Allen, *Dawson, Yukon Territory,* 18).

5. U.S.A., *Scouse and Byrnes v. Carbonneau,* Case 409, Deposition L. Byrnes, 1 August 1907, 13, 6. Polk's *Alaska-Yukon Gazetteer* for 1903 also lists miner William Scouse at the Fairview.

6. U.S.A., *Scouse and Byrnes v. Carbonneau,* Case 409, Deposition B. A. Carbonneau, 15 August 1906; Exhibit A; Deposition B. A. Carbonneau, 15 August 1906.

7. Ibid., Deposition L. E. Byrnes, 1 August 1907, 20.

8. This is an error. Mrs. Scouse still owed $650, her share of the machinery cost.

9. U.S.A., *Scouse and Byrnes v. Carbonneau,* Case 409, Exhibit B, extract of letter of 5 December 1904 from B. A. Carbonneau to J. B. Pattullo. The extract has numerous punctuation and spelling errors, partly corrected here. It is not clear whether they were Belinda's or made in transcription.

10. Belinda says in her letter to Pattullo, "I am a very poor writer, and I'll try and make one letter do both." Her sister-in-law, Betty Mulrooney, reported that Belinda would do anything she could to avoid writing a letter (interview by Mayer).

11. U.S.A., *Scouse and Byrnes v. Carbonneau,* Case 409, Deposition L. E. Byrnes, 1 August 1907, 11.

12. Ibid., Deposition B. A. Carbonneau, 15 August 1906.

13. See for example Beebe, *True Life Story.*

14. U.S.A., *Scouse and Byrnes v. Carbonneau,* Case 409, Deposition B. A. Carbonneau, 20 April 1907.

15. This is Fred Kammueler (referred to variously as Kamilla, Kamuller, Kammueller, or Camello). Belinda originally leased the Fairview Hotel to him in 1899, then to Julian Blaker in 1900. But according to Mabel Scouse, Kammueler was (again?) renting it in 1904, and documents showed he was a witness to the signing of the partnership agreement (U.S.A., *Scouse and Byrnes v. Carbonneau,* Case 409, Deposition Mrs. Z. A. Scouse, 8 September 1906; Complaint, 18 September 1905).

16. Ibid., Exhibit B, Carbonneau to Pattullo, 5 December 1904.

17. Ibid., Deposition B. A. Carbonneau, 15 August 1906.

18. Ibid., Plaintiff's exhibits, east 1/2 of Lot 2 Block 2 east, 3rd Avenue, 24 October 1904 and west 20 feet of the same lot, 17 April 1905; Answer of B. A. Carbonneau to Amended Complaint, 3 September 1906.

19. *Dawson Daily News,* 3 February 1905, p. 4, col. f; 7 March 1905, p. 2, col. f.

20. Phillips, *Alaska-Yukon Place Names*, 46; Naske and Rowinski, *Fairbanks: A Pictorial History*, 23.

21. *Fairbanks Telephone Directory*, 1906; *Tanana Directory*, 1907, 152.

22. See for example Cole, *Crooked Past*, 81. Guest (*Socioeconomic History*, 66) says that the Klondike actually experienced a recession in 1904, in large part due to the exodus to the Tanana valley.

23. Sometimes spelled Kelley.

24. U.S., *Scouse and Byrnes v. Carbonneau*, Case 409, Plaintiff's exhibits, Quitclaim to Carbonneau, Robinson and Kelley, 1 July 1905, recorded 25 September 1905.

25. Fairbanks, *Miscellaneous Documents*, vol. 1, 538, Dissolution of Partnership, 7 August 1905.

26. U.S., *Scouse and Byrnes v. Carbonneau*, Case 409, Defendant's exhibit A, Tozier to Carbonneau, 2 September 1906; Deposition Z. A. Scouse, 8 September 1906.

27. *Alaska-Yukon Magazine* 7 no. 4 (January, 1909): 315.

28. U.S., *Scouse and Byrnes v. Carbonneau*, Case 409, Deposition Z. A. Scouse, 8 September 1906.

29. Ibid., Supplemental Deposition, B. A. Carbonneau, September, 1906.

30. Ibid., Report of John F. Dillon, based on testimony 12–30 December 1907.

31. Ibid., Affidavit, John L. McGinn (Scouse's attorney), 20 April 1907.

32. Ibid., Deposition B. A. Carbonneau, 15 August 1906; Report of John F. Dillon; Affidavit, John L. McGinn (Scouse's attorney), 20 April 1907.

33. Vitzthum to Mayer, 27 January 1993. Consistent with this conjecture is the fact that, according to a family member, Belinda had at one time asked Alice for power of attorney (which Alice had refused). Furthermore, the deeds to and from A. Gowran for this property clearly refer to "her," that is, a female. While a masculine pronoun might legally serve for both males and females (for example, Belinda is referred to as "he" in her deed to A. Gowran), the feminine pronoun was used only for females. Fairbanks, *Deeds*, Vol. 6, 380, Carbonneau to Gowran, No. 15298, dated 15 September 1905. Filed for record 21 July 1906; Gowran to Mary Mulrooney, No. 16410, dated 15 February 1906. Filed for record 13 October 1906.

34. Fairbanks, *Deeds*, Vol. 7, p. 292, Gowran to Mary Mulrooney, No. 16410, dated 15 February 1906. Filed for record 13 October 1906.

35. Yakima, *Scouse and Byrnes v. AYIC*, Case 9439, Deposition of James Kelly, 19 August 1914.

36. *Dawson Daily News*, 2 May 1913. This article puts the timing as the fall of 1904, but Belinda went directly to Fairbanks from Dawson that fall. She was in New York in the spring of 1904 before returning to the Klondike to manage her mining interests.

37. Ibid. The fall of 1905 was the first opportunity Belinda would have had to check on her deposits. According to this article, the suits were not brought until 1911 (see also *New York Times*, 22 December 1914, p. 8), and so the theft could have been discovered at a later date than 1905.

38. Clark to Curwood, 15 December 1922.

39. Margaret was born in April of 1886. She signs herself Meggie Ann in Gauslin to Dougher, 5 December 1965. Courtesy of Rose Dougher Vitzthum.

40. Nellie was born in March of 1884 (U.S. Census, 1900, Archbald, Pennsylvania, Enum. District 2, 4 June 1900, Vol. 1, Sheet 1B, Line 68).

41. Betty Mulrooney to Johnston.

42. Yakima, *Scouse and Byrnes v. AYIC*, Case 9439, Opinion of the Court, Thomas E. Grady, Judge, (29 July 1916); U.S.A., *Scouse and Byrnes v. Carbonneau*, Case 409, Report of John F. Dillon, based on testimony 12–30 December 1907.

43. They arrived in Valdez on the *Oregon*, on Friday, 9 March, and left for Fairbanks the following week (*Valdez News*, 17 March 1906). That it was Margaret and Nell with Belinda is confirmed by an article in the *Fairbanks Daily Times* (10 January 1907), as well as by testimony from Nell several years later (Yakima, *Scouse and Byrnes v. AYIC*, Case 9439, Deposition of Mrs. W. F. Thompson, 18 March 1916).

44. Coming in at about the same time but by bicycle was attorney John A. Clark, who soon would represent Belinda in the legal action with Scouse and Byrnes. See his essay in Heller's *Sourdough Sagas* (163–93) for an entertaining and probably authentic account of trail experiences.

Chapter 22. The Dome City Bank: Business and Funny Business

1. According to L. D. Kitchener (*Flag over the North*, 297), Dome was founded sometime in 1905. However, the creek was mined as early as 1904.

2. *Fairbanks Sunday Times*, 10 November 1907, p. 6.

3. *Fairbanks Daily Times*, 7 November 1907.

4. Alaska, Secretary of State, *Affidavit*, Carbonneau and Mulrooney, 31 July 1907; *Domestic Corporations Record Book*, 52, p. 560, Incorporation papers, 17 August 1906, filed 27 September 1906.

5. *Fairbanks Daily News-Miner*, 5 May 1937, p. 4; *Yukon Sun*, 24 November 1903, p. 3, col. a.

6. James F. McElroy was an attorney and the brother of Mary McElroy (*Seattle Times*, 24 August 1919), to whom H. T. "Chief" Wills had been wed in the fall of 1903, when Belinda had been a member of the Seattle wedding party. Another brother, Matt J. McElroy, also had a Dawson connection. He rushed there in 1897 and stayed for a year (*Seattle Post-Intelligencer*, 3 March 1920). Belinda could have known James McElroy through either of these relations.

7. Johnston to DeArmond, 24 January 1989.

8. Betty Mulrooney, interview by Mayer.

9. Clark to Curwood, 15 December 1922. Few of the bank's financial records have been found. A bank ledger is said still to exist, but efforts to locate it have been unsuccessful.

10. The court actions were always in both names, with Mabel acting under a power of attorney for Bessy.

11. U.S., *Scouse and Byrnes v. Carbonneau*, Case 409, Report of John F. Dillon.

12. Ibid. Also, Lis Pendens, 4 April 1906. In later action they also would sue for assets in the Dome City Bank (Yakima, *Scouse and Byrnes v. AYIC* Case 9439, Second Amended Bill in Equity, 16 December 1915).

13. U.S., *Scouse and Byrnes v. Carbonneau*, Case 409, Amended Complaint, July, 1906; Answer of B. A. Carbonneau to Complaint, 3 September 1906; Defendant's Exhibit A, Filed 20 April 1907; Tozier to Carbonneau, 2 September 1906. See e.g. Attorney John A. Clark's first-person account of the fire and its aftermath in Heller (*Sourdough Sagas*, 211–215).

14. U.S., *Scouse and Byrnes v. Carbonneau*, Case 409, Affidavit, John L. McGinn (Scouse's attorney), 20 April 1907.

15. *Fairbanks Daily Times*, 16 June 1906. At twelve troy ounces to the pound, the 3,000

ounces would be worth about $60,000 at that time; equivalent to about $1,083,000 in 1998 consumer commodities (McCusker, "How Much Is That?" Table A-2, 329–332; *Consumer Price Index [1982–1984]*).

16. However, Belinda would also testify in the Scouse and Byrnes case that she was only a figurehead, that the bank interests were really her family's.

17. This incident may have occurred as early as the spring of 1905, for at that time a strike near Mt. McKinley led to a stampede from Fairbanks (*Dawson Daily News,* 20 February 1905, p. 4, col. f), and Belinda bought interests in claims on Ophir Creek in the McKinley District on 10 February 1905 (U.S.A., *Scouse and Byrnes v. Carbonneau,* Case 409, Affidavit, Exhibits, 18 January 1908, List of Claim Interests). However, in 1906 Belinda reported she went with Bettles to the Kantishna, a tributary of the Tanana River that drains the north side of Mt. McKinley, in the fall of 1905 (ibid., Deposition of B. A. Carbonneau, 15 August 1906, p. 28).

18. Gordon C. Bettles entered the Yukon basin in 1886, where he prospected, mined, traded, and helped publish the first newspaper in 1894 (Wickersham, *Old Yukon,* 145–152). Belinda knew him and his wife from Dawson.

19. Sophia Kokrine (Kokerine) Bettles was the daughter of an Eskimo woman and Gregory Kokrine, who came to Alaska from Russia but may have been from somewhere else originally (Waugaman to Mayer, 15 July 1998). Sophia married Gordon Bettles on 2 August 1893, at St. Michael, Alaska (Wickersham, *Old Yukon,* 148–149).

20. George Noble also was an early Dawsonite. See chapter 9.

21. Cronister was an early, pre-Klondike prospector in the Yukon basin (Gates, *Gold at Fortymile,* 156).

22. The thousand miles is an exaggeration. But the return trip was undoubtedly a long and difficult one. The summit of Denali (Mt. McKinley) is about 155 air miles from Fairbanks.

23. Since Belinda left for the Outside in September 1905, but apparently did not go Out again until the fall of 1908, this statement would favor a date early in 1905 for the prospecting trip.

24. Ricks, *Directory of Alaska Postmasters;* Dickerson, *120 Years of Alaska Postmasters.*

25. *Fairbanks Sunday Times,* 10 November 1907, p. 6. In 1908 Thomas appointed Margaret as administrator of his estate and willed her $5,000 and his horse (Thomas Collection, Alaska State Library). He had come from Spokane, Washington, first to Atlin, B.C., then to Dawson. He moved to the Fairbanks area in 1905, after which he was known as "Judge" Thomas.

26. *La Patrie* (Montreal), 10 February 1905, p. 1, col. f.

27. *Dawson Daily News,* 16 November 1906; Betty Mulrooney to Johnston, 31 March 1977.

28. *Dawson Daily News,* 27 December 1911, p. 3, cols. a–c.

29. See, for example, Radin, "Common Law of the Family," 213.

30. See, for example, Snell, "'The White Life for Two,'" 111–28.

31. England, *Divorce and Matrimonial Causes.*

32. When the Yukon became a territory in 1898 it received the English Matrimonial Causes Act of 1857. Accordingly, the Territorial Court potentially could have had jurisdiction over divorce; however, it apparently did not assume this power (although it could grant alimony [*Consolidated Ordinances, Yukon, 1902,* chap. 27; N.W.T., c. 29, s.1]). We found no confirmed records of divorce in the Territorial Court Records at the Yukon Archives before the 1940s. One case, Malander v. Malander (vol. 1432, file 13, no. 89) is a potential divorce. The Malanders had domestic disputes serious enough to be heard in police court (*Daily Klondike*

Nugget, 18 April 1902, p. 6, col. a). However, the file in the Territorial Court records contained only a note, "Received all the papers herein. Dated this 6th January 1903." No papers were included, so we could not determine what action was being taken nor what was the outcome of this case. A more thorough study of family law in the early history of the Yukon would be useful.

33. For more information on the institution of marriage in nineteenth-century Canada, see Backhouse, "'Pure Patriarchy.'"

34. U.S.A., *B. A. Carbonneau vs. C. E. Carbonneau,* Case 539, about 30 July 1906.

35. Johnston to DeArmond, 24 January 1989.

36. *Dawson Daily News,* 27 December 1911, p. 3, col. a.

37. Christine Johnston to Mayer, 11 November 1997.

38. *Dawson Daily News,* 27 December 1911, p. 3, col. a; 16 November 1906.

39. *Yukon World,* 8 February 1907, p. 4, col. a.

40. *Fairbanks Daily Times,* 10 January 1907, p. 4.

41. Jesse Noble arrived in Dawson from Whitehorse on the steamer *Dawson* on June 8. He left for Fairbanks on the *Cudahay* on 12 June. Nell, Agnes, and Jim arrived in Dawson on the *Dawson* on 24 June (*Dawson Daily News,* 24 June 1907; Betty Mulrooney to Johnston, 31 March 1977).

42. Alaska, Secretary of State, *Affidavit,* Carbonneau and Mulrooney, 31 July 1907.

43. The weight of the nugget and the date of its deposit are given in *Fairbanks News,* 11 February 1910.

44. *Seattle Post-Intelligencer,* 7 December 1908; Cole, *Crooked Past,* 114–116.

45. *Fairbanks Daily Times,* 16, 17, 19 and 24 July 1907. This claim is No. 3 A/D, RL, first tier, the claim in which Belinda had been interested.

46. *Fairbanks News,* 12, 14, and 17 January 1909.

47. Clark to Curwood, 15 December 1922.

48. U.S.A., Case 895.

49. U.S.A., Case 894.

50. U.S.A., *Scouse and Byrnes v. Carbonneau,* Case 409, Report of John F. Dillon.

51. *Fairbanks Daily Times,* 30 November 1907, 3.

52. U.S.A., *Scouse and Byrnes v. Carbonneau,* Case 409, Subpoenas.

53. *Yukon World,* 14 December 1907, p. 1, cols. c–e.

54. Carter and Perry, *Dawson Building Catalogue.* HA, Lots 10 and 11, Area 3. 27 July 1904.

55. *Yukon World,* 14 December 1907, p. 1, cols. c–e.

56. Alexander to Mayer, 21 April 1998.

57. Yakima, *Scouse and Byrnes v. AYIC,* Case 9439, Deposition of B. A. Carbonneau, 3 December 1915.

58. Carter and Perry, *Dawson Building Catalogue.* HA, Lots 10 and 11, Area 3. Sold to Joseph I. Seabrook September 28, 1908.

59. *Fairbanks Daily Times,* 16 May 1908.

60. U.S.A., *Scouse and Byrnes v. Carbonneau,* Case 409, Decree, 19 May 1908.

61. Ibid., Writ of Execution, 29 May 1908.

62. Ibid., Marshall's Return.

63. *Tanana Valley Directory 1907; Alaska Gazetteer and Directory, 1909–10.*

64. *Alaska Gazetteer and Directory, 1911–12.* The U.S. Census at Dome City, taken January, 1911, listed 313 inhabitants, most of whom where mining the nearby ground rather than living in town.

65. *Fairbanks News-Miner,* 29 January 1911, republished in *Dawson Daily News,* 22 February 1911, p. 4.

66. *Alaska Gazetteer and Directory, 1915–16.*

Chapter 23. Retrenching in Yakima, Washington

1. *Yakima Daily Republic,* 9 January 1909.

2. This and the following quotes in this paragraph are an imaginary conversation, based upon information from the cited sources and from Yakima informants.

3. Yakima, *Scouse and Byrnes v. AYIC,* Case 9439, Deposition of Louis M. Lang, 25 April 1916, 5.

4. *Yakima Daily Republic,* 9 January 1909.

5. *Yakima Morning Herald,* 26 January 1909.

6. There are also reports that pear trees were planted in the orchard.

7. Yakima, *Deeds,* Vol. 74, p. 616, Richardson and Richardson to Margaret Mulrooney and Henry Cook, 19 December 1908.

8. *Alaska-Yukon Magazine* 7, no. 4 (January 1909): 234, 299; Cole, *Crooked Past,* 116.

9. Today (1998) that home is at 620 South 48th Avenue, at the corner of Nob Hill Boulevard, with most of the original surrounding orchard land now subdivided into home lots.

10. *Yakima Daily Republic,* 20 February 1909; Yakima, *Scouse and Byrnes v. AYIC,* Case 9439, Deposition of Louis M. Lang, 25 April 1916, 12.

11. Kroll, interview by Mayer. This information was attributed to James Mulrooney, Belinda's brother.

12. *Yakima Daily Republic,* 20 February 1909. An article appearing about the same time in Fairbanks estimated the cost as $7,000 (*Fairbanks Times,* 22 February 1909). The $6,000 of 1909 would purchase consumer goods worth about $107,000 in 1998 (McCusker, "How Much Is That?" Table A-2, 329–332; *Consumer Price Index [1982–1984]*).

13. Yakima, *Scouse and Byrnes v. AYIC,* Case 9439, Deposition of Martin Andresen, 17 December 1914, 7.

14. Kroll, interview by Mayer; Yakima, *Scouse and Byrnes v. AYIC,* Case 9439, Interrogatories to be answered by Belinda A. Carbonneau, 5–6.

15. Much of the information about the furnishings of the house comes from the Hawkins Collection, while information about the house itself was gathered on a visit there by Mayer in 1979. At that time the castle was owned by Sarah and Dale Kroll, who kindly gave a tour and shared the information they had prepared for nominating the castle for the National Registry of Historic Places. See U.S.A., *Nomination Form, Carbonneau Castle.*

16. Wilfong and Lambert, interview by Mayer.

17. Kroll, interview by Mayer, quoting Forest Moore.

18. Wilfong and Lambert, interview by Mayer.

19. *Yakima Daily Republic,* 24 February 1909. On 30 May 1908, Agnes married Jay Johnston, a gold miner from Vault, Alaska. Vault Creek was the next creek to the west of Dome Creek. See map, fig. 21.1. Baby Charles was born 6 March 1909.

20. Roosevelt's hand-picked successor, William Howard Taft, would be inaugurated on March 4, 1909.

21. *Seattle Post-Intelligencer,* quoted in *Yakima Daily Republic,* 23 February 1909.

22. *Yakima Daily Republic,* 25 February 1909, p. 1.

23. Yakima, *Scouse and Byrnes v. AYIC*, Case 9439, Deposition of Louis M. Lang, 25 April 1916, 4–5.

24. *Yakima Daily Republic*, 11 August 1909.

25. Yukon, Mining Recorder, *Bonanza 40 A/D*, vol. 3, p. 420 f., 15 July 1904, Inst. 40239.

26. Ibid., Writ of Execution, 27 September 1907, Instr. 54222; transfer for $1.00, 26 June 1907, Instr. 53647.

27. Dawson, *Registered Documents*, Bill of Sale, Instr. 53647, 26 June 1907; notarized 2 August 1907; recorded 16 August 1907, microfilm roll 51.

28. Yukon, Mining Recorder, *Bonanza 40 A/D*, vol. 3, Assignment of Mortgage, 23 October 1907, (registered 1 September 1909), Instr. 58080.

29. Ibid., 4 February 1908, Instr. 56825; 5 February 1908 (The sequence suggests that Black carried out the transactions under authorization from Pattullo.); 20 July 1909, (registered 1 September 1909) Instr. 54222.

30. Ibid., 10 August 1909, (registered 1 September 1909), referring to Instr. 40239, 58080; 10 August 1909; Mulrooney to Barrette, registered 1 September 1909.

31. Yakima, *Scouse and Byrnes v. AYIC*, Case 9439, Deposition of H. H. Scales, 22 May 1916, 5.

32. Yakima, *Margaret Mulrooney v. Cook*, Case 5479, 4 September 1909; 4 January 1910.

33. Yakima, *Mortgages*, vol. 51, 298, 19 December 1908; vol. 64, 283, Satisfaction of Mortgage, 14 January 1910.

34. Yakima, *Deeds*, vol. 94, 567, 28 October 1909; vol. 102, 180, 15 February 1910; 181, 18 March 1910.

35. *Pennsylvania Statute Law 1920*. St. Paul, Minn.: West, 1921, §14570 (1893, June 8; P.L. 344, §2)

36. *Fairbanks News-Miner*, 20 August 1909. The raising of chickens is confirmed by Belinda's niece, Nell's daughter, Marion Thompson Thorgaard (Thorgaard to Vitzthum, 4 May 1982). It was possibly an interim enterprise until the fruit trees were mature enough to bear crops.

37. *Yakima Daily Republic*, 29 September 1909.

38. Kroll, interview by Mayer. This information was attributed to Vernie Eastman, Yakima. However, even in detailed newspaper accounts of Taft's visit, we found no evidence that he actually stopped at Belinda's in 1909, or that he would have had the time to do so.

39. Wilfong and Lambert, interview by Mayer.

40. Kroll, interview M. J. Mayer.

41. Dawson, *Death Records, Green's Mortuary*, 6 January 1909.

42. *Dawson Daily News*, 9 January 1909, p. 1, cols. b–g; p. 4, cols. f–h.

43. According to Pierre Berton, *Klondike Fever*, 420.

44. *Seattle Post-Intelligencer*, 12 October 1910, 1 d–f.

45. U.S. Census, 1910, Yakima County, Washington, 31 May 1910, Nob Hill Precinct, Enumeration District 283, Sheet 16A.

46. He was listed in Fairbanks newspapers as among the celebrants at surprise parties given for August Ruser and Judge George Thomas.

47. *Juneau Daily Record*, 9 July 1910. It is not clear whether Jesse was actually in court at the trial, however. See also, *Juneau Daily Alaska Dispatch*, 12 July 1910.

48. U.S. Census, 1910, Archbald, Lackawana County, Pennsylvania, 22 April 1910, Enumeration District 3, Sheet 15B.

49. In 1912 (Betty Mulrooney to Johnston, 31 March 1977).

50. Yakima, *Scouse and Byrnes v. AYIC*, Case 9439, Deposition of Martin Andresen, 17 December 1914, 14, 20.

51. Yakima, *Deeds,* vol. 119, 62, Agreement, 20 March 1911; vol. 124, 166, Easement, 13 February 1912.

52. Yakima, *Scouse and Byrnes v. AYIC,* Case 9439, Deposition of Martin Andresen, 17 December 1914, 5, 6.

53. *Fairbanks News-Miner,* 1 November 1911.

54. *Yakima Daily Republic,* 15 September 1910, p. 1, col. b.

55. Washington, *Articles of Incorporation, AYIC,* filed 6 September 1910, n. 28587.

56. For example *Yakima Daily Republic,* 7 December 1909; 15 September 1910, p. 1, col. b; Hall, interview by Mayer; Yakima, *Deeds,* vol. 106, 446, Deed, 1 September 1910.

57. *Fairbanks Times,* 28 January 1911.

58. See note 47 above and accompanying text for another version of the terms of the settlement.

59. *Dawson Daily News,* 22 February 1911, p. 4, quoting Belinda in the *Seattle Times.*

60. *Dawson Daily News,* 20 February 1911, p. 2, col. c, from a story in the *Seattle Times.*

61. Quoted in *Dawson Daily News,* 22 February 1911, p. 4.

62. Wickersham, *Diary,* 14 March 1911, 23 March 1911. Also supporting Belinda and Margaret in Seattle were "Judge" George Thomas of Fairbanks, who knew well all the personalities involved, and James F. McElroy, Seattle attorney and former trustee for the Dome City Bank at its founding. Newspaper stories implying that Wickersham paid the fine personally (e.g., *Dawson Daily News,* 28 March 1911, p. 4, col. a) are unfounded.

63. Yakima, *Scouse and Byrnes v. Carbonneau,* Case 6410, 19 January 1911.

64. There is a suggestion in coverage of Belinda's whipping of the bank clerk Ruser that many Alaskans considered all of the court actions against Belinda at this time as a form of persecution, and that Jesse Noble was behind all of them (*Dawson Daily News,* 20 February 1911, p. 2, col. c, from a story in the *Seattle Times*).

65. Yakima, *Scouse and Byrnes v. Carbonneau,* Case 6410, 28 February 1911. Recorded 1 March 1911.

66. Yakima, *Scouse and Byrnes v. AYIC,* Case 9439, 19 August 1914.

67. This is an overestimate of Belinda's assets in 1914. It may be an accurate estimate of her worth at the time of her marriage to Carbonneau. The $1 million in 1900 would purchase goods worth about $19.3 million in 1998 (McCusker, "How Much Is That?"; *Consumer Price Index [1982–1984]*).

68. Judge Ralph Kauffman of Kittitas County, quoted in *Yakima Daily Republic,* 15 September 1914.

69. Yakima, *Scouse and Byrnes v. AYIC,* Case 9439, Deposition of James Kelly, 31 August 1915.

70. *Yakima Daily Republic,* 9 May 1916, p. 3, col. c; 10 May 1916, p. 4, col. e; Yakima, *Scouse and Byrnes v. AYIC,* Case 9439, Decree, 28 July 1916.

71. *Yakima Daily Republic,* 9 May 1916, p. 3, col. c.

72. *Dawson Daily News,* 15 August 1916, p. 4, col. e.

73. Remington, *Washington Reports, vol.* 97. no. 13682, 7 August 1917, 701.

74. *Yakima Daily Republic,* 8 February 1915.

75. A review of the Harry Leon Wilson materials in the Bancroft Library, University of California, Berkeley, found nothing to either support or disprove an acquaintance between Wilson and Belinda.

76. Wilson, *Ma Pettengill;* "Ma Pettengill Mixes."

77. *Yakima Daily Republic,* 4 July 1916, p. 4, col. d; Scranton newspaper clipping, undated, courtesy of Rose Dougher Vitzthum.

78. *Dawson Building Catalog,* Titles.

79. *Yakima Daily Republic,* 15 July 1916, p. 1, col. a.

80. Yakima, *Scouse and Byrnes v. AYIC,* Case 9439, Deposition of Martin Andresen, 17 December 1914, p. 7.

81. Yakima, *Deeds,* vol. 138, 461, 16 October 1913; vol. 140, 295, 6 February 1914.

82. *Dawson Daily News,* 18 July 1912, 4 c; 5 May 1917.

83. Dawson City Museum, *Pan for Gold* data base, 1998; Coates and Morrison, *Sinking of the "Princess Sophia."*

84. The story of Carbonneau's death was carried in the *Dawson Daily News* (17 April 1919, p. 1, col. b) and in the *Fairbanks Daily News-Miner* (27 May 1919), where Nell Mulrooney Noble Thompson's husband was the owner and editor. It seems probable that the news would have reached Belinda fairly promptly through the Pioneers' grapevine, if not more directly.

Chapter 24. The Notorious Charles E. Carbonneau

1. England, *AFKS, Extraordinary Resolution,* 13 June 1901, rec. 11.

2. The company had to sell all assets to satisfy debts in 1909 (England, *GR(K)MC, Summary of Share Capital,* 14 January 1909, rec. 20).

3. *Daily Klondike Nugget,* 14 June 1902, p. 6, col. a; 17 June 1902, p. 1, col. h; 18 June 1902, p. 1, col. h; p. 2, col. a. We are not aware that he was ever tried or convicted of criminal behavior on either of these charges, however. The *Dawson Daily News* (2 May 1913) reported hearsay that Charles had been condemned to two years' imprisonment in connection with the Gold Run mining scheme, but we have found no confirmation of this.

4. *La Patrie* (Montreal), 10 February 1905, p. 1, col. f; *Le Journal* (Paris), 29 January 1905.

5. This and subsequent information about the company is from the *New York Times,* 14 April 1913, p. 2, col. c; 22 December 1914, p. 8.

6. *New York Times,* 14 April 1913, p. 2, col. d. We have not discovered what these other possible actions in Belgium and the United States involved. Although the case against Carbonneau was tried in 1913, according to a London *Times* article (5 April 1913, p. 3, col. d) it had been in process since 1909. Another account says Charles realized $1,750,000 from sale of bonds for the company in April 1913 (*Dawson Daily News,* 2 May 1913, quoting a story of 12 April from Paris).

7. *Dawson Daily News,* 2 May 1913; 16 November 1906.

8. *New York Times,* 15 April 1934, p. 24, col. a; 22 June 1919, II, p. 1, col. a, reported value as $20,000,000; 12 April 1908, V, p. 6, col. a.

9. Ibid., 15 April 1934, p. 24, col. a; 22 June 1919, II, p. 1, col. a; 20 July 1919, p. 7, col. c.

10. Ibid., 29 May 1913, p. 4, col. b.

11. Ibid., 14 April 1913, p. 2, col. c.

12. Ibid., 29 May 1913, p. 4, col. b.

13. About $292,000 (Mitchell, *British Historical Statistics,* 703), equivalent in 1998 to about $4,782,000 in consumer goods in the United States (McCusker, "How Much Is That?" Table A-2, 329–332; *Consumer Price Index [1982–1984]*). It is not clear whether the money was an investment, loan, or bribe.

14. *Times* (London), 5 April 1913, p. 3, col. d.

15. *New York Times,* 14 April 1913, p. 2, col. c.

16. *Times* (London), 5 April 1913, p. 3, col. d.

17. *New York Times,* 6 June 1913, p. 3, col. c.

18. Ibid.; *Juneau Alaska Daily Empire,* 2 August 1913.

19. *New York Times,* 22 December 1914, p. 8. In this article his name is spelled "Carboneau."

20. Ibid.

21. *Fairbanks Times,* 22 January 1915, p. 1; *Seattle Star,* 21 January 1915.

22. *Le Journal* (Paris), 6 February 1919, p. 2, col. a; *Le Petit Parisien,* 14 February 1919; *Le Journal* (Paris), 14 February 1919, p. 3, col. c.

23. *New York Times,* 22 June 1919, II, p. 1, col. d.

24. *La Presse* (Paris), 19 July 1919; *Le Figaro* (Paris), 20 July 1919. The fine in 1919 was in addition to the prison term and fine first imposed on Rochette in 1912, when he was also ordered to reimburse twenty-seven plaintiff investors 67,335 francs, it having been determined that over ten million francs had been swindled. Despite his conviction, Rochette continued his career as a promoter, speculator, and financier through the 1920s and early 1930s. In 1934 he committed suicide in a courtroom after being sentenced to two years for fraud (*New York Times,* 15 April 1934, p. 24, col. a).

25. The one exception was Belinda's involvement with the Eldorado-Bonanza Quartz and Placer Mining Company promotion. Like most of Charles's promotions, it apparently was a flop for investors.

26. For example Winslow and Solomon, "Entrepreneurs More Than Non-Conformists."

27. We estimate from 1905 through 1919.

28. Approximately 21.6 million people died worldwide from the flu. In the United States, ten times more people died of influenza (548,452) than were killed as U.S. soldiers in battles of World War I (53,402) and about five times more than overall deaths of U.S. forces in World War I (116,516) (Collier, *Plague of the Spanish Lady,* 305; *Information Please Almanac,* 385).

Chapter 25. Belinda Matures

1. In the U.S. Census (Yakima County, Washington, vol. 52, 10195, st. 2, ln. 31 f), enumerated 30 and 31 January 1920, all are listed at the same household on Glenn Side Drive, but no address is indicated. We do not know whether the apartment was considered a separate unit from the castle at this time.

2. Wilfong and Lambert, interview by Mayer

3. Ibid.

4. Jim Mulrooney to Kroll, interview by Mayer.

5. Wilfong, interview by Mayer.

6. Most people described Belinda's hair as dark brown.

7. Lambert, interview by Mayer.

8. Unfortunately but not surprisingly, the Gue sisters were unable to remember what those stories were when Mayer interviewed them sixty years later.

9. In the 1920 census Jim is described as the fruit farm foreman while Belinda is listed as corporation manager.

10. Kroll, interview by Mayer.

11. AYIC to Belinda A. Carbonneau, 13 August 1921 (Hall, interview by Mayer).

12. On 1 July 1923 (Vanderhoof to Mayer, 17 December 1996).

13. Pauline Schuchard to Belinda Carbonneau, Lots 7, 8 of Block 6, Plat Norris Addition to West Seattle (Seattle, *Deeds,* vol. 1244, p. 528, King County).

14. Mackay, "Saga of Belinda," 4–6; *Mount St. Vincent Founder's Day Program.*

15. *Mount St. Vincent Residents' Ledger,* 10 November 1924–3 January 1925. Belinda also may have worked in the kitchen of the home during this time (Jim Mulrooney to Kroll, interview by Mayer).

16. Yakima Federal Mortgage (Hall, interview by Mayer).

17. In 1925 all three are listed. In 1926, only Belinda is. None of them are listed in 1927. Then all three appear again in 1928. In 1929 only the Mulrooneys are there. *(Seattle City Directories.)*

18. That Belinda maintained a presence in Yakima in 1928 also is supported by Gladys Gue Wilfong, who recalled seeing Belinda as late as 1928, but not thereafter (Wilfong, interview by Mayer, 8).

19. Palmer, *With My Own Eyes,* 103. Although the original passage refers to Belinda as "Miss Mulvaney," from other writing of Palmer's we know he is talking about Miss Mulrooney. Compare for example "A Woman in the Klondyke," 529–34; *In the Klondyke,* 145–50.

20. Johnston letter to DeArmond, 24 January 1989; Janet Bouillon, interview by Mayer, 15 September 1996; Christine Johnston to Mayer, 11 November 1997.

21. According to Belinda's grand niece, Janet Noble Bouillon (interview by Mayer, 15 September 1996). A similar reference appears in the 1928 interviews (Hawkins).

22. Johnston to DeArmond, 24 January 1989.

23. Belinda is number 84 on the list of charter members (Rust Collection, Box 8, Folder 239, p. 25) and is shown as having paid dues through 12 April 1918 (ibid., Box 9, Folder 241, p. 82).

24. Helen Lyon Hawkins was born in St. Joseph, Missouri, in 1881, the daughter of Mary Rich and David Canfield Lyon. From 1901 until 1904, under the pen name Hannah Hinsdale, she was society editor of the *News-Press* in St. Joseph. She married Heinrich Guthartz (Henry Goodhart) Hawkins in the early 1900s, and by 1905 they had moved to Spokane, Washington, where they began raising a family. In about 1915 Hannah Hinsdale was again writing, this time for the *Spokesman-Review.* She apparently met Belinda Mulrooney at about the time she and her family moved to Yakima in 1925. (Quail Hawkins, interview by Mayer; *Spokane Spokesman-Review,* 10 July 1927, pt. 4, p. 1.)

25. According to Janet Bouillon, this may have been Belinda's priest in Seattle (interview by Mayer, 15 September 1996). We have found no traces of this other version, however.

26. In the foreword to the "New and Wonderful" (NW) manuscript, Hawkins says the interviews were conducted in 1928; however, the final page says it was twenty-seven years after Belinda's marriage, which would be 1927. The first few chapters of NW were submitted to an agent by December of 1928 (Hawkins Collection: Hawkins to Thompson, 1 December 1928). Therefore, Hawkins probably carried out the interviews between 1927 and 1928.

27. Belinda sold at least the castle and perhaps some acreage to C. A. Riemcke on 6 March 1928. She had previously mortgaged part of the property on 21 April 1927 to Addie Lomax (Hall, interview by Mayer).

28. This is probably not the apartments she had built for her parents much earlier, but it may be.

29. Wilfong and Lambert, interviewed by Mayer.

30. This is the Alex Miller cabin.

31. See note 27 above. George is the name reported by Sarah and Dale Kroll (interview by Mayer). However, the deed was in the name of a C. A. Riemcke (Hall, interview by Mayer).

32. Mrs. Riemcke to Kroll, interview by Mayer.

33. 4817–½ 37th Avenue SW (Seattle, *Property Records*).

34. She is first continuously listed in the *Seattle Directory* for 1930.

35. Seattle, *Death Records*, p. 702, no. 3993.

36. *Seattle City Directory.*

37. *Fairbanks News-Miner*, 7 November 1935, p. 4.

38. On 19 August 1931 to D. E. Bailey (Hall, interview by Mayer).

39. She also was released from the mortgage to Addie Lomax in 1934 (Hall, interview by Mayer).

40. Seattle, *Deeds*, vol. 1552, p. 8, William M. Christianson and wife to Mary Mulrooney, Lot 5 of Block 6, Plat Norris Addition to West Seattle, 5 July 1933; vol. 1622, p. 570, 28 February 1934.

41. Thorgaard to Vitzthum, 4 May 1982.

42. *Seattle City Directory*, 1934.

43. Marion Thorgaard and Betty Mulrooney.

44. Seattle, *Property Records*, 4811 37th Avenue SW.

45. Boarders other than family members are first indicated in the 1938 *Seattle City Directory*.

46. Betty Mulrooney, interview by Mayer. About this time Margaret married Alonzo Gauslin.

47. Bouillon, interview by Mayer, 29 September 1996.

48. Seattle, *Death Records*, p. 1273, no. 3887. Nell's husband W. F. Thompson had died in 1926. Four children—Robert Noble, and William, Richard, and Marion Thompson—survived her (*Fairbanks News-Miner*, 7 November 1935, p. 1).

49. *Fairbanks News-Miner*, 5 March 1936, p. 3; Seattle, *Death Records*, p. 625. Agnes was survived by husband Jay and two children, Charles and Anita.

50. *Seattle City Directory*, 1936, 1937.

51. Betty Mulrooney, interview by Mayer. Boeing Company acquired the land adjacent to the airport in the early to mid-1920s, and the airport was dedicated in 1928 (Frazelle to Mayer, 27 July 1997).

52. Seattle, *Death Records*, p. 171F.

53. Ibid., 60 Clark County, 2597.

54. *Seattle City Directory*, 1943–44.

55. Seattle, *Deeds*, vol. 2648, p. 39, Real Estate Contract, 29 July 1947.

56. Belinda's identification card, issued 18 June 1943 (Johnston collection); McCurdy, interview by Mayer. Associated Ship Builders was a joint venture between Puget Sound Bridge and Dredging Company and Lake Union Dry Dock Company to make mine sweepers.

57. Conover, "The Women's Page."

58. For example, Young, *Hall Young of Alaska*, 352–53; Young, *The Klondike Clan*, 218, 234, 238, 249, 382, 385.

59. Betty Mulrooney, interview by Mayer; Bouillon, interview by Mayer, 29 September 1996.

60. The Reverend Peter T. Rowe was the pioneering Episcopal Bishop of Alaska; therefore, Dawson was not in his territory, although he visited there. It was Reverend J. R. Bowen who established the Anglican Church in Dawson (Young, *Hall Young of Alaska*, 350). Rowe did establish one of the first churches at Fairbanks, and he and his wife were good friends of Belinda.

61. Father William Judge is not mentioned in this quote; however, in every other context when talking about the Dawson clergy, Belinda always included him, as she had great admiration for him. Therefore, we are assuming his being left out of the newsletter quote was

an oversight, most likely on the writer's part since Belinda was Catholic herself and had known Father Judge.

62. The Reverend S. Hall Young, Presbyterian minister, arrived in Dawson on 9 October 1897 (Young, *Hall Young of Alaska,* 316, 340).

63. Conover, "The Women's Page." Belinda is overlooking S. Hall Young's novel of 1916, *The Klondike Clan.*

64. Bouillon, interview by Mayer, 29 September 1996. Current Todd Ship Yard employment records only go back to 1947, at which time B. A. Carbonneau was not listed (courtesy of Maja Chaffe).

65. According to *Seattle Directories* the population increased by nearly 100,000 between 1940 and 1950, being 467,591 in 1950.

66. Cribbs, interview by Mayer, 18 March 1997 and 31 August 1997; *Seattle Directory.*

67. Irene Gilge placed these in the Yakima Valley Museum on 18 November 1980 (Yakima, *Deed of Gift*).

68. Cribbs, interview by Mayer, 18 April 1997; confirmed by Mulrooney family members.

69. Cautard to Mayer, 11 September 1996.

70. Charles Johnston to Mayer, 3 August 1988. However, we note that Belinda transferred her property on 37th Avenue SW to Marion N. Noble, nephew Bob's wife, on 16 October 1957 (Seattle, Deeds, vol. 3726, p. 416). And Margaret sold her house and lots to Dennis E. and Elizabeth Dunn, 19 September 1957 (ibid., vol. 3719, p. 630).

71. Bouillon to Mayer, 29 August 1998.

72. Hughes, interview by Mayer. The Hughes family were Belinda's neighbors to the south on 37th Avenue NE from about 1953.

73. A bottle of whiskey is what Belinda would suggest for neighbor Irene Gilge to bring when she visited (Hughes, interview by Mayer).

74. Bouillon, interview by Mayer, 29 September 1996; 15 September 1996.

75. *Mount St. Vincent Chronicles,* 21 October 1957.

76. Bouillon, interview by Mayer, 29 September 1996.

77. Providence Mount St. Vincent Nursing Center records. According to Assistant Archivist Mitchell (to Mayer, 19 June 1997), the home underwent a major renovation in 1967 which both reduced the number of beds and increased its rates. Sister Margaret had become so dependent that she felt lost without Belinda. Therefore, Margaret also was sent to Cascade Vista three months later (Charles Johnston to Mayer, 3 August 1988). Margaret died on 4 November 1973 (Seattle, *Death Records,* 17 A, no. 26506).

78. Betty Mulrooney, interview by Mayer.

79. Washington, *Certificate of Death,* no. 19864.

80. Nephew Robert Noble is listed as the informant on the death certificate, though it is hard to believe that describing Belinda as a housewife would occur to anyone who knew her well. However, Bob's daughter Janet Noble Bouillon explained that he probably did it to avoid any complications. (Bouillon, interview by Mayer, 29 September 1996).

Photographic Sources

Photographs and maps are reproduced with permission of the following (abbreviations used in figure legends are in parentheses):

Alaska State Library (ASL)
    Larss Collection
    James Wickersham Collection
Anchorage Museum of History and Art
Norman D. Anderson Collection
The Art Institute of Chicago
William F. Berry Collection
Norman Bolotin Collection
Janet Noble Bouillon Collection
California State University, Fresno (CSUF); Henry Madden Library, Sanoian Special Collections
Stan B. Cohen Collection
Dawson City Museum
    Belinda Carbonneau Collection
Robert N. DeArmond Collection
Division of Archives and Public Records, Puget Sound Regional Branch (DAPR, PS); Bellevue, Washington
Carol Gilge Cribbs Collection
Marjorie Gue Lambert and Gladys Gue Wilfong Collection
Charles Johnston Collection
Library of Congress
Manoogian Foundation
Melanie J. Mayer Collection
United States Park Service

University of Alaska, Fairbanks (UAF); Rasmuson Library
    Hazel Lindberg Collection
    R. Mackay Collection
    Falcon Joslin Collection
University of California, Berkeley (UCB); Bancroft Library
    Helen Lyons Hawkins Collection
University of Washington Libraries (UW); Special Collections, Manuscripts and University
    Archives Division
    Edith F. Larson Collection
Vancouver Public Library; Special Collections Division
Rose Dougher Vitzthum Collection
Candace Waugaman Collection
Yakima Valley Museum
    Belinda Mulrooney Carbonneau Collection
Yukon Archives
    Barley Collection
    Gillis Collection
    McLennon Collection

Photographers

Arnold, Charles Dudley
Barley, H. C.
Cantwell, George G.
Child
Curtis, Asahel
Ellingsen, E. O.
Fujiwara, F. D.
Hegg, Eric A.
LaRoche, Frank
Larss, P. E. and Duclos, J. E. N.
Prather, J. B.
Sether
Winter, Lloyd V. and Pond, E. P.

References

The sources cited in the text are listed here in the following categories: Published Books and Articles, Newspapers, Government Records in Public Archives, Unpublished Sources in Public Collections, and Personal Collections.

Published Books and Articles

Adney, Tappan. *The Klondike Stampede.* New York: Harper, 1900.

Ainsworth, M. D. S., and J. Bowlby. "An Ethological Approach to Personality Development." *American Psychologist* 46 (1991): 331–41.

Alaska Gazetteer and Directory. Seattle: R. L. Polk, 1909–10; 1911–12; 1915–16.

Alaska-Yukon Gazetteer. Seattle: R. L. Polk, 1903.

Alaska-Yukon Magazine 7, no. 4 (January 1909).

Allen, A. S., ed. *Dawson, Yukon Territory.* Dawson: Klondike Nugget Press, 1901.

Anderson, Norman D. *Ferris Wheel Newsletter* 23 (June 1995).

———. *Ferris Wheels: An Illustrated History.* Bowling Green, Ohio: Bowling Green State University Popular Press, 1992.

Armstrong, Neville. *Yukon Yesterdays: Thirty Years of Adventure in the Klondike.* London: John Long, 1936.

Backhouse, Constance B. "'Pure Patriarchy': Nineteenth-Century Canadian Marriage." *McGill Law Journal* 31 (1986): 264–312.

———. "Married Women's Property Law in Nineteenth-Century Canada." *Law and History Review* 6 (1988): 211–57.

Bancroft, Hubert Howe. *History of California.* Vol. 7, 1860–1890. San Francisco: History Company, 1890.

———. *The Book of the Fair.* 5 vols. Chicago and San Francisco: Bancroft, 1893.

Bankson, Russell A. *The Klondike Nugget.* Caldwell, Idaho: Caxton, 1935.

Basch, Norma. *In the Eyes of the Law: Women, Marriage and Property in Nineteenth-Century New York.* Ithaca, N.Y.: Cornell University Press, 1982.

B.C. Review (London), 11 October 1902, p. 184.

Beach, Rex. *The Winds of Chance.* New York: A. L. Burt, 1918.

Beebe, I. *The True Life Story of Swiftwater Bill Gates, by His Mother-in-Law, Mrs. Iola Beebe.* Seattle(?), c. 1908.

Berton, Pierre. *The Klondike Fever.* New York: Knopf, 1958. (Also published as *Klondike.* Toronto: McClelland and Stewart, 1958.)

Bettles, G. C. "Some Early Yukon River History." In *Sourdough Sagas,* edited by Herbert L. Heller, 109–14. New York: Ballantine, 1967.

Blackstone, Sir William. *Commentaries on the Laws of England.* 1765–69. 4th ed. Edited by Thomas M. Cooley and James DeWitt Andrews. Reprint, Chicago: Callaghan, 1899.

Bloom, Sol. *The Autobiography of Sol Bloom.* New York: G. P. Putnam, 1948.

Bolotin, Norman. *Klondike Lost.* Anchorage: Alaska Northwest, 1980.

Carter, Margaret, and Rita Perry. *Dawson Building Catalogue.* Parks Canada, National Historic Parks and Sites Branch, 1974.

Chambers, Anne. *Granuaile: The Life and Times of Grace O'Malley.* Dublin: Wolfhound Press, 1979.

Chicago City Directory, Lakeside Annual Directories of City of Chicago. Chicago: Chicago Directory Co., 1893. In *U.S. City Directories 1882–1901, Chicago, Illinois* (microfilm). New Haven, Conn.: Research Publications.

The Church at Home and Abroad. Philadelphia: Presbyterian Board of Publications, 1898.

Chused, Richard H. "The Oregon Donation Act of 1850 and Nineteenth Century Federal Married Women's Property Law." *Law & History Review* 44 (1984): 44–78.

Clark, Henry W. *History of Alaska.* New York: Macmillan, 1930.

Clark, John A. "Fairbanks' Great Fire." In *Sourdough Sagas,* edited by Herbert L. Heller, 211–15. New York: Ballantine, 1967.

———. "From Valdez to Fairbanks in 1906 by Bicycle, Blizzard and Strategy." In *Sourdough Sagas,* edited by Herbert L. Heller, 163–93. New York: Ballantine, 1967.

Clarkson, L. A. "Conclusion: Famine and Irish History." In *Famine: The Irish Experience 900–1900,* edited by E. Margaret Crawford, 220–36. Edinburgh: John Donald Publishers, 1989.

Coates, Ken, and Bill Morrison. *The Sinking of the "Princess Sophia."* Fairbanks: University of Alaska, 1991.

Cole, Terrence. *Crooked Past. The History of a Frontier Mining Camp: Fairbanks, Alaska.* Fairbanks: University of Alaska, 1984.

Collier, Richard. *The Plague of the Spanish Lady: The Influenza Pandemic of 1918–1919.* New York: Atheneum, 1974.

Conover, Pat. "The Women's Page." *Flood-tide* (Associated Ship Builders, Seattle), 1943.

Conway, Jill Ker. *True North.* New York: Knopf, 1994.

Crawford, E. Margaret, ed. *Famine: The Irish Experience 900–1900.* Edinburgh: John Donald, 1989.

Cusick, Daniel L. "Belinda, Queen of the Klondike." *Archbald (Penn.) Sunday Times,* 5 November 1967, A-8.

DeArmond, Robert N. *The Founding of Juneau.* Juneau: Gastineau Channel Centennial Association, 1967.

DeGraf, Anna. *Pioneering on the Yukon.* Hamden, Conn.: Archon, 1992.

Denison, Merrill. *Klondike Mike.* Seattle: Johnson, 1948.

Derks, Scott, ed. *The Value of a Dollar.* Detroit: Gale Research, 1994.

de Tocqueville, Alexis. *Democracy in America.* [1835, 1840]. Edited by J. P. Mayer. Translated by George Lawrence. Garden City, N.Y.: Doubleday, 1966.

Dickerson, Ora A. *120 Years of Alaska Postmasters, 1867–1987.* Scotts, Mich.: Cammarata, c. 1989.

Dill, W. S. [Madge H. L. Macbeth]. *The Long Day: Reminiscences of the Yukon.* Ottawa: Graphic, 1926.

Dranoff, Linda Silver. *Women in Canadian Law.* Toronto: Fitzhenry and Whiteside, 1977.

Emmons, G. T. *The Tlingit Indians.* Edited by F. de Laguna. American Museum of Natural History (New York), Anthropological Papers, no. 70. Seattle: University of Washington Press, 1991.

Fairbanks Telephone Directory, 1906.

Farr, Gail E., and Brett F. Bostwick. *Shipbuilding at Cramp and Sons.* Philadelphia: Philadelphia Maritime Museum, 1991.

Ferguson, M. L. *Ferguson's Dawson Yukon and Alaska Directory and Gazetteer, 1901.*

Filby, P. W., ed. *Philadelphia Naturalization Records.* Detroit: Gale Research, 1982.

Filby, P. W., and M. K. Meyer, eds. *Passenger and Immigration Lists Index.* Detroit: Gale Research, 1981.

Franklin, Stephen. "She Was the Richest Woman in the Klondike." *Vancouver Sunday Sun Weekend Magazine* 12, no. 27 (7 July 1962): 23.

Gates, Michael. *Gold at Fortymile Creek: Early Days in the Yukon.* Vancouver: University of British Columbia Press, 1994.

Gilbert, James. *Perfect Cities: Chicago's Utopias of 1893.* Chicago: University of Chicago Press, 1991.

Goldin, Claudia. "The Economic Status of Women in the Early Republic: Quantitative Evidence." *Journal of Interdisciplinary History* 16 (winter 1986): 375–404.

———. *Understanding the Gender Gap: An Economic History of American Women.* New York: Oxford University, 1990.

Green, Lewis. *The Gold Hustlers.* Vancouver: Dacher, 1994.

Greenhous, Brereton, ed. *Guarding the Goldfields.* Toronto: Dundurn, 1987.

Guest, Hal. *A History of the City of Dawson,* Microfiche Report Series 7. Heritage Presentation and Public Education, National Historic Sites, Parks Canada.

———. *Socioeconomic History of the Klondike Goldfields, 1896–1966.* Microfiche Report Series 181 (1985). Heritage Presentation and Public Education, National Historic Sites, Parks Canada.

Hales, Peter B. *Constructing the Fair: Platinum Photographs by C. D. Arnold of the World's Columbian Exposition.* Chicago: The Art Institute of Chicago, 1993.

Hansen, Gladys. *San Francisco Almanac.* San Rafael, Calif.: Presidio, 1980.

Hart, James D. *Companion to California.* New York: Oxford University Press, 1978.

Hartnoll, P., ed. *The Oxford Companion to the Theatre.* London: Oxford University Press, 1967.

Haskell, William B. *Two Years in the Klondike and Alaskan Gold Fields.* Hartford, Conn.: Hartford, 1898.

Heilbrun, Carolyn, and Judith Resnik. "Convergences: Law, Literature, and Feminism." In *Beyond Portia: Women, Law, and Literature in the United States,* edited by Jacqueline St. Joan and Annette Bennington McElhiney, 11–52. Boston: Northeastern University Press, 1997.

Heller, Herbert L., ed. *Sourdough Sagas.* New York: Ballantine, 1967.

Henderson, M. Allen. *How Con Games Work*. New York: Carol, 1994.

Higinbotham, Harlow N. *Report of the President to the Board of Directors of the World's Columbian Exposition, Chicago, 1892–1893*. Chicago: Rand McNally, 1898.

Hitchcock, Mary E. *Two Women in the Klondike*. New York: Putnam, 1899.

Hoppin, Martha J. *Country Paths and City Sidewalks: The Art of J. G. Brown*. Springfield, Mass.: Springfield Library and Museum Association, 1989.

Information Please Almanac. Edited by D. Golenpaul. New York: Simon and Schuster, 1963.

Information Please Almanac. New York: Houghton Mifflin, 1997.

Johnson, George F. "Yukon's Gold Yield $150,000,000." *Dawson Daily News Special Mining Edition*, 21 July 1909, p. 14, col. c.

Johnston, Alva. *The Legendary Mizners*. New York: Farrar, Straus and Young, 1953.

Judge, Charles J. *An American Missionary*. Boston: Catholic Foreign Mission Bureau, 1907.

Kanowitz, Leo. *Women and the Law: The Unfinished Revolution*. Albuquerque: University of New Mexico Press, 1969.

King, Jean Beach. *Arizona Charlie: A Legendary Cowboy, Klondike Stampeder, and Wild West Showman*. Phoenix: Heritage, 1989.

Kitchener, L. D. *Flag over the North*. Seattle: Superior, 1954.

Lerner, Gerda. "The Lady and the Mill Girl: Changes in the Status of Women in the Age of Jackson." *Midcontinent American Studies Journal* 10 (spring 1969): 5–14. Reprinted in *A Heritage of Her Own*, edited by Nancy Cott and Elizabeth Pleck, 2–19. New York: Simon and Schuster, 1979.

Lippincott's Gazetteer of the World. Philadelphia: Lippincott, 1886.

London, Jack. *A Daughter of the Snows*. 1902. Reprint, New York: Archer House, 1963.

Lucie, Patricia. "Marriage and Law Reform in Nineteenth-Century America." In *Marriage and Property: Women and Marital Customs in History*, edited by Elizabeth Craile. Aberdeen, Scotland: Aberdeen University, 1984.

Lynch, Jeremiah. *Three Years in the Klondike*. 1904. Reprint, Chicago: Donnelley, 1967.

Mackay, Wallace Vincent. "The Saga of Belinda." *Seattle Sunday Times, Charmed Land Magazine* (12 August 1962): 4–6.

Matheson, Robert E. *Special Report on Surnames in Ireland*. Dublin: His Majesty's Stationery Office, 1909.

May, Elaine Tyler. *Great Expectations*. Chicago: University of Chicago Press, 1980.

Mayer, Melanie J. *Klondike Women: True Tales of the 1897–98 Gold Rush*. Athens: Ohio University Press/Swallow Press, 1989.

McCusker, James J. "How Much Is That in Real Money? A Historical Price Index for Use as a Deflator of Money Values in the Economy of the United States." *Proceedings of the American Antiquarian Society* 101, no. 2 (1991): Table A2, 329–32.

McLain, John Scudder. *Alaska and the Klondike*. New York: McClure, Phillips, 1907.

Mitchell, B. R. *British Historical Statistics*. Cambridge: Cambridge University Press, 1988.

Mizner, Addison. *The Many Mizners*. New York: Sears, 1932.

Mokyr, Joel. "The Deadly Fungus: An Econometric Investigation into the Short-Term Demographic Impact of the Irish Famine, 1846–1851." *Research in Population Economics* 2 (1980): 237–77.

Morrison, David R. *The Politics of the Yukon Territory*. Vol. 12 of *Canadian Studies in History and Government*, edited by Goldwin French. Toronto: University of Toronto Press, 1968.

Muccigrosso, Robert. *The New World: Chicago's Columbian Exposition of 1893*. Chicago: Dee, 1993.

Naske, Claus M., and L. J. Rowinski. *Fairbanks: A Pictorial History*. Norfolk/Virginia Beach: Donning, 1981.

Newman, John J. *American Naturalization Processes and Procedures 1790–1985*. Indiana Historical Society, 1985.

Northern California State Directory for 1893–94. San Francisco Directory Company.

O'Connor, Richard. *High Jinks on the Klondike*. Indianapolis: Bobbs-Merrill, 1954.

Ogilvie, William. *Early Days on the Yukon and the Story of Its Gold Finds*. London: Lane, 1913.

O Gráda, Cormac. *Ireland before and after the Famine*. Manchester, England: Manchester University Press, 1988.

Palmer, Frederick. *In the Klondyke*. New York: Scribner's, 1899.

———. *With My Own Eyes*. New York: A. L. Burt, 1932.

———. "A Woman in the Klondyke." *Home Magazine* (Syracuse, N.Y.) 12, no. 6 (June 1899): 529–34.

Pelletier, E. LeRoy. *New York Times*, 23 January 1898, p. 1, col. g; p. 2, col. b.

———. *New York Times*, 8 May 1898, p. 6.

———. *New York Times*, 29 May 1898, p. 13, col. c.

Philadelphia City Directory. Philadelphia: Gopsill, 1890.

Phillips, James W. *Alaska-Yukon Place Names*. Seattle: University of Washington Press, 1973.

Pitcher, James S. *Sourdough Jim Pitcher: The Autobiography of a Pioneer Alaskan*. Anchorage: Alaska Northwest, 1985.

Prather, J. B. *The Land of the Midnight Sun*. Douglas, Alaska: Prather, 1900.

Radin, Max. "The Common Law of the Family." In *The National Law Library*. Vol. 6, *Legal Relations*, pt. 2. New York: Collier & Sons, 1939.

Ricks, Melvin B. *Directory of Alaska Post Offices and Postmasters*. Ketchikan, Alaska: Tongass, 1965.

Ross, Victor. *A History of the Canadian Bank of Commerce*. Toronto: Oxford University Press, 1922.

Sachs, Albie, and Joan Hoff Wilson. *Sexism and the Law: A Study of Male Beliefs and Legal Bias in Britain and the United States*. New York: Macmillan, 1978.

San Francisco Directory. San Francisco: Langley, 1894, 1895.

Seattle City Directory. Seattle: R. L. Polk, 1924; 1925; . . . 1958.

Siegel, Reva B. "The Modernization of Marital Status Law: Adjudicating Wives' Rights to Earnings, 1860–1930." *Georgetown Law Journal* 82 (1994): 2127–211.

Sinkevitch, Alice, ed. *AIA Guide to Chicago*. San Diego: Harcourt Brace, 1993.

Snell, James G. "'The White Life for Two': The Defense of Marriage and Sexual Morality in Canada, 1890–1914." *Histoire sociale-Social History (Ottawa)* 16 (1983): 111–28.

Solar, Peter. "The Great Famine Was No Ordinary Subsistence Crisis." In *Famine: The Irish Experience 900–1900*, edited by E. Margaret Crawford, 112–31. Edinburgh: John Donald, 1989.

Souvenir of a Ride on the Ferris Wheel at the World's Fair, Chicago. Chicago: American Engraving, 1893.

Statistical Bulletin of the Metropolitan Life Insurance Company, "Death Registration State If 1920."

Stiles, Bill. "Tanana Mines Yield Millions." *Alaska-Yukon Magazine* 7, no. 4 (January 1909): 274.

Tanana Valley Directory, 1907.

Weisberg, D. Kelly, "Barred from the Bar: Women and Legal Education in the United States, 1870–1890." *Journal of Legal Education* 28, no. 4 (1977): 485–507.

Who Was Who 1897–1915. 1920. Vol. 1. Reprint, London: Adam and Charles Black, 1962.

Wickersham, James. *Old Yukon: Tails, Trails and Trials.* Washington, D.C.: Washington Lawbook, 1938.

Wilson, Harry Leon. *Ruggles of Red Gap.* Garden City, N.Y.: Doubleday, 1915.

———. "Ma Pettengill Mixes." *Saturday Evening Post,* 15 December 1934, 14 ff.

———. *Ma Pettengill.* Garden City, N. Y.: Doubleday, 1919.

Winslow, Erik K., and George T. Solomon. "Entrepreneurs Are More Than Non-Conformists: They Are Mildly Sociopathic." *Journal of Creative Behavior* 21 (1987): 202–13.

Wortman, Marlene Stein, ed. *Women in American Law.* Vol. 1, *From Colonial Times to the New Deal.* New York: Holmes and Meier, 1985.

Wright, E. W., ed. *Lewis & Dryden's Marine History of the Pacific Northwest.* 1895. Reprint, Seattle: Superior, 1967.

Yeats, William Butler. "Remorse for Intemperate Speech." In *The Variorum Edition of the Poems of W. B. Yeats,* edited by P. Allt & R. K. Alspach, 506. New York: Macmillan, 1957.

Young, S. Hall. *The Klondike Clan.* New York: Fleming H. Revell, 1916.

———. *Hall Young of Alaska: "The Mushing Parson."* New York: Fleming H. Revell, 1927.

Zucker, Marvin A., and June Callwood. *Canadian Women and the Law.* Toronto: Copp Clark, 1971.

Newspapers

ARCHBALD, PENNSYLVANIA

Sunday Times

CHICAGO, ILLINOIS

Chicago Record
Chicago Tribune

DAWSON, YUKON

Dawson Daily News
Dawson Daily News Golden Clean-Up Edition, 1902
Dawson Daily News Special Mining Edition, 21 July 1909
Dawson Record
Klondike Miner
Klondike Miner and Yukon Advertiser
Klondike News, 1 April 1898
Klondike Nugget (Daily)
Klondike Semi-Weekly Nugget
Sunday Gleaner and Klondike Miner
Weekly News

Yukon Midnight Sun
Yukon Sun
Yukon Sun and Klondike Pioneer
Yukon Sun Special Edition, September 1900
Yukon World

FAIRBANKS, ALASKA
Fairbanks Daily Times
Fairbanks Evening News
Fairbanks News
Fairbanks News-Miner
Fairbanks Sunday Times
Fairbanks Times

JUNEAU, ALASKA
Alaska Daily Empire
Alaska Searchlight
Daily Alaska Dispatch
Daily Record

KANSAS CITY, KANSAS
Kansas City Star

LONDON, ENGLAND
Times

MONTREAL, QUEBEC
La Patrie

NEW YORK, NEW YORK
New York Times

PARIS, FRANCE
La Presse
Le Figaro
Le Journal
Le Petit Parisien

SAN FRANCISCO, CALIFORNIA
San Francisco Examiner

SANTA CRUZ, CALIFORNIA
Santa Cruz Sentinel

Seattle, Washington

Seattle Post-Intelligencer
Seattle Star
Seattle Sunday Times
Seattle Times

Skagway, Alaska

Daily Alaskan
Skaguay News

Spokane, Washington

Spokesman-Review

Valdez, Alaska

Valdez News

Vancouver, British Columbia

The Province
Sunday Sun

Yakima, Washington

Yakima Daily Republic
Yakima Morning Herald

Government Records in Public Archives

National

England

An Act to Amend the Law Relating to Divorce and Matrimonial Causes in England, *1857*. United Kingdom, 20 & 21 Vict., c. 85 ss2, 6, 7, 16–18, 27.

Anglo-French Klondyke Syndicate Limited. Record BT31/8212/59484. Public Records Office, Surrey, England.

Gold Run (Klondike) Mining Company Limited. Record BT31/10028/75003. Public Record Office, Surrey, England.

Canada

Correspondence Major J. M. Walsh, NWMP at Dawson, with Colonel Thomas B. D. Evans, Commander Yukon Field Force. Public Archives of Canada, Record Grp. 9, B1, vol. 280, ff76900.

Sessional Papers, Vol. 33, Fourth Session of the Eighth Parliament of the Dominion of Canada, 1899. No. 87B-87C. Copy of further report of William Ogilvie, Esq. and evidence accompanying the same. Ottawa: S. E. Dawson, 1899.

United States of America

Bradwell v. The State of Illinois, 83 U.S. Supreme Court Reports 130 (1873).

B. A. Carbonneau v. C. E. Carbonneau, about 30 July 1906. Case 539, U.S. District Court, Alaska, 3rd Div. National Archives, Anchorage branch.

Case 894, U.S. District Court, Fairbanks. National Archives, Anchorage Branch.

Case 895, U.S. District Court, Fairbanks. National Archives, Anchorage Branch.

Consumer Price Index (1982–84). See U.S. Bureau of Labor Statistics.

Department of Commerce. See U.S. Bureau of the Census and U.S. Bureau of Labor Statistics

Garden City Observation Wheel Company v. Ferris Wheel Company, et al. United States Circuit Court, Northern District of Illinois, 1894.

Prindle, L. M., F. J. Katz, C. C. Covert, C. E. Ellsworth, and A. G. Madden. *Mineral Resources of Alaska, Report of Investigations in 1908.* Bulletin 379-E. Fairbanks, Yukon-Tanana, and Lower Yukon Regions. Washington, D.C.: Government Printing Office, 1909.

Scouse and Byrnes v. Carbonneau, Complaint September 18, 1905. Case 409, U.S. District Court, Alaska, 3rd Div. National Archives, Anchorage Branch.

U.S. Bureau of Labor Statistics. *Consumer Price Index (1982–1984).* All Urban Consumers, U.S. city average, not seasonally adjusted, revised using 1982–1984 as base = 100. Available on World Wide Web at *http://stats.bls.gov/cpihome.htm.*

U.S. Bureau of the Census. Census of 1880, 1900, 1910, and 1920.

———. *Special Reports: Occupations at the Twelfth Census.* Supervised by William Hunt. Department of Commerce and Labor, Bureau of the Census. Washington, D.C.: Government Printing Office, 1904, pp. cxxv-cxxvi.

U.S. Department of the Interior, National Park Service. *Map of Chilkoot Trail,* Klondike Gold Rush National Historical Park, 1986.

———. *Nomination Form, National Registry of Historic Places Inventory, Carbonneau Castle,* 620 S. 48th Avenue, Yakima, Washington. U.S. Department of the Interior, National Park Service.

U.S. Geological Survey. See Prindle, L. M., et al.

STATE, PROVINCE, AND TERRITORY

Alaska Territory and State

Secretary of State. *Affidavit,* B. A. Carbonneau and M. Mulrooney, 31 July 1907, District of Alaska.

———. *Domestic Corporations Record Book,* 52, p. 560. Incorporation papers, filed 27 September 1906. Secretary of State, Juneau.

Northwest Territories

Ordinances of the Northwest Territories, 1886, 1898.

Revised Ordinances of the Northwest Territories, 1888.

Pennsylvania

Pennsylvania Statute Law 1920. St. Paul, Minn.: West, 1921.

Quarter Sessions Court Record. 6 August 1872. Philadelphia City Archives, Department of Records.

Washington State

Articles of Incorporation, Alaska and Yakima Investment Company. Filed 6 September 1910, no. 28587. Washington State Archives and Management Division, Olympia, Washington.

Certificates of Death. Department of Social and Health Services, Bureau of Vital Statistics.

Remington, Arthur, reporter. Washington Reports, Vol. 97. Cases Determined in the Supreme Court of Washington, June 15, 1917–August 17, 1917. Seattle / San Francisco: Bancroft-Whitney, 1918.

Yukon Territory. Yukon Archives, Whitehorse, unless otherwise indicated

Bonanza Townsite Record, Yukon Territory Records, RG 91, no. 9, File 1375. 31 May 1899 survey.

Consolidated Ordinances of the Yukon Territory, 1902.

Dawson Building Catalogue. Vol. 3, block HA, lot 11, area 3.

Finding Aid, Series 10, Mining Recorders Records (Placer). Northern Affairs Program, May 1983.

Free Miner's Certificates. Vol. 188; vol. 191.

Mining Recorder. Creeek Records (within each volume, entries are by claim number):

> Bonanza (Vols. 1, 2, 3)
>
> Bonanza Hills and Benches (Vol. 12)
>
> Bonanza Tributaries (Vol. 13)
>
> Dominion (Vol. 33)
>
> Eldorado (Vol. 22)
>
> Henderson (Vol. 133)
>
> Reindeer (Vol. 104)

———. Index of Original Locators (within each volume, entries are by creek): Vols. 182, 183, 184

———. Royalties (within each volume, entries are by claim number):

> Eldorado (Vol. 200)

Royal Canadian Mounted Police. Yukon Records, Register of Boats through Tagish, May 28-Oct. 22, 1898; RG 18, vol. 7.

———. Yukon Records, Register of Persons Inwards and Outward from Dec. 6, 1898 to April, 1899; RG 18, D4, vol. 5.

———. Yukon Records, Register of Persons Inwards from Dec. 18, 1898 to September, 1900; RG 18, D4, vol. 6.

Yukon Territorial Court. Records 1897–1950. Cases. Vol. 1420, File 277–02.

———. Cases. Vol. 1472, File 2.

———. Estates. Vol. 1453, no. 181.

Yukon Territorial Records, RG 91, vol. 17, File 4355, Concerning Liquor Permits 1898–1901.

CITY AND COUNTY

Chicago, Illinois

Chicago Police Department. The Chicago Police Reports, 1891–1894. 137.

Dawson, Yukon. Dawson City Museum

Mining Recorder Records, Gold Commissioner Records, Registered Documents, and Power of Attorney for Klondike District, microfilms.

Pan for Gold data base, 1997.

Death Records, Green's Mortuary. Dawson, 6 January 1909.

Fairbanks, Alaska

Deeds, vols. 6, 7, 1906. Recorder's Office.
Miscellaneous Documents, Vol. 1, 1905. Recorder's Office.

Seattle, Washington

Seattle Death Records, King County Washington. Seattle Public Library.
Deeds, King County. Secretary of State of Washington, Division of Archives and Records Management, Puget Sound Regional Branch, Bellevue, Washington.
Property Records, Seattle. Secretary of State of Washington, Division of Archives and Records Management, Puget Sound Regional Branch, Bellevue, Washington.

Sligo County, Ireland

Heritage and Genealogy Society, County Heritage Centre, Stephen Street.

Valuation of Tenements, Parish of Castleconnor, 45–46.

Parish of Castleconnor, Records of Births and Marriages.

Superintendent Registrar, Births, Deaths and Marriages. County Sligo, District of Castleconnor. Markeivicz House.

Yakima, Washington

Deed of Gift, Irene Gilge, November 18, 1980. Yakima Valley Museum and Historical Association, Archives and Manuscripts.
Deeds, Yakima County Assessor's Office.
Mortgages, Yakima County Assessor's Office.
Mulrooney, Margaret v. H. Cook, 4 September 1909. Case 5479, Superior Court, Yakima County.
Scouse, Z. A. and L. E. Byrnes v. Belinda A. Carbonneau, 19 January 1911. Case 6410, Superior Court, Yakima County.
Scouse, Z. A. and Lorene A. Byrnes v. Alaska and Yakima Investment Co. et al. Case 9439, Superior Court, Yakima County.
Superior Court Judgments, vol. T, p. 249. Yakima County, Washington.

Unpublished Sources in Public Collections

Arnold, Charles Dudley. *Photographs Documenting the World's Columbian Exposition.* 3 vols. Ryerson and Burnham Libraries, Art Institute of Chicago.
Carbonneau, Belinda A. Mulrooney. Collection of papers and photographs. Yakima Valley Museum, Yakima, Washington.
Carbonneau, Belinda Mulrooney, and Helen Lyons Hawkins. "New and Wonderful." 1928. University of California, Berkeley; Bancroft Library, BANC MSS 77/811928.
Clark, John A. Letter to James Oliver Curwood, 15 December 1922. VF Manuscripts, Archives, University of Alaska, Fairbanks.
Dun, R. G., and Company Collection, *Philadelphia, Pennsylvania.* Vol. 141, p. 124. Baker Library, Harvard University Graduate School of Business Administration.

Hartshorn, Florence. Dyea manuscript, p. 6, file 1–3. University of Washington Libraries, Special Collections, Manuscripts and University Archives Division, Seattle.

Hawkins, Helen Lyons. Collection of notes, supporting materials, and variations of a manuscript based upon interview of B. M. Carbonneau, including "Liar's License," "New and Wonderful," and "Miss Mulrooney, Queen of the Klondike." University of California, Berkeley; Bancroft Library, BANC MSS 77/81.

Johns, William Douglas. "The Early Yukon, Alaska and the Klondike Discovery As They Were before the Great Klondike Stampede Swept Away the Old Conditions by One Who Was There." Manuscript, c. 1940. University of Washington Libraries, Special Collections, Manuscripts and University Archives Division, Seattle. Also Candace Waugaman Collection, Fairbanks.

Kelcey, Barbara. "Lost in the Rush: The Forgotten Women of the Klondike Stampede." Master's thesis, University of Victoria, B.C., 1989.

Klein, Gerry W. "A History of Teck Corporation in the Yukon." World Goldpanning Championships Gold Symposium, Dawson, 1996.

Loiselle File. (Index of Marriages.) Archives nationales du Québec.

Marriage Register. St. Mary's Catholic Church, Dawson.

Mount St. Vincent Chronicles, 21 October 1957. Sisters of Providence Archives, Sacred Heart Province 1856, Seattle.

Mount St. Vincent Founder's Day Program, 31 May 1978. Sisters of Providence Archives, Sacred Heart Province 1856, Seattle.

Mount St. Vincent Residents' Ledger, 1924–1930(?). Sisters of Providence Archives, Sacred Heart Province 1856, Seattle.

Nelson, Bert Jr. Diary. University of Washington Libraries, Special Collections, Manuscripts and University Archives Division, Seattle.

Rust, Clara. Collection of Pioneer Women of Alaska. University of Alaska, Fairbanks; Rasmuson Library.

Thomas, George. Collection MS4 Box 1b. Alaska State Library, Historical Collections, Juneau.

Wade, F. C. Letter to Edith Wade, 20 April 1898. Frederick Coate Wade Papers, Vancouver Archives, Ms. 44.

Wickersham, James. Diaries. Alaska State Library, Historical Collections, Juneau.

Wilson, Harry Leon. Collection of papers and photographs. University of California, Berkeley, Bancroft Library.

Personal Collections

ROBERT N. DEARMOND

Correspondence with Charles Johnston, nephew of Belinda, son of Agnes Mulrooney Johnston; and George H. Mullins, Judge, Yakima County District Court
Photographs

JOHNSTON FAMILY

Correspondence: Betty Mulrooney to Charles Johnston

Papers:

    Statement by Belinda concerning accuracy of various accounts of her earlier life, about 1960?

    Identification card, Associated Ship Builders, Seattle. Issued 18 June 1943.

    Terms of Belinda's will

    Mulrooney/Carbonneau wedding menu

Photographs

MELANIE J. MAYER

Correspondence with:

    Steve Alexander, Companies House, Cardiff, England

    Norman D. Anderson, concerning Ferris wheels

    William F. Berry, grandson of Fred Berry

    Janet Noble Bouillon, grandniece of Belinda

    Jill Ten Cate, Archivist, Canadian International Bank of Commerce

    Debbie Cautard, Health Information Officer, Providence Mount St. Vincent Nursing Center, Seattle

    Michael Cirelli, independent researcher, Seattle

    Rebecca McDowell Cook, Secretary of State, Missouri

    Carol Gilge Cribbs, former neighbor of Belinda's in Seattle

    Robert N. DeArmond

    Virginia Cummings Devine, grandniece of Belle Brown Cummings

    Jack Frazelle, Assistant Manger, King County International Airport

    Michael Gates, Dawson Historian

    John M. Gould, Dawson Historian

    Lewis Green, former resident geologist at Whitehorse, Yukon, for the Geological Survey of Canada

    Martha J. Hoppin, Curator of American Art, Museum of Fine Arts, Springfield, Mass.

    Charles Johnston, nephew of Belinda, son of Agnes Mulrooney Johnston

    Christine Johnston, grandniece of Belinda, daughter of Charles Johnston

    Florence Nelson Long, independent researcher

    Terri Mitchell, Assistant Archivist, Sacred Heart Province Archives, Seattle

    Dean Vanderhoof, Research Assistant, Washington State Archives and Records Management, Olympia

    Rose Dougher Vitzthum, Connor family relative of Belinda's

    Candace Waugaman, collector of Alaskana

Interviews with:

    Janet Noble Bouillon, grandniece of Belinda; 15 September 1996, 29 September 1996

    Carol Gilge Cribbs, former neighbor of Belinda's in Seattle; 18 March 1997; 18 April 1997; 31 August 1997

    Gladys Gue Wilfong and Marjorie Gue Lambert, 13 November 1979

    Ray Hall, Yakima County Assessor; 27 September 1996

    Quail Hawkins, daughter of Helen Lyon Hawkins; 5 October 1991

    Ann Hughes, former neighbor of Belinda's in Seattle; 16 April 1997

Christine and Emogene Johnston, grandniece and niece-in-law of Belinda; 28 February 1998

Sarah and Dale Kroll, owners of Carbonneau Castle, Yakima; 20 October 1979

James McCurdy, son of H. W. McCurdy, founder of Associated Ship Builders; 3 March 1998, 31 August 1998

Betty Freeman Mulrooney, sister-in-law of Belinda; 20 October 1979

Robert Murray, former resident of Lackawana valley, Pennsylvania; 16 December 1997

Photographs

ROSE DOUGHER VITZTHUM

Correspondence:

Belinda Mulrooney Carbonneau and Margaret Mulrooney Gauslin to Margaret Dougher

Betty Mulrooney to Charles Johnston, c. 1978

Marion Thompson Thorgaard to RDV

Photographs

Connor family genealogy

CANDACE (MRS. WILLIAM) WAUGAMAN

Photographs

Alaskana

Index

Page numbers in boldface type refer to illustrations.